Drupal 10 Module Development

Develop and deliver engaging and intuitive enterprise-level apps

Daniel Sipos

BIRMINGHAM—MUMBAI

Drupal 10 Module Development

Group Product Manager: Alok Dhuri
Publishing Product Manager: Uzma Sheerin
Senior Editor: Kinnari Chohan
Technical Editor: Maran Fernandes
Copy Editor: Safis Editing
Project Coordinator: Deeksha Thakkar
Proofreader: Safis Editing
Indexer: Tejal Soni
Production Designer: Ponraj Dhandapani
Developer Relations Marketing Executives: Rayyan Khan and Deepak Kumar

First published: October 2017
Second edition: March 2019
Third edition: August 2020
Fourth edition: April 2023

Production reference: 1040423

Published by Packt Publishing Ltd.
Livery Place
35 Livery Street
Birmingham
B3 2PB, UK.

ISBN 978-1-83763-180-3

www.packtpub.com

Contributors

About the author

Daniel Sipos is a senior web developer specializing in Drupal. He's been working with Drupal sites since version 6, and started out, like many others, as a site builder. He's a self-taught programmer with many years' experience working professionally on complex Drupal projects. In his spare time, he runs Webomelette, a Drupal website where he writes technical articles, tips, and techniques related to Drupal development.

I would like to acknowledge my colleagues and friends who have kept and continue to keep me on my toes with everything related to Drupal. They are, in no particular order, Antonio De Marco, Francesco Sardara, and Hernani Borges de Freitas.

About the reviewer

Martin Postma has been a contributing member of Drupal.org since 2007 under the nickname LOLANDESE.

Apart from his development skills, his participation in a team also brings people on board by sharing his knowledge and guiding them towards more cooperation using the Agile/Scrum tool set.

After living in several countries, he now works remotely in a small hamlet at nearly 1000 meters of altitude in the Italian Alps near Turin. He enjoys hosting hikers in his BNBs. If you are a Drupalist that needs to gear down in a beautiful remote place, feel free to pay him a visit. Search for: "Independent chalet with breathtaking view" villar pellice and book his accommodation through one of the two major vacation rental platforms. He loves to talk about Drupal.

Table of Contents

6

Data Modeling and Storage   127

7

Your Own Custom Entity and Plugin Types   189

11

Caching   355

12

JavaScript and the Ajax API   373

13

Internationalization and Languages   399

14

Batches, Queues, and Cron   409

15

16

17

18

Drupal Security   541

Index   547

Other Books You May Enjoy   558

Preface

Welcome to the latest edition of *Drupal 10*. In this updated edition, we will continue our exploration of Drupal as a powerful web-based content management system that is designed with developers in mind. While Drupal is useful out of the box, we will focus on how to extend its functionality to create even more powerful websites and applications.

This book will cover the most common ways that a Drupal website can be extended, as well as exploring various subsystems and APIs that can help you structure and model your business requirements. We will use a practical, example-based approach to illustrate complex topics and make them easier to understand.

As before, this book is aimed at developers who are familiar with Drupal and want to take their skills to the next level. Whether you are a seasoned Drupal developer or just getting started, this book will help you leverage the power of Drupal 10 to create amazing websites and applications.

So, let's embark on this journey together and discover the true potential of Drupal 10.

Who this book is for

This book is for Drupal developers who want to create custom modules for Drupal sites based on their specific business requirements. It is also suitable for Drupal site builders and PHP developers with basic object-oriented programming skills who want to improve their Drupal module development skills. While some experience with Symfony is helpful, it is not required.

What this book covers

Chapter 1, Developing for Drupal 10, provides an introduction to module development in Drupal. In doing so, it introduces you to the various subsystems and outlines the requirements for running a Drupal 10 application.

Chapter 2, Creating Your First Module, gets the ball rolling with the creation of the first Drupal module of the book. Its primary focus is to explore the most common things module developers need to know from the get-go.

Chapter 3, Logging and Mailing, is about the tools available for doing something every web-based application does and/or should be doing, that is, sending emails and logging events.

Chapter 4, Theming, presents the theme system from a module developer's perspective in Drupal 10.

Chapter 5, Menus and Menu Links, explores the world of menus in Drupal and shows how to programmatically create and work with menu links.

Chapter 6, Data Modeling and Storage, looks at the various types of storage available in Drupal, from the state system to configuration and entities.

Chapter 7, Your Own Custom Entity and Plugin Types, takes a hands-on approach in terms of creating a custom configuration and content entity type, as well as a custom plugin type for wiring up a practical functional example.

Chapter 8, The Database API, presents the database abstraction layer and discusses how we can work directly with data stored in custom tables.

Chapter 9, Custom Fields, walks through the creation of the three plugins necessary for creating a custom field that can be used on a Drupal content entity type.

Chapter 10, Access Control, explores the world of access restrictions in Drupal, from roles and permissions to route and entity access checks.

Chapter 11, Caching, looks at the various cache mechanisms available for module developers to improve the performance of their functionality.

Chapter 12, JavaScript and the Ajax API, introduces module developers to the specificities of writing JavaScript in Drupal, as well as the powerful Ajax system, which can be used to build advanced interactions.

Chapter 13, Internationalization and Languages, covers the practices that Drupal module developers need to observe in order to ensure that the application can be properly translated.

Chapter 14, Batches, Queues, and Cron, explores the various ways module developers can structure their data-processing tasks in a reliable way.

Chapter 15, Views, looks at the various ways module developers can programmatically interact with views and even expose their own data to them.

Chapter 16, Working with Files and Images, explores the various file and image APIs that allow module developers to store, track, and manage files in Drupal.

Chapter 17, Automated Testing, explores the various types of automated tests that developers can write for their Drupal applications so as to ensure stable and resilient code.

Chapter 18, Drupal 10 Security, explores the most common security principles that need to be observed when developing Drupal 10 modules.

To get the most out of this book

You don't need much to follow along with this book. A local environment setup capable of installing and running Drupal 10 (preferably with Composer) should suffice.

If you are using the digital version of this book, we advise you to type the code yourself or access the code from the book's GitHub repository (a link is available in the next section). Doing so will help you avoid any potential errors related to the copying and pasting of code.

Download the example code files

You can download the example code files for this book from GitHub at `https://github.com/PacktPublishing/Drupal-10-Module-Development-Fourth-Edition`. If there's an update to the code, it will be updated in the GitHub repository.

We also have other code bundles from our rich catalog of books and videos available at `https://github.com/PacktPublishing/`. Check them out!

Download the color images

We also provide a PDF file that has color images of the screenshots and diagrams used in this book. You can download it here: `https://packt.link/XUWE3`.

Conventions used

There are a number of text conventions used throughout this book.

`Code in text`: Indicates code words in text, database table names, folder names, filenames, file extensions, pathnames, dummy URLs, user input, and Twitter handles. Here is an example: "Hook implementations typically go inside a `.module` file, so let's create one in our module folder called `hello_world.module` and place an opening PHP tag at the top."

A block of code is set as follows:

```
/**
 * @file
 * Hello World module file.
 */
```

Any command-line input or output is written as follows:

```
../vendor/bin/phpunit tests/Drupal/Tests/Core/Routing/
UrlGeneratorTest.php
```

Bold: Indicates a new term, an important word, or words that you see onscreen. For instance, words in menus or dialog boxes appear in **bold**. Here is an example: "Users can now reach this page from the module administration page by clicking on the **Help** link for each individual module that has this hook implemented."

> **Tips or important notes**
> Appear like this.

Get in touch

Feedback from our readers is always welcome.

General feedback: If you have questions about any aspect of this book, email us at customercare@ packtpub.com and mention the book title in the subject of your message.

Errata: Although we have taken every care to ensure the accuracy of our content, mistakes do happen. If you have found a mistake in this book, we would be grateful if you would report this to us. Please visit www.packtpub.com/support/errata and fill in the form.

Piracy: If you come across any illegal copies of our works in any form on the internet, we would be grateful if you would provide us with the location address or website name. Please contact us at copyright@packt.com with a link to the material.

If you are interested in becoming an author: If there is a topic that you have expertise in and you are interested in either writing or contributing to a book, please visit authors.packtpub.com.

Share Your Thoughts

Once you've read *Drupal 10 Module Development*, we'd love to hear your thoughts! Scan the QR code below to go straight to the Amazon review page for this book and share your feedback.

https://packt.link/r/1837631808

Your review is important to us and the tech community and will help us make sure we're delivering excellent quality content.

Download a free PDF copy of this book

Thanks for purchasing this book!

Do you like to read on the go but are unable to carry your print books everywhere?

Is your eBook purchase not compatible with the device of your choice?

Don't worry, now with every Packt book you get a DRM-free PDF version of that book at no cost.

Read anywhere, any place, on any device. Search, copy, and paste code from your favorite technical books directly into your application.

The perks don't stop there, you can get exclusive access to discounts, newsletters, and great free content in your inbox daily

Follow these simple steps to get the benefits:

1. Scan the QR code or visit the link below

https://packt.link/free-ebook/9781837631803

2. Submit your proof of purchase
3. That's it! We'll send your free PDF and other benefits to your email directly

1

Developing for Drupal

Drupal is a web-based **Content Management System** (**CMS**). While it is useful out of the box, it is designed with developers in mind. The purpose of this book is to explain how Drupal can be extended in many ways and for many purposes. To this end, the version we will use will be the latest one at the time of writing this book—Drupal 10.

In this book, we will cover a wide range of development topics. We'll discuss how to create a Drupal module, and as we go through the chapters, we'll cover many concepts and tips that will help you build what you need. The goal is not only to explain how things work but also to go through some examples in order to demonstrate this. Since no book can contain everything, I hope that after reading this book, you'll be able to expand on your knowledge on your own by using the resources I reference and by looking into the Drupal core code itself. As helpful as such a book can be for learning any kind of software development, if you really want to progress, you will need to apply the knowledge you have learned and explore the source code yourself. Only by doing this will you be able to understand complex systems with many dependencies and layers.

This chapter introduces the terminology, tools, and processes for developing modules in Drupal. While subsequent chapters focus on code, this chapter focuses on concepts. We'll talk about the architecture of Drupal and how you can hook into Drupal at strategic places to extend it to accomplish new tasks.

The major topics we will be covering in this chapter are as follows:

- An introduction to Drupal development
- How did we get to Drupal 10?
- Drupal architecture
- The major subsystems of Drupal
- Tools for developing in Drupal

By the end of this chapter, you will understand the architectural aspects of Drupal and be ready to start writing code.

Introducing Drupal (for developers)

Out of the box, Drupal traditionally has all the standard functions of a web-based CMS:

- Visitors can view published information on the site, navigate through menus, view listings, individual pages, and so on.
- Users can create accounts and leave comments.
- Administrators can manage the site configuration and control the permissions of users.
- Editors can create, preview, and then publish content when it is ready.
- Content can be syndicated to RSS, where feed readers can pick up new articles as they are published.
- With several built-in themes, even the look and feel of the site can be easily changed.

However, Drupal 8 improved on these and introduced some more powerful capabilities. For example, advanced multilingual support, content moderation, layout building, REST API, and many other features are now available out of the box. And yes, I did mean Drupal 8 because all this started with that version and has been continuing with the subsequent ones.

How did we get to Drupal 10?

Drupal 10 does not represent a great milestone in the traditional sense. It does, but not one comparable in scale to the release of Drupal 8.0 when the entire world cheered and the stock markets rallied. Rather, Drupal 10 represents proof that some decisions were made wisely when the time came to change the release approach that Drupal was accustomed to.

Before Drupal 8, every few years, a major version of Drupal was released. And with these releases came the joy of getting all the new features and leaving the old behind. But what also came was the pain of upgrading to these new releases. No more, said Drupal 8, which has been steadily introducing new features and functionality with each minor release until now. To the point that we have reached the end of the Drupal 9 release cycle and have gone into Drupal 10 in almost the same way as we've been going from one minor release to another, say, from 9.4 to 9.5. But then what is the difference?

In semantic versioning, minor releases mean that new features can be added as long as **backward compatibility** (**BC**) is ensured on all existing public APIs. This means that even if in 8.5, you realize a public API is stupid and want to change it, you must ensure that in 8.6 it remains functional. In a deprecated state, sure, but still compatible. Most of the time, these APIs simply delegate to the new, shiny ones. But as time goes on, the codebase gets full of this deprecated code that should not be used anymore. Enter major releases, such as Drupal 9 or Drupal 10.

Major releases allow the removal of all the deprecated code and instruct developers and users of the software to ensure that they are compatible with all the new APIs and that they ditch the old ones. So, this is exactly what Drupal 10 is doing: removing all the deprecated code from 9.5 and calling it Drupal 10. The two will be identical in many respects. The same thing happened when Drupal 9 was released.

Why *now*, though? Why not in 4 years? Or 5? Apart from the growing codebase full of useless code and the increasing difficulty of managing these deprecations, Drupal also faces the challenge of maintaining its dependencies. Ever since it "got off the island" and started relying on other open-source libraries, it also became dependent on their life cycles. Here, the most notable is Symfony, the popular framework of reusable PHP components. Drupal 8 used Symfony 3 that has no longer been supported since 2021, and therefore the end of life of Drupal 8 needed to coincide with that. Upgrading to Symfony 4 meant breaking BC, so a new major version of Drupal was also needed (at the time, Drupal 9). Now, with Drupal 10, we jump to using Symfony 6.

Besides, there are plenty of libraries that stand to be updated as well, such as Twig to version 3, which is also great.

Where does this leave our book? Everything you will learn about in this book will be compatible with Drupal 10. Many of the things will also be compatible with Drupal 9, especially later versions of it, and with slight adjustments. For this reason, going forward, I will refrain from making mentions of specific versions of Drupal because it makes less and less sense to do so. Except, of course, when it becomes germane to my point to be specific about the version.

Developing for Drupal

As fantastic as these features are, they will certainly not satisfy the needs of all users. To that end, Drupal's capabilities can be easily extended with modules, themes, and installation profiles. Take a look at Drupal's main website, `https://drupal.org/`, and you will find thousands of modules that provide new features and thousands of themes that transform the look and feel of the application or website.

The flexible way Drupal can be extended and transformed through the module and theme mechanisms has led many to claim that Drupal isn't just a CMS but also a **Content Management Framework (CMF)**, capable of being re-tooled to specific needs and functional requirements.

Establishing whether Drupal is rightly called a CMS or CMF is beyond our purpose here, but it is certain that Drupal's most tremendous asset is its extensibility. Want to use a directory server for authentication? There's a Drupal module for that. Want to export data to **Comma-Separated Value (CSV)** files? There are several modules for that (depending on what data you want to export). Interested in Facebook support, integration with Twitter, or adding a Share This button? Yup, there are modules for those too—all of which are available on Drupal.org and provided and maintained by developers like you.

Want to integrate Drupal with that custom tool you wrote to solve your specific business needs? There may not be a module for that, but with a little bit of code, you can write your own. In fact, that is the subject of this book—providing you with the knowledge and tools to achieve your own goals.

In summary, the purpose of this book is to get you ramped up (as quickly as possible) for Drupal module development, using the latest version, 10. As we move chapter by chapter, we will cover the APIs and tools that you will use to build custom Drupal sites, and we won't stick to theory. Most chapters provide working, practically oriented example code designed to show you how to implement the concepts we will be talking about. We will follow Drupal coding conventions and utilize Drupal design patterns in an effort to illustrate the correct way to write code within the Drupal development context.

While I certainly can't write the exact code to meet your needs, my hope is that the code mentioned in these chapters can serve as a foundation for your bigger and better applications.

So let's get started with a few preliminary matters to better understand Drupal.

Technologies that drive Drupal

Drupal has gone through a series of different best practices for when it comes to how it should be installed. But the reality is that they are simply tailored to different needs. The most common, and the most recommended by this author, is the Composer-based approach with the Drupal community-promoted project here: `https://www.drupal.org/docs/develop/using-composer/starting-a-site-using-drupal-composer-project-templates`.

You can read more about how to install Drupal there, so I will not go into detail here. Instead, let's talk a bit about the technologies that power (or are needed by) Drupal 10.

PHP

Drupal is written in the PHP programming language. PHP is a widely supported, multiplatform, and web-centric scripting language. Since Drupal is written in PHP, this book will largely feature code written in PHP, albeit with Drupal standard practices kept in mind.

It is very important to note that the minimum version of PHP required for Drupal 10 to run (and install via Composer) is 8.1. Therefore, PHP 7.4 is no longer supported as it reached its end of life in November 2022 and PHP 8.0 is expected to reach its end of life 1 year later.

Databases and MySQL

Drupal uses the powerful **PHP Data Objects** (**PDO**) library that is standard in PHP. This library is an abstraction layer that allows developers to support numerous databases, including MySQL, PostgreSQL, SQLite, and MariaDB.

The minimum database versions for Drupal 10 are as follows:

- MySQL 5.7.8/MariaDB 10.3.7/Percona Server 5.7.8 or higher with PDO and an InnoDB-compatible primary storage engine

- PostgreSQL 12 or higher (with the pg_trm extension enabled)

- SQLite 3.26 or higher (with the json1 extension enabled)

The web server

Apache has long been the predominant web server, but it is by no means the only server. While Drupal was originally written with Apache in mind, many other web servers (including IIS, Lighttpd, and Nginx) can run Drupal.

We do not explicitly cover the web server layer anywhere in this book, primarily because development rarely requires working at that low level. However, Drupal expects a fair amount of processing from the web server layer, including the handling of URL rewriting.

The two most common web servers you'll typically run Drupal on are Apache and Nginx, with the following minimum version requirements for Drupal 10 (same as with Drupal 9):

- Apache 2.4.7 or higher

- Nginx 1.1 or higher

HTML, CSS, and JavaScript

The de facto web data format is HTML styled with **Cascading Style Sheets** (**CSS**). Client-side interactive components are scripted with JavaScript. As Drupal developers, we will encounter all three of these technologies in this book. Although you don't need to be a JavaScript ninja to understand the code here, you will get the most out of this book if you are comfortable with these three technologies.

Drupal architecture

In the previous section, we introduced the technologies that drive Drupal. However, how do they all fit together? How is the code organized? In this section, let me give you a quick overview of this architecture.

Drupal core, modules, and themes

From an architectural standpoint, we can break up Drupal into three pieces: its core, modules, and themes.

When we discuss Drupal core, we can interpret it in two ways. A more restrictive interpretation sees it as the functionality covered by all the code it ships with, excluding modules and themes. The more widespread interpretation sees it as the total code base it ships with (*out of the box*).

Although the most widespread interpretation is the latter (not least because it differentiates all the functionalities its standard installation contains versus all others provided by contributed modules and themes), it is interesting to consider the first one as well, even if just for a minute. Because in doing so, we can distinguish, architecturally speaking, the base code from the modules and themes that provide various functionalities and layouts. And why is this distinction interesting? Because at the bridge between the two come into play the hooks and events that will also allow us to inject ties to our own functionality.

The core libraries are made up of code belonging to the Drupal project and those from the wider PHP community, which Drupal borrows under open source licensing. This latter approach was new in Drupal 8, continued in Drupal 9 and 10, and has been regarded by many as a positive shift toward getting off the Drupal island and embracing outside libraries, frameworks, and communities.

Essentially, the core libraries provide the functions and services used throughout Drupal. For example, helpers for interacting with the database, translating between languages, sanitizing user data, building forms, encoding data, and many such utilities are found in Drupal's core libraries.

The modules (both core and contributed) are where most of the actual business logic is encapsulated. If enabled, they can provide functionality or extend the existing one. Most of the core modules are needed and cannot be disabled due to their importance in the standard Drupal installation. However, contributed ones can be installed and uninstalled as needed.

The themes (both core and contributed) are an important part of the theme system and are used by the presentation layer. They provide HTML templates within which content and data can be rendered to the user, as well as CSS styling and even client-side scripting for some nice visual interactions. Themes can extend other themes and can also contain some PHP logic to process the data before being rendered.

Now that we have seen what the core libraries, modules, and themes do, let's talk briefly about hooks and events to understand how they are all connected.

Hooks, plugins, and events

Hooks are a very typical Drupal procedural concept that allow Drupal core and modules to gather data from other modules and themes (or expose it). By doing this, the latter can provide new functionality or alter existing one. It is the responsibility of the code that *invokes* the hook to make use of whatever the hook *implementations* return. The format for whatever the latter needs to return is usually described in the hook documentation.

Concretely, hooks work by scanning installed modules and themes and looking for a function that follows a specific naming pattern (in other words, a *hook implementation*). This is, in most cases, in the following format—module_name_hook_name. Additionally, there are also *alter* hooks, which have the word *alter* tacked on to the end of the function name and are used to change data passed as a reference to the hook implementation. We will see examples of hooks later in the book. Don't worry.

> **Note**
>
> Developers with a background in **Object-Oriented Programming (OOP)** or with a strong knowledge of design patterns might recognize this as being similar to the event-handling paradigm captured in the Passive Observer pattern. When some particular event occurs, Drupal allows modules the opportunity to respond to that event.

In previous versions of Drupal, up until Drupal 8, hooks were KING. Yes, I wrote this in capital letters; my *Caps Lock* did not get stuck. This is because they were *the* way to add or extend functionality in modules. As such, they were the single most important aspect of Drupal programming. Since Drupal 8, however, although still important, they have taken a backseat to new concepts, such as plugins and events. There is talk of having them removed completely at some point, but let's wait and see because they are still here.

Since Drupal 8, I dare to say that plugins have become king. Much of the logic that used to be tied to Drupal via hooks is now added in through **plugins** (not to be confused with WordPress plugins). Drupal plugins are discoverable bits of functionality, centralized by a manager, that are used for certain tasks and features. We will see more about plugins and provide many examples later in the book.

A third extension point introduced in Drupal 8 is the event system. Unlike the first two, however, this is not specific to Drupal, but is, in fact, the actual Symfony `EventDispatcher` component (`https://symfony.com/doc/current/components/event_dispatcher.html`). Events are primarily used in Drupal to intercept certain actions or flows in order to either stop or modify them. Many *request-to-response tasks* that were handled via hooks in the past are now handled by dispatching events to check whether any modules are interested in, for example, delivering the response to the user.

Services and the dependency injection container

Another architecturally important element of Drupal is the Symfony dependency injection component (`https://symfony.com/doc/current/components/dependency_injection.html`), specifically represented by the service container.

This component is a staple of modern OOP PHP programming and as such has become foundational to Drupal since version 8. It allows us to create *services* that can be injected into various places of our code in order to handle certain functional (and often swappable) tasks. Additionally, they can also be used as an extension point because the service container is able to group services that have very specific responsibilities and use them to do something automatically. In other words, simply by defining a service, we can provide our own functionality or even change existing logic.

We will encounter many services, and we will see how we can declare our own later in this book.

From request to response

Now that we have listed the most important architectural components of Drupal, let's briefly see how these are used in delivering responses to the requests a user makes on a Drupal website. To this end, we will analyze a simplified example of a handled request:

1. A user accesses the `http://example.com/node/123` URL in a web browser.

2. The browser contacts the web server at `example.com` and requests the resource at `/node/123`.

3. The web server recognizes that the request must be handled by PHP and starts up (or contacts) a PHP environment to handle the request.

4. PHP executes Drupal's front controller file (`index.php`), which then creates a new `Request` object from the resource that was requested.

5. Symfony's `HttpKernel` handles this request object by dispatching a number of events, such as `kernel.request`, `kernel.controller`, `kernel.response`, and `kernel.view`.

6. The route that maps to that request is identified through the `kernel.request` event.

7. The route controller is identified, and the `kernel.controller` event is used to perform any alterations on the responsible controller, as well as to resolve the arguments that need to be passed to it. In our case, this route is registered by the Node module through the main Entity system, which identifies the entity ID, loads it, and builds the markup to be returned as part of the response.

8. If the respective controller (or handler) returns something other than a `Response` object, the `kernel.view` event is dispatched to check whether there is any code that can transform that into a `response` object. In most cases, controllers typically return render arrays, which are transformed into `response` objects.

9. Once a response is created, the front controller returns it to the browser and terminates the request.

In this context, as module developers, we spend most of our time inside controllers and services trying to figure out what we need to return to the page. We then rely on Drupal to transform our render array into a proper response to the user, but we can also return one ourselves directly. Moreover, the theme system comes into play here, as well as the block system, because our content gets wrapped into a block that is placed in a region surrounded by other regions that contain other blocks. If it sounds complicated now, don't worry; we will cover in detail all these aspects with examples, and it will become clear in no time. You are not expected to know what render arrays are, for example.

Drupal's major subsystems

In the previous section, we took a brief look at Drupal's architecture. Now we will refine our perspective a bit. We will walk through the major subsystems that Drupal has to offer.

Routing

It all starts with a route, doesn't it? Most interactions with a Drupal website begin with a use (or system) accessing a certain path (or resource). This translates into a route, which maps that resource to a flow that (hopefully) returns a successful response back, or at least a graceful failure.

The Symfony `Routing` component (`http://symfony.com/doc/current/components/routing.html`) is the chief actor in this play.

In *Chapter 2, Creating Your First Module*, we will see how we can define our own route and map it to a controller that will render our page. We will cover a few of the more important route options and take a look at how we can control access to these routes.

Entities

Progressively, entities have become a very powerful way of modeling data and content in Drupal. The most famous type of entity has always been the `Node`, and it has been historically the cornerstone of content storage and display. Since Drupal 8, the entire entity system has been revamped to make any other entity types potentially just as important. They have been brought to the forefront and have been properly connected with other systems.

All entity types can have multiple `bundles`, which are different *variations* of the same entity type and can have different fields on them (while sharing some base fields) – fields store data.

Drupal core still ships with the `Node` entity type, with a few bundles such as Basic Page and Article in its standard installation profile. In addition, it comes with a few other entity types, such as `User`, `Comment`, `File`, and so on.

These are not the only types of entities we have, though. The aforementioned examples are all **content** entity types. Drupal 8, however, also introduced the configuration entity types. The former are used for modeling content, but in reality, they are for anything that holds data that can be stored in the database and is specific to that environment. They are not used for storing configuration, though. Users and content are great examples, as they do not need to be (usually) deployable from one environment to another. The latter, on the other hand, are exportable items of configuration, of which there can be more than one. For example, a content entity bundle is a great example because there can be more than one bundle for a certain content entity type; they have some metadata and information stored that can differ from bundle to bundle, and they need to be deployed on all environments. That is, they are fundamental to the correct functioning of the site.

Understanding the entity system is indispensable for development in Drupal because it provides a powerful way to model custom data and content.

Now that we have an idea of what entities are, let's take a look at how data is actually stored on these entities.

Fields

I have alluded in the previous section to how certain entity bundles can have various fields. This means that each entity type bundle can have any number of fields that are responsible for holding data. Additionally, each entity type itself can have fields for storing data. Okay, but what? Let's break this down.

There are two types of fields in Drupal—base fields and configurable fields. The former are fields that are defined in code for a given entity type and that are present across all *bundles*, whereas the latter are usually created and configured in the UI and attached to a *bundle* of that entity type (and exported via configuration).

Fields can also be of multiple types, depending on the data they store. You can have string (or text) fields, numeric fields, date fields, email fields, and so on. As developers, we can create our own field types if the existing ones are not good enough for our data.

In this book, we will take a look at how we can define base fields on a certain entity type and create our own field type with its own data input widget and output formatter. Site builders can then use this field type on any entity type.

Menus

Any site needs some sort of navigation, right? Drupal not only maintains content but also provides details about how the site itself is organized. That is, it keeps a structure of how content is related.

The principal way that it does this is through the menu subsystem. The latter provides APIs to generate, retrieve, and modify elements that describe the site structure. Put in common parlance, it handles the system's navigational menus.

Menus are hierarchical; that is, they have a tree-like structure. A menu item can have multiple children, each of which may have its own children, and so on. In this way, we can use the menu system to structure our site into sections and subsections.

In this book, we will see how we can work programmatically with menus and menu links.

Views

Listing content and data is always an important capability that CMSes covet, and this is what Views does in Drupal. And it does it well.

The purpose of the Views module is to expose data and content in a way that allows the creation of configurable listings. It includes things such as filters, sorts, display options, and many other features. As developers, we often find a need to write our own field or filter plugin to work with Views or expose data from our custom entities or external data sources.

Views is tied to the general architecture and used for most list pages (especially, admin pages) provided by Drupal core. Although it's a very site-building-oriented tool, in this book, we will take a look at how we can create plugins that extend its capabilities to offer even more options for site builders.

Forms

Unless your site has three pages and five paragraphs of text, the likelihood that you will need to capture user input via some type of form is very high. Also, if you've been coding PHP applications, you will know how forms have always been a pain from the point of view of securely and efficiently rendering and processing the submitted data. As soon as you use a PHP framework such as Symfony or Laravel, you will note that an API is in place to take much of that load off your shoulders.

The same goes for Drupal and its powerful Form API. Historically, it has been a great abstraction over having to output your own form elements and deal with posted values. It allows you to define your own form definition in OOP and handle validation and submission in a logical way. Its rendering and processing are taken care of by Drupal securely, so you don't have to worry about any of that.

In this book, we will encounter some forms and see how they actually work in practice.

Configuration

The centralized Drupal configuration system, although it stores all configuration in the database, allows it all to be exported into YAML files (and then reimported). This means committing it to the version control system (Git). So, from a development point of view, we have a good relationship between the features we are coding and the configuration they depend on (for example, a new field).

Configuration is of two kinds—simple and complex (configuration entities we noted in the *Entities* section). The difference between the two is that simple configuration is always singular. In other words, there is only one instance of itself. For example, the site name and email address are stored inside such a configuration item. You wouldn't expect the need for more than one instance of these two value items. However, in the case of the complex configuration, you would. For example, a View definition is such a configuration entity because it follows a certain schema and we can have multiple View definitions. Makes sense, doesn't it? If not, it will when we dive deeper into the configuration system.

Plugins

Plugins are an elegant solution to an important problem— encapsulating functionality. Right off the bat, you should not confuse them with things such as WordPress plugins, which are more akin to Drupal modules. Instead, you should think of plugins as components of reusable code that can be used and managed by a central system. Typically, they are used when a system handles a task in a certain way (plugin A) but allows other modules to provide different ways to handle that task (plugin B or C).

You can also look at plugins as being similar to entities (somehow): except not used for data storage, but for functionality. Instead of creating a type of data that gets stored, you create a type of functionality that is used. Plugins and entities usually work hand in hand, especially when it comes to manipulating data in different ways.

An important aspect of how they work is their discoverability. Most plugin types are discovered via something called *Annotations*. Annotations are a form of DocBlock comments, borrowed from the Doctrine library (`https://www.doctrine-project.org/projects/doctrine-annotations/en/latest/index.html`), by which we can describe classes, methods, and even properties with certain metadata. This metadata is then read to determine what that item is without the need to instantiate the class. In Drupal, we use annotations only at a class level to denote that it is a plugin implementation with certain characteristics.

> **Note:**
> Annotations are very similar in concept to PHP 8 attributes, which will someday replace the Doctrine annotations. The plan is, in fact, to deprecate the latter over the course of the Drupal 10 release cycle.

The second most common discoverability method for plugins is via a YAML file, and a popular example of those is menu links (as we will see later in the book). However, for now, you should know that plugins are very widely used, and we will create quite a few plugins in this book.

The theme system

The responsibility for theming a given piece of data is spread out over Drupal core, modules, and the themes themselves. So, as a module developer, it is important to know that both modules and themes can theme data or content.

In this book, we will focus on the aspects that happen at the module level. We will not concern ourselves with styling, but instead, we will work primarily with theming definitions and templates that are needed within the module. Typically, it is best practice to ensure that modules are able to theme their data. If done right, themes can then come into play to style the output or override that theming to change the presentation altogether.

The templating system used by Drupal is Twig (`https://twig.symfony.com`), which with Drupal 10, has been upgraded to version 3.

Caching

The last major subsystem that I will include here is the caching layer. Since version 8, Drupal has gone to great lengths to improve the performance of building pages and rendering data. To this end, the caching system has become an important part to consider whenever we either do complex or heavy calculations or render content.

From a module developer's perspective, there are two main pillars of the caching system. The first one provides developers with a cache backend to store the results of complex data calculations. These can be read in the next requests to avoid the need for reprocessing that task. This goes hand in hand with the cache invalidation that happens when something in the system changes that requires the calculations to be redone. The second pillar is the render cache, which allows developers to wrap their output with metadata that describes when the cache of that output needs to be invalidated.

We will see these in action in a later chapter dedicated to caching.

Other subsystems

There are other subsystems in Drupal of varying importance. I chose to include the previous ones because I deemed them to be the most important to be introduced upfront and especially from the point of view of a module developer. However, as we progress through the book, we will definitely encounter others.

Tools for developing in Drupal

Drupal is a sophisticated platform, and from the glimpse provided in this chapter, we can already see that there are numerous systems and structures to keep track of. In this section, I will mention a few tools that simplify or streamline the development process.

Going forward, I assume that you have your own web server stack and your own PHP development tools. However, if not, you can check out the currently available options for running a Drupal site. However, the most flexible development environment, in my opinion, is the Docker-based one. You can easily get started with a pre-made and well-documented stack here: `https://github.com/wodby/docker4drupal`.

All the code we write in this book can be found in the GitHub repository referenced in the introductory pages. However, a quick-to-set-up Docker-based environment is also provided there. So, with just a few commands, you can have a Drupal site up and running, and you can test the code of each individual chapter with ease. Do make sure you check it out and try using it. Simply follow the instructions in the repository README file.

As for a code editor, I personally use PhpStorm (as many others do), but you are free to use whatever IDE you want because Drupal itself doesn't require anything special. Do, however, use some sort of IDE because it will make your life much easier.

Additionally, while running a PHP debugger is certainly not necessary, you may find running Xdebug or the Zend Debugger to be useful. I personally recommend a PHP debugger wholeheartedly, not only for debugging itself but also for understanding the processes that happen under the hood.

Version control

Any software development needs to happen through a version-controlled environment. By now, Drupal universally uses Git. So, you should make sure that you have Git installed locally, even if just to be able to check out the code examples we write in this book, which are hosted on GitHub.

Composer

As I alluded to earlier, installing Drupal is best done via the recommended project. However, you may also install it straight from Git by checking out the latest tag or commit in the `Drupal.org` Git repository (`https://www.drupal.org/project/drupal/git-instructions`). If you do this, you will need to install its dependencies via Composer, and Drupal has many.

To this end, you will need to have Composer available in your development environment and have a basic understanding of how to use it.

The API site and coding standards

A lot of background knowledge is required for writing good Drupal code. Of course, the aim of a book such as this is to try to provide as much of that background knowledge as possible. However, self-documentation and research still remain key, and there are a number of resources that a Drupal developer should have on hand.

The first is the official online API documentation. Just about every function in Drupal is documented using inline code documentation. The Doxygen program is then used to extract that documentation and format it. You can access the full API documentation online at `http://api.drupal.org`.

Along with using the Drupal APIs, we strive to comply with Drupal's coding conventions. Best practices in software development include keeping code clean, consistent, and readable. One aspect of this is removing nuances in code formatting by following a fixed standard.

This is particularly important on a platform such as Drupal, where thousands of developers all contribute to the code. Without coding standards, the code would become a cluttered mishmash of styles, and valuable development time will be spent merely deciphering code instead of working on it.

The Drupal site has a manual on coding standards that each Drupal developer needs to become familiar with (`https://www.drupal.org/docs/develop/standards/coding-standards`). It won't happen overnight; you will get better with experience, but you can also configure your IDE to, for instance, flag any issues with your code formatting.

A third resource is the change records database (`https://www.drupal.org/list-changes/drupal`). On this page, you'll find an inventory of the most important API and usage changes with some handy explanations. Since Drupal 10 will ship new functionality every 6 months, this database is very important to follow.

The developer (Devel) module

In your development environment, you can install a handy module called Devel (`http://drupal.org/project/devel`), which provides several sophisticated tools designed to help developers create and debug Drupal code.

The following are a few of the features of this module:

- Functions used for dumping objects and arrays into formatted Drupal output
- Tools for analyzing database usage and performance
- A content generator for quickly populating your site with testing content

Drush (the Drupal shell)

Sometimes, it is much easier to run some tasks with a single command in a console. Drush (`https://github.com/drush-ops/drush`) provides a command-line Drupal interface and it can be used to execute tasks with a few keystrokes at the console.

When developing, we often have to clear caches, run specific tasks, or deploy data to a remote server. Drush can help accomplish tasks like these. Additionally, we can write our own Drush commands that perform various custom tasks, for example, to be used in cron jobs. So having Drush installed is a must for any serious Drupal developer.

Developer settings

While doing local development, it's beneficial to (sometimes) disable things such as caching in order to be quicker. To do so, we can use local settings that disable caching, prevent CSS and JavaScript file aggregation, and do other similar things.

These settings are found inside the `example.settings.local.php` file in the `/sites` folder of the installation. To benefit from these, you will need to make sure that they are included in your main `settings.php` file (either by copying them inside or including a file like this).

A word of caution—do keep in mind that by developing with caching disabled at all times, you run the risk of overlooking certain aspects that won't work properly with caching enabled (such as invalidations). So, do try to toggle these settings on or off to ensure that a production-like environment will work just as well as under your development conditions.

Drupal check

In order to facilitate upgrading code from Drupal 9 to 10, a nice tool has been created by the community that statically runs over your code and points out all the use of deprecated code you may have. It's a command-line utility called `drupal-check` that is easily installable and can greatly speed up this process. Of course, you can rely also on the IDE to flag deprecated warnings.

The tool can be found here: `https://github.com/mglaman/drupal-check`.

Summary

This chapter has been an overview of Drupal for developers. We saw what technologies Drupal uses. We took a look at Drupal's architecture. We took a cursory glance at several prominent subsystems of Drupal. We also got a feel for which developer-oriented tools are to be used while working with Drupal.

Starting with the next chapter, we will be working with code. In fact, each of the subsequent chapters will focus on practical aspects of working with Drupal.

In the next chapter, we will create our first Drupal module with the obligatory `Hello World` example.

2
Creating Your First Module

Now that we have covered some of the introductory aspects of Drupal module development, it's time to dive right into the meat of what we are doing here—module creation.

Here are some of the important topics that we will cover in this chapter:

- Creating a new Drupal module – the files that are necessary to get started
- Creating a route and controller
- Creating and using a service
- Creating a form
- Creating a custom block
- Working with links
- Using the Event Dispatcher

Concretely, in this chapter, we will create a new custom module called *Hello World*. In this module, we will define a route that maps to a controller and that outputs this age-old programming message. This will be our first win.

Next, we will define a service that our Controller will use to pimp out our message. After all, we don't want the same message presented to the user all day long. This simple example, however, will illustrate what services are and how to interact with the service container to make use of them.

Then, we will create a form where an administrator will be able to override the message shown on our page. It will be stored in configuration, and we will alter our service to make use of that configuration. The key takeaway here will be the use of the Form API. However, we will also discuss how to store some basic configuration values and add dependencies to our existing services.

Finally, we want to become a bit more flexible. Why should users only be greeted on a specific page? We will create a custom block that can be placed anywhere on the site and will display the same message. Here, we will see how block plugins are defined and how they can expose their own configuration forms to be more flexible.

Although not strictly related to our *Hello World* example, we will also look at how to work with links programmatically in Drupal. This is a very common task that any Drupal developer needs to do very often. This is why we will get in it out of the way early.

Moreover, we will also look at using the Event Dispatcher component and, more importantly, subscribing to events. We'll illustrate this with a fairly common example of when you'd need to do this—performing redirects from incoming requests.

By the end of this chapter, you should have the foundational knowledge necessary to build your own module from scratch. Moreover, you should be able to understand and implement some of the most used techniques in Drupal module development.

Creating a module

Creating a simple Drupal module is not difficult. You only need one file for it to be recognized by the core installation and to be able to enable it. In this state, it won't do much, but it will be installable. Let's first look at how to do this, and then we will progressively add meat to it in order to achieve the goals set out at the beginning of the chapter.

Modules go inside the /modules folder of the Drupal application. Inside the /modules folder, there can be a /contrib folder, which stores contributed modules, and a /custom folder, where we put the modules we write custom for the specific application. And that is where we will place our custom module, called *Hello World*.

We will start by creating a folder called hello_world. This will also be the module's machine name used in many other places. Inside, we will need to create an *info* file that describes our module. This file is named hello_world.info.yml. This naming structure is important—first, the module name, then info, followed by the .yml extension. You will hear this file often referred to as the module's info file (due to it having had the .info extension in past versions of Drupal).

Inside this file, we will need to add some minimal information that describes our module. We will go with something like this:

```
name: Hello World
description: Hello World module
type: module
core_version_requirement: ^10
package: Custom
```

Some of this is self-explanatory, but let's see what these lines mean:

- The first two key-value pairs represent the human-readable name and description of the module.

- The `type` key means that this is a module *info* file rather than a theme.

- The `core_version_requirement` key specifies that this module works with version 10 of Drupal, and it won't be installable on previous or future versions.

- Finally, we place this in a generic `Custom` package so that it gets categorized in this group on the modules' administration screen.

That is pretty much it. The module can now be enabled either through the UI at `/admin/modules` or via Drush using the `drush en hello_world` command.

> **Note**
>
> Using the `core_version_requirement` key, we can semantically specify which version of Drupal the module works with. For example, this would indicate the module is compatible with Drupal 9 as well: `^9.5 || ^10`.

Before we move on, let's see what other options you can add (and probably will need to add at some point or another) to the `info` file:

Module dependencies: If your module depends on other modules, you can specify this in its info file like so:

```
dependencies:
   - drupal:views
   - ctools:ctools
```

The dependencies should be named in the `project:module` format, where `project` is the project name as it appears in the URL of the project on Drupal.org and `module` is the machine name of the module.

Configuration: If your module has a general configuration form that centralizes the configuration options of the module, you can specify the route of that form in the info file. Doing so will add a link to that form on the `admin/modules` UI page where modules are being installed:

```
configure: module_name.configuration_route_name
```

The module as it stands doesn't do much. In fact, it does nothing. However, do pat yourself on the back, as you have created your first Drupal module. Before we move on to the interesting stuff we planned out, let's implement our first hook, responsible for providing some helpful information about our module.

Your first hook implementation

As we hinted at in the first chapter, when Drupal encounters an event for which there is a hook (and there are hundreds of such events), it will look through all modules for matching hook implementations. Now, how does it find the matching implementations? It looks for the functions that are named in the `module_name_hook_name` format, where `hook_name` is replaced by the name of the hook being implemented and `module_name` is the module machine name. The name of a hook is whatever comes after `hook_`. We will see an example next when we implement `hook_help()`. However, once it finds the implementations, it will then execute each of them, one after another. Once all hook implementations have been executed, Drupal will continue its processing.

Hook implementations typically go inside a `.module` file, so let's create one in our module folder called `hello_world.module` and place an opening PHP tag at the top. Then, we can have the following `hook_help()` implementation inside (and typically all other hook implementations):

```php
use Drupal\Core\Routing\RouteMatchInterface;

/**
 * Implements hook_help().
 */
function hello_world_help($route_name, RouteMatchInterface
    $route_match) {
  switch ($route_name) {
    case 'help.page.hello_world':
      $output = '';
      $output .= '<h3>' . t('About') . '</h3>';
      $output .= '<p>' . t('This is an example module.') .
    '</p>';
      return $output;

    default:
  }
}
```

As you can see, the name of the function respects the previously mentioned format—module_name_hook_name—because we are implementing `hook_help`. So, we replaced `hook` with the module name and `hook_name` with `help`. Moreover, this particular hook takes two parameters that we can use inside it, though in our case, we only use one, that is, the route name.

The purpose of this hook is to provide Drupal with some help text about what this module does. You won't always implement this hook, but it's good to be aware of it. The way it works is that each new module receives its own route inside the main module, where users can browse this info—ours is `help.page.hello_world`. So, in this implementation, we will tell Drupal (and, more specifically, the core `Help` module) the following: if a user is looking at our module's help route (page), show the info contained in the `$output` variable. And that's pretty much it.

According to the Drupal coding standards, the DocBlock message above the hook implementation needs to contain at least a line in the format you see above. A second line could, in certain cases, document the logic taking place in the hook, especially if we were doing something complex or not immediately obvious. It's good to help others understand what we are doing.

Users can now reach this page from the module administration page by clicking on the **Help** link for each individual module that has this hook implemented. Do remember to clear the cache first, though. Easy, right?

Figure 2.1: Hello World example module

Even though we are not really providing any useful info through this hook, implementing it helped us understand how hooks work and what the naming convention is for using them. Additionally, we saw an example of a traditional (procedural) Drupal extension point that module developers can use. In doing so, we literally extended the capability of the **Help** module by allowing it to give more info to users.

Before we move on, let's quickly add a file comment to ensure we respect the Drupal coding standards. So, we add the following to the top of the `.module` file:

```
/**
 * @file
 * Hello World module file.
 */
```

> **Note**
>
> In order to keep the code examples on the pages of the book concise, going forward, I will skip certain formatting required for respecting the Drupal coding standards. In the GitHub repository, however, all the code should be fully correct.

Now, let's move on to creating something of our own.

Route and controller

The first real piece of functionality we set out to create was a simple Drupal page that outputs the age-old *Hello World* string. To do this, we will need two things—a route and a controller. So, let's start with the first one.

The route

Inside our module, we will need to create our routing file that will hold all our statically defined routes. The name of this file will be `hello_world.routing.yml`. By now, I assume that you understand what the deal is with the file naming conventions in a Drupal module. However, in any case, this is another YAML file in which we will need to put YAML-formatted data:

```
hello_world.hello:
  path: '/hello'
  defaults:
    controller: Drupal\hello_world\Controller\
        HelloWorldController::helloWorld
    _title: 'Our first route'
  requirements:
    _permission: 'access content'
```

This is our first route definition. It starts with the route name (`hello_world.hello`), followed by all the necessary info about it underneath, in a YAML-formatted multidimensional array. The standard practice is to have the route name start with the module name it is in, followed by route qualifiers as needed.

So, what does the route definition contain? There can be many options here, but for now, we will stick with the simple ones that serve our purpose.

> **Note**
>
> For more info about all the route configuration options, visit the relevant documentation page at `https://www.drupal.org/docs/drupal-apis/routing-system/structure-of-routes`. It is a good resource to keep on hand.

First, we have a path key, which indicates the path we want this route to work on. Then, we have a `defaults` section, which usually contains info relevant to the handlers responsible for delivering something when this route is accessed. In our case, we set the controller and method responsible for delivering the page, as well as its title. Finally, we have a `requirements` section, which usually has to do with conditions that need to be met for this route to be accessible (or be hit)—things such as permissions and format. In our case, we will require users to have the `access content` permission, which most visitors will have. Don't worry; we will cover more about access in *Chapter 10, Access Control*.

That is all we need for our first route definition. Now, we will need to create the Controller that maps to it and can deliver something to the user.

Before we do that, let's look at an example of a very common routing requirement you will most likely have to use really soon. We don't need this for the functionality we're building in this chapter, so I won't include it in the final code. However, it's important that you know how this works.

Route variables

A very common requirement is to have a variable route parameter (or more) that gets used by the code that maps to the route, for example, the ID or path alias of the page you want to show. These parameters can be added by wrapping a certain path element in curly braces, like so:

```
path: '/hello/{param}'
```

Here, {param} will map to a $param variable that gets passed as an argument to the controller or handler responsible for this route. So, if the user goes to the hello/jack path, the $param variable will have the jack value and the controller can use that.

Additionally, Drupal comes with parameter converters that transform the parameter into something more meaningful. For example, an entity can be autoloaded and passed to the Controller directly instead of an ID. Also, if no entity is found, the route acts as a 404, saving us a few good lines of code. To achieve this, we will also need to describe the parameter so that Drupal knows how to autoload it. We can do so by adding a route option for that parameter:

```
options:
    parameters:
      param:
        type: entity:node
```

So, we have now mapped the {param} parameter to the node entity type. Hence, if the user goes to hello/1, the node with the ID of 1 will be loaded (if it exists).

We can do one better. If instead of {param}, we name the parameter {node} (the machine name of the entity type), we can avoid having to write the parameters option in the route completely. Drupal will figure out that it is an entity and will try to load that node by itself. Neat, no?

So, keep these things in mind the next time you need to write dynamic routes.

Namespaces

Before moving on with the Controller we set out to write, let's break down the namespace situation in Drupal and how the folder structure needs to be inside a module.

Drupal uses the PSR-4 namespace autoloading standard. In effect, this means that the namespace of all Drupal core and module classes starts with \Drupal. For modules, the base namespace is \

Drupal\module_name, where module_name is the machine name of the module. This then maps to the /src folder found inside the module directory (for main integration files). For PHPUnit tests, we have a different namespace, as we will see in *Chapter 17, Automated Testing*.

So essentially, we will need a /src folder inside our module to place all our classes that need to be autoloaded. So, we can go ahead and create it.

The Controller

Now that we have found where we must place our Controller, let's begin by creating a Controller folder inside our module's /src folder. Although not mandatory, this is standard practice for Controller placement. Inside this folder, we can have our first Controller class file: HelloWorldController.php.

Inside the file, we again have something simple (after the opening PHP tags):

```php
namespace Drupal\hello_world\Controller;

use Drupal\Core\Controller\ControllerBase;

/**
 * Controller for the salutation message.
 */
class HelloWorldController extends ControllerBase {

  /**
   * Hello World.
   *
   * @return array
   *    Our message.
   */
  public function helloWorld() {
    return [
      '#markup' => $this->t('Hello World'),
    ];
  }
}
```

As expected, we start with the namespace declaration. If you read the previous section, the namespace choice will make sense. Then, we have our Controller class, which extends ControllerBase, which happens to provide some helper tools (such as the StringTranslationTrait, which I will explain later in *Chapter 13, Internationalization and Languages*). If you recall our route definition, we referenced a helloWorld method on this Controller class.

If you've worked with previous versions of Drupal, this array (called a *render array*) will be familiar. Otherwise, what you need to know right now is that we are returning simple markup with the

`Hello World` text wrapped in the translation service I hinted at in the previous paragraph. After the Controller returns this array, there will be an `EventSubscriber` that takes this array, runs it through the Drupal theme layer, and returns the HTML page as a response. The actual content returned in the Controller will be wrapped in the `Main page content` block, which is usually placed in the main content region of the theme.

Now, our simple Controller is done. If we clear the cache and go to `/hello`, we should encounter a new page that outputs the **Our first route** title and the **Hello World** content. Success!

> **Note**
>
> You can clear the cache by going to **Admin** -> **Configuration** -> **Development** -> **Performance** or by running the `drush cache-rebuild` command.

Figure 2.2: Controller interface

Services

Why don't I like this approach?

Even if for the moment not much is happening in it, I don't want the Controller making decisions on how to greet my users. First of all, Controllers need to stay lean. I want my users to be greeted a bit more dynamically, depending on the time of day, and that will increase the complexity. Second of all, maybe I will want this greeting to be done elsewhere as well, and there is no way I am copy-pasting this logic somewhere else, nor am I going to misuse the Controller just to be able to call that method. The solution? We delegate the logic of constructing the greeting to a service and use that service in our Controller to output the greeting.

What is a service?

A service is an object that gets instantiated by a Service Container and is used to handle operations in a reusable way, for example, performing calculations and interacting with the database, an external API, or any number of things. Moreover, it can take dependencies (other services) and use them to help out. Services are a core part of the **dependency injection (DI)** principle that is commonly used in modern PHP applications.

If you don't have any experience with these concepts, an important thing to note is also that they are globally registered with the service container and are (usually) instantiated only once per request. This means that altering them after you have requested them from the container means that they stay altered even if you request them again. In essence, they are singletons. So, you should write your services in such a way that they stay immutable, and most of the data they need to process is either from a dependency or passed in from the client that uses it (and does not affect it). Although this is the case for most services, there are some that work differently, in that they get re-created with each request. But these examples are rare, and we should not overload the job at hand by talking about them here.

> **Note**
>
> Many Drupal core service definitions can be found inside the `core.services.yml` file located in the root `/core` folder. So, if you are ever looking for service names to use, your best bet is to look there. Additionally, core modules also have service definitions inside their respective `*.services.yml` files. So, make sure that you also check there.

The HelloWorldSalutation service

Now that we have a general idea as to what a service is, let's create one to see all this in practice.

As I mentioned earlier, I want my greetings to be more dynamic, that is, I want the salutation to depend on the time of day. So, we will create a `HelloWorldSalutation` class that is responsible for doing that and place it in the `/src` folder (our module's namespace root) in a file naturally called `HelloWorldSalutation.php`:

```php
namespace Drupal\hello_world;

use Drupal\Core\StringTranslation\StringTranslationTrait;

/**
 * Prepares the salutation to the world.
 */
class HelloWorldSalutation {

  use StringTranslationTrait;
```

```
/**
 * Returns the salutation
 */
public function getSalutation() {
  $time = new \DateTime();
  if ((int) $time->format('G') >= 00 && (int) $time->
      format('G') < 12) {
    return $this->t('Good morning world');
  }

  if ((int) $time->format('G') >= 12 && (int) $time->
      format('G') < 18) {
    return $this->t('Good afternoon world');
  }

  if ((int) $time->format('G') >= 18) {
    return $this->t('Good evening world');
  }
}
}
```

> **Note**
>
> From now on, I will not always mention the file name that a particular class goes into. So, you can safely assume one file per class, named after the class itself. Moreover, I assume that the namespace business is also clear, so I won't explain it again.

Let's see what else we did here. First, we used the `StringTranslationTrait` in order to expose the translation function. Second, we created a rudimentary method that returns a different greeting depending on the time of day. This could probably have been done better, but for the purposes of this example, it works just fine.

> **Note**
>
> In this example, I used the native PHP `time()` function to get the current time, and that's OK. But you should know that Drupal has its very own `Drupal\Component\Datetime\Time` service that we can use to get the current time. It also has additional methods for requesting time-specific information, so make sure you check it out and use it when appropriate.

Now that we have our class, it's time to define it as a service. We don't want to be going `new HelloWorldSalutation()` all over our code base, but instead, register it with the Service Container and use it from there as a dependency. How do we do that?

First, we will need, yet again, a YAML file: `hello_world.services.yml`. This file starts with the `services` key and under that, we will have all the service definitions of our module. So, our file will look like this (for now):

```
services:
  hello_world.salutation:
    class: Drupal\hello_world\HelloWorldSalutation
```

This is the simplest possible service definition you can have. You give it a name (`hello_world.salutation`) and map it to a class to be instantiated. It is standard practice to have the service name start with your module name.

Once we clear the cache, the service will get registered with the Service Container and will be available to use.

> **Note**
>
> If there is any reason to believe that you will have more than one salutation service, you should create an interface that this class can implement. This way, you'll be able to always type-hint that interface instead of the class and make the implementations swappable. In fact, having interfaces is a best practice.

Tagged services

Service definitions can also be tagged in order to inform the container if they serve a specific purpose. Typically, these are picked up by a collector service that uses them for a given subsystem. As an example, if we wanted to tag the `hello_world.salutation` service, it would look something like this:

```
hello_world.salutation:
  class: Drupal\hello_world\HelloWorldSalutation
  tags:
    - {name: tag_name}
```

Tags can also get a priority, as we will see in some examples later in this book.

Before we go and use our service in the Controller we created, let's take a breather and run through the ways you can make use of services once they are registered.

Using services in Drupal

There are essentially two ways of using services—statically and injected. The first is done using a static call to the service container, whereas the second uses dependency injection to pass the object through the constructor (or in some rare cases, a setter method). However, let's check out how, why, and what the real difference is.

Statically, you would use the global \Drupal class to instantiate a service:

```
$service = \Drupal::service('hello_world.salutation');
```

This is how we use services in .module files and, in rare cases, classes that are not exposed to the service container and into which we cannot inject.

A few popular services also have shorthand methods on the \Drupal class; for example, \Drupal::entityTypeManager(). I recommend that you inspect the \Drupal class and take a look at the ones with shorthand methods available.

It is not good to use the static method of service instantiation inside a Controller, service, plugin, or any other class where dependency injection is an option. The reason is that it defeats much of the purpose of using a service, as it couples the two, making it a nightmare to test. Inside hook implementations and other Drupal-specific procedural code, on the other hand, we have no choice, and it is normal to do so.

Moreover, just because a piece of code is inside a .module file, it doesn't mean that it should be there. In general, these modules should only contain things such as hook implementations or any other implementations that require a certain naming convention to be respected. They should also be lean and have their work delegated to services.

The proper way to use services is to inject them where needed. Admittedly, this approach is a bit more time-consuming but, as you progress, it will become second nature. Also, since there are a few different ways to inject dependencies (based on where you do so), we will not cover them here. Instead, we will see how they work throughout this book, at the right time. We will look at a very important example right now in the next section.

Injecting the service into our Controller

Let's now continue with our module and take a look at how to inject the newly created service into our Controller.

We will need to add some code to the Controller (typically at the beginning of the class so that we can immediately identify the presence of this code when looking at it):

```
/**
 * @var \Drupal\hello_world\HelloWorldSalutation
 */
protected $salutation;

/**
 * HelloWorldController constructor.
 *
 * @param \Drupal\hello_world\HelloWorldSalutation
 *     $salutation
```

```
  */
  public function __construct(HelloWorldSalutation
      $salutation) {
    $this->salutation = $salutation;
  }

/**
 * {@inheritdoc}
 */
public static function create(ContainerInterface
    $container) {
  return new static(
    $container->get('hello_world.salutation')
  );
}
```

In addition to this, ensure that you include the relevant *use* statements at the top of the file:

```
use Drupal\hello_world\HelloWorldSalutation;
use Symfony\Component\DependencyInjection
    \ContainerInterface;
```

So, what is going on here? First, we give the Controller a constructor method, which takes our service as an argument and stores it as a property. For me, this is usually the very first method in the class. But how does this constructor get its argument? It gets it via the create() method, which receives the Service Container as a parameter and is free to choose the service(s) needed by the Controller constructor. This is usually my second method in a class. I prefer this order because it's very easy to check whether these methods are present. Also, their presence is important, especially when inheriting and observing what the parent is injecting.

OK, but how does this injection business work in reality?

In a nutshell, after the route is found and the responsible Controller is resolved, a check is made to see whether the latter implements ContainerInjectionInterface. Our Controller does so via its parent, ControllerBase. If it does, the Controller gets instantiated via the create() method, and the container is passed to it. From there, it is responsible for creating a new static version of itself with the required services from the container—not that complicated, really!

The create() method is a staple practice in the Drupal dependency injection pattern, so you will see it quite a lot. However, one thing to keep in mind is that you should never pass the entire container to the class you instantiate with it because you are no longer doing dependency injection then.

A note about ControllerBase, which we are extending—it is a standard practice to extend it, but not mandatory, as controllers are nothing more than simple callables. It provides some nice traits, implements the interfaces that are required, and immediately shows what the purpose of the class is.

However, from the point of view of dependency injection, I advise against using the helper methods that return services (for example, `entityTypeManager()`). They, unfortunately, load services statically, which is not the best practice in this case. You should instead inject them yourself, as we did just now.

OK, let's turn back to our example. Now that we have the service injected, we can use it to render the dynamic salutation:

```
return [
   '#markup' => $this->salutation->getSalutation(),
];
```

There we have it. Now our greeting is dependent on the time of day and our Controller is dependent on our salutation service.

One thing I would like to specify about our example is that I disregarded caching for the sake of simplicity. With caching turned on, the page would be cached and served with potentially the wrong salutation. However, in *Chapter 11, Caching*, we will cover all these intricacies, so there is no point in complicating our example now.

Invoked Controllers

Now that we know what routes, Controllers, and services are, I'd also like to quickly note that Controllers can be defined as services and *invoked* by the routing system. In other words, just as we defined our `hello_world.salutation` service, we could define another one that would act as a Controller and reference that service ID in the routing file instead of the fully qualified class name. Then, for Drupal to know which method inside the service to call when a user accesses the route, we would need to implement the magic `__invoke` method inside the service. The rest would work pretty much in the same way.

This capability was introduced in Drupal 8.7 and is typical of the Action-Domain-Responder architectural pattern. We won't use it going forward but it's good to know that it's available.

The Form API

Our page displays a greeting dynamically, depending on the time of day. However, we now want an administrator to specify what the greeting should actually be, in other words, to override the default behavior of our salutation if they so choose.

The ingredients for achieving this will be as follows:

- A route (a new page) that displays a form where the administrator can set the greeting
- A configuration object that will store the greeting

In building this functionality, we will also look at how to add a dependency to our existing service. So, let's get started with our new route, which naturally goes inside the `hello_world.routing.yml` file we have already created:

```yaml
hello_world.greeting_form:
  path: '/admin/config/salutation-configuration'
  defaults:
    _form: Drupal\hello_world\Form\SalutationConfigurationForm
    _title: 'Salutation configuration'
  requirements:
    _permission: 'administer site configuration'
```

Most of this route definition is the same as we saw earlier. There is one change, though, in that it maps to a form instead of a Controller. This means that the entire page is a form page. Also, since the path is within the administration space, it will use the administration theme of the site. What is left to do now is to create our form class inside the /Form folder of our namespace (a standard practice directory for storing forms, but not mandatory).

Due to the power of inheritance, our form is actually very simple. However, I will explain what goes on in the background and guide you on your path to building more complex forms. So, here we have our form:

```php
namespace Drupal\hello_world\Form;

use Drupal\Core\Form\ConfigFormBase;
use Drupal\Core\Form\FormStateInterface;

/**
 * Configuration form definition for the salutation
 *      message.
 */
class SalutationConfigurationForm extends ConfigFormBase {

  /**
   * {@inheritdoc}
   */
  protected function getEditableConfigNames() {
    return ['hello_world.custom_salutation'];
  }

  /**
   * {@inheritdoc}
   */
  public function getFormId() {
    return 'salutation_configuration_form';
```

```php
  }

  /**
   * {@inheritdoc}
   */
  public function buildForm(array $form, FormStateInterface
    $form_state) {
    $config = $this->config('hello_world.custom
        _salutation');

    $form['salutation'] = [
      '#type' => 'textfield',
      '#title' => $this->t('Salutation'),
      '#description' => $this->t('Please provide the
          salutation you want to use.'),
      '#default_value' => $config->get('salutation'),
    ];

    return parent::buildForm($form, $form_state);
  }

  /**
   * {@inheritdoc}
   */
  public function submitForm(array &$form,
    FormStateInterface $form_state) {
    $this->config('hello_world.custom_salutation')
      ->set('salutation', $form_state->
        getValue('salutation'))
      ->save();

    parent::submitForm($form, $form_state);
  }
}
```

Clearing the cache and navigating to `admin/config/salutation-configuration` will present you with your simple configuration form via which you can save a custom salutation message:

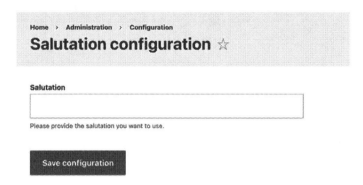

Figure 2.3: Salutation configuration form

Later, we will make use of that value. However, first, let's talk a bit about forms in general, and then this form in particular.

A form in Drupal is represented by a class that implements `FormInterface`. Typically, we either extend from `FormBase` or `ConfigFormBase`, depending on what its purpose is. In this case, we created a configuration form, so we extended it from the latter class.

There are four main methods that come into play in this interface:

- `getFormId()`: Returns a unique, machine-readable name for the form.
- `buildForm()`: Returns the form definition (an array of form element definitions and some extra metadata, as needed).
- `validateForm()`: The handler that gets called to validate the form submission. It receives the form definition and a `FormStateInterface` object that contains, among other things, the submitted values. You can flag invalid values on their respective form elements, which means that the form is not submitted but refreshed (with the offending elements highlighted).
- `submitForm()`: The handler that gets called when the form is submitted (if validation has passed without errors). It receives the same arguments as `validateForm()`. You can perform operations such as saving the submitted values or triggering some other kind of flow.

Defining a form, in a nutshell, means creating an array of form element definitions. The resulting form is very similar to the render array we mentioned earlier. When creating your forms, you have many form element types to use. A complete reference of what they are and what their options are (their definition specificities) can be found on the Drupal Form API reference page (`https://api.drupal.org/api/drupal/elements/10.0.x`).

From a dependency injection point of view, forms can receive arguments from the service container in the same way that we injected the salutation service into our Controller. As a matter of fact, `ConfigFormBase`, which we are extending in our example, injects the `config.factory` service because it needs to use it for reading and storing configuration values. Drupal is full of these helpful classes that we can extend and that provide a bunch of useful boilerplate code that is very commonly used across the Drupal ecosystem.

If the form you are building is not storing or working with configuration, you will typically extend from `FormBase`, which provides some static methods and traits, as well as implements some interfaces. The same word of caution goes for using its helper service methods as it went for the ones in `ControllerBase`: if you need services, you should always inject them.

Let's turn to our form class and dissect it a bit now that we know a thing or two about forms.

We have the `getFormId()` method. Check. We also have `buildForm()` and `submitForm()`, but not `validateForm()`. The latter is not mandatory, and we don't need it for our example, but if we did, we could have something like this:

```
/**
 * {@inheritdoc}
 */
public function validateForm(array &$form,
    FormStateInterface $form_state) {
  $salutation = $form_state->getValue('salutation');
  if (mb_strlen($salutation) > 20) {
    $form_state->setErrorByName('salutation', $this->
        t('This salutation is too long'));
  }
}
```

In this validation handler, we basically check whether the submitted value for the `salutation` element is longer than 20 characters. If so, we set an error on that element (to turn it red usually) and specify an error message on the form state specific to this error. The form will then be refreshed (with the error presented) and the submit handler will not be called.

For the purposes of our example, this is, however, not necessary, so I will not include it in the final code.

> **Note**
>
> Form validation error messages, by default, are printed at the top of the page. However, with the core **Inline Form Errors** module, we can have the form errors printed right beneath the actual elements. This is much better for accessibility, as well as for clarity when dealing with large forms. Note that the standard Drupal 10 installation doesn't have this module enabled, so you'll have to enable it yourself if you want to use it.

If we turn back to our form class, we also see a strange `getEditableConfigNames()` method. This is required by the `ConfigFormBaseTrait`, which is used in the `ConfigFormBase` class that we are extending. It needs to return an array of configuration object names that this form intends to edit. This is because there are two ways of loading configuration objects: for editing and for reading (immutable). With this method, we inform it that we want to edit that configuration item.

As we see on the first line of `buildForm()`, we are using the `config()` method of the previously mentioned trait to load up our editable configuration object from the Drupal configuration factory. This is to check the value that is currently stored in it. Then, we define our form elements (in our case, one—a simple text field). For `#default_value` (the value present in the element when the user goes to the form), we put whatever is in the configuration object. The rest of the element options are self-explanatory and pretty standard across all element types. Consult the Form API reference to see what other options are available and for which element types. Finally, at the end of the method, we also call the parent method because that provides the form's submit button, which for our purposes is enough.

The last method we need is the submit handler, which loads up the editable configuration object, puts the submitted value in it, and then saves it. Finally, it also calls the parent method, which then simply sends a success message to the user on the screen using the `Messenger` service—a standard way of showing the user a success or error message.

That is pretty much it; this will work just fine.

From the point of view of configuration, we used `ConfigFormBase` to make our lives easier and combine the form aspect with that of the configuration storage. In a later chapter, we will talk more about the different types of storage and talk about how to work with configuration objects. So, no worries if you are left a bit unclear about how configuration works.

> **Note**
>
> As I mentioned in this book's introduction, learning by reading code is important. So, to learn about all the existing Drupal form elements, check out their individual classes that implement `Drupal\Core\Render\Element\FormElementInterface` where you can also see code comments as to how they should be used.

Altering forms

Before going ahead with our proposed functionality, I would like to open a parenthesis and discuss forms in a bit more detail. An important thing that you will do as a module developer is alter forms defined by other modules or Drupal core. So, it behooves us to talk about it early on and what better moment than now, when defining the form itself is still fresh in our minds?

Obviously, the form we just created belongs to us and we can change it however we want. However, many forms out there have been defined by other modules and there will be just as many times that you will want to make changes to them. Drupal provides us with a very flexible, albeit still procedural, way of doing so—a suite of *alter* hooks; but what are *alter* hooks?

The first thing we did in this chapter was implement hook_help(). That is an example of an invoked hook by which a caller (Drupal core or any module) asks other modules to provide input. This input is then aggregated in some way and made use of. The other type of hooks we have in Drupal is the *alter* hooks, which are used to allow other modules to make changes to an array or an object before that array or object is used for whatever it is used for. So, in the case of forms, there are some alter hooks that allow modules to make changes to the form definition before it's processed for rendering.

You may be wondering why I am saying that to make changes to a form, we have more than one *alter* hook. Let me explain by giving an example of how other modules could alter the form we just defined (this will not be included in our code base):

```
/**
 * Implements hook_form_alter().
 */
function my_module_form_alter(&$form, \Drupal\Core\
    Form\FormStateInterface $form_state, $form_id) {
  if ($form_id === 'salutation_configuration_form') {
    // Perform alterations.
  }
}
```

In the code above, we implement the generic hook_form_alter(), which gets fired for all forms when being built, and we do so inside a module called my_module. The first two arguments are the form and form state (the same as we saw in the form definition), the former being passed by reference. This is the typical *alter* concept—we make changes to an existing variable and don't return anything. The third parameter is the form ID, the one we defined in the getFormId() method of our form class. We check to ensure that the form is correct and then we can make alterations to the form.

This is, however, almost always the wrong approach, because the hook is fired for all forms indiscriminately. Even if we don't do anything for most of them, it's still a useless function call, not to mention that if we want to alter 10 forms in our module, there will be a lot of `if` conditionals in there—the price we pay for procedural functions. Instead, though, we can do this:

```
/**
 * Implements hook_form_FORM_ID_alter().
 */
function my_module_form_salutation_configuration_form
    alter(&$form, \Drupal\Core\Form\FormStateInterface
        $form_state, $form_id) {
  // Perform alterations.
}
```

Here, we are implementing `hook_form_FORM_ID_alter()`, which is a dynamic alter hook in that its name contains the actual ID of the form we want to alter. So, with this approach, we ensure that this function is called only when it's time to alter OUR form (or a specific form). The other benefit is that if we need to alter another form, we can implement the same kind of hook for that and have our logic neatly separated.

Custom submit handlers

So, up to this point, we have seen how other modules can make changes to our form. That means adding new form elements, changing existing ones, and so on. But what about our validation and submit handlers (those methods that get called when the form is submitted)? How can those be altered?

Typically, for the forms that we defined as we did, it's pretty simple. Once we alter the form and inspect the `$form` array, we can find a `#submit` key, which is an array that has one item: `::submitForm`. This is simply the `submitForm()` method on the form class. So, what we can do is either remove this item and add our own function or simply add another item to that array:

```
/**
 * Implements hook_form_FORM_ID_alter().
 */
function my_module_form_salutation_configuration_form
    alter(&$form, \Drupal\Core\Form\FormStateInterface
        $form_state, $form_id) {
  // Perform alterations.
  $form['#submit'][] = 'hello_world_salutation_
    configuration_form_submit';
}
```

And the callback we added to the `#submit` array above can look like this:

```
/**
 * Custom submit handler for the form_salutation_
      configuration form.
 *
 * @param $form
 * @param \Drupal\Core\Form\FormStateInterface $form_state
 */
function my_module_salutation_configuration_form_submit
      (&$form, \Drupal\Core\Form\FormStateInterface
         $form_state) {
  // Do something when the form is submitted.
}
```

So, the cool thing is that you can choose to tack on your own callback or replace the existing one. Keep in mind that the order they are in that array is the order in which they get executed. So, you can also change the order if you want.

There is another case though. If the submit button on the form has a `#submit` property specifying its own handler, the default form `#submit` handlers we saw just now won't fire anymore. This was not the case with our form. So, in that situation, you will need to add your own handler to that form's submit element array instead.

Finally, when it comes to the validation handler, it works the same as with the submit handler, but it all happens under the `#validate` array key.

Feel free to experiment with altering existing forms and inspecting the variables they receive as arguments.

Rendering forms

Staying on forms for just a bit longer, let's quickly learn how to render forms programmatically. We have already seen how to map a form to a route definition so that the page being built contains the form when accessing the route path. However, there are times when we need to render a form programmatically, either inside a Controller or a block, or wherever we want. We can do this using the `FormBuilder` service.

The form builder can be injected using the `form_builder` service key or used statically via the shorthand:

```
$builder = \Drupal::formBuilder();
```

Once we have it, we can build a form, like so:

```
$form = $builder->getForm('Drupal\hello_world\Form\
    SalutationConfigurationForm');
```

In the code above, $form will be a render array of the form that we can return, for example, inside a Controller. We'll talk more about render arrays a bit later, and you'll understand how they get turned into actual form markup. However, for now, this is all you need to know about rendering forms programmatically—you get the form builder and request from it the form using the fully qualified name of the form class.

With this, we can close the parenthesis on forms.

Service dependencies

In the previous section, we created a form that allows administrators to set up a custom salutation message to be shown on the page. This message is stored in a configuration object that we can now load in our HelloWorldSalutation service. So, let's do just that with a two-step process.

First, we will need to change our service definition to give our service an argument—the configuration factory (the service responsible for loading config objects). This is how our service definition should look now:

```
hello_world.salutation:
  class: Drupal\hello_world\HelloWorldSalutation
  arguments: ['@config.factory']
```

The addition is the arguments key, which is an array of service names proceeded by @. In this case, config.factory is the responsible service name, which, if we check in the core.services. yml file, we can note that it maps to the Drupal\Core\Config\ConfigFactory class.

So, with this change, the HelloWorldSalutation class will receive an instance of ConfigFactory. All we need to do now is adjust our class to actually receive it:

```
/**
 * @var \Drupal\Core\Config\ConfigFactoryInterface
 */
protected $configFactory;

/**
 * HelloWorldSalutation constructor.
 *
 * @param \Drupal\Core\Config\ConfigFactoryInterface
 *     $config_factory
 */
```

```
public function __construct(ConfigFactoryInterface
    $config_factory) {
  $this->configFactory = $config_factory;
}
```

There's nothing too complicated going on here. We added a constructor and set the config factory service on a property. We can now use it to load our configuration object that we saved in the form. However, before we do that, we should also *use* the ConfigFactoryInterface class at the top of the file:

```
use Drupal\Core\Config\ConfigFactoryInterface;
```

Now, at the top of the getSalutation() method, we can add the following bit:

```
$config = $this->configFactory->get
      ('hello_world.custom_salutation');
$salutation = $config->get('salutation');
if ($salutation !== "" && $salutation) {
  return $salutation;
}
```

With this addition, we are loading the configuration object we saved in the form, and from it, we request the salutation key, where, if you remember, we stored our message. If there is a value in there, we will return it. Otherwise, the code will continue, and our previous logic of time-based greeting will apply.

So now, if we reload our initial page, the message we saved through the form should show up. If we then return to the form and remove the message, this page should default back to the original dynamic greeting. Neat, right? Don't forget to clear the caches before you check this because we changed our service definition and that requires a cache clear.

> **Note**
> If you are not seeing the changes on the page after editing/removing the salutation message, ensure you have the caches on your local site disabled as we have not yet taken that into account so early in our journey.

Let's now look at how we can create a custom block that we can place anywhere we like and that will output the same thing as our page.

Blocks

Blocks are plugins. However, the blocks you create in the UI are content entities and the placement of blocks (of both types) in the block layout are configuration entities. So, the block system is a good example of how entities and plugins work hand in hand in Drupal. We will talk in more detail about plugin types and entities later in the book.

So, how do we create a custom block plugin? All we need is one class, placed in the right namespace—`Drupal\module_name\Plugin\Block`. In this case (with plugins), folder naming is important. The plugin discoverability is dependent on the plugin type itself, and this one has the `Plugin\Block` namespace bit in it. But enough talk; let's create a simple block that just renders the same as our Controller did previously, and I will explain things along the way.

Our first block plugin

So, this is our plugin class—`HelloWorldSalutationBlock`—which does just that:

```
namespace Drupal\hello_world\Plugin\Block;

use Drupal\Core\Block\BlockBase;
use Drupal\Core\Plugin\ContainerFactoryPluginInterface;
use Symfony\Component\DependencyInjection\
    ContainerInterface;
use Drupal\hello_world\HelloWorldSalutation;

/**
 * Hello World Salutation block.
 *
 * @Block(
 *   id = "hello_world_salutation_block",
 *   admin_label = @Translation("Hello world salutation"),
 * )
 */
class HelloWorldSalutationBlock extends BlockBase
    implements ContainerFactoryPluginInterface {

  /**
   * The salutation service.
   *
   * @var \Drupal\hello_world\HelloWorldSalutation
   */
  protected $salutation;

  /**
```

```
   * Constructs a HelloWorldSalutationBlock.
   */
  public function __construct(array $configuration,
    $plugin_id, $plugin_definition, HelloWorldSalutation
      $salutation) {
    parent::__construct($configuration, $plugin_id,
      $plugin_definition);
    $this->salutation = $salutation;
  }

  /**
   * {@inheritdoc}
   */
  public static function create(ContainerInterface
    $container, array $configuration, $plugin_id,
      $plugin_definition) {
    return new static(
      $configuration,
      $plugin_id,
      $plugin_definition,
      $container->get('hello_world.salutation')
    );
  }

  /**
   * {@inheritdoc}
   */
  public function build() {
    return [
      '#markup' => $this->salutation->getSalutation(),
    ];
  }
}
```

Before even going through the explanation, you should know that clearing the cache and placing this block through the block management UI will do what we wanted. However, let's understand what is going on here first.

Perhaps the strangest thing you'll note is the DocBlock comment at the top of the class. This is called an *annotation* and denotes that this class is a `Block` plugin and contains its static definition. As I mentioned in the first chapter, annotations are the most common discovery mechanisms for plugins in Drupal core. They will most likely be replaced by PHP attributes in Drupal 11 but for the moment, we still use them. In this case, the plugin definition we need is made up of an ID and an administration label.

> **Note**
>
> Properly defined plugin types have an `AnnotationInterface` implementation, which describes the properties that can or should be used in the annotation. So, if you are unsure as to what needs to be there, look for this class for that specific plugin type.

Then, we see that our class extends `BlockBase` and also implements `Container FactoryPluginInterface`. The former, like `ControllerBase` and `FormBase` we saw earlier, provides a number of helpful things a block plugin needs. However, we cannot really get around extending this class because block plugins are quite complex, working with things such as context and configuration. So, ensure that you always extend this class. The latter is, however, optional. That interface makes this block plugin container-aware, that is, at the moment of instantiation, it uses the `create()` method to build itself using the service container for dependencies. And sure enough, we have our `create()` method as well.

Before moving on to the actual block building, we need to talk a bit about dependency injection in plugins. As you can see, the signature of this `create()` method is different from the one we saw in the Controller. This is also why we are using a different container-aware interface. The reason is that plugins are constructed with a few extra parameters: `$configuration`, `$plugin_id`, and `$plugin_definition`. The first contains any configuration values that are needed by the plugin, the second is the ID set in the plugin annotation (or other discovery mechanisms), and the third is an array that contains the metadata of this plugin (including all the info found in the annotation). However, apart from this, it's business as usual when it comes to dependency injection. If a plugin type base class doesn't implement this interface, you can do so yourself directly in your plugin. This works with most plugins, save for a few exceptions that cannot be made container-aware, but this happens very rarely.

Finally, we have a `build()` method, which is responsible for building the block content. It needs to return a render array (just like our Controller did), and as you can see, we are using our injected service and returning the same greeting. That is pretty much what we need to do in order to achieve our goal. There are other important aspects to block plugins we will cover later, such as caching and access, but we have specific chapters for those topics.

Block configuration

Before we close the book on our custom block plugin, let's take a look at how we can add a configuration form to it. This way, we can practice using some more Form API elements and see how we can store and use block configuration.

Even though our functionality is complete (for the moment), let's imagine that we need a Boolean-like control on our block configuration so that when an administrator places the block, they can toggle something, and that value can be used in the `build()` method. We could achieve this with three to four methods in our plugin class.

First, we would need to implement the `defaultConfiguration()` method, in which we describe the items of configuration that we are storing for this block and the default values for these items. So, we could have something like this:

```
/**
 * {@inheritdoc}
 */
public function defaultConfiguration() {
  return [
    'enabled' => 1,
  ];
}
```

We return an array of keys and values that will be in the configuration. Also, since we said we are going with a Boolean field, we use the number 1 as the value of a fictitious key named `enabled`.

Next, we would need to implement the `blockForm()` method, which provides our form definition for this configuration item:

```
/**
 * {@inheritdoc}
 */
public function blockForm($form, FormStateInterface
    $form_state) {
  $config = $this->getConfiguration();

  $form['enabled'] = array(
    '#type' => 'checkbox',
    '#title' => $this->t('Enabled'),
    '#description' => $this->t('Check this box if you want
        to enable this feature.'),
    '#default_value' => $config['enabled'],
  );

  return $form;
}
```

With the appropriate extra `use` statement at the top of the file:

```
use Drupal\Core\Form\FormStateInterface;
```

As you can see, this is a typical Form API definition for one form element of the `checkbox` type. Additionally, we are using the handy `getConfiguration()` method of the parent class to load up the configuration values that get saved with this block. If none have been saved, note that the `enabled` key will be present in it with the default value we set above (1).

Lastly, we would need the submit handler that will do what's necessary to "store" the configuration. I used inverted commas because we don't actually have to do anything related to storage, but just map the value submitted in the form to the relevant key in the configuration. The block system does it for us:

```
/**
 * {@inheritdoc}
 */
public function blockSubmit($form, FormStateInterface
    $form_state) {
  $this->configuration['enabled'] = $form_state->
    getValue('enabled');
}
```

It couldn't be simpler than this. Now, if we placed our custom block somewhere, the form we are presented with would incorporate our form element that allows us to toggle the enabled key. What remains to be done is to make use of this value inside the build() method. We could do that similarly to how we loaded the configuration values inside the buildForm() method:

```
$config = $this->getConfiguration();
```

Alas, we don't really need this configuration in our example block, so we won't be adding it to our code. However, it is important for you to know how to do it, so we covered it here. Moreover, before moving on, I also want to specify that you can use an optional method to handle validation on the configuration form. The method name is blockValidate(); it has the same signature as blockSubmit() and works the same way as the validation handler we saw when we built our standalone form. So, I won't repeat that here.

Working with links

One of the principal characteristics of a web application is the myriad of links between its resources. They are in fact the glue that brings the internet together. So, in this section, I want to show you a few common techniques used while working with links programmatically.

There are two main aspects when talking about link building in Drupal—the URL and the actual link tag itself. So, creating a link involves a two-step process, but can also be shortened into a single call via some helper methods.

The URL

URLs in Drupal are represented with the Drupal\Core\Url class, which has several static methods that allow you to create an instance of it. The most important of these is ::fromRoute(), which takes a route name, route parameters (if any are needed for that route), and an array of options to create a new instance of Url. There are other such methods available that turn all sorts of other things into a `Url` instance, most notably the `::fromUri()` method, which takes an internal or external URI. These methods can be very helpful, especially when dealing with dynamically obtained data. However, when hardcoding, it's always best to work with route names because that allows you to later change the actual path behind that route without affecting your code.

Using the `$options` array, there are many options that can be passed to `Url` when instantiating it. You can pass an array of query parameters, a fragment, and others. These will then help construct a URL as complex as you need without having to deal with strings yourself. I suggest that you check out the documentation above the `::fromUri()` method because it describes them all. Also, keep in mind that the options are pretty much the same, regardless of the method that you use to create the `Url` object.

The link

Now that we have a `Url` object, we can use it to generate a link. We can do this in two ways:

- Use the `LinkGenerator` service (named `link_generator`) and call its `generate()` method by passing the link text and the `Url` object we have obtained. This will return a `GeneratedLink` object, which contains the actual string representation of the link as well as some cache metadata.

- Use the `\Drupal\Core\Link` class, which wraps a render element (we will talk more about render elements in the `Theming` chapter) to represent the link.

Let's take a look at an example of both, from start to finish.

Consider this example of generating a link using the service:

```
$url = Url::fromRoute('my_route', ['param_name' =>
    $param_value]);
$link = \Drupal::service('link_generator')->generate('My
    link', $url);
```

We can then directly print `$link` because it implements the `__toString()` method.

Now, consider this example of generating a link using the `Link` class:

```
$url = Url::fromRoute('my_other_route');
$link = Link::fromTextAndUrl('My link', $url);
```

We now have `$link` as a `Link` object whose `toRenderable()` method returns a render array of `#type => 'link'`. Behind the scenes, at render time, it will also use the link generator to transform that into a link string.

If we have a `Link` object, we can also use the link generator ourselves to generate a link based on its own data:

```
$link = \Drupal::service('link_generator')->
    generateFromLink($link_object);
```

Which way to link?

As we saw, we have a few ways to create links and URL representations, but when it comes to creating a link, which method should we use? There are advantages and disadvantages to each one.

When it comes to the URL, as mentioned, it's a good idea to stick to hardcoding routes rather than URIs. However, if you are working with dynamic data, such as user input or stored strings, the other methods are perfectly valid. I recommend that you look at the `Url` class in detail because you will be using it quite a bit as you develop Drupal modules.

Regarding the actual links, using the service to generate a link means that you are creating a string at that point in the code. This means that it cannot be altered later in the process. Instead, using the `Link` class falls nicely in line with the entire render array rationale of delaying the actual generation to the last possible moment. We will talk more about render arrays later. Generating links early on could also have consequences with the render system and cache bubbling, so it's always better to stick with the `Link` objects or render arrays like `#type =>'link'`.

When it comes to entities, you can and should use the helper methods on the base entity classes to generate links and URLs to these entities. We will talk more about entities later in this book.

Event Dispatcher and redirects

A common thing you'll have to do as a module developer is to intercept a given request and redirect it to another page, and often, this will have to be dynamic, depending on the current user or other contextual info. What we have to do in order to achieve this is to subscribe to the `kernel.request` event (remember this from the previous chapter?) and then change the response directly. However, before seeing an example of this, let's take a look at how we can perform a simpler redirect from within a Controller. You know, since we're on the subject.

Redirecting from a Controller

In this chapter, we have written a Controller that returns a render array. We know from the previous chapter that this is picked up by the theme system and turned into a response. In *Chapter 4*, *Theming*, we will go into a bit more detail and see how this process is done. However, this render pipeline can also be bypassed if the Controller returns a response directly. Let's consider the following example:

```
return new \Symfony\Component\HttpFoundation\Response('my
    text');
```

This will bypass much of that processing and return a blank white page with only the `my text` string on it. The `Response` class we're using is from the Symfony HTTP Foundation component.

However, we also have a handy `RedirectResponse` class that we can use, and it will redirect the browser to another page:

```
return new \Symfony\Component\HttpFoundation\
    RedirectResponse('/node/1');
```

The first parameter is the URL where we want to redirect to. Typically, this should be an absolute URL; however, browsers nowadays are smart enough to handle a relative path as well. So, in this case, the Controller will redirect us to that path.

> **Note**
>
> Typically, when returning redirect responses, you'll want to use a child class of `RedirectResponse`. For example, we have the `LocalRedirectResponse` and `TrustedRedirectResponse` classes, which both extend from `SecuredRedirectResponse`. The purpose of these utilities is to ensure that redirects are safe.

Redirecting from a subscriber

Many times, our business logic dictates that we need to perform a redirect from a certain page to another if various conditions match. In these cases, we can subscribe to the request event and simply change the response, essentially bypassing the normal process, which would have gone through all the layers of Drupal. However, before we see an example, let's talk about the Event Dispatcher for just a bit.

The central player in this system is the `event_dispatcher` service, which is an instance of the `ContainerAwareEventDispatcher` class. This service allows the dispatching of named events that take a payload in the form of an `Event` object, which wraps the data that needs to be passed around. Typically, when dispatching events, you'll create an `Event` subclass with some handy methods for accessing the data that needs to be passed around. Finally, instances of `EventSubscriberInterface` "listen" to events that have certain names and can alter the `Event` object that has been passed. Essentially, then, this system allows subscribers to change data before the business logic uses it for something. In this respect, it is a prime example of an extension point in Drupal. Finally, registering event subscribers is a matter of creating a service tagged with `event_subscriber` that implements the interface I mentioned earlier.

Let's now take a look at an example event subscriber that listens to the `kernel.request` event and redirects to the home page if a user with a certain role tries to access our *Hello World* page. This will demonstrate both how to subscribe to events and how to perform a redirect. It will also show us how to use the current route match service to inspect the current route.

Let's create this subscriber by first writing the service definition for it:

```
hello_world.redirect_subscriber:
  class: Drupal\hello_world\EventSubscriber\
    HelloWorldRedirectSubscriber
  arguments: ['@current_user']
  tags:
    - { name: event_subscriber }
```

As you can see, we have the regular service definition with one argument and with the event_ subscriber tag. The dependency is the service that reflects the current user (either logged in or anonymous) in the form of an AccountProxyInterface. This is a wrapper to the AccountInterface, which represents the actual current user. Also, when I say *user*, I mean an object that has certain data about the user and not the actual entity object with all the field data. It's the user session, basically. Certain things about the user are, however, accessible from the AccountInterface, such as the ID, name, roles, and email. I recommend that you check out the interface for more info. However, for our example, we will use it to check whether the user has the non_grata role, which will trigger the redirect I mentioned.

Next, let's look at the event subscriber class itself:

```
namespace Drupal\hello_world\EventSubscriber;

use Drupal\Core\Session\AccountProxyInterface;
use Symfony\Component\EventDispatcher\
    EventSubscriberInterface;
use Symfony\Component\HttpFoundation\RedirectResponse;
use Symfony\Component\HttpKernel\Event\RequestEvent;

/**
 * Redirects to the homepage when the user has the
    "non_grata" role.
 */
class HelloWorldRedirectSubscriber implements
    EventSubscriberInterface {

  /**
   * @var \Drupal\Core\Session\AccountProxyInterface
   */
  protected $currentUser;

  /**
   * HelloWorldRedirectSubscriber constructor.
   *
   * @param \Drupal\Core\Session\AccountProxyInterface
```

```php
      $currentUser
   */
  public function __construct(AccountProxyInterface
    $currentUser) {
    $this->currentUser = $currentUser;
  }


  /**
   * {@inheritdoc}
   */
  public static function getSubscribedEvents() {
    $events['kernel.request'][] = ['onRequest', 0];
    return $events;
  }


  /**
   * Handler for the kernel request event.
   *
   * @param \Symfony\Component\HttpKernel\Event\
       RequestEvent $event
   */
  public function onRequest(RequestEvent $event) {
    $request = $event->getRequest();
    $path = $request->getPathInfo();
    if ($path !== '/hello') {
      return;
    }

    $roles = $this->currentUser->getRoles();
    if (in_array('non_grata', $roles)) {
      $event->setResponse(new RedirectResponse('/'));
    }
  }
}
```

As expected, we store the current user as a class property so that we can use it later. Then, we implement the `EventSubscriberInterface::getSubscribedEvents()` method. This method needs to return a multidimensional array, which is basically a mapping between event names and the class methods to be called if that event is intercepted. This is how we register methods to listen to one event or another, and we can listen to multiple events in the same subscriber class if we want. It's typically a good idea to separate these, however, into different, more topical classes. The callback method name is inside an array whose second value represents the priority of this callback compared to others you or other modules may define. The higher the number, the higher the priority, which means the earlier in the process it will run. Do check the documentation on the interface itself for a good description of the ways you can subscribe to events.

In our example, we listen to the `kernel.request` event I mentioned in the previous chapter. This event is dispatched by Symfony's `HttpKernel`, passing an instance of `RequestEvent`, which basically wraps the `Request` object. If we inspect this class, we can see that it has a `setResponse()` method on it, which we can use to set the response. If a subscriber provides one, it stops the event propagation (none of the other listeners with a lower priority are given a chance) and the response is returned.

So, in our `onRequest()` callback method, we check the current path being requested, and if it is ours and the current user has the `non_grata` role, we set the `RedirectResponse` onto the event to redirect it to the home page. This will do the job we set out to do. If you go to the `/hello` page as a user with that role, you should be redirected to the home page.

This being said, I don't like many aspects of this implementation. So, let's fix them.

First, we hardcoded the `kernel.request` event name (I did—I can't blame you for that). Any decent code that dispatches events will use a class constant to define the event name and the subscribers should also reference that constant. Symfony has the `KernelEvents` class just for that purpose. Check it out and see what other events are dispatched by the `HttpKernel`, as they are all referenced there.

So, instead of hardcoding the string, we can have this:

```
$events[KernelEvents::REQUEST][] = ['onRequest', 0];
```

Second, the way we do the path handling in the `onRequest()` method is all sorts of wrong. We are hardcoding the `/hello` path in this condition. What if we change the route path because our boss wants the path to be `/greeting`? I also don't like the way we passed the path to the `RedirectResponse`. The same thing applies (although in the case of the home page, not so much): what if the path we want to redirect to changes? Let's fix these problems using routes instead of paths. They are system-specific and are unlikely to change because of business requirements.

The problem is that we are unable to understand which route is being accessed from the `Request` object. Instead, we can use the `current_route_match` service—a very popular one you'll use often—which gives us loads of info about the current route. So, let's inject that into our event subscriber. By now, you should know how to do this on your own (check the final code if you still have trouble). Make sure you type-hint the service with the interface it implements: `RouteMatchInterface` and set it to the `routeMatch` class property. Once that is done, we can do this instead:

```
public function onRequest(RequestEvent $event) {
    $route_name = $this->routeMatch->getRouteName();

    if ($route_name !== 'hello_world.hello') {
        return;
```

```
    }

    $roles = $this->currentUser->getRoles();
    if (in_array('non_grata', $roles)) {
        $url = Url::fromUri('internal:/');
        $event->setResponse(new LocalRedirectResponse($url->
            toString()));
    }
}
```

From the `CurrentRouteMatch` service, we can figure out the name of the current route, the entire route object, parameters from the URL, and other useful things. Do check out the class for more info on what you can do, as I guarantee that they will come in handy.

Instead of checking against the path name, we now check against the route name. So, if we change the path in the route definition, our code will still work. Then, instead of just adding the path to the `RedirectResponse`, we can build it first using the `Url` class we learned about in the previous section. Granted, in our example, it is probably overkill but had we redirected it to a known route, we could have built it based on that, and our code would have been more robust. Additionally, using the `Url` class, we can also check other things, such as access, and its `toString()` method simply turns it into a string that can be used for the `RedirectResponse`. Finally, instead of the simple `RedirectResponse`, we are using the `LocalRedirectResponse` class as we are redirecting to a local (safe) path.

With this, we will get the same redirect, but in a much cleaner and more robust way. Of course, only after adjusting the *use* statements at the top by removing the one for the `RedirectResponse` and adding the following:

```
use Drupal\Core\Routing\RouteMatchInterface;
use Drupal\Core\Routing\LocalRedirectResponse;
use Symfony\Component\HttpKernel\KernelEvents;
use Drupal\Core\Url;
```

> **Note**
>
> Again, for the sake of not overloading you with too much information, I omitted a very important aspect here: caching. So, our redirect works, but not very well. We will fix it when we learn about caching in *Chapter 11, Caching*.

Dispatching events

Since we have discussed how to subscribe to events in Drupal, we should also take a look at how we can dispatch our own events. After all, the Symfony Event Dispatcher component is one of the principal vectors of extensibility in Drupal.

To demonstrate this, we will create an event to be dispatched whenever our `HelloWorldSalutation::getSalutation()` method is called. The purpose is to inform other modules that this has happened and potentially allow them to alter the message that comes out of the configuration object—not really a solid use case, but good enough to demonstrate how we can dispatch events.

The first thing that we will need to do is to create an event class that will be dispatched. It can go into the root of our module's namespace:

```php
namespace Drupal\hello_world;

use Symfony\Contracts\EventDispatcher\Event;

/**
 * Event class to be dispatched from the
 *   HelloWorldSalutation service.
 */
class SalutationEvent extends Event {

  const EVENT = 'hello_world.salutation_event';

  /**
   * The salutation message.
   *
   * @var string
   */
  protected $message;

  /**
   * @return mixed
   */
  public function getValue() {
    return $this->message;
  }

  /**
   * @param mixed $message
   */
  public function setValue($message) {
    $this->message = $message;
  }
}
```

The main purpose of this event class is that an instance of it will be used to transport the value of our salutation message. This is why we created the `$message` property on the class and added the getter and setter methods. Moreover, we use it to define a constant for the actual name of the event that will be dispatched. Finally, the class extends from the base `Event` class that comes with Symfony.

Next, it's time to inject the Event Dispatcher service into our `HelloWorldSalutation` service. We have already injected `config.factory`, so we just need to add a new argument to the service definition:

```
arguments: ['@config.factory', '@event_dispatcher']
```

Of course, we will also receive it in the constructor and store it as a class property:

```
/**
 * @var \Symfony\Component\EventDispatcher\
        EventDispatcherInterface
 */
protected $eventDispatcher;

/**
 * HelloWorldSalutation constructor.
 *
 * @param \Drupal\Core\Config\ConfigFactoryInterface
        $config_factory
 * @param \Symfony\Contracts\EventDispatcher\
        EventDispatcherInterface $eventDispatcher
 */
public function __construct(ConfigFactoryInterface
    $config_factory, EventDispatcherInterface
        $eventDispatcher) {
  $this->configFactory = $config_factory;
  $this->eventDispatcher = $eventDispatcher;
}
```

We will also have the obligatory *use* statement for the `EventDispatcherInterface` at the top of the file:

```
use Symfony\Contracts\EventDispatcher\
    EventDispatcherInterface;
```

Now, we can make use of the dispatcher. So, instead of the following code inside the `getSalutation()` method:

```
if ($salutation !== "" && $salutation) {
  return $salutation;
}
```

We can have the following:

```
if ($salutation !== "" && $salutation) {
    $event = new SalutationEvent();
    $event->setValue($salutation);
    $event = $this->eventDispatcher->dispatch($event,
        SalutationEvent::EVENT);
    return $event->getValue();
}
```

So, with the above, we decided that if we are to return a salutation message from the configuration object, we want to inform other modules and allow them to change it. We first create an instance of our Event class and feed it the relevant data (the message). Then, we dispatch the named event and pass the event object along with it. Finally, we get the data from that instance and return it.

Pretty simple, isn't it? What can subscribers do? It's very similar to what we saw regarding the example on redirects in the previous section. All a subscriber needs to do is listen for the SalutationEvent::EVENT event and do something based on that. The main thing that it can do is use the setValue() method on the received event object to change the salutation message. It can also use the stopPropagation() method from the base Event class to inform the Event Dispatcher to no longer trigger other listeners that have subscribed to this event.

Summary

In this chapter, we covered a great deal of info about the things you need to know when developing Drupal modules. The first thing we did was create our very own module skeleton that can be installed on a Drupal site. Then, we saw how to create a new page at a specific path (route) and show some basic data on that page. Nothing too complex, but enough to illustrate one of the most common tasks you will do as a module developer. We then took that to a new level and abstracted the logic for that data calculation into a service. Not only that, but we also saw how we can use that service and, more importantly, how we *should* use it. Next, we saw how we can work with the Form API to allow administrators to add some configuration to the site. Also, since we talked about forms, we saw how we can alter existing ones defined by other modules—a useful technique for any module developer.

Next, we created our first custom block, which allowed us to reuse our service and be more flexible with where we show our data.

Then, we looked at how to create URLs and links programmatically. In the functionality we built in this module, we don't need any links, yet. However, it is common practice to work with them, so we had to learn early how to generate links and work with URLs properly in Drupal.

In the last section, we explored the Symfony *Event Dispatcher* component, something that allows us to dispatch and subscribe to events. We saw some examples of how we can subscribe to one of the main Kernel events in order to redirect the page, but we also saw how to dispatch our own event. The latter was meant to allow subscribers to make changes to our data.

Most of the topics we covered in this chapter were meant to give you an initial boost and the tools to start developing modules in Drupal. They represent the absolute most common things—I believe—that any new Drupal developer encounters and has to know.

In the next chapter, we will look at two important aspects most applications will need to use. One is logging—the better your site logs its errors and important actions, the easier it will be to debug and trace back issues. Another is mailing. Websites usually need to send out emails to users in one way or another, so it's important that we see how that works in Drupal.

3

Logging and Mailing

In the previous chapter, we learned about some of the more common things most Drupal module developers will have to know, starting with the basics, that is, creating a Drupal module.

In this chapter, we will take things further and cover some other important tasks a developer will have to perform:

- We will look at how logging works in Drupal. In doing so, we will cover some examples by expanding on our *Hello World* module.

- We will look at the Mail API in Drupal, namely, how we can send emails with the default setup (PHP mail). However, more than that, I will show you how to create your own email system to integrate with your (perhaps external) mail service; remember plugins? This will be yet another good example of using a plugin to extend existing capabilities.

- At the end of the chapter, we will also look at the Drupal token system. We'll do so in the context of us replacing certain *tokens* with contextual data so that the emails we send out are a bit more dynamic.

By the end of this chapter, you should be able to add logging to your Drupal module and feel comfortable sending emails programmatically. Additionally, you'll understand how tokens work, and as a bonus, see how you can define your own tokens.

Logging

The main logging mechanism in Drupal is a database log through which client code can use an API to save messages into the `watchdog` table. The messages in there are cleared after they reach a certain number, but meanwhile, they can be viewed in the browser via a handy interface (at `admin/reports/dblog`):

Figure 3.1: Viewing Recent log messages

Alternatively, a core module that is disabled by default, Syslog, can be used to complement/replace this logging mechanism with the Syslog of the server the site is running on. For the purposes of this book, we will focus on how logging works with any mechanism, but we will also look at how we can implement our own logging system.

The Drupal logging theory

Before going ahead with our example, let's cover some theoretical notions regarding the logging framework in Drupal. In doing so, we'll try to understand the key *players* we will need to interact with.

First, we have the `LoggerChannel` object, which represents a category of logged messages. Moreover, it is an object through which we do the actual logging, via logger plugins that are injected into it and which implement `LoggerInterface` (we will see about these in a minute). But for now, it's enough to know that the *logger channel* also implements this interface and it simply delegates to the inner plugins that implement the same interface.

To this end, the *logger channel* is created by our second main *player*, `LoggerChannelFactory`, a service that is normally our main *contact point* with the logging framework as client code.

To understand these things better, let's consider the following example of a simple usage:

```
\Drupal::logger('hello_world')->error('This is my error
    message');
```

That's it. We just used the available registered loggers to log an error message through the `hello_world` channel. This is our own custom channel that we just came up with on the fly and that simply categorizes this message as belonging to the `hello_world` category (the module we started in the previous chapter). Moreover, you'll see that I used the static call for getting the logging service. Under the hood, the logger factory service is loaded, a channel is requested from it, and the `error()` method is called on that channel:

```
\Drupal::service('logger.factory')->get('hello_world')->
   error('This is my error message');
```

When you request a channel from `LoggerChannelFactory`, you give it a name, and based on that name, the factory creates a new instance of `LoggerChannel`, which is the default channel class. The factory will then pass to that channel all the available loggers so that when we call any of the `RfcLoggerTrait` logging methods on it, it will delegate to each of the loggers to do the actual logging.

We also have the option of creating our own, more specific channel. An advantage of doing this is that we can inject it directly into our classes instead of the entire channel factory. Also, we can do it in a way where we don't even require the creation of a new class, but it will inherit from the default one. We'll see how to do that in the next section.

The third main *player* is the `LoggerInterface` implementation, which follows the PSR-3 standard and is responsible for doing the actual logging of the messages. This object has a number of methods to do so in different ways (different levels), but `log()` is the central one.

As an example, if we look at the `DbLog` class (which implements `LoggerInterface` and which is the database logging implementation we mentioned earlier) we note that it uses the `RfcLoggerTrait`. This trait is great cause it takes care of all the individual `LoggerInterface` methods, leaving `DbLog` to implement only `log()`.

The `LoggerInterface` implementation (such as `DbLog`) is then registered as a service using the `logger` tag, which in turn means it gets registered with `LoggerChannelFactory` (which acts as a service collector).

As we saw in *Chapter 2, Creating Your First Module*, tags can be used to categorize service definitions and we can have them collected by another service for a specific purpose. In this case, all services tagged with `logger` have a standard "purpose", and they are gathered and used by `LoggerChannelFactory`.

I know this has been quite a lot of theory, but these are some important concepts to understand. Don't worry; as usual, we will go through some examples.

Our own logger channel

I mentioned earlier how we can define our own logger channel so that we don't have to always inject the entire factory. So, let's take a look at how to create one for the *Hello World* module we're now writing.

Most of the time, all we have to do is add such a definition to the services definition file:

```
hello_world.logger.channel.hello_world:
   parent: logger.channel_base
   arguments: ['hello_world']
```

Before talking about the actual logger channel, let's see what this weird service definition means, because this is not something we've seen before. I mean, where's the class?

The `parent` key means that our service will inherit the definition from another service. In our case, the parent key is `logger.channel_base`, and this means that the class used will be `Drupal\Core\Logger\LoggerChannel` (the default one). If we look closely at the `logger.channel_base` service definition in `core.services.yml`, we also see a `factory` key. This means that this service class is not being instantiated by the service container but by another service, namely the `logger.factory` service's `get()` method.

The `arguments` key is also slightly different in that we don't have the @ sign. That is because this sign is used to denote a service name, whereas our argument is a simple string. As a bonus tidbit, if the string is preceded and followed by a `%`, it denotes a parameter that can be defined in any `*.services.yml` file (like a variable).

Getting back to our example then, if you remember the logger theory, this service definition will mean that requesting this service will perform, under the hood, the following task:

```
\Drupal::service('logger.factory')->get('hello_world');
```

It uses the logger factory to load a channel with a certain argument. So, now we can inject our `hello_world.logger.channel.hello_world` service and call any of the `LoggerInterface` methods on it directly in our client code.

Our own logger

Now that we have a channel for our module, let's assume that we also want to log messages elsewhere. They are fine to be stored in the database, but let's also send an email whenever we encounter an error log. In this section, we will only cover the logging architecture needed for this and defer the actual mailing implementation to the second part of this chapter when we discuss mailing.

The first thing that we will need to create is the `LoggerInterface` implementation, which typically goes in the `Logger` folder of our namespace. So, let's call ours `MailLogger`. And it can look like this:

```
namespace Drupal\hello_world\Logger;

use Drupal\Core\Logger\RfcLoggerTrait;
use Psr\Log\LoggerInterface;

/**
 * A logger that sends an email when the log type is
   "error".
 */
```

```
class MailLogger implements LoggerInterface {

  use RfcLoggerTrait;

  /**
   * {@inheritdoc}
   */
  public function log($level, \Stringable|string $message,
    array $context = []): void {
    // Log our message to the logging system.
  }
}
```

The first thing to note is that we are implementing the PSR-3 `LoggerInterface`. This will require a bunch of methods, but we will take care of most of them via the `RfcLoggerTrait`. The only one left to implement is the `log()` method, which will be responsible for doing the actual logging. For now, we will keep it empty.

By itself, having this class does nothing. We will need to register it as a tagged service so that `LoggingChannelFactory` picks it up and passes it to the logging channel when something needs to be logged. Let's see what that definition looks like:

```
hello_world.logger.mail_logger:
  class: Drupal\hello_world\Logger\MailLogger
  tags:
    - { name: logger }
```

As it stands, our logger doesn't need any dependencies. However, note the property called `tags` with which we tag this service with the `logger` tag. This will register it as a specific service that another service (called a collector) looks for – just like we discussed in the previous chapter. In this case, the collector is `LoggingChannelFactory`.

Clearing the cache should enable our logger. This means that when a message is being logged, via any channel, our logger is also used, together with any other enabled loggers (by default, the database one). So, if we want our logger to be the only one, we will need to disable the DB Log module from Drupal core.

We will continue working on this class later in this chapter when we cover sending out emails programmatically.

Now that we have all the tools at our disposal, and more importantly, understand how logging works in Drupal, let's add some logging to our module.

Logging for Hello World

There is one place where we can log an action that may prove helpful. Let's log an info message when an administrator changes the greeting message via the form we wrote. This could happen at one of two moments: whenever the salutation configuration is changed or when the actual form is submitted. Technically, in this case, the former is the more appropriate one because this configuration could also be changed via the code (API), so it stands to reason that logging would be needed then as well. However, to keep things simpler, let's handle it in the submit handler of `SalutationConfigurationForm`.

If you remember my rant in the previous chapter, there is no way we should use a service statically if we can instead inject it, and we can easily inject services into our form. So, let's do this now.

First of all, `FormBase` already implements `ContainerInjectionInterface`, so we don't need to implement it in our class, as we are extending from it somewhere down the line. Second of all, the `ConfigFormBase` class we are directly extending already has `config.factory` injected, so this complicates things for us a bit—well, not really. All we need to do is copy over the constructor and the `create()` methods, add our own service, store it in a property, and pass the services the parent needs to the parent constructor call. It will look like this:

```
/**
 * @var \Drupal\Core\Logger\LoggerChannelInterface
 */
protected $logger;

/**
 * SalutationConfigurationForm constructor.
 *
 * @param \Drupal\Core\Config\ConfigFactoryInterface
 *   $config_factory
 *    The factory for configuration objects.
 * @param \Drupal\Core\Logger\LoggerChannelInterface
 *   $logger
 *    The logger.
 */
public function __construct(ConfigFactoryInterface
  $config_factory, LoggerChannelInterface $logger) {
  parent::__construct($config_factory);
  $this->logger = $logger;
}
```

```
/**
 * {@inheritdoc}
 */
public static function create(ContainerInterface
  $container) {
  return new static(
    $container->get('config.factory'),
    $container->get('hello_world.logger.
      channel.hello_world')
  );
}
```

And the relevant *use* statements at the top:

```
use Drupal\Core\Config\ConfigFactoryInterface;
use Drupal\Core\Logger\LoggerChannelInterface;
use Symfony\Component\DependencyInjection\
  ContainerInterface;
```

As you can see, we get all the services that any of the parents need, plus the one we want (the logger channel) via the create() method. Also, in our constructor, we store the channel as a property and then pass the parent arguments to the parent constructor. Now, we have our hello_world logger channel available in our configuration form class. So, let's use it.

At the end of the submitForm() method, let's add the following line:

```
$this->logger->info('The Hello World salutation has been
  changed to @message.', ['@message' => $form_state->
    getValue('salutation')]);
```

We are logging a regular information message. However, since we also want to log the message that has been set, we use the second argument, which represents an array of context values. Under the hood, the database logger will extract the context variables that start with @, !, or % with the values from the entire context array. This is done using the LogMessageParser service. If you implement your own logger plugin, you will have to handle this yourself as well—but we'll see that in action soon.

And now we are done with logging a message when the salutation configuration form is saved.

Logging recap

In this first section, we saw how logging works in Drupal. Specifically, we covered a bit of theory so that you understand how things play together and you don't just mindlessly use the logger factory without having a clue what goes on under the hood.

As examples, we created our own logging channel, which allows us to inject it wherever we need it without always having to go through the factory. We will use this channel going forward for the *Hello World* module. Additionally, we created our own logger implementation. It won't do much now, except getting registered, but we will use it in the next section to send emails when errors get logged to the site.

Finally, we used the logging framework (and our channel) in the salutation configuration form to log a message whenever the form is submitted. In doing so, we also passed the message that was saved so that it also gets included in the log. This should already work with the database log, so go ahead and save the configuration form and then check the logging UI for that information message. We defined some new services, so make sure you clear the caches first if you haven't already.

Now that we know how to log things in our application, let's turn our attention to the Drupal Mail API.

Mail API

Our goal for this section is to see how we can send emails programmatically in Drupal. In achieving this goal, we will explore the default mail system that comes with the core installation (which uses PHP mail), but also create our own system that can theoretically use an external API to send mails. We won't go all the way with the latter because it's beyond the scope of this book. We will stop after covering what needs to be done from a Drupal point of view.

In the next and final section, we will look at tokens so that we can make our mailings a bit more dynamic.

The theory behind the Mail API

Like before, let's first cover this API from a theoretical point of view. It's important to understand the architecture before diving into examples.

Sending emails programmatically in Drupal is a two-part job. The first thing we need to do is define something of a *template* for the email in our module. This is not a template in the traditional sense, but rather a procedural data wrapper for the email you want to send. It's referred to in code as the *key* or *message ID*, but I believe that *template* is a better word to describe it. And you guessed it, it works by implementing a hook.

The second thing that we will need to do is use the Drupal mail manager to send the email using one of the defined *templates*. If this sounds confusing, don't worry—it will become clear with the example.

The *template* is created by implementing hook_mail(). This hook is a special one, as it does not work like most others. It gets called by the mail manager when a client (some code) is trying to send an email for the module that implements it.

The MailManager is a plugin manager that is also responsible for sending the emails using a mail system (plugin). The default mail system is PhpMail, which uses PHP's native mail() function to send out emails. To create our own mail system means creating a new plugin. Also, the plugin itself is the one delivering the emails, the manager simply deferring to it. As you can see, we can't go even a chapter ahead without creating plugins.

Each mail plugin needs to implement MailInterface, which exposes two methods—format() and mail(). The first one does the initial preparation of the mail content (message concatenation and so on), whereas the latter finalizes and sends it.

However, how does the mail manager know which plugin to use? It checks a configuration object called system.mail, which stores the default plugin (PhpMail) and can also store overrides for each individual module and any module and *template* ID combination. So, we can have multiple mail plugins each used for different things. A quirky thing about this configuration object is that there is no admin form where you can specify which plugin does what. You must adjust this configuration object programmatically as needed. One way you can manipulate this is via hook_install() and hook_uninstall() hooks. These hooks are used to perform some tasks whenever a module is installed/uninstalled. So, this is where we will change the configuration object to add our own mail plugin a bit later.

However, now that we have looked at a few bits of theory, let's see how we can use the default mail system to send out an email programmatically. Do you remember our unfinished logger from the previous section? That is where we will send our email whenever the logged message is an error.

Implementing hook_mail()

As I mentioned earlier, the first step for sending mail in Drupal is implementing hook_mail(). In our case, it can look something like this:

```
/**
 * Implements hook_mail().
 */
function hello_world_mail($key, &$message, $params) {
  switch ($key) {
    case 'hello_world_log':
      $message['from'] = \Drupal::config('system.site')->
        get('mail');
      $message['subject'] = t('There is an error on your
```

```
        website');
        $message['body'][] = $params['message'];


        break;
    }
}
```

This hook receives three parameters:

- The message key (template) that is used to send the mail

- The message of the email that needs to be filled in

- An array of parameters passed from the client code

As you can see, we are defining a key (or *template*) named `hello_world_log`, which has a simple static subject, and as a body, it will have whatever comes from the `$parameters` array in its `message` key. Since the *From* email is always the same, we will use the site-wide email address that can be found in the `system.site` configuration object. You'll note that we are not in a context where we can inject the configuration factory as we did when we built the form. Instead, we can use the static helper to load it.

Additionally, you'll notice that the body is itself an array. This is because we can build (if we want) multiple items in that array that can later be *imploded* as paragraphs in the mail plugin's `format()` method. This is in any case what the default mail plugin does, so here we need to build an array.

Another useful key in the `$message` array is the `header` key, which you can use to add some custom headers to the mail. In this case, we don't need to because the default `PhpMail` plugin adds all the necessary headers. If we write our own mail plugin, we can then add our headers in there as well—and all other keys of the `$message` array for that matter. This is because the `$message` array is passed around as a reference, so it keeps getting built up in the process, from the client call to the `hook_mail()` implementation, to the plugin.

That is about all we need to do with `hook_mail()`. Let's now see how to use this in order to send out an email.

Sending emails

We wanted to use our `MailLogger` to send out an email whenever we are logging an error. So let's go back to our class and add this logic.

This is how we can start our `log()` method:

```
/**
 * {@inheritdoc}
```

```
*/
public function log($level, \Stringable|string $message,
  array $context = []): void {
  if ($level !== RfcLogLevel::ERROR) {
    return;
  }

  $to = $this->configFactory->get('system.site')->
    get('mail');
  $langcode = $this->configFactory->get('system.site')->
    get('langcode');
  $variables = $this->parser->parseMessagePlaceholders
    ($message, $context);
  $markup = new FormattableMarkup($message, $variables);
  \Drupal::service('plugin.manager.mail')->
    mail('hello_world', 'hello_world_log', $to, $langcode,
      ['message' => $markup]);
}
```

First, we said that we only want to send mails for errors, so in the first lines, we check whether the attempted log is of that level and return early otherwise. In other words, we don't do anything if we're not dealing with an error and rely on other registered loggers for those.

Next, we determine who we want the email to be sent to and the langcode to send it in (both are mandatory arguments of the mail manager's `mail()` method). We opt to use the site-wide email address (just as we did for the *From* value). We use the same configuration object as we used earlier in the `hook_mail()` implementation. Don't worry—we will shortly take care of injecting the config factory into the class.

> **Note**
>
> When we talk about langcode, we refer to the machine name of a language object. In this case, that is what is being stored for the site-wide default language. Also, we'll default to that for our emails. In a later chapter, we will cover more aspects regarding internationalization in Drupal.

Then, we prepare the message that is being sent out. For this, we use the `FormattableMarkup` helper class to which we pass the message string and an array of variable values that can be used to replace the placeholders in our message. We can retrieve these values using the `LogMessageParser` service the same way as the `DbLog` logger does. So, with this, we are basically extracting the placeholder variables from the entire context array of the logged message.

Lastly, we use the mail plugin manager to send the email. The first parameter to its `mail()` method is the module we want to use for the mailing. The second is the key (or *template*) we want to use for it (which we defined in `hook_mail()`). The third and fourth are self-explanatory, while the fifth is the `$params` array we encountered in `hook_mail()`. If you look back at that, you'll notice that we used the `message` key as the body. Here, we populate that key with our markup object, which has a `_toString()` method that renders it with all the placeholders replaced.

You may wonder why I did not inject the Drupal mail manager as I did the rest of the dependencies. Unfortunately, the core mail manager uses the logger channel factory itself, which in turn depends on our `MailLogger` service. So, if we make the mail manager a dependency of the latter, we find ourselves in a circular loop. So, when the container gets rebuilt, a big fat error is thrown. It might still work, but it's not right. So, I opted to use it statically, because, in any case, this method is very small and would be difficult to test due to its expected result being difficult to assert (it sends an email). Sometimes, you have to make these choices, as the alternative would have been to inject the entire service container just to trick it. However, that is a code smell and would not have helped anyway had I wanted to write a test for this class.

Even if I did not inject the mail manager, I did inject the rest. So, let's look at what we need now at the top of the class:

```php
/**
 * @var \Drupal\Core\Logger\LogMessageParserInterface
 */
protected $parser;


/**
 * @var \Drupal\Core\Config\ConfigFactoryInterface
 */
protected $configFactory;


/**
 * MailLogger constructor.
 *
 * @param \Drupal\Core\Logger\LogMessageParserInterface
 *   $parser
 * @param \Drupal\Core\Config\ConfigFactoryInterface
 *   $config_factory
 */
public function __construct(LogMessageParserInterface
  $parser, ConfigFactoryInterface $config_factory) {
```

```
    $this->parser = $parser;
    $this->configFactory = $config_factory;
}
```

And finally, all the relevant *use* statements that we were missing:

```
use Drupal\Core\Logger\LogMessageParserInterface;
use Drupal\Core\Config\ConfigFactoryInterface;
use Drupal\Component\Render\FormattableMarkup;
use Drupal\Core\Logger\RfcLogLevel;
```

Finally, let's quickly also adjust the service definition of our mail logger:

```
hello_world.logger.mail_logger:
    class: Drupal\hello_world\Logger\MailLogger
    arguments: ['@logger.log_message_parser',
      '@config.factory']
    tags:
      - { name: logger }
```

We simply have two new arguments—nothing new to you by now.

Clearing the caches and logging an error should send the logged message (with the placeholders replaced) to the site email address (and from the same address) using the PHP native `mail()` function. Congratulations! You just sent out your first email programmatically in Drupal.

Altering someone else's emails

Drupal is powerful not only because it allows us to add our own functionality but also because it allows us to alter existing functionality. An important vector for doing this is the *alter* hooks system. Remember those from *Creating Your First Module*? These are hooks that are used to change the value of an array or object before it is used for whatever purpose it was going to be used for. When it comes to sending emails, we have an alter hook that allows us to change things on the mail definition before it goes out: `hook_mail_alter()`. For our module, we don't need to implement this hook. However, for the sake of making our lesson complete, let's see how we could use this hook to, for example, change the header of an existing outgoing email:

```
/**
 * Implements hook_mail_alter().
 */
function hello_world_mail_alter(&$message) {
```

```
  switch ($message['key']) {
    case 'hello_world_log':
      $message['headers']['Content-Type'] = 'text/html;
        charset=UTF-8; format=flowed; delsp=yes';
      break;
  }
}
```

So, what is going on here? This hook implementation gets called in each module it is implemented in. It's not like hook_mail() in this respect as it allows us to alter emails sent from any module. However, in our example, we will just alter the mail we defined earlier.

The only parameter (passed by reference as is usual with alter hooks) is the $message array, which contains all the things we built in hook_mail(), as well as the key (*template*) and other things added by the mail manager itself, such as the headers. So, in our example, we are setting an HTML header so that whatever is getting sent out *could be* rendered as HTML. After this hook is invoked, the mail system formatter is also called, which, in the case of the PhpMail plugin, transforms all HTML tags into plain text, essentially canceling out our header. However, if we implement our own plugin, we can prevent that and successfully send out HTML emails with proper tags and everything.

So, that is basically all there is to altering existing outgoing mail. Next, we will see how we can create our own mail plugin that uses a custom external mail system. We won't go into detail here, but we will prepare the architecture that will allow us to bring in the API we need and use it easily.

Custom mail plugins

In the previous section, we saw how we can use the Drupal mail API to send emails programmatically. In doing so, we used the default PHP mailer, which although is good enough for our example, might not be good enough for our application. For example, we might want to use an external service via an API.

In this section, we will see how this works. To this end, we will write our own mail plugin that does just that, and then simply tell Drupal to use that system instead of the default one. Yet another plugin-based, non-invasive, extension point.

Before we start, I would like to mention that we won't go into any kind of detail related to the potential external API. Instead, we will stop at the Drupal-specific parts, so the code you will find in the repository won't do much—it will be used as an example only. It's up to you to use this technique if you need to.

The mail plugin

Let's start by creating our Mail plugin class, and if you remember, plugins go inside the Plugin folder of our module namespace. And mail plugins belong inside a Mail folder. This is what a simple skeleton mail plugin class can look like:

```
namespace Drupal\hello_world\Plugin\Mail;

use Drupal\Core\Mail\MailFormatHelper;
use Drupal\Core\Mail\MailInterface;
use Drupal\Core\Plugin\ContainerFactoryPluginInterface;
use Symfony\Component\DependencyInjection\
  ContainerInterface;

/**
 * Defines the Hello World mail backend.
 *
 * @Mail(
 *   id = "hello_world_mail",
 *   label = @Translation("Hello World mailer"),
 *   description = @Translation("Sends an email using an
 *       external API specific to our Hello World module.")
 * )
 */
class HelloWorldMail implements MailInterface,
  ContainerFactoryPluginInterface {

  /**
   * {@inheritdoc}
   */
  public static function create(ContainerInterface
    $container, array $configuration, $plugin_id,
      $plugin_definition) {
    return new static();
  }

  /**
   * {@inheritdoc}
   */
  public function format(array $message) {
    // Join the body array into one string.
    $message['body'] = implode("\n\n", $message['body']);
```

```
    // Convert any HTML to plain-text.
    $message['body'] = MailFormatHelper::htmlToText
        ($message['body']);
    // Wrap the mail body for sending.
    $message['body'] = MailFormatHelper::wrapMail
        ($message['body']);


    return $message;
}


/**
 * {@inheritdoc}
 */
public function mail(array $message) {
    // Use the external API to send the email based on the
        $message array
    // constructed via the `hook_mail()` implementation.
}
}
```

As you can see, we have a relatively easy plugin annotation; no unusual arguments there. Then, you will note that we implemented the mandatory `MailInterface`, which comes with the two methods implemented in the class.

I mentioned the `format()` method earlier and said that it's responsible for doing certain processing before the message is ready to be sent. Our implementation is a copy from the `PhpMail` plugin to exemplify just what kind of task would go there. However, you can do whatever you want in here, for example, allow HTML tags. Imploding the body is something you will probably want to do anyway, as it is kind of expected that the mail body is constructed as an array by `hook_mail()`.

The `mail()` method, on the other hand, is left empty. This is because it's up to you to use the external API to send the email. For this, you can use the `$message` array we encountered in the `hook_mail()` implementation.

Lastly, note that `ContainerFactoryPluginInterface` is another interface that our class implements. If you remember, that is what plugins need to implement in order for them to become container-aware (for the dependencies to be injectable). Since this was only example code, it doesn't have any dependencies, so I did not include a constructor and left the `create()` method empty. Most likely, you will have to inject something, such as a PHP client library that works with your external API. So, it doesn't hurt to see this again.

That is pretty much it for our plugin class. Now, let's see how we can use it because for the moment, our `hello_world_log` emails are still being sent with the default PHP mailer.

Using mail plugins

As I mentioned earlier, there is no UI in Drupal to select which plugin the mail manager should use for sending emails programmatically. It figures it out inside the `getInstance()` method by checking the `system.mail` configuration object, and more specifically, the `interface` key inside that (which is an array).

By default, this array contains only one record, that is, `'default' => 'php_mail'`. That means that, by default, all emails are sent with the `php_mail` plugin ID. In order to get our plugin in the mix, we have a few options:

- We can replace this value with our plugin ID, which means that all emails will be sent with our plugin.

- We can add a new record with the key in the `module_name_key_name` format, which means that all emails sent for a module with a specific key (or *template*) will use that plugin.

- We can add a new record with the key in the `module_name` format, which means that all emails sent for a module will use that plugin (regardless of their key).

For our example, we will set all emails sent from the `hello_world` module to use our new plugin. We can do this using the `hook_install()` implementation, which runs whenever the module is installed.

Install (and uninstall) hooks need to go inside a `.install` PHP file in the root of our module. So this next function goes inside a new `hello_world.install` file. Also, if our module has already been enabled, we will need to first uninstall it and then install it again to get this function to fire:

```php
/**
 * Implements hook_install().
 */
function hello_world_install($is_syncing) {
  if ($is_syncing) {
    return;
  }

  $config = \Drupal::configFactory()->
    getEditable('system.mail');
  $mail_plugins = $config->get('interface');
  if (in_array('hello_world', array_keys($mail_plugins))) {
```

```
        return;
    }


    $mail_plugins['hello_world'] = 'hello_world_mail';
    $config->set('interface', $mail_plugins)->save();
}
```

The first thing we do is check whether the module is installed as part of a configuration sync, and if it is, we do nothing. There are two main reasons for this. First, when modules are installed as part of a configuration sync (such as deployment to another environment), we cannot rely on what configuration has already been imported. Second, the assumption is that when we install this module locally via normal means and then export the site configuration to files, the configuration change we make will be exported as well. So, when we sync this configuration on another environment, our changes will be reflected. We will talk more about configuration later.

Next, we load the configuration object as editable (so we can change it), and if we don't yet have a record with hello_world in the array of mail plugins, we set it and map our plugin ID to it. Lastly, we save the object.

The opposite of this function is hook_uninstall(), which goes in the same file and—expectedly— gets fired whenever the module is uninstalled. Since we don't want to change a site-wide configuration object and tie it to our module's plugin, we should implement this hook as well. Otherwise, if our module gets uninstalled, the mail system will fail because it will try to use a nonexistent plugin. So, let's tie up our loose ends:

```
/**
 * Implements hook_uninstall().
 */
function hello_world_uninstall($is_syncing) {
  if ($is_syncing) {
    return;
  }


  $config = \Drupal::configFactory()->
    getEditable('system.mail');
  $mail_plugins = $config->get('interface');
  if (!in_array('hello_world', array_keys($mail_plugins)))
  {
    return;
  }
```

```
    unset($mail_plugins['hello_world']);
    $config->set('interface', $mail_plugins)->save();
}
```

As you can see, what we did here is basically the opposite. If the record we set previously exists, we unset it and save the configuration object. And the same logic about the configuration sync applies equally.

So now, any mails sent programmatically for the `hello_world` module will use this plugin. Easy, right? However, since the plugin we wrote is not ready, the code you find in the repository will have the relevant line from the `hook_install()` implementation commented out so that we don't actually use it.

> **Note**
>
> If you are following along, in order to get the `hook_install()` hook fired, you need to first uninstall the `hello_world` module and install it back.

Mail API recap

In this section, we talked about the mail API by covering some theoretical aspects first, as we are already starting to get used to it. We saw what modules need to have in order to send out emails and how we can alter emails being sent by other modules we don't control. Finally, we saw how extendable the mail system is using plugins and how we can write our own to control exactly how and what mechanism we use for sending out emails.

Let's now switch gears and talk about tokens and why they are important for us as module developers.

Tokens

The last thing we will cover in this chapter is the Token API in Drupal. We will cover a few bits of theory and, as usual, demonstrate them via examples on our existing *Hello World* module code. We will do this in the context of the emails we are sending out for error logs.

It would be nice if we could include some personalized information in the mail text without having to hardcode it in the module code or configuration. For example, in our case, we might want to include the username of the current user that is triggering the error log that is being emailed.

Let's first understand how the Token API works, before going into our *Hello World* module.

The Token API

Tokens in Drupal are a standard formatted placeholder, which can be found inside a string and replaced by a real value extracted from a related object. The format they use is `type:token`, where `type` is the machine-readable name of a token type (a group of related tokens), and `token` is the machine-readable name of a token within this group.

The power of the Token API in Drupal is not only given by its flexibility but also by the fact that it is already a popular API. It is flexible because you can define groups that contain related tokens, linked by the data object that contains their value (for example, a node object or user object). It is popular because in previous versions of Drupal, it was the contributed module many others were dependent on to define their own tokens, and it is now available in Drupal core with many tokens already defined out of the box. So, you'll find many existing tokens that you can use in your code, and if not, you can define your own.

There are three main components of this API—at least from the point of view of a Drupal module developer. These components are two hooks—`hook_token_info()` and `hook_tokens()`—and the `Token` service, which is used to perform the replacement.

The first hook is used to define one or more token types and tokens. It essentially registers them with the system. The second is fired when a token is found inside a string (a replacement is attempted by the service) and is used to do the replacement of the tokens based on the data that is passed to it from the service. For example, the User module defines two token types and a number of tokens using `user_token_info()`. With `user_tokens()`, it checks whether the token is one of its own and tries to replace it with the contextual data (either a user object or the currently logged-in account object). To read the documentation related to each of these in detail and to see an extended example, you can find them either on the Drupal.org API page or inside the `token.api.php` file. There, you will also find *alter* hooks that correspond to these two and can be used to alter either the defined token information or logic to replace these tokens written by other modules or Drupal core.

The `Token` service is what we can use as module developers if we have to replace tokens found inside a string. We will see how this is used in the next section.

Using tokens

To quickly demonstrate how we can use tokens, let's include in our `hello_world_log` mails some information about the current user at the time the email is being sent out. This will naturally coincide with the user that is signed in at the time the error is being logged.

For this, we will need to alter our `hook_mail()` implementation. In there, we will use the `current_user` service, add another string to our mail body, and, of course, replace a token:

```
/**
 * Implements hook_mail().
```

```
  */
function hello_world_mail($key, &$message, $params) {
  switch ($key) {
    case 'hello_world_log':
      $message['from'] = \Drupal::config('system.site')->
        get('mail');
      $message['subject'] = t('There is an error on your
        website');
      $message['body'][] = $params['message'];
      $user_message = 'The user that was logged in:
        [current-user:name].';
      $message['body'][] = \Drupal::token()->
        replace($user_message, ['current-user' =>
          \Drupal::currentUser()]);


      break;
  }
}
```

As you can see, we are adding a new "paragraph" to our email. This is a simple string that informs us about the user that was logged in. However, in doing so, we use the Token service (statically) to replace that piece of string with the token value. The replace() method of the service takes a string and optionally an array of data objects keyed by the type (group) of the tokens they should be used for.

The choice of token and type in this case is important. The User module defines the user and current-user types. The difference between the two, if you check inside user_tokens(), is that the latter simply delegates to the former after it loads a full user entity. We could, alternatively, have done that ourselves and then passed the user type, but why should we? If somebody has done that for us already, we should not have to do it again. And what we pass to the current-user token type as a data object to be used in the replacement process is the AccountProxy (current user session).

So, that's it. Now, the email message will get an extra line that contains the dynamically generated username of the currently logged-in user at the time the error happened. Under the hood, the Token service scans the string, extracts the token, and calls all hook_tokens() implementations. The User module is the one that can return the replacement for this token based on the user object it receives.

Defining new tokens

We just saw how we can programmatically use existing tokens inside our strings and get them replaced with minimal effort. All we need is the token service and the data object that can be used to replace the token. Keep in mind that there are tokens that don't even require any data objects due to their global nature. The hook_tokens() implementation will take care of that—let's see how.

In the previous chapter, we created functionalities for a dynamic *Hello World* message: either calculated on the fly or loaded from a configuration object. How about we expose that message as a token? That would make its usage more flexible because our string becomes exposed to the entire token system.

As mentioned earlier, we will start with the hook_token_info() implementation:

```php
/**
 * Implements hook_token_info().
 */
function hello_world_token_info() {
  $type = [
    'name' => t('Hello World'),
    'description' => t('Tokens related to the Hello World
      module.'),
  ];

  $tokens['salutation'] = [
    'name' => t('Salutation'),
    'description' => t('The Hello World salutation
      value.'),
  ];

  return [
    'types' => ['hello_world' => $type],
    'tokens' => ['hello_world' => $tokens],
  ];
}
```

In here, we will need to define two things—the types and the tokens. In our case, we are defining one of each. The type is hello_world and comes with a human-readable name and description in case it needs to be rendered somewhere in the UI. The token is salutation and belongs to the hello_world type. It also gets a name and description. In the end, we return an array that contains both.

What follows is the `hook_tokens()` implementation in which we handle the replacement of our token:

```
/**
 * Implements hook_tokens().
 */
function hello_world_tokens($type, $tokens, array $data, array
$options, BubbleableMetadata $bubbleable_metadata) {
  $replacements = [];
  if ($type == 'hello_world') {
    foreach ($tokens as $name => $original) {
      switch ($name) {
        case 'salutation':
          $replacements[$original] = \Drupal::service
            ('hello_world.salutation')->getSalutation();
          $config = \Drupal::config
            ('hello_world.custom_salutation');
          $bubbleable_metadata->addCacheableDependency
            ($config);
          break;


      }
    }
  }

  return $replacements;
}
```

There is a bit more going on here, but I'll explain everything. This hook gets fired whenever a replacement of tokens is attempted on a string. And it's fired for each type that has been found inside that string, `$type` being the first argument. Inside `$tokens`, we get an array of tokens located in that string, which belong to `$type`. The `$data` array contains the objects needed to replace the tokens (and passed to the `replace()` method), keyed by the type. This array can be empty (as it will be in our case).

Inside the function, we loop through each token of this group and try to replace it. We only know of one, and we use our `HelloWorldSalutation` service to determine the replacement string.

Finally, the function needs to return an array of all replacements found (which can be multiple if multiple tokens of the same type are found inside a string).

The `bubbleable_metadata` parameter is a special cache metadata object that describes this token in the cache system. It is needed because tokens get cached, so if any dependent object changes, the cache needs to be invalidated for this token as well. By default, all objects inside the `$data` array are read and included in this object. However, in our case, it is empty, yet we still depend on a configuration object that can change—the one that stores the overridden salutation message. So, we will need to add a dependency on that configuration object even if the actual value for the salutation we compute uses the same `HelloWorldSalutation` service we used before. So, we have a simple example here, but with a complex twist. We will talk more about caching later in the book.

That's all there is to defining our token. It can now also be used inside strings and replaced using the `Token` service. Something like this:

```
$final_string = \Drupal::token()->replace('The salutation
    text is: [hello_world:salutation]');
```

As you can see, we pass no other parameters. If our token was dependent on an entity object, for example, we would have passed it in the second parameter array and made use of it inside `hook_tokens()` to compute the replacement.

Tokens recap

The token system is an important part of Drupal because it allows us to easily transform raw data into useful values using placeholder strings. It is a widely used and flexible system that many contributed modules build upon. The great thing about tokens is the UI component. There are modules that will allow users to define strings in the UI which contain tokens that can be replaced by the system. Also, this is something you can do as a module developer.

Summary

In this chapter, we discussed many things. We saw how logging works in Drupal, how the mail API can be used programmatically (and extended), and how the token system can be employed to make our text more dynamic.

While going through this chapter, we also enriched our *Hello World* module. So, apart from understanding the theory about logging, we created our own logging channel service and logger plugin. For the latter, we decided to send out emails when log messages were of the *error* type. In doing this, we looked at the Mail API and how we can use it programmatically. We saw that, by default, PHP's native `mail()` function is used to send out emails. But we can create our own plugin very easily in order to use whatever external service we want—yet another great example of extensibility via plugins.

Lastly, we looked at tokens in Drupal. We saw what components make up the API, how we can programmatically use existing tokens (replace them with the help of contextual data), and how we can define our own tokens for others to use. These are the main tenets of extensibility (and sharing)—using something someone else has exposed to you and exposing something for someone else to use.

In the next chapter, we will look at another great topic—theming.

4
Theming

The most obvious part of Drupal's theming system is the **Appearance** admin page found at `admin/appearance`, which lists all the themes installed on your website:

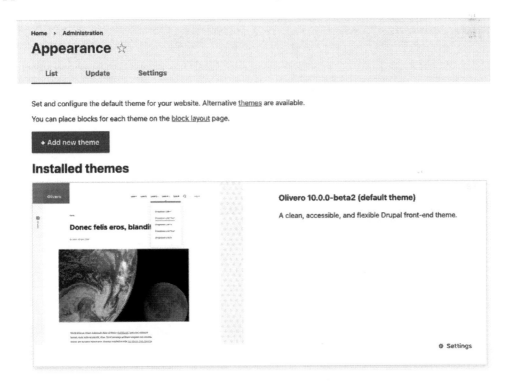

Figure 4.1: Appearance admin page

When you choose a theme from the **Appearance** page, you are applying a specific graphic design to your website's data and functionality. However, the applied theme is in reality only a small part of the entire theming layer.

This book focuses mostly on building modules that encapsulate chunks of functionality. However, since we're ultimately building a web application, everything output by our functionality will need to be marked up with HTML. In Drupal, this process of wrapping data in HTML and CSS is called theming.

In this chapter, we will discuss how our module integrates with the theme layer. We will talk about the architecture of the system, theme templates, hooks, render arrays, and others. Then, we will provide some practical examples.

The major topics we will cover in the chapter are as follows:

- Theme hooks, templates, and suggestions
- Render arrays and layouts
- Assets and libraries
- Theming our Hello World module using the lessons learned

Business logic versus presentation logic

We start this chapter by discussing an important architectural choice that modern applications make: how to turn data into presentation.

So, what would be the best way to get our data and functionality marked up? Do we simply wrap each piece of data in HTML and return the whole thing as a giant string, as shown in the following example?

```
return '<div class="wrapper">' . $data . '</div>';
```

No, we don't. Like all other well-designed applications, Drupal separates its business logic from its presentation logic.

Traditionally, the primary motivations for this separation of concerns are as follows:

- To make the code easier to maintain
- To make it possible to easily swap out one layer's implementation without having to rewrite the other layer

As we will see, Drupal takes the "swapability" aspect quite far. You may think that the theme you select on the **Appearance** page is responsible for applying the HTML and CSS for the website. This is true, but only to some extent. There are thousands of contributed modules on Drupal.org. Also, you can write a bunch of your own. Should the theme be responsible for marking up all of those modules' data? Obviously not.

Since a module is most intimately familiar with its own data and functionality, it is its own responsibility to provide the default theme implementation—that initial look and feel that is independent of design and that should display the data correctly regardless of the theme. However, as long as the module uses the theme system properly, a theme will be able to override any HTML and/or CSS by swapping the module's implementation with its own.

In other words, after data is retrieved and manipulated inside the module (the business logic), it will need to provide the default theme implementation to wrap it inside its markup. Sometimes, a particular theme will need to override this implementation to achieve a specific design goal. If the theme provides its own implementation, Drupal will use that theme implementation instead of the module's default implementation. This is usually called *overriding*. Otherwise, the default fallback will still be there. The theme also provides the option of applying styling via CSS only and leaving the markup provided by the module intact.

Twig

Theme engines are responsible for doing the actual output via template files. Since Drupal 8, this is handled by the Twig engine created by SensioLabs (the people responsible for the Symfony project). Hence, all template files in Drupal have the `.html.twig` extension.

Theme hooks

Since we have covered some of the principles behind the Drupal theme system—most notably, the separation of concerns—let's go a bit deeper and see how they are actually put into practice. This all starts with the theme hooks. Yes, Drupal loves to call things *hooks*.

Theme hooks define how a specific piece of data should be rendered. They are registered with the theme system by modules (and themes) using `hook_theme()`. In doing so, they get a name, a list of variables they output (the data that needs to be wrapped with markup), and other options.

The modules and themes that register theme hooks also need to provide an implementation (one that will be used by default).

As an example, let's take a look at two common ways of registering a theme hook that we'll often find. For this, we will use Drupal core examples that already exist:

```
function hook_theme($existing, $type, $theme, $path) {
  return [
    'item_list' => array(
      'variables' => array('items' => array(), 'title' =>
        '', 'list_type' => 'ul', 'wrapper_attributes' =>
          array(), 'attributes' => array(), 'empty' =>
            NULL, 'context' => array()),
    ),
    'select' => array(
      'render element' => 'element',
    ),
  ];
}
```

In the above `hook_theme()` example, I included two theme hooks from Drupal core. One is based on variables, whereas the other is based on a render element. There are, of course, many more options that can be defined here, and I strongly encourage you to read the `Drupal.org` API documentation page for this hook.

However, right off the bat you can see how easy it is to register a theme hook. In the first case, we have `item_list`, which, by default (if not otherwise specified), will map to the `item-list.html.twig` file for outputting the variables. In its definition we find the variables it uses, with some handy defaults in case they are not passed in from the client. The second theme hook is `select`, which doesn't use variables but a render element (which we will discuss soon). Also, its template file is easy to determine based on the name: `select.html.twig`. I encourage you to check out both of these template files in the core code (provided by the System module).

In addition to the actual implementation, the modules and themes that register a theme hook can also provide a default template preprocessor. The responsibility of this is to "preprocess" (that is, prepare) data before being sent to the template. For example, if a theme hook receives an entity (a complex data object) as its only variable, a preprocessor can be used to break that entity into tiny pieces that are needed to be output in the template (such as title and description).

Template preprocessors are simple procedural functions that follow a naming pattern and are called by the theme system before the template is rendered. As I mentioned earlier, the modules and themes that register a theme hook can also provide a default preprocessor. So, for a theme hook named `component_box`, the default preprocessor function would look like this:

```
function template_preprocess_component_box(&$variables) {
    // Prepare variables.
}
```

The function name starts with the word `template` to denote that it is the original preprocessor for this theme hook, then follows the conventional `preprocess` word, and ends with the name of the theme hook. The argument is always an array passed as a reference and contains some info regarding that theme hook, and more importantly, the data variables that were defined with the theme hook and passed to it from the calling code. That is what we are usually working within this function. Also, since it's passed by a reference, we don't return anything in this function, but we always manipulate the values directly in the `$variables` array. In the end, the template file can print out variables named after the keys in this array. The values will be, of course, the values that map to those keys.

Another module (or theme) can override this preprocessor function by implementing its own. However, in its naming, it needs to replace the word `template` with the module name (to avoid collisions). If one such override exists, both preprocessors will be called in a specific order. The first is always the default one, followed by the ones defined by modules, and then the ones defined by themes. This is another great extension point of Drupal because altering data or options found inside the preprocessor can go a long way in customizing the existing functionality to your liking.

As an alternative to following the previous naming convention, you also have the option to specify the preprocessor function names in the `hook_theme()` definition when you register it. However, I recommend that you stick to the default naming convention because it's much easier to spot what the purpose of the function is. As you become more advanced, you'll, in turn, appreciate being able to quickly understand these *convention* functions at a quick glance.

I mentioned a bit earlier that modules and themes can also override theme hooks defined by other modules and themes. There are two ways to do this.

The most common one is for a theme to override the theme hook. This is because of the rationale I was talking about earlier—a module defines a default implementation for its data, but a theme can then take over its presentation with ease. Also, the way themes can override a theme hook is by simply creating a new Twig file with the same name as the original and placing it somewhere in its `templates` folder. If that theme is enabled, it will be used instead. A less common but definitely valid use case is for a module to override a theme hook defined by another module. For example, this might be because you need to change how data is rendered by a popular contributed module. To achieve this, you will need to implement `hook_theme_registry_alter()` and change the template file used by the existing theme hook. It's also worth adding that you can change the entire theme hook definition using this hook if you want, not just the template. Moreover, since we mentioned this hook, note that theme hooks, upon definition, are stored and cached in a theme *registry* for optimized performance, and that registry is what we are altering with this hook. This also means that we regularly need to clear the cache when we make changes to the theme registry.

All this is good and fine, but the business logic still has to interact with the theme system to tell it which particular theme hook to use. And we do so by using something called *render arrays*, which contain the theme hook information, the variables, and any other metadata on how that component needs to be rendered. We will also talk about render arrays in this chapter.

Theme hook suggestions

A great thing about theme hooks is that they are reusable. However, one problem you'll encounter is that theme hook templates lose context when a theme hook is reused. For example, the `item_list` theme hook, whose definition we saw in the previous section, has no idea what list it is theming. And this makes it difficult to style differently depending on what that content is. Fortunately, we can provide context to the theme system by using a theme hook pattern instead of the original theme hook name, and this pattern looks something like this:

```
base_theme_hook__some_context
```

The parts of the pattern are separated with a double underscore and together they are called a *theme hook suggestion*. But how does this work?

Client code (the render arrays, as we will soon see), when using a theme hook to render a piece of data, can append the context to the theme hook, turning it into a suggestion. The theme system will then check for the following:

- If there is a template file that matches that suggestion (inside a theme), it uses it instead of the original theme hook template.

- Alternatively, if there is a theme hook registered that has that actual name, it uses that instead.

- Alternatively, it checks for the base theme hook and uses that instead (the fallback).

In this case, the caller (the render array) is responsible for "proposing" a suggestion. For example, consider the following render array:

```
return [
  '#theme' => 'item_list__my_list',
  '#items' => $items,
];
```

The base theme hook is `item_list`, which is rendered using the `item-list.html.twig` template file provided by Drupal core. If there is no `item-list--my-list.html.twig` template file in the theme, and there is no `item_list__my_list` theme hook registered, the default `item_list` theme hook will be used. Otherwise, we will follow the order that I mentioned before. A module can register that suggestion as a hook, which will be used instead. However, a theme can override that further by just creating the template file with that name.

And all this is done so that when rendering something with a reusable theme hook, we give the possibility to determine what exactly is being themed. However, the example we saw just now is static in the sense that we hardcoded `my_list` as the theme hook suggestion. We can do better than that.

A module that registers a theme hook can also provide a list of suggestions that should go with that theme hook automatically. It does so by implementing `hook_theme_suggestions_HOOK()`, where HOOK is the theme hook name. This hook is fired at runtime by the theme system, trying to determine how a certain render array needs to be rendered. It receives as argument the same `$variables` array as the template preprocessors do. This means that we can make use of those variables and dynamically provide theme hook suggestions. We will see an example of this later in the chapter.

Moreover, as module developers, we can also provide a list of theme hook suggestions to theme hooks registered by other modules or Drupal core. We can do so by implementing `hook_theme_suggestions_HOOK_alter()`, where we receive the available suggestions for that theme hook in addition to the variables.

In summary, theme hook suggestions are a powerful way of adding some context to the generic theme hooks that are responsible for rendering multiple things.

Render arrays

Render arrays are a core part of the Render API that is responsible for transforming markup *representations* into actual markup.

Acknowledging my limits as a writer, I will defer to the definition found in the Drupal.org documentation, which best describes what render arrays are:

> *... a hierarchical associative array containing data to be rendered and properties describing how the data should be rendered.*

Simple, but powerful.

One of the principal reasons behind having render arrays is that they allow Drupal to delay the actual rendering of something into markup to the very last moment. This means we simply construct render arrays and by the end of the request, Drupal will know how to turn them into markup. This way, modules and themes can intercept them at various levels in the process and make alterations.

We will now talk about render arrays and the different aspects of working with them.

The structure of a render array

Render arrays are rendered by the `renderer` service (`RendererInterface`), which traverses the array and recursively renders each level. Each level of the array can have one or more elements, which can be of two types: properties or children. The properties are the ones whose keys are preceded by a # sign, whereas children are the ones whose keys are not preceded by that sign. The children can themselves be an array with properties and children. However, each level needs to have at least one property in order to be considered a level because it is responsible for telling the render system how that level needs to be rendered. As such, property names are specific to the Render API and to the actual thing they need to render, while the names of children can be flexible. In addition to these two types (yes, I lied, there can be more than two), we can also have the variables defined by a theme hook, which are also preceded by the # sign. They are not properties per se but are known by the theme system because they have been registered inside `hook_theme()`.

There are many properties that the Render API uses to process a render array. Some of them are quite important, such as `#cache` and `#attached`. However, there are a few that are mandatory in order for a render array to make sense, in that they define its core responsibility. The following are the properties that describe what the render array should do and each render array should have at least one of these.

#type

The `#type` property specifies that the array contains data that needs to be rendered using a particular *render element*. Render elements are plugins (yes, plugins) that encapsulate a defined renderable component. They essentially wrap another render array, which can use a theme hook or a more complex render array to process the data they are responsible for rendering. You can think of them as essentially standardized render arrays.

There are two types of render elements: generic and form input elements. Both have their respective plugin types, annotations and interfaces. They are similar in that they both render a standardized piece of HTML; however, form input elements have the complexity of having to deal with form processing, validation, data mapping, and so on. Remember that when we defined our form in *Chapter 2, Creating Your First Module,* we encountered arrays with # signs. These were (form) render elements with different options (properties).

To find examples of these two types of render elements, look for plugins that implement the `ElementInterface` and `FormElementInterface` interfaces.

#theme

The `#theme` property ties in strongly with what we've been talking about earlier in this chapter—theme hooks. It specifies that the render array needs to render some kind of data using one of the theme hooks defined. Together with this property, you will usually encounter other properties that map to the name of the variables the theme hook has registered in `hook_theme()`. These are the variables the theme system uses to render the template.

This is the property you will use in your business logic to convey that your data needs to be rendered using a specific theme hook. There are many theme hooks that have been already registered by Drupal core and contributed modules that make the life of a Drupal developer much easier. Just look inside `drupal_common_theme()` for a bunch of common theme hooks that you can perhaps use. And, of course, you can define your own.

#markup

Sometimes, registering a theme hook and a template for outputting some data can be overkill. Imagine that all you have is a string you need to wrap in a `<span>` tag or something. In this case, you can use the `#markup` property, which specifies that the array directly provides the HTML string that needs to be output. Note, however, that the provided HTML string is run through `\Drupal\Component\Utility\Xss::filterAdmin` for sanitization (mostly, XSS protection). This is perfectly fine because if the HTML you are trying to include here is stripped out, it's a good indication that you are overusing the `#markup` property and should instead be registering a theme hook.

Going a bit further than just simple markup is the `#plain_text` property via which you can specify that the text provided by this render array needs to be escaped completely. So basically if you need to output some simple text, you have the choice between these two for very fast output.

Now, if you remember in *Chapter 2, Creating Your First Module*, at some point our controller returned this array:

```
return [
  '#markup' => $this->t('Hello World')
];
```

This is the simplest render array you'll ever see. It has only one element, a tiny string output using the #markup property. Later in this chapter, we will adjust this and use a render array provided by our HelloWorldSalutation service in order to make things a bit more *themeable*. That will be the section where we put into practice many of the things we learn here.

However, as small as you see this array here, it is only part of a larger hierarchical render array that builds up the entire Drupal page and that contains all sorts of blocks and other components. Also responsible for building this entire big thing is the Drupal render pipeline.

The render pipeline

In *Chapter 1, Developing for Drupal 10*, when we outlined a high-level example of how Drupal handles a user request in order to turn it into a response, we touched on the notion of a render pipeline. So let's see what this is about, as there are essentially two render pipelines to speak of: the Symfony render pipeline and the Drupal one.

As you know, Drupal uses many Symfony components, one of which being the HTTP Kernel component (http://symfony.com/doc/current/components/http_kernel.html). Its main role is to turn a user request (built from PHP super globals into a Request object) into a standardized response object that gets sent back to the user. These objects are defined in the Symfony HTTP Foundation component (https://symfony.com/doc/current/components/http_foundation.html). To assist in this process, it uses the Event Dispatcher component to dispatch events meant to handle the workload on multiple layers. As we saw, this is what happens in Drupal as well.

Controllers in Drupal can return one of two things—either a Response object directly or a render array. If they return the first, the job is almost done, as the Symfony render pipeline knows exactly what to do with that (assuming the response is correct). However, if they return a render array, the Drupal render pipeline kicks in at a lower level to try to turn that into a Response. We always need a Response.

The kernel.view event is triggered in order to determine who can take care of this render array. Drupal comes with the MainContentViewSubscriber which listens to this event and checks the request format and whether the controller has returned a render array. Based on the former, it instantiates a MainContentRendererInterface object (which, by default—and most of the time—will be the HTML-based HtmlRenderer) and asks it to turn the render array into a Response. Then, it sets the Response onto the event so that the Symfony render pipeline can continue on its merry way.

In addition to the HTML renderer, Drupal comes with a few others that need to handle different types of requests:

- The `AjaxRenderer` handles Ajax requests and integrates with the Ajax framework. We'll see examples of Ajax-powered functionalities later in the book.

- The `DialogRenderer` handles requests meant to open up a dialog on the screen.

- The `ModalRenderer` handles requests meant to open up a modal on the screen.

Returning to the HTML renderer, let's see what *it* does to turn our render arrays into actual relevant HTML on a Response object. Without going into too much detail, here is a high-level description of what it does:

- Its first goal is to build a render array that has `#type => 'page'` as a property because this is the render element responsible for the entire page. Meaning that if the Controller returned it, it doesn't have to do much. However, usually controllers don't include that, so it dispatches an event to determine who can build this render array.

- By default, the `SimplePageVariant` plugin is used for building up the page array, but with the Block module enabled, the `BlockPageVariant` plugin is used, taking things even further down some levels in the render pipeline. The main content area gets wrapped with blocks in the sidebar, header, footer, and so on.

- Once it has the page render array, it wraps it into yet another render element, which is `#type => 'html'` (responsible for things such as the `<head>` elements).

- Once it has the main render array of the entire page, it uses the `Renderer` service to traverse it and do the actual rendering at each level (and there can be many). It does so by translating render elements (`#type`), theme hooks (`#theme`), simply marked-up text bits (`#markup`), or plain text bits (`#plain_text`) into their respective HTML representations.

So, as you see, the render pipeline starts at Symfony level, goes down into Drupal territory when it encounters render arrays, but continues going down to build each component found on a page around the main content returned by the Controller. Then, it comes back up those levels, all the way until a great render array is created and can be turned into HTML. Also, as it goes back up, various metadata can bubble up to the main render array.

I purposefully left out caching from this equation, which although very important, we will cover in a later chapter. However, suffice to say, cache metadata is one such example that bubbles up from the lower levels all the way to the top and is gathered to determine page-level caching. But more on that later.

If you had problems understanding this complex pipeline, don't worry, you can always come back to this description later. You don't have to know all these intricacies to proceed with the book but it's good to have this explanation handy, especially to dig into the code to better try to understand it.

Now that we know more about render arrays, how they are structured, and the pipeline they go through, we can talk a bit about asset management from a module development perspective. Because even though it is usually a theme responsibility, module developers often have to add and use CSS and JS files to their modules, and it all happens in render arrays.

Assets and libraries

Working with CSS and JS files in Drupal is done using *libraries*. So, let's see how they work by going through some examples.

There are three steps to adding assets to your page:

- Creating your CSS/JS file
- Creating a library that includes them
- Attaching that library to a render array

Libraries

Assuming that you already have the CSS/JS files, libraries are defined inside a `module_name.libraries.yml` file in the module root folder. A simple example of a library definition inside this file would look like this:

```yaml
my-library:
  version: 1.x
  css:
    theme:
      css/my_library.css: {}
  js:
    js/my_library.js: {}
```

This is a standard YAML notation by which we define a library called `my-library` and provide some information about it. We can specify a version number and then add as many CSS and JS file references as we need. The file paths are relative to the module folder this library definition is in, and we can add some options between the curly braces (more advanced, but we will see an example in a moment).

Additionally, you'll note that the CSS file has an extra level key called `theme`. This is to indicate the type of CSS to be included and can be one of the following (based on SMACSS (`https://smacss.com/`) standards):

- `base`: Usually contains CSS reset/normalizers and HTML element styling
- `layout`: High-level page styling, such as grid systems

- `component`: UI elements and reusable components
- `state`: Styles used in client-side changes to components
- `theme`: Visual styling of components

The choice here is also reflected in the weighting of the CSS file inclusion, the latter being the "heaviest"—it will be included last.

Another important aspect of using libraries in any application is the ability to include externally hosted files (usually from a CDN). Let's take a look at an example library definition that uses externally hosted files:

```
angular.angularjs:
  remote: https://github.com/angular/angular.js
  version: 1.4.4
  license:
    name: MIT
    url: https://github.com/angular/angular.js/blob/
      master/LICENSE
    gpl-compatible: true
  js:
    https://ajax.googleapis.com/ajax/libs/angularjs/
      1.4.4/angular.min.js: { type: external, minified:
        true }
```

This example is taken from a Drupal.org example (`https://www.drupal.org/docs/8/creating-custom-modules/adding-stylesheets-css-and-javascript-js-to-a-drupal-8-module`) on defining libraries in Drupal. However, as you can see, the structure is the same as our previous example, except that it has some more meta information regarding the external library. And instead of a local path reference, we have a remote URL to the actual resource. Moreover, we also see some options within the curly braces with which we can specify that the file is actually externally located and minified.

An important note when it comes to JS in Drupal is that it doesn't include all libraries such as jQuery by default. It does so only when and where it's needed. This has, therefore, brought the concept of library dependencies to the forefront, as certain scripts require other libraries to be loaded for them to work.

Let's assume that `my-library` depends on jQuery and specify it as a dependency. All we need to add to our library definition is the following:

```
dependencies:
  - core/jquery
```

Keep in mind that the dependencies key is at the same YML level as css and js.

With this, we declare the Drupal core jQuery library to be required by our library. This means that if we use our library somewhere and jQuery is not included, Drupal will process the dependencies and include them all. A side benefit of this is that dependencies are always included before our scripts, so we can also control that.

The core/jquery notation indicates that the extension (module or theme) that defines the jquery library is Drupal core. If it had been a module or theme, core would have been replaced by the module or theme machine name. So, for example, to use our new library as a dependency somewhere, it would be referenced as module_name/my-library.

Attaching libraries

The most common way you'll be using libraries is by attaching them to your render arrays. This approach implies that the library is needed for the rendering of that component so that if said component is missing from the page, the library assets are no longer included.

Here is what a render array would look like with the previous library we defined attached to it:

```
return [
  '#theme' => 'some_theme_hook',
  '#some_variable' => $some_variable,
  '#attached' => [
    'library' => [
      'my_module/my-library',
      ],
    ],
];
```

The #attached property is important here, and it signifies that we are essentially attaching something to the render array, which in our case happens to be a library.

However, you may have cases in which the library you need is not linked to a specific render array (a component on the page) but to the entire page itself—all pages or a subset. To attach libraries to an entire page, you can implement hook_page_attachments(). Consider the following example:

```
function hook_page_attachments(array &$attachments) {
  $attachments['#attached']['library'][] = 'my_module/my-
    library';
}
```

This hook is called on each page, so you can also attach libraries contextually (for example, if the user has a specific role or something like that). Moreover, there is also the hook_page_attachments_alter() hook, which you can use to alter any existing attachments (for example, to remove attachments from the page).

Another way you can attach libraries is inside a preprocess function. We talked about preprocess functions earlier in this chapter; it's simple to achieve:

```
function my_module_preprocess_theme_hook(&$variables) {
    $variables['#attached']['library'][] = 'my_module/
      my_library';
}
```

All you have to do is add the #attached key (if it doesn't already exist) to the variables array.

These three methods of attaching libraries are the most common ones you'll encounter and use yourself. However, there are a few other ways and places where attachments can be added—you can alter an existing render element definition and you can attach libraries directly to a Twig file. I recommend that you read the Drupal.org documentation (https://www.drupal.org/docs/creating-modules/adding-assets-css-js-to-a-drupal-module-via-librariesyml) for more information on these methods.

Common theme hooks

In this section, we will look at three common theme hooks that come with Drupal core that you are likely to use quite often. The best way to understand them is, of course, by referring to an example of how to use them. So, let's get to it.

Lists

One of the most common HTML constructs are lists (ordered or unordered), and any web application ends up having many of them, either for listing items or for components that do not even look like lists. But for the purposes of marking up, an ul or ol fits the bill best. Luckily, Drupal has always had the item_list theme hook, which is flexible enough to allow us to use it in almost all cases.

The item_list theme hook is defined inside drupal_common_theme(), is preprocessed (by default) in template_preprocess_item_list(), uses the item-list.html.twig template by default, and has no default theme hook suggestions (because it's so generic and registered outside the context of any business logic). If we inspect its definition, we'll note that it takes a number of variables that build up its flexibility. Let's take a look at an example of how to use it.

Imagine that we have the following array of items:

```
$items = [
   'Item 1',
   'Item 2'
];
```

The simplest way we can render this as an `<ul>` is as follows:

```
return [
   '#theme' => 'item_list',
   '#items' => $items
];
```

Do note that the respective `<ul>` is wrapped in a `<div class="item_list">` and that the items in our array can also be render arrays themselves.

If we want to change the list into an `<ol>`, we set the `#list_type` variable to `ol`. We can even have a title heading (`<h3>`) before the list if we set the `#title` variable. Moreover, we can add more attributes on the `<div>` wrapper. For more information on how the other options work, I suggest that you inspect the template file and preprocessor function. However, these are the ones you'll most often use.

Links

In *Chapter 2, Creating Your First Module*, we briefly looked at how we can work with links programmatically and how to build and render them in two different ways. We also noted that it's better to use the `#link` render element (and we now understand what this is) if we want the link to be alterable somewhere down the line. Now, let's take a look at how we can build a list of links using the helpful `links` theme hook.

The `links` theme hook takes an array of links to be rendered, optional attributes, an optional heading, and a flag to set the active class dynamically. It then uses the `links.html.twig` template to construct a `<ul>`, much like the `item_list` hook.

The most important variable here is the array of links, as it needs to contain individual arrays with the following keys: `title` (the link text), `url` (a `Url` object), and `attributes` (an array of attributes to add to each link item). If you look inside the `template_preprocess_links` preprocessor, you'll see that it takes each of these items and transforms them into a render array with the `#type => 'link'` (the render element).

In addition to the array of links, we can also pass a heading (just like with `item_list`) and a flag for setting the active class—`set_active_class`. The latter will make it add an `is-active` class onto the `<li>` item in the list and the link itself if the link matches the current route. Handy stuff, isn't it? However, for more information, check out the documentation above the `template_preprocess_links()` implementation. Now, let's see a quick example of using this in practice:

```php
$links = [
  [
    'title' => 'Link 1',
    'url' => Url::fromRoute('<front>'),
  ],
  [
    'title' => 'Link 2',
    'url' => Url::fromRoute('hello_world.hello'),
  ]
];

return [
  '#theme' => 'links',
  '#links' => $links,
  '#set_active_class' => true,
];
```

That is all. We build an array of link data and then construct the render array using the `links` theme hook. We also use the `set_active_class` option just for kicks. This means that the `is-active` class will be present on the first link if this is rendered on the home page or on the second link if rendered on the *Hello World* page. As simple as that.

Tables

The last common theme hook we will look at now will help you build tables. It has always been a Drupal best practice to use the theme hook when building tables rather than creating the markup yourself. This is also, in part, because it has always been very flexible. So, let's take a look.

The `table` theme hook takes a bunch of variables, many of them optional. The most important, however, are the `header` (an array of header definitions) and `rows` (a multidimensional array of row definitions). It's not worth repeating all the possible options you have for building tables here because they are all very well documented above the `template_preprocess_table()` preprocessor function. So, do check there for more information. Instead, we'll focus on a simple use case of rendering a table, and we'll do so via an example:

```
$header = ['Column 1', 'Column 2'];
$rows = [
  ['Row 1, Column 1', 'Row 1, Column 2'],
  ['Row 2, Column 1', 'Row 2, Column 2']
];

return [
  '#theme' => 'table',
  '#header' => $header,
  '#rows' => $rows,
];
```

So, as you can see, we have the two critical variables. We have the list of header items and the rows (whose cells are in the array in the same order as the header). Of course, you have many more options, including attributes at all levels of the table, a handy sorting capability that makes it easy to integrate with a database query, and more. I strongly encourage you to explore these options in the documentation.

Attributes

In the previous three examples of theme hooks, we encountered the concept of `attributes` in the context of using them to render HTML elements. Attributes here are understood in the same way as with HTML. For example, `class`, `id`, `style`, and `href` are all HTML element attributes. Why is this important?

The reusability of theme hooks makes it so that we cannot hardcode all our HTML attributes in the Twig template files. We can have some, including classes, but we will always need to allow business logic to inform the theme hook of certain attribute values it needs printed on the HTML element. For example, an `active` class on a link. This is why we have this concept of attributes.

Most theme hooks you'll see have attributes in some form or another, with the variable usually being called `$attributes`, `$wrapper_attributes`, or something of that nature. Also, this variable always needs to be a multidimensional array with the attribute data you want passed. The keys in this array are the name of the attribute, whereas the value is the attribute value. If the value can have multiple items, such as classes, it will also be an array. Consider the following example:

```
$attributes = [
  'id' => 'my-id',
  'class' => ['class-one', 'class-two'],
  'data-custom' => 'my custom data value'
];
```

As you can see, we have some common attributes, but you can also make up your own as needed (usually in the form of data attributes). However, in no way is this mandatory, and you can add only the ones you actually need. Do always, though, read the documentation on the theme hook to see how they are used and which elements are actually going to get them.

From an API point of view, Drupal handles attributes via a handy class called `Attribute`. You'll note that many template preprocessors will take that array and construct a new `Attribute` object for manipulating them with more ease. Additionally, such an object is also renderable because it implements the `MarkupInterface` and Twig will know directly how to transform it into a string. And to make dealing with attribute collections easier, a helper class called `AttributeHelper` was introduced.

So, keep that in mind if you are writing your own theme hooks and need to handle attributes with more class (pun intended).

Layouts

As part of the Drupal 8 release cycle, the Layouts API has been introduced to provide contributed modules with a unified approach for defining layouts. For example, modules such as Panels and Layout Builder make use of this API to define layouts that contain regions and that can render content and all sorts of things inside.

We won't be using layouts going forward in this book but it's important you know how to work with them in case you need them. So, let's quickly talk about how you, as a module developer, can define and make use of layouts programmatically.

Defining layouts

Simply put, layouts are plugins. But unlike the plugins we've seen before, these are defined in YAML files instead of annotations above a class. One of the reasons for this is that layouts are more *definition* than functionality, so they don't necessarily require classes. They can be simply defined in a few lines inside a YAML file.

Although not necessarily, YAML-based plugins are typically defined inside a file named `module_name.plugin_type_name.yml` found in the root of the module defining the plugin. So in the case of layouts, this would be `module_name.layouts.yml`. But what does a definition contain?

Let's imagine we want to define a two-column layout with a left and right region. Our simplest definition could look like this:

```
two_column:
  label: 'Two column'
  category: 'My Layouts'
  template: templates/two-column
```

```
regions:
  left:
    label: Left region
  right:
    label: Right region
```

So what do we learn from this definition?

- First, we have a name and category, which are mandatory. These can be used in whatever UI to show information about the layout.

- Second, we specify the template that should render this layout. The corresponding theme hook gets defined under the hood. In the case above, the template file would be in the `templates` folder and would be called `two-column.html.twig`.

- Lastly, we define the regions of the layout with a label for each. The `left` and `right` keys are important as they are the machine names of the regions.

- As a bonus, if we wanted to attach a library, we could add another line to this definition, like so:

```
library: my_module/my_library
```

Before the layout registration is complete, we'd also need to create the template file we referenced. And it could look like this:

```
<div class="two-column">
  <div class="left-region">
    {{ content.left }}
  </div>
  <div class="right-region">
    {{ content.right }}
  </div>
</div>
```

In the template, we have access to the `content` variable on which we can access the values of the regions we can print.

And that's pretty much it. Clearing the cache (and enabling the Layout Discovery module) would register this layout with the system.

Rendering a layout

OK, but registering a layout doesn't help us with much. Unless, of course, we use *Layout Builder* or some contributed module that uses layouts for various things. In which case we'd already be providing great value. But what if we want to use this layout ourselves? In other words, render stuff with it.

The simplest way of rendering something with this layout could look like this:

```
$layoutPluginManager = \Drupal::service
  ('plugin.manager.core.layout');
$layout = $layoutPluginManager->createInstance
  ('two_column');

$regions = [
  'left' => [
    '#markup' => 'my left content',
  ],
  'right' => [
    '#markup' => 'my right content',
  ],
];

return $layout->build($regions);
```

Without going into too much detail about the plugin system (yet), but with the above we use the Layout plugin manager to create a new instance of the layout we defined (whose machine name is two_column). Then we prepare the data to print inside the layout in the $regions array. As you can see, the array construct mirrors the regions in the layout. Finally, we build the layout by passing the regions data. And that is it. The resulting render array would render the template with the content printed in the corresponding regions.

Theming our Hello World module

The HelloWorldController we built in *Chapter 2, Creating Your First Module*, currently uses a service to retrieve the string to be used as the salutation and then returns a simple markup render array with it. Let's imagine now that we want to output this message but wrap it in our own specific markup. To make an easy thing complicated, we want to break up the salutation string into parts so that they can be styled slightly differently. Additionally, we want to allow others to override our theme using suggestions that depend on whether or not the salutation has been overridden via the configuration form. So, let's see how we can do these things.

To get things started, this is the markup we are after:

```
<div class="salutation">
  Good morning <span class="salutation-target">world</span>
</div>
```

The first thing we need to do is to define our own theme hook capable of outputting this. To this end, we implement `hook_theme()`:

```
/**
 * Implements hook_theme().
 */
function hello_world_theme($existing, $type, $theme, $path)
{
  return [
    'hello_world_salutation' => [
      'variables' => ['salutation' => NULL, 'target' =>
        NULL, 'overridden' => FALSE],
    ],
  ];
}
```

For now, we only return one theme hook called `hello_world_salutation`, which takes the variables you can see. Each of them has a default value in case one is not passed from the client (through the render array). The first two are obvious, but we also want to have a flag on whether or not the salutation has been overridden. This will help with the theme hook suggestions.

By default, if we don't specify a template filename, this theme hook will look for a Twig template with the name `hello-world-salutation.html.twig` inside the `/templates` folder of our module. Since this is good enough for us, let's go ahead and create it:

```
<div {{ attributes }}>
  {{ salutation }}
  {% if target %}
    <span class="salutation-target">{{ target }}</span>
  {% endif %}
</div>
```

Twig notation is easy to understand. {{ }} means that we are printing a variable with that name (which can even be a render array) and {% %} refers to control structures, such as *if statements or loops*. Do check out the Twig documentation (https://twig.symfony.com/) for more information if you are unsure.

> **Note**
>
> There are some great ways to debug what values end up being printed in the Twig template. You can use the native Twig dump() function, which will output things using the PHP var_dump(), or you can install the Devel module and use the kint() function, which will format things in a more readable way.

We wrapped the target variable in an *if* statement so that if by any chance it's missing, we don't print an empty <span> tag. It's best practice to have your template mirror the possibilities of the theme hook being called with the defaults.

Finally, we also have an attributes array, which we are printing on the wrapper. We did not define this, but each theme hook comes with it. The variable is an Attribute object, as we discussed earlier, which gets printed into a string of the individual attributes.

Now, instead of printing the class, we want directly in the template, we will use the preprocessor to make things more dynamic.

So let's implement the preprocessor next:

```
/**
 * Default preprocessor function for the
   hello_world_salutation theme hook.
 */
function template_preprocess_hello_world_salutation
  (&$variables) {
  $variables['attributes'] = [
    'class' => ['salutation'],
  ];
}
```

As I mentioned earlier, at this stage we are still working with an array of attributes. The theme system will turn it into the Attribute object before rendering the template, which in turn will know how to handle that.

Other modules or themes can now implement this preprocessor themselves and change the classes (or any other wrapper attributes) as they need. Had we hardcoded the class in the template file, they would have had to override the entire template—which, although still a viable option, is overkill if you just need to add a class.

Now, let's allow themers to have different implementations for our salutation message depending on whether or not it is overridden by an admin. I know this particular example is quite a stretch in terms of usefulness, but it allows us to demonstrate the approach, which is very useful.

So, as we discussed, we can define a suggestion for our theme hook:

```
/**
 * Implements hook_theme_suggestions_HOOK().
 */
function hello_world_theme_suggestions_hello_world
  _salutation($variables) {
  $suggestions = [];

  if ($variables['overridden'] === TRUE) {
    $suggestions[] = 'hello_world_salutation__overridden';
  }

  return $suggestions;
}
```

If you remember, our theme hook had the `overridden` variable which can be used for this flag. So, in our theme hook suggestion implementation, we check for it, and if it's true, we add our suggestion. This function gets called on the fly at the time of rendering and the most specific suggestion encountered is used if, of course, the salutation is overridden. If that is the case, it will try `hello_world_salutation__overridden`, and if not found, it will fall back to `hello_world_salutation`, which exists.

Themes can now have two different templates that render the salutation in two different ways, depending on whether or not the message has been overridden:

- `hello-world-salutation.html.twig`
- `hello-world-salutation--overridden.html.twig`

OK, our theme hook is now ready for use. Let's use it.

Since our theme template breaks our salutation message up into pieces, and can even receive the overridden flag, it will not be enough to just use this theme hook in the HelloWorldController. Instead, we will need to go back to our service and have it return the render array responsible for outputting the salutation. After all, business logic knows the structural aspects of how a certain component needs to be rendered. Theming just needs to style and alter that based on the flexibility offered by a good functional implementation.

However, let's not override the getSalutation() method on the service, but instead create a new one called getSalutationComponent(). This will then return the render array, which can output the whole thing:

```php
/**
 * Returns the Salutation render array.
 */
public function getSalutationComponent() {
  $render = [
    '#theme' => 'hello_world_salutation',
  ];

  $config = $this->configFactory->get
    ('hello_world.custom_salutation');
  $salutation = $config->get('salutation');

  if ($salutation !== "" && $salutation) {
    $event = new SalutationEvent();
    $event->setValue($salutation);
    $this->eventDispatcher->dispatch($event,
      SalutationEvent::EVENT);
    $render['#salutation'] = $event->getValue();
    $render['#overridden'] = TRUE;
    return $render;
  }

  $time = new \DateTime();
  $render['#target'] = $this->t('world');

  if ((int) $time->format('G') >= 00 && (int) $time->
    format('G') < 12) {
```

```
    $render['#salutation'] = $this->t('Good morning');
    return $render;
  }

  if ((int) $time->format('G') >= 12 && (int) $time->
      format('G') < 18) {
    $render['#salutation'] = $this->t('Good afternoon');
    return $render;
  }

  if ((int) $time->format('G') >= 18) {
    $render['#salutation'] = $this->t('Good evening');
    return $render;
  }
}
```

This is how it will look. We start by creating the render array that uses our new theme hook. Then, we look in the configuration object and if there is a message stored in there, we use that, set the overridden flag to true, and return the render array. You'll note that we didn't set a target, which means that it won't get printed in the template file (as expected). If, however, it is not overridden, we proceed with our previous logic and set the message dynamically while keeping the target the same. You can easily see how this now maps to what the theme hook and template expect for the different cases.

A couple of points to be made before going forward.

First, I want to reiterate the warning that due to things such as caching, the dynamic salutation message won't work as expected. We'd need to set some cache metadata to prevent this render array from being cached in order for it to work. However, we will see more about that in *Chapter 11, Caching*.

Second, you will have noted that the variables we defined in the theme hook show up preceded by a # sign, as if they were properties known to the render system. As I said earlier, they are in fact not properties, but they are known by the theme system as variables because we defined them as such. So, it's important to be able to distinguish these kinds of things when reading code that you didn't write yourself. There are, of course, many properties you don't know off the top of your head, but with experience, you'll be able to read the code, figure out the source, and understand what it means. In this, the difference between a good developer and a great one is the ability of the latter to figure things out by reading the source code rather than relying on documentation.

Third, you can see quite some code duplication here between the two methods. This is not great but I leave you to come up with more creative ways of refactoring this service to avoid this.

Now, we have a service that can return a string representation of our message, and a fully-fledged renderable component. It follows that we edit our Controller and have it return this component instead of its own render array:

```
/**
 * Hello World.
 *
 * @return array
 */
public function helloWorld() {
    return $this->salutation->getSalutationComponent();
}
```

You'll note that we don't need the `#markup` property anymore, as we have our own render array. For the `salutation` token and the block we created, let's not use this component but rely on the string version. This way we keep both options in the code for you to see.

Summary

The Drupal theming system is complex and thus impossible to cover fully in one chapter of a module development book. However, we did go through the basics necessary to get you started—understanding the core tenets of the theme system, some of its most important Drupal specificities, and practical use cases.

We started this chapter by discussing the abstract principle of separating business from presentation logic—a principle that is used by many modern web applications. We saw why it is critical for flexible and dynamic theming. Next, we discussed a great deal about how Drupal does this separation—the mighty theme hooks that act as a bridge between the two layers. Here, we also covered some of the highly used practices surrounding them—preprocessor functions and theme hook suggestions for added flexibility. Then, we covered how the business logic can actually use theme hooks—the render arrays (perhaps one of the most important Drupal constructs). Also, since we were on the subject, we outlined the Drupal and Symfony render pipeline to get a better understanding of the process that builds the entire page render array. Next, we discussed libraries and how we can "attach" them to render arrays. We will definitely see some more examples later in the book when we talk about JavaScript.

Finally, we started transitioning into the practical aspects of theming a module by exemplifying a few common theme hooks found in Drupal core. In doing so, we also encountered the topic of Attributes, an important one to understand when dealing with making theme hooks more dynamic.

We ended the chapter with an overhaul of our *Hello World* salutation message to create a themable component. We did so by putting into practice much of what we learned about theme hooks earlier on: we defined a theme hook and corresponding template, a preprocess function, as well as a theme hook suggestion, and built a render array dynamically to fire them all. Not a bad day in the life of a Drupal module developer.

In the next chapter, we will look at menus and the different types of menu links in Drupal. What kind of web application would it be without any menu links in it?

5

Menus and Menu Links

Navigation is an important part of any web application. The ability to create menus and links easily in order to connect pages together is a core aspect of any content management system. Drupal is fully equipped with both the site-building capabilities and a developer API to easily build and manipulate menus and links.

In this chapter, we will discuss menus and menu links from a Drupal module developer perspective. In doing so, we will touch upon a few key aspects:

- The general architecture of the menu system in Drupal
- Manipulating and rendering menus
- Defining various types of menu links

By the end of this chapter, you should be able to understand what menus and menu links are, how to use them in your code, and how to define menu links in your module. So let's get started.

The menu system

Before we get our hands dirty with menus and menu links, let's talk a bit about the general architecture behind the menu system. To this end, I want to go through its main components, what some of its key players are, and what classes you should be looking at. As always, no great developer has ever relied solely on a book or documentation to figure out complex systems.

Menus

Menus are configuration entities represented by the following class: `Drupal\system\Entity\Menu`. I mentioned in *Chapter 1, Developing for Drupal 10*, that we have something called configuration entities in Drupal, which we will explore in detail later in this book. However, for now, it's enough to understand that menus can be created through the UI and become an exportable configuration. Additionally, this exported configuration can also be included inside a module so that it gets imported when the module is first installed. This way, a module can ship with its own menus. We will see how this latter aspect works when we talk about the different kinds of storage in Drupal. For now, we will work with the menus that come with Drupal core.

Each menu can have multiple menu links, structured hierarchically in a tree with a maximum depth of 9 links. The ordering of the menu links can be done easily through the UI or via the weighting of the menu links, if defined in code.

Menu links

At their most basic level, menu links are YAML-based plugins (like the Layout plugins we saw in the previous chapter). To this end, regular menu links are defined inside a `module_name.links.menu.yml` file and can be altered by other modules by implementing `hook_menu_links_discovered_alter()`. When I say regular, I mean those links that go into menus. We will see shortly that there are also a few other types.

There are a few important classes you should check out in this architecture though: `MenuLinkManager` (the plugin manager) and `MenuLinkBase` (the menu link plugins base class that implements `MenuLinkInterface`).

Menu links can, however, also be content entities. The links created via the UI are stored as entities because they are considered content. The way this works is that for each created `MenuLinkContent` entity, a plugin derivative is created. We are getting dangerously close to advanced topics that are too early to cover. But in a nutshell, via these derivatives, it's as if a new menu link plugin is created for each `MenuLinkContent` entity, making the latter behave as any other menu link plugin. This is a very powerful system in Drupal.

Menu links have a few properties, among which is a path or route. When created via the UI, the path can be external or internal or can reference an existing resource (such as a user or piece of content). When created programmatically, you'll typically use a route.

Multiple types of menu links

The menu links we've been talking about so far are the links that show up in menus. There are also a few different kinds of links that show up elsewhere but are still considered menu links and work similarly.

Local tasks

Local tasks, also known as tabs, are grouped links that usually show up above the main content of a page (depending on the region where the tabs block is placed). They are usually used to group together related links that deal with the current page. For example, on an entity page, such as the node detail page, you can have two tabs—one for viewing the node and one for editing it (and maybe one for deleting it)—in other words, local tasks:

Figure 5.1: Local tasks

Local tasks take access rules into account, so if the current user does not have access to the route of a given tab, the link is not rendered. Moreover, if that means only one link in the set remains accessible, that link doesn't get rendered as there is no point. So, for tabs, a minimum of two links are needed for them to show up.

Modules can define local task links inside a `module_name.links.task.yml` file, whereas other modules can alter them by implementing `hook_menu_local_tasks_alter()`.

Local actions

Local actions are links that relate to a given route and are typically used for operations. For example, on a **List** page, you might have a local action link to create a new list item, which will take you to the relevant form page.

In the following screenshot, we can see a local action link used to create a new user on the main user management page:

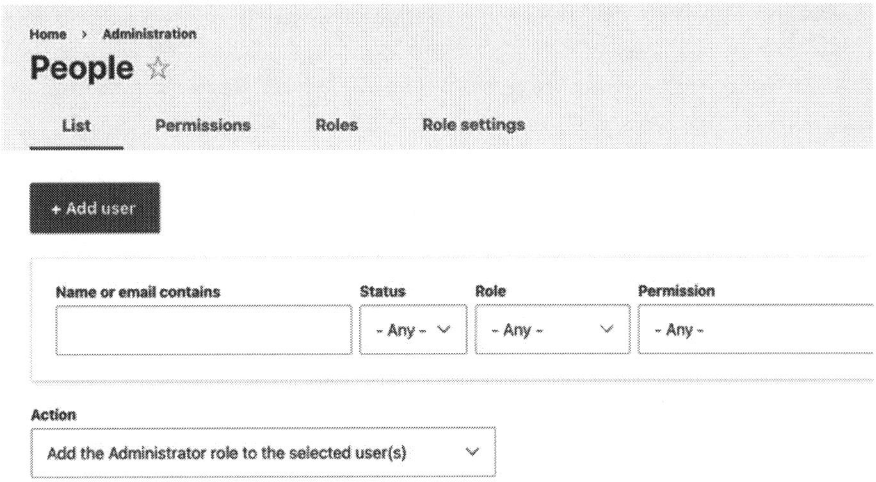

Figure 5.2: Local actions

Modules can define local action links inside a `module_name.links.action.yml` file, whereas other modules can alter them by implementing `hook_menu_local_actions_alter()`.

Contextual links

Contextual links are used by the Contextual module to provide handy links next to a given component (a render array). You probably encountered this when hovering over a block, for example, and getting that little icon with a dropdown that has the **Configure block** link:

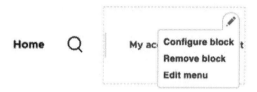

Figure 5.3: Contextual links

Contextual links are tied to render arrays. In fact, any render array can show a group of contextual links that have previously been defined.

Modules can define contextual links inside a `module_name.links.contextual.yml` file, whereas other modules can alter them by implementing `hook_contextual_links_alter()`.

MenuLink trees

As I mentioned in the section about menus, menu links are stored hierarchically inside a menu. This hierarchy is represented via a menu link tree. There are a few key players here we should go over.

We have the `MenuLinkTree` service, which is the interface used to load and prepare the tree of a certain menu. The loading is deferred to the `MenuTreeStorage` service, which does so on the basis of a `MenuTreeParameters` object that contains metadata on certain restrictions to be applied on the menu links that are loaded. We will see some examples of this a bit later.

What comes out of the `MenuLinkTree` service is an array of `MenuLinkTreeElement` objects. These are essentially value objects that wrap the `MenuLinkInterface` plugins and that provide some extra data about their placement in the tree they are loaded in. One such important piece of information is the subtree (the array of `MenuLinkTreeElement` objects that are below it).

Menu link tree manipulators

When loading a menu link tree, you get the entire tree that fits the specified parameters. However, when using that tree, you probably want to perform some checks and remove certain items. A common example is to remove the menu links to which the user doesn't have access. This is where manipulators come into place.

The MenuLinkTree service has a transform() method that alters a tree based on an array of manipulators. The latter take the form of callables, typically service names with specific methods. So, the actual manipulators are services that traverse the tree and make alterations to the tree items, their order, and so on.

Menu active trail

A menu trail is a list (array) of menu link plugins that are the parents of a menu link. For the active trail, that specific menu link represents the current route (if there is a menu link for that route).

The Drupal menu system also has a service that can be used to determine the active trail of the current route if used by a menu link. By passing a menu name to look inside of, the MenuActiveTrail service returns an array of plugin IDs of the parents all the way up to the menu root, if the current route is in fact an active link. There is also a method that can be used to check that: getActiveLink().

Now that we have covered some theory about the menu system, it's time to get our hands dirty with some code.

Rendering menus

The first thing we will look at is how to work with menus programmatically with the view of rendering them in our module. For this, we will work with the default **Administration** menu that comes with Drupal core and has many links in it, at various levels. Note that the code we write in this section will not be included in the code repository.

Drupal core provides a block, called SystemMenuBlock, which can be used to render any menu inside a block. However, let's see how we can do this ourselves instead.

The first thing we will need to do is get the MenuLinkTree service. We can inject it, or, if that's not possible, get it statically via the helper \Drupal class:

```
$menu_link_tree = \Drupal::menuTree();
```

Next, we will need to create a MenuTreeParameters object so that we can use it to load our menu tree. There are two ways we can do this. We can either create it ourselves and set our own options on it or we can get a default one based on the current route:

```
$parameters = $menu_link_tree->
  getCurrentRouteMenuTreeParameters('admin');
```

Providing the name of a menu (in our case, `admin`), this method gives us a `MenuTreeParameters` instance with the following options set on it:

- The links in the active trail of the current route are marked as expanded, that is, they will show up in the resulting tree that we load.

- The children of the links in the active trail that have the "expanded" property set are also included in the resulting tree.

Essentially, this set of parameters gives us a tree within the context of the current route we are on. In other words, it will load all the root links in the menu and all the children of the root link that are in the active trail of the current route. It will leave out the children of the other root links.

You can, of course, further customize this set of parameters or create one from scratch. For example, if we want to load only the tree of a root link inside a menu, we could do it as follows:

```
$parameters = new MenuTreeParameters();
$parameters->setRoot($plugin_id);
```

In this example, `$plugin_id` is the ID of the menu link that should be at the root of the tree (defined in the YAML file or derived through a derivative).

I encourage you to look inside the `MenuTreeParameters` class and explore the other options you have for loading a tree.

For our example, we want to work with the entire menu tree of the **Administration** menu, so just instantiating a new `MenuTreeParameters` object will be enough, as we want to load all links in the menu. We can do this as follows:

```
$tree = $menu_link_tree->load('admin', $parameters);
```

Now, we have an array of `MenuLinkTreeElement` objects inside the `$tree` variable, which contain, among others, the following:

- The link property, which is the menu link plugin

- The subtree property, which is an array of `MenuLinkTreeElement` objects going down the tree

- Various metadata about the link within the tree (depth, whether in the active trail, whether it has children, access, and so on)

However, it is important to note that notwithstanding any `MenuTreeParameters` we may have had, we are now sitting on top of all menu links in that menu, regardless of any access check. It is our responsibility to make sure that we don't render links to pages the user has no access to (as they will get a 403 error when they get there). To do this, we use the manipulators we discussed earlier, which are simple methods on a service.

The Drupal menu system comes with a few handy manipulators that can be found inside the `DefaultMenuLinkTreeManipulators` service. Most of the time, these will be sufficient for you:

- Access (handled by the `checkAccess()` method): Checks whether the user has access to the links in the tree. If they don't, the link becomes an instance of `InaccessibleMenuLink`, and any links in its subtree are cleared out.

- Node Access (handled by the `checkNodeAccess()` method): Checks whether the user has access to the Node entity linked to by the menu link. If you know that the menu has links to Nodes, you can use this before the regular access check because it's a bit more performant.

- Index and Sort (handled by the `generateIndexAndSort()` method): Creates unique indexes in the tree and sorts it by them.

- Flatten (handled by the `flatten()` method): Flattens the menu tree to one level.

If these are not enough, you can add your own manipulators as needed. All you have to do is define a service that has a public method and then reference it when transforming the tree. However, speaking of transforming, let's go ahead and use the access check manipulator to ensure that the current user has access to our tree links:

```
$manipulators = [
  ['callable' => 'menu.default_tree_manipulators:
    checkAccess']
];
$tree = $menu_link_tree->transform($tree, $manipulators);
```

As I mentioned earlier, we use the `transform()` method on the service and pass an array of callables. The latter are nothing more than the service name, followed by `:` and the method name to be used (as shown in the code above). So if you create your own service, you can reference it the same way.

Now, each `MenuLinkTreeElement` that remains in the tree has its `access` property filled with an instance of `AccessResultInterface` (a system of denoting access that we will talk more about in *Chapter 10, Access Control*). If the link is not accessible, it becomes an instance of `InaccessibleMenuLink`, so we know that we cannot render it, and even if we did render it, it will go to the home page rather than the 403.

Now, to render the tree, all we have to do is turn this tree into a render array:

```
$menu = $menu_link_tree->build($tree);
```

Inside `$menu`, we now have a render array that uses the `menu` theme hook with a theme hook suggestion based on the menu name. So, in our case, it is `menu__admin`. Remember what these are from the previous chapter?

The `menu` theme hook will use the `menu.html.twig` (or `menu--admin.html.twig` if it exists inside a theme) file to render the menu links inside a simple, albeit hierarchical, HTML list.

As a quick recap from the theming chapter, at this point you have a few options for gaining full control over the output of the menu:

- Creating a new theme hook and mimicking what the `build()` method does to build the render array

- Altering the theme registry to switch out the template with your own

- Overriding the template inside a theme

- Implementing a preprocessor for the theme hook and altering variables there

So, as you can see, you have many options. The choice you make depends on what you need to achieve, how happy you are with what the default markup is, and so on.

Working with menu links

Now that we know how to load and manipulate trees of menu links, let's talk a bit more about the regular menu links. In this section, we will look at how our module can define menu links and how we can work with them programmatically once we get our hands on them from a tree or somewhere else.

Defining menu links

In our *Hello World* module, we defined a couple of routes, one of which maps to the `/hello` path. Let's now create a link to that path that goes inside the main menu that is shipped with Drupal core.

As I mentioned, menu links are defined inside a `*.links.menu.yml` file. So, let's create that file for our module and add our menu link definition in it:

```
hello_world.hello:
  title: 'Hello'
  description: 'Get your dynamic salutation.'
  route_name: hello_world.hello
  menu_name: main
  weight: 0
```

In a typical YAML notation, we have the machine name (in this case, also the plugin ID) `hello_world.hello`, followed by the relevant information below it. These are the most common things you will define for a menu link:

- The `title` is the menu link title whereas the `description` is, by default, set as the `title` attribute on the resulting link tag.

- The `route_name` indicates the route to be used behind this link.

- The `menu_name` indicates the menu that it should be in; this is the machine name of the menu.

- The `weight` can be used to order links within the menu.

- `parent` can be used to indicate another menu link the current one should be a child of (as such, you can build the hierarchy).

Once this is in, you should clear the cache and check out the links in the menu. You'll note that you can edit it, but some things cannot be changed through the UI due to them being defined in code.

Note that links that are created as a result of plugin derivatives, such as the ones created in the UI, have machine names (plugin IDs) in the following format:

```
main_plugin_id:plugin_derivative_id
```

The `main_plugin_id` is the ID of the menu link plugin that is responsible for deriving multiple links, whereas the `plugin_derivative_id` is the ID given to each individual derivative. For example, in the case of `MenuLinkContent` entities, the format is like this:

```
menu_link_content:867c544e-f1f7-43aa-8bf7-22fcb08a4b50
```

The UUID in this example is the UUID of the menu link content entity, which happens to be the plugin derivative ID.

Manipulating menu links

I mentioned earlier that `MenuLinkTreeElement` objects wrap individual menu links, but what can you do with these programmatically if you choose to work with this data yourself and not rely on the menu theme hook? Let's cover a few common things you can do.

The most important thing to do is to access the menu link plugin. You can do so directly, as it is a public property on the `MenuLinkTreeElement`:

```
$link = $data->link;
```

Now, you can work with the `$link` variable, which is an instance of `MenuLinkInterface`, and often, an actual `MenuLinkDefault` instance that extends the `MenuLinkBase` class.

So, if we inspect that interface, we can see a few handy methods. The most common of these will be the getters for the menu link definition we saw earlier when defining the plugin. The `getUrlObject()` is also an important method that transforms the route of the menu link into a `Url` object that we already know how to use. If the menu link is created in the UI, it could be that it has no route but only a path, in which case, this method will still be able to construct a common `Url` object based on that path.

If you have your hands on a menu link that is not from a tree where you have already handled access, you can ask the `Url` object to check access before using it:

```
$access = $url->access();
```

If the link is not routed, the access will always return TRUE because it means that the link is external, or, in any case, no access check can be done. We will talk more about the access system in a separate chapter.

Defining local tasks

Let's now take a look at an example of how we can define local task links by heading back to our *Hello World* module. On the `/hello` page, let's add two local tasks—one for the regular `/hello` page, and the other for the configuration form where the salutation can be changed. This is a good example of using local tasks (tabs), as the configuration form is strictly related to what is on the page and is used to make changes to it.

As I mentioned, local tasks go inside a `*.links.task.yml` file. So, let's create one for our module with two links in it:

```
hello_world.page:
  route_name: hello_world.hello
  title: 'Hello World'
  base_route: hello_world.hello
hello_world.config:
  route_name: hello_world.greeting_form
  title: 'Configuration'
  base_route: hello_world.hello
  weight: 100
```

As usual, the topmost lines are the machine name (plugin IDs) of the links, and we have the definitions under them. We have a `route_name` property again to specify what route these links should go to, a `title` for the link title, and a `base_route`. The latter is the route the local task should show up on. As you can see, both our links will show up on the `/hello` page. The `weight` property can be used to order the tabs.

If you clear the cache and go to that page (as a user who has access to both routes), you'll be able to see the following two tabs:

Home

Our first route ☆

Good afternoon world

Figure 5.4: Hello World local tasks

If you visit as an anonymous user, neither will show up for the reason I mentioned earlier.

Defining local actions

Nothing about our Hello World module calls for defining a local action link. So instead of doing that, let's check out one that actually makes sense. If you navigate to the `admin/content` screen, you'll see the `+ Add content` button. It looks exactly the same as the example we saw earlier on the user management page. That is a local action link for this route. The `+` styling indicates that these links are primarily used to add or create new items relevant to the current route.

This local action link is defined in the `node` module inside the `node.links.action.yml` file, and it looks like this:

```
node.add_page:
  route_name: node.add_page
  title: 'Add content'
  appears_on:
    - system.admin_content
```

Again, we have the machine name (plugin ID) and the definition. I hope that `route_name` and `title` are, by now, clear to you. A new thing here, though, is the `appears_on` key that is used to indicate the routes (plural) on which this action link should show up. So, a key feature is that one action link can exist on multiple pages.

Defining contextual links

Contextual links are a bit more complicated than the other types of links we've seen before, but nothing is too challenging for us. Let's see how we can add contextual links to our salutation component so that users can navigate to the configuration form via a contextual link.

First, we will need to create the `*.links.contextual.yml` file and define the link:

```
hello_world.override:
  title: 'Override'
  route_name: hello_world.greeting_form
  group: hello_world
```

Nothing too complicated here. Again, we have a `title` link and a `route_name`. Additionally, we have a `group` key, which indicates the group name that this link will be a part of. We will reference this later.

Next, we will need to alter our theme hook template file because the contextual links are printed in a `title_suffix` variable that is available in all theme hooks and is used by various modules to add miscellaneous data to templates. The Contextual module is one such example. So, we will need to get that printed. This is what it will look like now:

```
<div {{ attributes }}>
  {{ title_prefix }}
  {{ salutation }}
  {% if target %}
      <span class="salutation--target">{{ target }}
        </span>
  {% endif %}
  {{ title_suffix }}
</div>
```

You'll note that we included the `title_prefix` variable to keep things nice and consistent. Usually, these will be empty, so no need to worry.

Our `hello_world_salutation` theme hook defines individual variables rather than a render element. In such cases, inside a general preprocessor, the Contextual module looks at the first defined variable to check whether there are any contextual links defined. In the case of theme hooks that use render elements, it checks that element instead.

This is what the contextual links definition looks like inside a render array, and also what we need to add for our use case (we will see the final block of code below):

```
'#contextual_links' => [
  'hello_world' => [
    'route_parameters' => []
  ],
]
```

Here, we defined that the `hello_world` group of contextual links should be rendered here. Also, we specified an array of route parameters, which, in our case, is empty. This is because, typically, the contextual links are just that—contextual, meaning that they usually work with an entity or something that has an ID, and its route requires a parameter. So, here is where we can supply that because as we've seen, the `*.links.contextual.yml` definition is static and generic.

> **Note**
>
> The `#contextual_links` property is, in fact, a render element itself that gets replaced with another render element (`contextual_links_placeholder`). The latter outputs a simple text placeholder in the HTML, which gets replaced with the correct links via JavaScript.

So, now that we know how to make use of the contextual links, let's alter our Hello World salutation component to make use of this. This is what it looks like now:

```
public function getSalutationComponent() {
  $render = [
    '#theme' => 'hello_world_salutation',
    '#salutation' => [
      '#contextual_links' => [
        'hello_world' => [
          'route_parameters' => []
        ],
      ]
    ]
  ];

  $config = $this->configFactory->get
    ('hello_world.custom_salutation');
  $salutation = $config->get('salutation');
```

```php
    if ($salutation !== "" && $salutation) {
      $event = new SalutationEvent();
      $event->setValue($salutation);
      $this->eventDispatcher->dispatch($event,
        SalutationEvent::EVENT);
      $render['#salutation']['#markup'] = $event->getValue();
      $render['#overridden'] = TRUE;
      return $render;
    }

    $time = new \DateTime();
    $render['#target'] = $this->t('world');

    if ((int) $time->format('G') >= 00 && (int) $time->
      format('G') < 12) {
      $render['#salutation']['#markup'] = $this->t('Good
        morning');
      return $render;
    }

    if ((int) $time->format('G') >= 12 && (int) $time->
      format('G') < 18) {
      $render['#salutation']['#markup'] = $this->t('Good
        afternoon');
      return $render;
    }

    if ((int) $time->format('G') >= 18) {
      $render['#salutation']['#markup'] = $this->t('Good
        evening');
      return $render;
    }
  }
```

The main changes are as follows. First, we have already defined the #salutation variable at the top and made it into a render array. As you remember, these are highly nestable. In this render array, we added our #contextual_links render element. Second, every time we need to set the value for the salutation string below, we do so in a `#markup` element this time, because, as we saw in the previous chapter, we need a property that defines how the render array gets rendered.

So now if you clear the cache and navigate to the `/hello` page, you should be able to hover over the salutation and see the contextual links icon pop up and contain our `Override` link. You should land on the salutation **configuration** form when you click on the link but also note a `destination` query parameter in the URL:

Figure 5.5: Hello World contextual links

The destination query parameter is used by Drupal to return the user to the page they previously were on after they submitted a form on that page. This is a handy trick to keep in mind, as it is a very popular UX technique.

Summary

In this chapter, we covered a lot of ground for working with menus and menu links. We started by getting an overview of the architecture of the menu system in Drupal. I threw many classes and hooks at you because I am a firm believer that the best way to learn is to dig into the code.

We also saw what types of menu links there are in Drupal. We not only have regular links that belong to actual menus, but all sorts of other utility link systems, such as local tasks, local actions, and contextual links.

Then, we got our hands dirty and started with a practical example of how to load menu links in a tree, manipulate them, and finally, turn them into a render array. Right after that, we looked at how we can define all these types of menu links and how to understand them if we need to work with them programmatically.

In the next chapter, we will look at one of the most important aspects of any kind of content management framework—the different types of data storage we can have in Drupal and how we can work with them.

6

Data Modeling and Storage

We have gone through five chapters already in this book, but we have yet to cover a topic that has to do with one of the main purposes of a CMS—data storage. Okay, we hinted at it in the previous chapter and saw an example of a configuration object in *Chapter 2*. However, we merely scratched the surface of what is possible. It's now time to go ahead and dive into everything related to how you can store data in Drupal.

In this and the next chapter, we will talk about a lot of things related to storage and data manipulation, as well as see a lot of examples in the process. The focus of this chapter will, however, be more theoretical. There is a lot of ground to cover, as there are many APIs and concepts that you will need to understand. However, we will still see plenty of code examples to demonstrate in practice what we are talking about. In the next chapter, though, to make up for it, we will almost entirely work with code and build a few functionalities.

More concretely, however, this chapter will be divided into three main logical parts (not necessarily represented by headings).

First, we will talk about your options for data storage. We will talk about the State system with its key/value store, tempstore, user data, configuration, and finally, entities—the big one. We will leave the cache out of this because it will be covered in *Chapter 11*, *Caching*. We will see examples of all these options and go into the architectural details necessary to understand how they work.

Second, we will dive deep into the Drupal Entity API to understand the architecture behind it—how data is stored and, more importantly, modeled. I am referring to the `TypedData` system here.

Finally, we will look at how we can manipulate entities; in other words, how we can work with them and extract data—basically, the day-to-day of working with entities. One of the main topics here will be, of course, querying and loading entities. Moreover, we will also cover the validation aspect of this process.

The main topics we will cover in the chapter are:

- Different types of data storage: State, Configuration, Entities, Fields, etc.

- The TypedData API

- Interacting with the Entity API

By the end of this chapter, you should be able to understand a great deal about storage in Drupal and make decisions on which options to choose for your requirements. You'll know the differences and the reasons for using one over another. Moreover, you'll get a good understanding of the Entity API, which, in turn, will allow you to navigate more easily through Drupal code and work with the entity system. Lastly, and probably the most common thing Drupal developers do, you'll be able to work with entities: perform CRUD operations, read and write field values, and more of this good stuff.

So, let's begin.

Different types of data storage

Storing and using data is a critical part of any (web) application. Without somehow persisting data, we wouldn't be able to build much of anything. However, different uses of data warrant different systems for storing and manipulating it. For the purposes of this chapter, I will use the word *data* to mean almost anything that has to be persisted somewhere, for any given time.

Since Drupal 8, various layered APIs have been introduced to tackle common use cases for data storage. The strength of these new systems is mirrored in the fact that we rarely, if ever, need to even use the mother of all storage APIs, the Database API. This is because everything has been abstracted into different layers that help us handle most of what we need.

The State API

The State API is a key/value database storage and the simplest way you can store some data in Drupal. One of its main purposes is to allow developers to store information that relates to the *state* of the system (hence the name). And because the *state* of the system can be interpreted in various ways, think of this as simple information related to the current environment (Drupal installation) that is not editorial (content). An example would be the timestamp of the last time the cron ran or any flags or markers that the system sets to keep track of its tasks. It is different from caching in the sense that it is not meant to be cleared as often, and only the code that sets it is responsible for updating it.

One of the main characteristics of this system is the fact that it is not designed for human interaction. I mean this in the sense that it is the application itself that needs to make use of it. The option for humans is the configuration system, which we will talk about in detail in a later section.

So now that we know about the State API, let's jump into the technicalities and see what it's made of and how we can use it.

The State system revolves around the `Drupal\Core\State\StateInterface`, which provides all the methods we need to interact with it. This interface is implemented by the `State` service, which we can inject into our classes or use statically via the `\Drupal::state()` shorthand. Once we have that, things could not be easier, as the interface tells us exactly what we can do.

We can set a value:

```
\Drupal::state()->set('my_unique_key_name', 'value');
```

Or we can get a value:

```
$value = \Drupal::state()->get('my_unique_key_name');
```

We can also set/get multiple values at once (how convenient!):

```
\Drupal::state()->setMultiple(['my_unique_key_one' =>
  'value', 'my_unique_key_two' => 'value']);


$values = \Drupal::state()->getMultiple(
  ['my_unique_key_one', 'my_unique_key_two']);
```

Isn't that easy? We can also get rid of them:

```
\Drupal::state()->delete('my_unique_key_name');
\Drupal::state()->deleteMultiple(['my_unique_key_one',
  'my_unique_key_two']);
```

There are a couple of things to note here.

First, the key names you choose live in a single namespace, so it's recommended that you prefix them with your module name—`my_module.my_key`. That way, you avoid collisions.

Second, the values you store can also be more complex than simple strings. You can store any scalar value but also objects as they get serialized and deserialized automatically. Be careful, though, about which objects you plan on storing and ensure they can get properly serialized/deserialized.

By now, you are probably wondering where these values end up. They go into the `key_value` table, namespaced under the `state` collection. Also, the latter is a nice segue into a talk about the underlying system that powers the State API: the key/value store.

Note that the State system is only one implementation of an underlying framework of key/value stores. If you look at the `State` service, you will note that it uses the `KeyValueFactoryInterface` (which by default is implemented by the `KeyValueDatabaseFactory`). This, in turn, creates a key/value storage instance (by default, the `DatabaseStorage`), which implements the public API to interact with the store. If you look at the `key_value` table in the database, you'll note other collections besides *state*. Those are other implementations specific to various subsystems, such as the Entity API and System schema. Guess what? You can easily write your own and customize it to your needs. However, the reason why the State API was created was so that module developers can use it. So, odds are that you won't have to implement your own.

TempStore

The next system we will look at is the *TempStore* (temporary store).

The tempstore is a key/value, session-like storage system for storing temporary data across multiple requests. Imagine a multistep form or a wizard with multiple pages as great examples of tempstore use cases. You can even consider "work in progress", that is, something not yet permanently saved somewhere but kept in the tempstore so that a certain user can keep working on it until it's finished. Another key feature of the tempstore is that entries can have an expiration date, at which point they get automatically cleared. So, that user had better hurry up.

There are two kinds of tempstore APIs: private and shared ones. The difference between the two is that with the first one, entries strictly belong to a single user, whereas with the second one, they can be shared between users. For example, the process of filling in a multistep form is the domain of a single user, so the data related to that must be private to them. However, that form can also be open to multiple users, in which case the data can either be shared between the users (quite uncommon) or used to trigger a locking mechanism that blocks user B from making changes while user A is editing (much more common). So, there are many options, but we will see some examples soon.

First, though, let's look at some of the key players in this system.

We start with the `PrivateTempStore` class, which provides the API for dealing with the private tempstore. It is not a service because to use it, we must instantiate it via the `PrivateTempStoreFactory`. So, that is what we have to inject into our classes if we want to use it. The latter has a `get($collection)` method, which takes a collection name that we decide upon and creates a new `PrivateTempStore` object for it. If you look closely, the storage it uses is based on the `KeyValueStoreExpirableInterface`, which is very similar to the `KeyValueStoreInterface` used by the State API. The only difference is that the former has an expiration date, which allows the automatic removal of old entries. By default, the storage used in Drupal is the `DatabaseStorageExpirable`, which uses the `key_value_expire` table to store the entries.

Up to this point, the `SharedTempStore` is strikingly similar to the private one. It is instantiated using the `SharedTempStoreFactory` service and uses the same underlying database storage by default. The main difference is the namespace occupied in the `key_value_expire` table, which is composed as `tempstore.shared.collection_name`, as opposed to `tempstore.private.collection_name`.

Additionally, when asking the factory for the `SharedTempStore`, we have the option of passing an owner for whom we retrieve it. Otherwise, it defaults to the current user (the logged-in user ID or the anonymous session ID). Also, the way we interact with it and its purpose, more than anything, differ.

So, let's take a look at how we can work with the private and the shared tempstores.

Private TempStore

The following is a simple example of what we just talked about:

```
$factory = \Drupal::service('tempstore.private');
$store = $factory->get('my_module.my_collection');
$store->set('my_key', 'my_value');
$value = $store->get('my_key');
```

First, we get the `PrivateTempStoreFactory` service and ask it for the store identified by a collection name we choose. It's always a good idea to prefix it with your module name to avoid collisions. If another module names its own collection `my_collection`, it's not going to be pretty (even if the store is private).

Next, we use very simple setters and getters to set values similar to how we did with the State API.

If you run this code as user 1 (the main admin user), you'll note a new entry in the `key_value_expire` database table. The collection will be `tempstore.private.my_module.my_collection`, while the name will be `1:my_key`. This is the core principle of the private tempstore: each entry name is prefixed with the ID of the user who is logged in when the entry was created. Had you been an anonymous user, it would have been something like this: `4W2kLm0ovYlBneHMKPBUPdEM8G EpjQcU3_-B3X6nLh0:my_key`, where that long string is the session ID of the user.

The entry value will be a bit more complex than with the State API. This time it will always be a serialized `stdClass` object, which contains the actual value we set (which itself can be any scalar value or object that can be properly serialized), the owner (the user or session ID), and the last updated timestamp.

Lastly, we have the `expire` column, which, by default, will be one week from the moment the entry was created. This is a "global" timeframe set as a parameter in the `core.services.yml` definition file and can be altered in your own services definition file if you want. However, it is still global.

We can also delete entries like so:

```
$store->delete('my_key');
```

And we can also read the information I mentioned before about the entry (the last update date, owner):

```
$metadata = $store->getMetadata('my_key');
```

This returns the stdClass object that wraps the entry value, but without the actual value.

Shared TempStore

Now that we've seen how the private tempstore works, let's look at the shared one. The first thing we need to do in order to interact with it is to use the factory to create a new shared store:

```
$factory = \Drupal::service('tempstore.shared');
$store = $factory->get('my_module.my_collection');
```

However, unlike the private tempstore, we can pass a user identifier (ID or session ID) as a second parameter to the get() method to retrieve the shared store of a particular owner. If we don't, it defaults to the current user (logged in or anonymous).

Then, the simplest way we can store/read an entry is like before:

```
$store->set('my_key', 'my_value');
$value = $store->get('my_key');
```

Now, if we quickly jump to the database, we can see that the value column is the same as before, but the collection reflects that this is the shared store and the key is no longer prefixed by the owner. This is because another user should be able to retrieve the entry if they like. And the original owner can still be determined by checking the metadata of the entry:

```
$metadata = $store->getMetadata('my_key');
```

Also, we can delete it exactly as with the private store:

```
$store->delete('my_key');
```

Okay. But what else can we do with the shared store that we cannot do with the other one?

First, we have two extra ways we can set an entry. We can set it if it doesn't already exist:

```
$store->setIfNotExists('my_key', 'my_value');
```

Alternatively, we can set it if it doesn't exist or belongs to the current user (that is, the user owns it):

```
$store->setIfOwner('my_key', 'my_value');
```

Both these methods will return a Boolean, indicating whether the operation was successful or not. And essentially, they are handy to check for collisions. For example, if you have a big piece of configuration that multiple users can edit, you can create the entry that stores the work in progress only if it doesn't exist, or if it exists and the current user owns it (virtually overwriting their own previous work, which may be okay).

Then, you also have the `getIfOwner()` and `deleteIfOwner()` methods, which you can use to ensure that you only use or delete the entry if it belongs to the current user.

All this fuss, and for what? Why not just use the private store? This is because, in many cases, a flow can only be worked on by a single person at a time. So, if somebody started working on it, you will need to know this so you can prevent others from working on it. Moreover, you can allow certain users to "kick out" the previous user from the flow if they "went home without finishing it." They can then continue or clear out all the changes. It all depends on your use case.

Also, as a final point, the shared tempstore also works with the same expiration system as the private one.

Tempstore recap

So, there we have two different, albeit similar, tempstores that you can use for various cases. If you need to store session-like data available to the user across multiple requests but it is private to them, you can use the `PrivateTempStore`. Alternatively, if this data needs to be used by either multiple users at the same time or the opposite, preventing multiple users from working on something at the same time, you can use the `SharedTempStore`.

Both have an easy-to-understand API with simple methods and you can be flexible in terms of creating your own collections for whichever use case you need.

The UserData API

Now, I want to briefly talk about another user-specific storage option, provided by the User module, called *UserData*.

The purpose of the UserData API is to allow the storage of certain pieces of information related to a particular user. Its concept is similar to the State API in that the type of information stored is not configuration that should be exported. In other words, it is specific to the current environment (but belonging to a given user rather than a system or subsystem).

Users are content entities who can have fields of various data types. These fields are typically used for structured information pertaining to the user, for example, a first and a last name. However, if you need to store something more irregular, such as user preferences or a flag that a given user has done something, UserData is a good place to do that. This is because the information is either not something structured or is not meant for the users themselves to manage. So, let's see how this works.

The UserData API is made up of two things—the `UserDataInterface`, which contains the methods we can use to interact with it (plus developer documentation), and the `UserData` service, which implements it and can be used by the client code (us):

```
$user_data = \Drupal::service('user.data');
```

We are now ready to use the three methods on the interface:

- `get()`
- `set()`
- `delete()`

The first three arguments of all these methods are the same:

- `$module`: to store data in a namespace specific to our module name, thereby preventing collisions
- `$uid`: to tie data to a given user—it doesn't have to be the current user
- `$name`: the name of the entry being stored

Naturally, the `set()` method also has the `$value` argument, which is the data being stored, and this can be any scalar value or serializable object.

Together, all these arguments make for a very flexible storage system. We can essentially, for one module, store multiple entries for a given user and it doesn't stop there. Since that is possible, many of these parameters are optional. For example, we can get all the entries for a given module at once or all the entries for a given module and user combination at once. The same goes for deleting them. But where does all this data go?

The user module defines the `users_data` database table whose columns pretty much map to the arguments of these methods. The extra `serialized` column is there to indicate whether the stored data is serialized. Also, in this table, multiple records for a given user can coexist.

That is all there is to say about the UserData API. Use it wisely. Now, it's time to turn to the configuration API, one of the biggest subsystems in Drupal.

Configuration API

The Configuration API is one of the most important topics a Drupal developer needs to understand. There are many aspects to it that tie it into other subsystems, so it is critical to be able to both use and understand it properly.

In this section, we will cover a lot about the configuration system. We start by understanding what configuration is and what it is typically used for. Then, we will go through the different options we have for managing configuration in Drupal, both as a site builder and a developer using the Drush commands. Next, we will talk about how configuration is stored, where it belongs, and how it is defined in the system. We will also cover a few ways in which configuration can be overridden at different levels. Finally, we look at how we can interact with simple configuration programmatically. So, let's begin with an introduction.

Introduction

Configuration is the data that the proper functioning of an application relies upon. It is those bits of information that describe how things need to behave and helps control what code does. In other words, it configures the system to behave in a certain way with the expectation that it could also configure it to behave in a different way. To this end, configuration can be as simple as a toggle (turning something on or off) or as complicated as containing hundreds of parameters that describe an entire process.

What is configuration used for?

Configuration is used for storing everything that must be synchronized between the different environments (for example, moving from development to production). As such, it differs from the other types of data storage we have seen so far in that they were specific to one environment and configuration is not.

Another way of looking at configuration is by examining the role of a traditional site builder. They typically navigate the UI and configure the site to behave in a certain way: show this title on the home page, use this logo, show this type of content on the home page, and so on. As we mentioned, the result of these actions materializes into configuration that the site builder expects will travel easily to the acceptance environment where it can be reviewed, and finally, to production.

Some configuration can actually be critical to the proper functioning of the application. Certain code might break without a parameter having a value it can use. For example, if there is no site-wide email address set, what email will the system use to send its automated mail? For this reason, many of these configuration parameters come with sane defaults (upon installation). However, this also shows that configuration is a part of the application and just as important as the actual code.

Managing configuration

As we will see in a bit, Drupal stores configuration data in the database (for performance reasons), but it makes it all exportable to YAML files. So, a typical flow for managing it will have you perform changes in the UI, export the configuration, commit it into Git, and deploy the code upstream to the next environment. There, it's just a matter of importing what has been exported.

The import, export, and synchronization can be done both via Drush and through the UI at `admin/config/development/configuration`:

Figure 6.1: Configuration sync UI

The typical flow is for the active site configuration to be synchronized with the one in the YAML files. This means importing into the database all the configurations that are different in the YAML files from those in the database. These YAML files are inside the configuration `sync` folder, which should be committed to Git (you can configure in the `settings.php` file which directory should be the `sync` folder) and the opposite is to export the active configuration to the YAML files in order to commit them into Git.

The UI allows provides also a nice `Diff` interface to see what is different in YAML compared to the database:

View changes of system.site

Active	Staged
langcode: en	langcode: en
uuid: bb6d1577-4593-4d72-b16f-357050141974	uuid: bb6d1577-4593-4d72-b16f-357050141974
- name: 'Drupal 10'	+ name: 'Drupal 10 module development'
mail: danny@webomelette.com	mail: danny@webomelette.com
slogan: ''	slogan: ''

Back to 'Synchronize configuration' page.

Figure 6.2: Diff interface between YAML and the database

In this screenshot, we can see that the YAML files contain a small change in the site name configuration. Clicking on **Import all** will bring the database in line with the YAML files.

The first time you install a Drupal site, the configuration sync folder will be empty. It is up to you to do a manual export of all the active configuration and put it there. You can do so via the UI manual export tool or via Drush:

```
drush config-export
```

You would perform this step every time you make configuration changes through the UI that you want exported into YAML files.

Then, you can synchronize either in the UI as we've seen, or through Drush with the following command:

```
drush config-import
```

As a Drupal developer, you will be mostly using these two Drush commands.

Different types of configuration

Drupal comes with two distinct types of configuration—simple and configuration entities. Let's see what the difference is.

Simple configuration is the type that stores basic data, typically represented by scalar values such as integers or strings (or sets of such data). On the other hand, configuration entities are more complex and use the same CRUD API as the content entities.

Typically, simple configuration items are one of a kind. A module, for instance, may create and manage a configuration item that enables or disables one of its features. Most likely, this module needs this configuration to know what it should do about that feature. However, even if it doesn't, it is still a singular item that relates to that piece of functionality. And this configuration does not, however, have to be a small thing. It can contain lots of data needed for the module.

Configuration entities, on the other hand, are multiple instances of the same configuration type. For example, a View is a configuration entity and a given site can have an unlimited number of Views. It can even have none. We will talk more about configuration entities when we cover entities in general.

Configuration storage

Configuration is essentially stored in two places:

- The active storage (by default in the database)
- The sync storage (by default, the YAML files)

Here is an example of a simple configuration YAML file:

```yaml
my_string: 'Hello!'
my_int: 10
my_boolean: true
my_array:
  my_deep_string: 'Yes, hello!'
```

The name of this file is given by the ID you need to use with the Configuration API to read this data.

In addition to the actual data, you can have a `dependencies` key under which you can list what this configuration item depends on:

```yaml
dependencies:
  module:
    - drupal:views
  theme:
    - bootstrap
  config:
    - system.site
```

There are three types of dependencies: modules, themes, and other configuration items.

If you remember in *Chapter 2, Creating Your First Module*, we created a configuration object with the `hello_world.custom_salutation` ID in which we stored a simple value:

```yaml
salutation: 'Whatever the user set in the form'
```

And we did so programmatically through our form and did not provide a YAML file. This meant that our code for displaying the salutation did not depend on this configuration item existing or having a value of some kind. Had it been mandatory for our code to work, we could have created it upon module installation. There are two ways this can be done.

The most common way is to do so statically. Inside the `config/install` folder of a module, we can have YAML configuration files that get imported when the module is installed. However, if the values we need to set in this configuration are unknown (they need to be retrieved dynamically), we can do so in a `hook_install()` implementation (remember those from *Chapter 3, Logging and Mailing?*). There we can try to get our value and create the configuration object containing it.

> **Note**
>
> Configurations found inside the `config/install` folder of the module will not be imported when the module is installed if they have unmet dependencies; that is, if whatever they depend on does not exist in the system. As a matter of fact, the module itself would not install.

As a bonus, you can also provide configuration files with the module that should only be imported if their dependencies are met. In other words, optional configuration. These go in the `config/optional` folder of the module. If dependencies of these configurations are not met, the module will install correctly but without those configurations. Moreover, if later the dependencies are met, these optional configurations do get also imported automatically. Keep in mind, however, that optional configuration is reserved for configuration entities as it does not make sense with simple configurations.

Schema

For various systems to properly interact with the configuration items, configuration schemas have been introduced. Schemas are a way to define the configuration items and specify what kind of data they store, be it strings, Booleans, integers, and so on. They are, of course, notated in YAML format and go inside the `config/schema` folder of a module.

There are three main reasons why configuration needs a schema definition:

- *Multilingual support*: As we will see later, configuration is translatable in Drupal. However, in order to know which parts of the configuration can be translated, the schema system has been brought in to provide this additional layer. This way, configuration items that ship with contributed modules can get their own translations on the `localize.drupal.org` website. Moreover, users can provide translations for these in the UI because now the system knows which bits are translatable.

- *Configuration entities*: Configuration entities require schema definitions in order for the proper identification in the persistence layer of the data types that need to be exported with them. Moreover, schemas are used for the validation of configuration entity data.

- *Typecasting*: The configuration schema ensures that the configuration API is able to always typecast the values to their right data types properly.

Let's look at a configuration example provided by Drupal core to see how the schema works, namely the `system.mail` configuration provided by the `System` module. Remember in *Chapter 3*, *Logging and Mailing*, we talked about how this configuration item controls the mail plugin used for sending out emails? Well, by default, this is what it looks like:

```
interface:
  default: 'php_mail'
```

It's a very simple multidimensional array. So, if we now look in the `system.schema.yml` file for the schema definition, we will find the definitions for all the configuration items that come with the System module. The top-level line represents the name of the configuration item, so if we scroll down, we will find `system.mail`:

```
system.mail:
  type: config_object
```

```
label: 'Mail system'
mapping:
 interface:
   type: sequence
   label: 'Interfaces'
   sequence:
     type: string
     label: 'Interface'
```

If we look past the irony of the schema being five times bigger than the actual configuration, we can get a pretty good understanding of what this configuration item is all about. And more importantly, Drupal itself can too.

We can see that the system.mail configuration is of the config_object type. This is one of the two main types of configurations, the other being config_entity. The label key is used to indicate the human-readable name of this item, whereas the mapping key contains the definition of its individual elements. We can see the interface has the label Interfaces and the type sequence. The latter is a specific type that denotes an array in which the keys are not important. Whenever we want the keys to be taken into account, we use mapping (as it's done at the top level of this schema definition). And since we are looking at a sequence type, the individual items inside it are also defined as a string type with their own label.

Let's now write our own schema definition for the example configuration file we saw before:

```
my_string: 'Hello!'
my_int: 10
my_boolean: true
my_array:
  my_deep_text: 'Yes, hello, is anybody there?!'
```

If this configuration was found inside a file called my_module.settings.yml, this would be the corresponding schema definition:

```
my_module.settings:
  type: config_object
  label: 'Module settings'
  mapping:
    my_string:
      type: string
      label: 'My string that can also be of type text if
        it was longer'
```

```
    my_boolean:
      type: Boolean
      label: 'My boolean'
    my_array:
      type: mapping
      label: 'My array in which the keys are also
        important, hence not a sequence'
      mapping:
        my_deep_text:
          type: text
          label: 'My hello string'
```

As a bonus piece of information, any `config_object`-typed configuration inherits the following property:

```
langcode:
  type: string
  label: 'Language code'
```

This helps with the multilingual system and invites us to add a `langcode` property to each configuration item.

Most of the properties we've seen so far have been `type`, `label`, `mapping`, and `sequence`. There are two more that you should be aware of:

- `translatable`: very important as it indicates whether a data type can be translated. By default, the `text` and `label` types are already set to translatable, so you don't need to do so yourself.

- `nullable`: indicates whether the value can be left empty. If missing, it's considered required.

Here are some types you can use to define configuration:

- Scalar types: `string`, `integer`, `boolean`, `email`, `float`, `uri`, and `path`

- Lists: `mapping` and `sequence`

- Complex (extending scalar types): `label`, `path`, `text`, `date_format`, and more.

Make sure you check out the `core.data_types.schema.yml` file where most of these are defined.

Before we move on, let's make sure we create the configuration schema for the configuration item we created programmatically in *Chapter 2, Creating Your First Module*, namely the one storing the overridden salutation message. So, inside the `/config/schema` folder of the *Hello World* module, we can have the `hello_world.schema.yml` file with the following:

```
hello_world.custom_salutation:
  type: config_object
  label: 'Salutation settings'
  mapping:
   salutation:
     type: string
     label: 'The salutation message'
```

That takes care of some technical debt we introduced back when we didn't know about configuration schemas.

Overrides

We saw that configuration exists in the database, but belongs in organized and well-described YAML files. For the configuration from the YAML files to be used, they need to be imported—either via synchronization or upon module installation for those provided by modules. So, this means that the database still holds the active configuration.

To make things more dynamic, the Configuration API also provides an override system by which we can, at various levels, override the active configuration on the fly. We have three different layers at which we can do this: global, module, and language overrides.

The Configuration API then incorporates these overrides in a way that prevents them from leaking into the active configuration. We will see examples when we talk about how to interact with the Configuration API in general.

Global overrides

The global override happens via the global $config variable. It's available in the settings.php file for site-wide overrides:

```
$config['system.maintenance']['message'] = 'Our own message
    for the site maintenance mode';
```

In this example, we changed, on the fly, the message used for the site maintenance mode. Why you would want to do that is beside the point, but you may have some other configuration that would benefit from being overridable like this. In any case, you can see the array notation we use. The first key is the name of the configuration item (the name of the file minus the .yml extension) and then we have the key of the individual element in the configuration file. If this were to be nested, we'd be traversing further down.

Global config overrides are a great place where you can use environment-specific and/or sensitive data such as API keys. Things like this should never be exported to the sync storage. Instead, you can define a configuration object in the module and have it installed without a value. Then, using the global override, you provide the value specific to the relevant environment.

Module overrides

Although you can simply use the global `$config` array, that is not really the place where modules should be tinkering. First, because it's a global variable and it's never a good idea to change global variables. That should be left to the `settings.php` file. Second, because there is no way of controlling priority if multiple modules try to change it in the same way. Instead, we have the module override system that we can use.

Via the module overrides, we can create a service with the `config.factory.override` tag (remember what tagged services are?) and in this service, handle our overrides. To exemplify this, let's use this system to override the maintenance mode message. Inside our Hello World module, we can have the following service class:

```php
namespace Drupal\hello_world;

use Drupal\Core\Cache\CacheableMetadata;
use Drupal\Core\Config\ConfigFactoryOverrideInterface;
use Drupal\Core\Config\StorageInterface;

/**
 * Overrides configuration for the Hello World module.
 */
class HelloWorldConfigOverrides implements
  ConfigFactoryOverrideInterface {

  /**
   * {@inheritdoc}
   */
  public function loadOverrides($names) {
    $overrides = [];
    if (in_array('system.maintenance', $names)) {
      $overrides['system.maintenance'] = ['message' => 'Our
        own message for the site maintenance mode.'];
    }
```

```
      return $overrides;
  }


  /**
   * {@inheritdoc}
   */
  public function getCacheSuffix() {
    return 'HelloWorldConfigOverrider';
  }


  /**
   * {@inheritdoc}
   */
  public function createConfigObject($name, $collection =
    StorageInterface::DEFAULT_COLLECTION) {
    return NULL;
  }


  /**
   * {@inheritdoc}
   */
  public function getCacheableMetadata($name) {
    return new CacheableMetadata();
  }
}
```

Here, we have to implement the `ConfigFactoryOverrideInterface` interface, which comes with four methods:

- In `loadOverrides()`, we provide our overridden configuration values.
- In `getCacheSuffix()`, we return a simple string to be used in the static cache identifier of our overrides.
- In `createConfigObject()`, we don't actually do anything, but we could create a Configuration API object that would be used during installation or synchronization.
- In `getCacheableMetadata()`, we return any cache metadata related to our override. We don't have any, so we return an empty object.

Since this is a service, we can inject dependencies and make use of them if we want to calculate the overrides. Depending on this calculation, it can become important to set some proper cache metadata as well, but we will cover caching in another chapter.

Next, we register this as a tagged service:

```
hello_world.config_overrider:
  class: Drupal\hello_world\HelloWorldConfigOverrides
  tags:
    - { name: config.factory.override, priority: 5 }
```

We set the priority to 5 and, with this, we can control the order in which modules get their chance at overriding configuration. A higher priority will take precedence over a lower one.

And that's it. Clearing the cache will register this service and alter our configuration. If you now put the site in maintenance mode, you will notice that the message is the one we set here. However, if you go to the maintenance mode administration page at admin/config/development/maintenance, you will still see the original message. This is so that administrators do not, by accident, save the override value into the configuration storage.

Language overrides

Although we will talk some more about the multilingual features of Drupal, let's briefly note the possibility of language overrides.

If we enable configuration translation and add some more languages to our site, we can translate configuration items that are translatable (as described by their schema). In doing so, we override the default configuration for a particular language, an override that gets stored in the configuration storage and can be exported to YAML files.

We can make use of this override programmatically, even if we are not in a specific language context. This is what the code would look like, assuming we have an override in French for our maintenance mode message and we want to use that:

```
$language_manager = \Drupal::service('language_manager');
$language = $language_manager->getLanguage('fr');
$original_language = $language_manager->
  getConfigOverrideLanguage();
$language_manager->setConfigOverrideLanguage($language);
$config = \Drupal::config('system.maintenance');
$message = $config->get('message');
$language_manager->setConfigOverride
  Language($original_language);
```

This looks a bit complicated, but it's not really. First, we load the language manager service and get the Language object for our language (the one we want to get the overridden value for). Then, we keep track of the original configuration override language (which is essentially the current language) but also set the French language as the one to be used going forward. Finally, we load the `system.maintenance` configuration object and read its message in French before restoring the original language on the language manager. This is a quick way to illustrate an approach by which we can temporarily switch language contexts for configuration overrides. And this will be the way to load configuration entities in a different language than the current one.

The language override is in fact a complex version of the module override, provided by the core language module and integrated with its services for creating an API. So, I do encourage you to explore the code to better understand how this works.

Priority

We have three layers for configuration overrides: global, modules, and languages. This is also the order of the actual priority they have. Global overrides take precedence over everything else, while module overrides take precedence over the language overrides. This is why, if we have overridden the `system.maintenance` configuration in the module, we cannot use the language override in our code. So, keep this in mind.

Interacting with simple configuration

Now that we have talked about what the Drupal configuration system is, it's time to talk about the API itself and how we can interact with it. In this section, we will focus only on simple configuration, as we will talk more about configuration entities when we cover all entities.

In *Chapter 2, Creating Your First Module*, we already became somewhat exposed to the Configuration API in our `SalutationConfigurationForm` where we stored and read a simple configuration value. Now, it's time to go a bit deeper to understand the API and look at some more examples of how we can use it.

The class that represents a simple configuration object is `Drupal\Core\Config` and it wraps around the data found in one individual configuration item. Moreover, it helps to interact with the underlying storage system in order to persist the configuration (by default, into the database). In addition, it handles the overrides we talked about earlier automatically.

An important subclass of `Config` that we work with a lot is `ImmutableConfig`. Its purpose is to prevent changes being made to the configuration object, and as such, it is for read-only uses.

The way we get to use instances of these classes is through the `ConfigFactory` service, which has two handy methods for getting a configuration object:

```
$factory = \Drupal::service('config.factory');
$read_only_config = $factory->get
```

```
  ('hello_world.custom_salutation');
$read_and_write_config = $factory->getEditable
  ('hello_world.custom_salutation');
```

The get() method returns an ImmutableConfig object that is read-only, while the getEditable() method returns a Config object that can also be used for changing the configuration values. The way we do this is via the set() and save() methods:

```
$read_and_write_config->set('salutation', 'Another
  salutation');
$read_and_write_config->save();
```

Very simple. We also have the setData() method, which allows us to change the entire data of the configuration item at once. As a parameter, it expects an associative array of values.

If you cannot inject the ConfigFactory but must rely on the static call, the Drupal class has a shortcut for loading config objects directly:

```
$config = \Drupal::config('system.maintenance');
```

The config() method takes the name of the configuration as a parameter and returns an ImmutableConfig object.

To read the data, we have a few options. We can read one element from the config:

```
$value = $read_and_write_config->get('salutation');
```

If the element is nested, we can traverse down via the dot (.) notation:

```
$config = $factory->get('system.site');
$value = $config->get('page.403');
```

This will return the value set for the 403 page in the system.site configuration. We can also get all the values by simply not passing any parameters to the get() method, which would return an associative array.

If you remember our discussion about the configuration overrides, by default, the get() method will return the values as they have been overridden through the module or globally (or as a language if the language manager has a different language set for configuration). However, if we want, we can also retrieve the original value:

```
$config = $factory->get('system.maintenance');
$value = $config->getOriginal('message', FALSE);
```

The second parameter of `getOriginal()` indicates whether to apply overrides and, by default, it is TRUE. So this way, we get the configuration value that is set in the active storage.

Finally, we can also clear configuration values or the entire objects themselves. For example, consider the following code:

```
$config->clear('message')->save();
```

It will remove the `message` key from the configuration object and save it without that value. Alternatively, we can also remove the entire thing:

```
$config->delete();
```

That is pretty much it. The power of this API also stems from its simplicity.

Configuration recap

In this section, we have covered a lot of ground when it comes to the Configuration API. We've seen what configuration is and what types of configuration we have, as well as how we can manage it in Drupal. Then, we've seen how it's stored—in a database and YAML files—and how we can describe configuration using schemas. Finally, we looked at how we can interact with simple configuration as module developers, right after we went over the different ways we can override existing configuration.

In the next section, we will talk about entities and see also more about configuration entities.

Entities

We have finally reached the point where we will talk about the most complex, robust, and powerful system for modeling data and content in Drupal—the Entity API.

The Entity API integrates seamlessly with the multilingual system to bring fully translatable content and configuration entities. This means that most data you store can be translated easily into multiple languages.

Content versus configuration entity types

Let's start by establishing some basic terminology in order to prevent confusion down the line:

- Entities are instances of a given entity type. Thus, we can have one or more entities of a certain type, the latter being like a blueprint for individual entities.

- Entity types can be of two kinds: content and configuration.

We talked a little bit about configuration entities in the previous section. There, we saw that they are multiple instances of a certain *type* of configuration, as opposed to simple configuration, which is only one set of configuration values. Essentially, configuration entities are exportable sets of configuration values that inherit much of the same handling API as content entities.

Here are some examples of configuration entity types:

- **View**: A set of configuration values that make up a view
- **Image style**: Defines how an image needs to be manipulated in that given style
- **Role**: Defines a role that can be given to a user

Content entities, on the other hand, are not exportable and are the most important way we can model and persist data in Drupal. These can be used for content and all sorts of other structured data used in your business logic that needs to be persisted but not deployed to other environments.

Here are some examples of content entity types:

- Node
- Comment
- User
- Taxonomy Term

Apart from the exportability aspect, the main difference between content and configuration entities is the type of fields they use. The latter uses simpler fields, the combination of which gets stored as one entity "record" in the database (and exported to YAML). The content entity fields are complex and structured, both in modeling and in the persistence layer (the database).

Moreover, configuration entities also lack bundles. Bundles are yet another categorization of entities that sit below the content entity type. That means that each content entity type can have (but it doesn't have to have) one or more bundles, to which configurable fields can be attached. And not to throw more confusion at you, but bundles are in fact configuration entities themselves (as they need to be exported).

The Entity API is very flexible in terms of the types of data that you can store. Content entity types come with several different field types for various forms of data, from primitive values to more complex ones such as dates or references.

Content entities can also be made revisionable. This means content entity types can be configured to keep in store older versions of the same entity with some extra metadata related to the change process.

In this section and going forward, I will illustrate the most common features of entities by way of exemplifying two entity types:

- **Node**: The most prolific content entity type that comes with Drupal core and that is typically used as the main content modeling entity type
- **NodeType**: The configuration entity type that defines Node bundles

In the next chapter, we will learn how to create our own. But after everything we will learn in this one, it will be a breeze.

Entity type plugins

Entity types are registered with Drupal as plugins. Yes, again. The `Drupal\Core\Entity\Annotation\EntityType` class is the base annotation class for these plugins and you will mainly see two subclasses (annotations): `ContentEntityType` and `ConfigEntityType`. These are used to register content and configuration entity types, respectively.

The annotations classes map to the plugin classes used to represent the entity types. The base class for these is `Drupal\Core\Entity\EntityType`, which is then extended by another `ContentEntityType` and `ConfigEntityType`. These plugin classes are used to represent the entity types in the system and are a good resource for seeing what kind of data we can use on the annotation of these plugins. At a quick glance, we can already see that the differences between the two types are not so big.

The plugin manager for entity types is the `EntityTypeManager`, an important service you will probably interact with a lot as a Drupal developer. Among other things we will see later, it is responsible for managing the entity type plugins using the regular annotation-based discovery method.

The Node entity type is defined in `Drupal\node\Entity\Node`, where you will see a huge annotation at the top of the class. The NodeType configuration entity type, on the other hand, is found in `Drupal\node\Entity\NodeType`. You can spot the difference in the annotation they use.

Identifiers

The entity type annotations start with some basic information about them: an ID, a label, and things like that. For example, consider the Node entity:

```
 *    id = "node",
 *    label = @Translation("Content"),
 *    label_singular = @Translation("content item"),
 *    label_plural = @Translation("content items"),
 *    label_count = @PluralTranslation(
 *      singular = "@count content item",
```

```
*       plural = "@count content items"
*    ),
```

These are used in various places in the system to properly reference the entity type by machine and human-readable names.

Bundles

The Node entity type happens to have bundles, which is the reason why we have a `bundle_label` property as well:

```
bundle_label = @Translation("Content type"),
```

We can deduce that Node has bundles by the fact that it references the ID of the plugin that defines the bundle configuration entity type:

```
bundle_entity_type = "node_type",
```

Lo and behold, that is the NodeType's `ConfigEntityType` plugin ID. In its plugin annotation, we can find the reverse `bundle_of` property, which references the Node entity type. This is not mandatory for all configuration entity types but is used for the ones that act as content entity bundles. For example, the `View` configuration entity type does not have this.

In addition, we also find on the Node plugin annotation the route to where the bundles are configured:

```
field_ui_base_route = "entity.node_type.edit_form",
```

This is a route defined for the NodeType configuration entity.

As I mentioned earlier, bundles do not exist for configuration entities.

Database tables

Another important bit of information for content entities is the database table name they will use for storage:

```
base_table = "node",
data_table = "node_field_data",
```

The `node` table in this case holds the primary information about the entities such as the ID, UUID, or bundle, while the `node_field_data` table holds field data, which is singular and not translatable. Otherwise, these fields get their own database tables automatically. I will explain how field data is stored a bit later.

Entity keys

The Entity API defines a set of *keys* that are consistent across all entity types and by which common entity information can be retrieved. Since not all entity types need to have the same fields for storing that data, there is a mapping that can be done in the annotation for these:

```
 *    entity_keys = {
 *        "id" = "nid",
 *        "revision" = "vid",
 *        "bundle" = "type",
 *        "label" = "title",
 *        "langcode" = "langcode",
 *        "uuid" = "uuid",
 *        "status" = "status",
 *        "published" = "status",
 *        "uid" = "uid",
 *        "owner" = "uid",
 *    },
```

The Node entity type has a relatively comprehensive example of entity keys. As you can see, the unique identifier field for Nodes has always been `nid`. However, the common identifier for entities across the system is `id`. So, a mapping here facilitates that.

Links

Each entity type has a series of links the system needs to know about. Things like the canonical URL, the edit URL, the creation URL, and so on. For the node entities, we have the following:

```
 *    links = {
 *        "canonical" = "/node/{node}",
 *        "delete-form" = "/node/{node}/delete",
 *        "delete-multiple-form" = "/admin/content/
 *          node/delete",
 *        "edit-form" = "/node/{node}/edit",
 *        "version-history" = "/node/{node}/revisions",
 *        "revision" = "/node/{node}/revisions/{node_revision}
 *          /view",
 *        "create" = "/node",
 *    }
```

Like the entity keys, these links are meant to ensure some commonality between entity types (depending on their enabled capabilities).

One thing to note about these paths is that they need to be defined as routes. So, you can find them inside the `node.routing.yml` file (where you also find the routes used by the NodeType configuration entity type). Alternatively, though, these routes can be defined dynamically in order to prevent duplication. This can be done using a route provider handler. We will talk about handlers soon but also see a concrete example in the next chapter. In case you were wondering where the missing routes for the Node links are, check the `NodeRouteProvider` that registers them.

Entity translation

Entities are translatable across the board—like almost everything else in Drupal. To mark an entity type as such, all we need is the following in the plugin annotation:

```
translatable = TRUE,
```

This exposes the entity type to all the multilingual goodness. However, as we will see a bit later, individual fields also need to be declared as translatable.

Entity revisions

All content entity types can be made revisionable (and publishable) with minimal effort. Since Node is such an example, we can check out how it's built to understand this better.

First, the annotation needs to have the database table information where revisions are stored. This mirrors exactly the original tables we saw before:

```
revision_table = "node_revision",
revision_data_table = "node_field_revision",
```

Second, the annotation needs to have the entity keys for the revision ID and the published status we saw earlier:

```
*    entity_keys = {
*      "revision" = "vid",
*      "published" = "status",
*    },
```

Third, also in the annotation, the revision metadata keys need to be referenced:

```
*    revision_metadata_keys = {
*      "revision_user" = "revision_uid",
*      "revision_created" = "revision_timestamp",
```

```
*        "revision_log_message" = "revision_log"
*    },
```

These map to table columns in the revision table. And to ensure that all the necessary columns get created, the entity type class should extend from `EditorialContentEntityBase`, which provides the necessary field definitions for this. But it's also good to know that this base class already implements the `EntityPublishedInterface`, which allows you to make the entity type publishable.

Finally, the entity fields themselves are not automatically revisionable, so a flag needs to also be set on them. Again, we will see that in a minute when we talk about the fields.

Configuration export

Configuration entity types have a few extra options on their plugin definitions that relate to the exportability of the entities. By default, several configuration entity fields are persisted and exported. However, the `config_export` property needs to be used to declare which other fields should be included in the export. For example, the NodeType configuration entity type defines the following:

```
*    config_export = {
*        "name",
*        "type",
*        "description",
*        "help",
*        "new_revision",
*        "preview_mode",
*        "display_submitted",
*    }
```

Keep in mind that, without this definition, the configuration schema is used as a fallback to determine which fields to persist. If the configuration entity type doesn't have a schema (which it should though), no extra fields will get persisted. It is, however, recommended that all config entity types declare the `config_export` key in their annotation.

Additionally, configuration entity types have a prefix that is used for the namespace in the configuration system. This is also defined in the plugin annotation:

```
config_prefix = "type",
```

Handlers

The last main group of settings (that we will cover here) found on the entity type plugin annotations are the handlers. Handlers are the objects used by the Entity API to manage various tasks related to entities. The Node entity type is a good example to look at because it defines quite a lot of them, giving us an opportunity to learn:

```
*    handlers = {
*      "storage" = "Drupal\node\NodeStorage",
*      "storage_schema" = "Drupal\node\NodeStorageSchema",
*      "view_builder" = "Drupal\node\NodeViewBuilder",
*      "access" = "Drupal\node\NodeAccessControlHandler",
*      "views_data" = "Drupal\node\NodeViewsData",
*      "form" = {
*        "default" = "Drupal\node\NodeForm",
*        "delete" = "Drupal\node\Form\NodeDeleteForm",
*        "edit" = "Drupal\node\NodeForm",
*        "delete-multiple-confirm" = "Drupal\node\Form\
*          DeleteMultiple"
*      },
*      "route_provider" = {
*        "html" = "Drupal\node\Entity\NodeRouteProvider",
*      },
*      "list_builder" = "Drupal\node\NodeListBuilder",
*      "translation" = "Drupal\node\NodeTranslationHandler"
*    },
```

As we immediately notice, these are all simple references to classes. So, when in doubt, it's always a good idea to go and see what they do and how they work. But let's briefly talk about all of them and see what their main responsibilities are:

- The storage handler is one of the most important. It does everything that has to do with CRUD operations and interacting with the underlying storage system. It is always an implementation of EntityStorageInterface and a parent of the ContentEntityStorageBase or ConfigEntityStorage classes. If the entity type does not declare one, it will default to SqlContentEntityStorage (since we are using a SQL database most of the time) or ConfigEntityStorage for configuration entities.

- The `storage_schema` handler is not something you will deal with too much. Its purpose is to handle the schema preparations for the storage handler. It will default to the `SqlContentEntityStorageSchema` if one is not provided, and it will take care of the database tables needed for the entity type definition.

- The `view_builder` handler is an `EntityViewBuilderInterface` implementation responsible for creating a render array out of an entity with the purpose of preparing it for display. If one is not specified, it defaults to `EntityViewBuilder`.

- The `access` handler is an `EntityAccessControlHandlerInterface` implementation responsible for checking access for any of the CRUD operations on a given entity of the respective type. If one is not provided, the default `EntityAccessControlHandler` is used; it also triggers the access hooks modules can implement to have a say in the access rules of a given entity. We will talk a lot more about access in a dedicated chapter later on.

- The `views_data` handler is an `EntityViewsDataInterface` implementation responsible for exposing the respective entity type to the Views API. This is used so that Views can properly understand the entity and its fields. By default, it uses the generic `EntityViewsData` if one is not provided.

- The `form` handlers are `EntityFormInterface` implementations used for various types of entity manipulations such as create, edit, and delete. The referenced classes are forms that are used for managing the entities.

- The `route_provider` handlers are `EntityRouteProviderInterface` implementations responsible for dynamically providing routes necessary for the respective entity type. The Node entity type defines one for HTML pages, but others can be created for different kinds of HTTP formats as well.

- The `list_builder` handler is an `EntityListBuilderInterface` implementation responsible for building a listing of entities of the respective type. This listing is typically used on the administration screen for managing the entities. This is an important one to have since without it, the admin listing won't work. The default implementation is `EntityListBuilder`.

- The `translation` handler is a `ContentTranslationHandlerInterface` implementation responsible for exposing entities of this type to the Translation API.

We can add our own handlers to any entity type, be it one we define or one defined by Drupal core, and then use it via the entity type manager. If we define the entity type, it's enough to include it in the annotation like all the others. Otherwise, we do it using `hook_entity_type_alter()`.

Then, we can use the handler like so:

```
\Drupal::entityTypeManager()->hasHandler('node',
  'my_handler');
\Drupal::entityTypeManager()->getHandler('node',
  'my_handler');
```

Fields

The principal way data is modeled by entities is through fields. Entities themselves are essentially just a collection of different types of fields that hold various types of data.

Configuration entity fields

Configuration entities have relatively simple fields due to their storage handling. We can store complex configuration but there is no complex database schema to reflect that. Instead, we have the configuration schema layer, which describes configuration entities so the Entity API can understand the types of data they store and represent. We talked about this earlier in the chapter when we looked at the configuration system. But let's examine the NodeType configuration entity type to better understand its fields.

The fields on configuration entities are essentially declared as class properties. So, we can see that NodeType has fields such as `$description`, `$help`, and others. As I mentioned a bit earlier, the plugin annotation includes a reference to the class properties that are to be persisted and exported. As you can imagine, a class should be allowed to also have some properties that are not actually field values that need to be exported.

The configuration entity class can also have some specific getter and setter methods for its fields, but can also rely on the `ConfigEntityBase` parent class' `set()` and `get()` methods for setting and accessing field values. Things are relatively simple to understand.

Now, let's check out the NodeType configuration schema found in `node.schema.yml` and see what that is all about:

```
node.type.*:
  type: config_entity
  label: 'Content type'
  mapping:
   name:
     type: label
     label: 'Name'
   type:
     type: string
     label: 'Machine-readable name'
   ....
  new_revision:
    type: Boolean
    label: 'Whether a new revision should be created by
      default'
  ...
```

This is just a sample of the schema definition without some of the fields because we already know how to read those. However, there are some things that are new though.

We can see the wildcard notation, which indicates that this schema should apply to all configuration items that start with that prefix. So, essentially, to all entities of a certain type. In this case, the entity type name is `type`, as denoted in the NodeType annotation's `config_prefix` property. Of course, the namespace is prefixed by the module name.

Next, we see that the type is `config_entity`, which is the other major complex type, besides `config_object`, which is used to denote simple configuration (and which we saw earlier). Both types are extensions of the `mapping` type with some extra information. In the case of configuration entities, the extra values are the definitions for the fields that automatically get exported—`uuid`, `langcode`, `status`, `dependencies`, and `third_party_settings`. This means that these fields exist on all configuration entities of any type and are always persisted/exported.

Lastly, we have the schema definitions for each individual field, such as `name`, `type`, and more. So, now the system knows that the `new_revision` field should be treated as a Boolean, or that the `name` field is translatable (since it is of the type `label`, which extends the simple `string` type and has the translation flag).

So, as you can see, the field matrix of a configuration entity type is not so complex to understand. Content entities are much more complex, and we will talk about those next.

Content entity fields

Content fields can be of two types: base fields and configurable fields. Moreover, very important to understand is that content entity fields are built on top of the low-level TypedData API. The latter is a complex system for modeling data in code and is widely used in Drupal. Unfortunately, it is also one of the APIs least understood by developers. Not to worry, in the next section, I will break it down for you. Since we still don't know anything about it, we will now talk about fields from a higher-level perspective.

Base fields

Base fields are the fields closest to a given entity type, things like the title, creation/modification date, publication status, and so on. They are defined in the entity type class as `BaseFieldDefinition` implementations and are installed in the database based on these definitions. Once installed, they are no longer configurable from a storage point of view from the UI (except in some cases, in which certain aspects can be overridden). Additionally, some display and form widget configuration changes can still be made (also depending on whether the individual definitions allow this).

Let's check out the Node entity type's `baseFieldDefinitions()` method and see an example of a base field definition:

```
$fields['title'] = BaseFieldDefinition::create('string')
  ->setLabel(t('Title'))
```

```
  ->setRequired(TRUE)
  ->setTranslatable(TRUE)
  ->setRevisionable(TRUE)
  ->setSetting('max_length', 255)
  ->setDisplayOptions('view', [
    'label' => 'hidden',
    'type' => 'string',
    'weight' => -5,
  ])
  ->setDisplayOptions('form', [
    'type' => 'string_textfield',
    'weight' => -5,
  ])
  ->setDisplayConfigurable('form', TRUE);
```

This is the definition of the Node `title` field. We can deduce that it is of the `string` type due to the argument passed to the `create()` method of the `BaseFieldDefinition` class. The latter is a complex data definition class on top of the TypedData API.

Other common types of fields that can be defined are `boolean`, `integer`, `float`, `timestamp`, `datetime`, `entity_reference`, `text_long`, and many others. You can find out what field types you can use by checking the available `FieldType` plugins provided by Drupal core and any other modules. These are the same types of fields that can be used by configurable fields in the UI. In a later chapter, we will see how we can write our own custom field type.

The field definition can have several options, which may also differ depending on the type of field being defined. I will skip the obvious ones here and jump to the `setTranslatable()` and `setRevisionable()` methods and ask you to remember when we saw earlier how the Node entity type plugin annotation indicated that Nodes are translatable and revisionable. This is where the fields themselves are configured to that effect. Without these settings, they'd be left out of the translation capability and revisions.

> **Note**
>
> If you take a look at how the `baseFieldDefinitions()` method starts, you'll see that it inherits some fields from the parent class as well. This is where common field definitions are inherited from, which allows the entity type to be revisionable and publishable.

The `setSetting()` method is used to provide various options for the field type. In this case, it's used to indicate the maximum length, which is also mirrored in the table column in the database. Then, we have the display options that configure the view formatter, as well as the form widget the field should use. They reference the plugin IDs of the `FieldFormatter` (`string`) and `FieldWidget` (`string_textfield`) plugin types, respectively. In a later chapter, we will see how we can define our own field plugins that can be used for both base and configurable fields.

Lastly, we have the `setDisplayConfigurable()` method, which is used to enable/disable configuration changes on the form widget or display through the UI. In this case, only the form widget is exposed to changes.

Not all these options and configurations are always used or mandatory. It depends on what type of field we are defining, how we want the field to be configured, and whether defaults are okay for us. An important option that can be used on all field types is cardinality—whether the field can have more than one value of the same type. This allows a field to store multiple values that follow the same data definition on that entity field.

If we create our own entity type and want to later add or modify a base field, we can do that in the same place as we originally defined them—in the entity class. However, for entities that do not "belong" to us, we need to implement some hooks in order to contribute our own changes. To provide a new base field definition to an existing entity type, we can implement `hook_entity_base_field_info()` in our module and return an array of `BaseFieldDefinition` items, just as we saw before with the Node entity type. Alternatively, we can implement `hook_entity_base_field_info_alter()` and alter existing base field definitions to our liking. Do keep in mind that this latter hook might be changed in the future, although at the time of writing, no great priority has been given to that.

Configurable fields

Configurable fields are typically created through the UI, **attached to an entity type bundle**, and exported to code. The part highlighted in bold is a critical difference between these and base fields in that base fields exist on all bundles of an entity type. You should already be familiar with the UI for creating a configurable field:

Figure 6.3: Selecting a field type

They also use the TypedData API for their definitions, as well as the same field type, widget, and formatter plugins we talked about earlier. Architecturally speaking, the main difference between base and configurable fields is that the latter are made up of two parts: storage configuration (`FieldStorageConfig`) and field configuration (`FieldConfig`). These are both configuration entity types whose entities, together, make up a configurable field. The former defines the field settings that relate to how the field is stored. These are options that apply to that field across all the bundles of an entity type it may be attached to (such as cardinality, field type, and so on). The latter defines options for the field specific to the bundle it is attached to. These can, in some cases, be overrides of the storage config but also new settings (such as the field description, whether it is required, and more).

The easiest way to create configurable fields is through the UI. Just as easily, you get them exported into code. You could alternatively write the field storage configuration and field configuration yourself and add them to your module's `config/install` folder, but you can achieve the same thing more easily if you just export them through the UI.

Moreover, you can use a couple of hooks to make alterations to existing fields. For example, by implementing `hook_entity_field_storage_info_alter()`, you can alter field storage configurations, while with `hook_entity_bundle_field_info_alter()`, you can alter field configurations, as they are attached to an entity type bundle.

Field storage

We saw earlier how configuration entities are persisted and exported based on the configuration schema and plugin definition. Let's quickly talk about how the fields used on content entities are stored in the database.

Base fields, by default, end up in the entity base table (the one defined in the plugin annotation as `base_table`). This makes things more performant than having them in individual tables. However, there are quite a lot of exceptions to this.

If the entity type is translatable, a "data" table gets created where records of the same entity base field values in different languages can be stored. This is the table the Node entity type plugin annotation declared with the `data_table` property. If this property is missing, the table name will, by default, be `[base_table]_field_data`.

Moreover, if the field cardinality of a given field is higher than 1, a new table is created for the field with the name `[entity_type_name]__[field_name]`, where multiple records for the same field can be stored.

If the entity and field have translation enabled and the respective field cardinality is higher than 1, the "data" table holds the records for an entity in all languages it is translated into, while the `[entity_type_name]__[field_name]` table holds all the value records in all languages for a given field.

Configurable fields, on the other hand, always get a separate field data table named `[entity_type_name]__[field_name]`, where multiple values for the same field (in multiple languages) can be stored.

Entity types recap

The Entity API is quite complex. We have only begun our journey to understanding the different kinds of entity types, bundles, fields, and so on. We have so far talked about the differences between configuration and content entity types and what exactly they are made up of. To this end, we also touched upon the different types of fields they can use and how the data in these fields is stored.

However, there is still a lot to understand about entities, especially content entities, which will be our focus in the next sections. We are going to first look at the TypedData API to better understand how content entity field data is modeled. As of now, that is still a black box. Next, we'll look at how to work with the API to query, create, and manipulate entities (both content and configuration). Finally, we'll talk a bit about the Validation API the content entities and fields use consistently to ensure they hold proper data. So, let's get to it.

TypedData

To really understand how entity data is modeled, we need to understand the TypedData API. Unfortunately, this API remains quite a mystery for many. But you're in luck because, in this section, we're going to get to the bottom of it.

Why TypedData?

It helps to understand things better if we first talk about why this API was needed in the first place. It all has to do with the way PHP as a language *is*, compared to others, and that is, loosely typed. This means that in PHP, it is very difficult to use native language constructs to rely on the type of certain data or understand more about that data. The difference between the string `"1"` and integer `1` is a very common example.

Since PHP 7, we have type-hinting for scalar values in function parameters, which is good, but still not enough. Scalar values alone are not going to cut it if you think of the difference between `1495875076` and `2495877076`. The first is a timestamp while the second is an integer. Even more importantly, the first has meaning while the second one does not. At least seemingly. Maybe I want it to have some meaning because it is the specific formatting for the IDs in my package tracking app.

What is TypedData?

The TypedData API is a low-level and generic API that essentially does two things from which a lot of power and flexibility are derived.

First, it wraps "values" of any kind of complexity. More importantly, it forms "values." This can range from a simple scalar value to a multidimensional map of related values of different types that together are considered one value. Let's take, for example, a New York license plate: `405-307`. This is a simple string but we "wrap" it with TypedData to give it meaning. In other words, we know programmatically that it is a license plate and not just a random PHP string. But wait, that plate number can be found in other states as well (possibly, I have no idea). So, to better define a plate, we need also a state code: *NY*. This is another simple string wrapped with TypedData to give it meaning—a state code. Together, they can become a slightly more complex piece of TypedData: a US license plate, which has its own meaning.

Second, as you can probably infer, it gives meaning to the data that it wraps. If we continue our previous example, the US license plate TypedData now has plenty of meaning. So, we can programmatically ask it what it is and all sorts of other things about it, such as what is the state code for that plate. And the API facilitates this interaction with the data.

As I mentioned, due to this flexibility, a lot of power can be built on top. Things like data validation are very important in Drupal and rely on TypedData. As we will see later in this chapter, validation happens at the TypedData level using constraints on the underlying data.

The low-level API

Now that we have a basic understanding of the principles behind TypedData and why we need it, let's start exploring the API, starting from the smallest pieces and moving up.

There are two main pillars of this API: `DataType` plugins and data definitions.

DataType plugins

DataType plugins are responsible for defining the available types of data that can be used in the system. For example, the `StringData` plugin is used to model a simple primitive string. Moreover, they are responsible for interacting with the data itself; things like setting and accessing the respective values.

The DataType plugins are managed by the `TypedDataManager` and are annotated by the `DataType` annotation class. They implement the `TypedDataInterface` and typically extend the `TypedData` base class or one of its subclasses.

There are three main types of DataType plugins out there, depending on the interface they implement:

- First, there is the `TypedDataInterface` I mentioned before; this is typically used for simple primitive values such as strings or integers.

- Second, there is the `ListInterface`, which is used to form a collection of other `TypedData` elements. It comes with methods specific to interacting with lists of elements.

- Third, there is `ComplexDataInterface`, which is used for more complex data formed of multiple properties that have names and can be accessed accordingly. Going forward, we will see examples of all these types.

The best way to understand how these plugins are used is to first talk about data definitions as well.

Data definitions

Data definitions are the objects used to store all that meaning about the underlying data we talked about. They define the type of data they can hold (using an existing `DataType` plugin) and any kind of other meaningful information about that data. So, together with the plugins, the data definitions are one mean data modeling machine.

At the lowest level, they implement the `DataDefinitionInterface` and typically extend the `DataDefinition` class (or one of its subclasses). Important subclasses of `DataDefinition` are `ListDefinition` and `ComplexDefinitionBase`, which are used to define more complex data types. And as you might expect, they correlate to the `ListInterface` and `ComplexDataInterface` plugins I mentioned earlier.

Let's see an example of a simple usage of data definitions and DataType plugins by modeling a simple string—`my_value`.

It all starts with the definition:

```
$definition = DataDefinition::create('string');
```

The argument we pass to the `create()` method is the `DataType` plugin ID we want to define our data with. In this case, it is the `StringData` plugin.

We already have some options out of the box for defining our string data. For example, we can set a label:

```
$definition->setLabel('Defines a simple string');
```

We can also mark it as read-only or set whatever "settings" we want into the definition. However, one thing we don't do is deal with the actual value. This is where the DataType plugin comes into play. The way this happens is that we create a new plugin instance, based on our definition and a value:

```
/** @var \Drupal\Core\TypedData\TypedDataInterface $data */
$data = \Drupal::typedDataManager()->create($definition,
  'my_value');
```

We used the `TypedDataManager` to create a new instance of our definition with our actual string value. What we get is a plugin that we can use to interact with our data, understand it better, change its value, and so on:

```
$value = $data->getValue();
$data->setValue('another string');
$type = $data->getDataDefinition()->getDataType();
$label = $data->getDataDefinition()->getLabel();
```

We can see what kind of data we are dealing with, its label, and other things. Let's look at a slightly more complex example and model the license plate use case we talked about earlier.

We first define the number:

```
$plate_number_definition = DataDefinition::
  create('string');
$plate_number_definition->setLabel('A license plate
  number.');
```

Then, we define the state code:

```
$state_code_definition = DataDefinition::create('string');
$state_code_definition->setLabel('A state code');
```

We are keeping these generic because nobody says we cannot reuse these elsewhere; we might need to deal with state codes in another place.

Next, we create our full plate definition:

```
$plate_definition = MapDataDefinition::create();
$plate_definition->setLabel('A US license plate');
```

We use the `MapDataDefinition` here which, by default, uses the Map DataType plugin. Essentially, this is a well-defined associative array of properties. So, let's add our definitions to it:

```
$plate_definition->setPropertyDefinition('number',
  $plate_number_definition);
$plate_definition->setPropertyDefinition('state',
  $state_code_definition);
```

This map definition gets two named property definitions: `number` and `state`. Now, you can see the hierarchical aspect of the `TypedData` API.

Finally, we instantiate the plugin:

```
/** @var \Drupal\Core\TypedData\Plugin\DataType\Map
  $plate */|
$plate = \Drupal::typedDataManager()->create
  ($plate_definition, ['state' => 'NY', 'number' =>
    '405-307']);
```

The value we pass to this type of data is an array whose keys should map to the property names and values to the individual property definitions (which in this case are strings).

Now, we can benefit from all the goodness of the `TypedData` API:

```
$label = $plate->getDataDefinition()->getLabel();
$number = $plate->get('number');
$state = $plate->get('state');
```

The `$number` and `$state` variables are `StringData` plugins that can then be used to access the individual values inside:

```
$state_code = $state->getValue();
```

Their respective definitions can be accessed in the same way that we did before. So, we managed in these few lines to properly define a US license plate construct and make it intelligible by the rest of our code. Next, we will look at even more complex examples and inspect how content entity data is modeled using `TypedData`. Configuration entities, as we saw, rely on configuration schemas to define the data types. Under the hood, the schema types reference `DataType` plugins themselves. So, behind the scenes, the same low-level API is used. To keep things a bit simpler, we will look at content entities, where this API is much more explicit and you will actually have to deal with it.

Content entities

Let's now examine entities and fields and see how they make use of the TypedData API for modeling the data they store and manage. This will also help you better understand how data is organized when you are debugging entities and their fields.

The main place where data is stored and modeled is fields. As we saw, we have two types: base fields and configurable fields. However, when it comes to TypedData, they do not differ very much. They both use the `FieldItemList` DataType plugin (either directly or a subclass). In terms of definitions, base fields use `BaseFieldDefinition` instances while configurable fields use `FieldConfig` instances. The latter are slightly more complicated because they are configuration entities themselves (to store the field configuration), but that implement down the line the `DataDefinitionInterface`. So, they combine the two tasks. Moreover, base fields can also use `BaseFieldOverride` definition instances, which are essentially also configuration entities and are used for storing alterations made through the UI to the fields defined as base fields. Just like the `FieldConfig` definitions, these extend the `FieldConfigBase` class because they share the same exportable characteristics.

In addition to fields, entities themselves have a TypedData plugin that can be used to wrap entities and expose them to the API directly—the `EntityAdapter`. These use an `EntityDataDefinition` instance, which basically includes all the individual field definitions. Using plugin derivatives, each entity type gets an `EntityAdapter` plugin instance dynamically.

Let's now examine a simple base field and understand the usage of the TypedData API in the context of fields. The `BaseFieldDefinition` class extends `ListDataDefinition`, which is responsible for defining multiple items of data in a list. Each item in the list is an instance of `DataDefinitionInterface` as well, so you can see the same kind of hierarchy as we had with our license plate example. But why is one field a list of items?

You probably know that when you create a field, you can choose how many items this one field can hold—its cardinality. You typically choose one but you can choose many. The same is true with all types of fields. Regardless of the cardinality you choose, the data is modeled as a list. If the field has a cardinality of one, the list will only have one item. It is as simple as that. So, if base field definitions are lists of definitions, what are the individual item definitions? The answer is extensions of `FieldItemDataDefinition`.

In terms of DataType plugins, as I mentioned, we have the `FieldItemList` class, which implements the `ListInterface` I mentioned earlier as one of the more complex data types. The individual items inside are subclasses of `FieldItemBase` (which extends the Map DataType we encountered earlier). So, we have the same kind of data structure. But just to make matters slightly more complicated, another plugin type comes into play here—`FieldType`. The individual field items are actually instances of this plugin type (which extend `FieldItemBase` and down the line a `DataType` plugin of some kind). So, for instance, a text field will use the `StringItem` FieldType plugin, which inherits a bunch of logic from the Map DataType. So, you can see how the TypedData API is at a very low level and things can be built on top of it.

So now, if we combine what we have learned and look at a base field, we see the following: a `FieldItemList` data type using a `BaseFieldDefinition` (or `BaseFieldOverride`) data definition. Inside each item is a `FieldItemBase` implementation (a `FieldType` plugin extending some sort of `DataType` plugin) using a `FieldItemDataDefinition`. So, not that complicated after all. We will put this knowledge to good use in the final section of this chapter when we see how we can interact with entities and field data. I am not throwing all these notions at you just for the sake of it.

The configurable fields work in almost the same way, except that the definition corresponding to the `FieldItemList` is an instance of `FieldConfig` (which is also a configuration entity that stores the settings for this field, and which is similar to the `BaseFieldOverride`). However, it is also a type of list definition with the individual list items being the same as in base fields.

TypedData recap

So, as we've seen, the scope of understanding the TypedData API in Drupal is quite broad. We can make things very simple, as with our first example, but then hit some really complicated territory with its use in the entity system. The point of this section has been to make you aware of this API, understand its reasoning, see a couple of simple examples, and break down all the components that are used in the Entity API.

However, I admit, it must have been quite a difficult section to follow. All this terminology and theory can be daunting. But don't worry if you didn't fully understand everything, that's fine. It's there for you to reference as we go through the next section because we will apply all that knowledge and you will see why it's useful to be aware of it. In other words, we will now focus on interacting with entities (both content and configuration) and in doing so, make heavy use of the functionality made possible by the TypedData API. But do also take the time to navigate the code and see the classes I mentioned.

Interacting with the Entity API

In this final section of the chapter, we're going to cover the most common things you will be doing with content and configuration entities. These are the main topics we will discuss going forward:

- Querying and loading entities

- Reading entities

- Manipulating entities (update/save)

- Creating entities

- Rendering entities

- Validating entity data

So, let's hit it.

Querying entities

One of the most common things you will do as a programmer is query stuff, such as data in the database. The Entity API offers a layer that reduces the need to query the database directly. In a later chapter, we will see how we can still do that when things become more complex. For now, since most of our structured data belongs in entities, we will use the entity query system for retrieving entities.

If you remember when we spoke about the entity type handlers, one of them was the storage handler that provides the API for CRUD operations on the entities. This is the handler we will use to access the entity query. And we do this via the `entity_type.manager` service (`EntityTypeManager`):

```
$query = \Drupal::entityTypeManager()->getStorage('node')
   ->getQuery();
```

We request the storage handler, which can then give us the query factory for that entity type. In this example, I used a static call but, as always, you should inject the service where you can.

Building queries

Now that we have an entity query factory on our hands, we can build a query that is made up of conditions and all sorts of typical query elements. Here's a simple example of querying for the last 10 published article nodes:

```
$query
   ->condition('type', 'article')
   ->condition('status', TRUE)
   ->range(0, 10)
   ->accessCheck(FALSE)
   ->sort('created', 'DESC');
$ids = $query->execute();
```

The first thing you can see is that the methods in the factory are chainable. We have some expected methods to set conditions, the range, sorting, and so on. As you can already deduce, the first parameter is the field name and the second is the value. An optional third parameter can also be the operator for the condition. Moreover, the name of the `$ids` variable also tells you what the result of the `execute()` method is: the IDs of the entities found (keyed by their revision IDs). Also important to note is the call to `accessCheck()` (mandatory since Drupal 9.2), which allows us to specify whether access to those entities by the current user should be taken into account.

> **Tip**
>
> I strongly recommend you check out the `\Drupal\Core\Entity\Query\QueryInterface` class for some documentation about these methods, especially the `condition()` method, which is the most complex.

Here is a slightly more complex condition that would return nodes of two different types:

```
->condition('type', ['article', 'page'], 'IN')
```

Additionally, you can also use condition groups, with OR or AND conjunctions:

```
$query
    ->condition('status', TRUE);
  $or = $query->orConditionGroup()
    ->condition('title', 'Drupal', 'CONTAINS')
    ->condition('field_tags.entity.name', 'Drupal',
      'CONTAINS');
  $query->condition($or);
  $ids = $query->execute();
```

In the previous query, we see a few new things. First, we create a condition group of the type OR in which we add two conditions. One of them checks whether the node title field contains the string `'Drupal'`. The other checks whether any of the entities referenced by the `field_tags` field (in this case, taxonomy terms) have the string `'Drupal'` in their names. So, you can see the power we have in traversing into referenced entities. Finally, we use this condition group as the first parameter to the `condition()` method of the query (instead of the field name and value).

> **Note**
>
> Entity queries (especially for the Node entity type) take access restrictions into account, as they are run from the context of the current user. This means that, for example, a query for unpublished nodes triggered on a page hit by an anonymous user may not return results, but would if triggered by an administrator. This is handled with the mandatory `accessCheck(FALSE)` instruction on the query. We will talk more about node access in a later chapter.

Configuration entities work in the same way. We get the query factory for that entity type and build a query. Under the hood, the query is of course run differently due to the flat nature of the storage.

Each configuration entity gets one record in the database, so they need to be loaded and then examined. Moreover, the conditions can be written to also match the nested nature of configuration entity field data. For example:

```
$query = \Drupal::entityTypeManager()->getStorage('view')
  ->getQuery();
$query->condition('display.*.display_plugin', 'page');
$ids = $query->execute();
```

This query searches for all the View configuration entities that have the display plugin of the type `'page'`. The condition essentially looks inside the `display` array for any of the elements (hence the `*` wildcard). If any of these elements has a `display_plugin` key with the value `'page'`, it's a match. This is what an example view entity looks like in YAML format:

```
...
  base_field: nid
  display:
    default:
      display_options:
        ...
      display_plugin: default
      display_title: Master
    ...
    page_1:
      display_options:
        ...
      display_plugin: page
      display_title: Page
```

I removed a bunch of data from this entity just to keep it short. But as you can see, we have the `display` array, with the `default` and `page_1` elements, and each has a `display_plugin` key with a plugin ID.

Loading entities

Now that we have our entity IDs found by the query, it's time to load them. It couldn't be simpler to do so. We just use the storage handler for that entity type (and we get that from the entity type manager):

```
$nodes = \Drupal::entityTypeManager()->getStorage('node')
  ->loadMultiple($ids);
```

This will return an array of `EntityInterface` objects (in this case, `NodeInterface`). Or if we have only one ID to load:

```
$nodes = \Drupal::entityTypeManager()->getStorage('node')
  ->load($id);
```

This will return a single `NodeInterface` object.

The entity type storage handler also has a shortcut method, which allows you to perform simple queries and load the resulting entities in one go. For example, if we wanted to load all article nodes:

```
$nodes = \Drupal::entityTypeManager()->getStorage('node')
  ->loadByProperties(['type' => 'article']);
```

The `loadByProperties()` method takes one parameter: an associative array that contains simple field value conditions that need to match. Behind the scenes, it builds a query based on these and loads the returning entities. Do keep in mind that you cannot have complex queries here and access checks will NOT be taken into account in the query being built under the hood (`accessCheck(FALSE)`). So, for full control, just build the query yourself.

Reading entities

So, we have our entity loaded and we can now read its data. For content entities, this is where the TypedData knowledge comes into play. Before we look at that, let's see quickly how we can get the data from configuration entities. Let's inspect the Article `NodeType` for this purpose:

```
/** @var \Drupal\node\Entity\NodeType $type */
$type = \Drupal::entityTypeManager()->
  getStorage('node_type')->load('article');
```

The first and simplest thing we can do is inspect the individual methods on the entity type class. For example, `NodeType` has a `getDescription()` method, which is a handy helper for getting the description field:

```
$description = $type->getDescription();
```

This is always the best way to try to get the field values of configuration entities because you potentially get return type documentation that can come in handy for your IDE. Alternatively, the `ConfigEntityBase` class has the `get()` method, which can be used to access any of the fields:

```
$description = $type->get('description');
```

This is going to do the same thing and it is the common way any field can be accessed across the different configuration entity types. The resulting value is the raw field value, in this case, a string.

Apart from the typical field data, we have the entity keys (if you remember from the entity type plugin definitions). These are common for both configuration and content entities and the relevant accessor methods are found on the `EntityInterface`. Here are some of the more common ones:

```
$id = $type->id();
$label = $type->label();
$uuid = $type->uuid();
$bundle = $type->bundle();
$language = $type->language();
```

The resulting information naturally depends on the entity type. For example, configuration entities don't have bundles (some content entity types don't either). So, the `bundle()` method will return the name of the entity type if there are no bundles. By far, the most important one is `id()`. You will often also use `label()` as a shortcut to the primitive field value of the field used as the label for the entity. There are other entity keys as well that individual entity types can declare. For example, entity types that extend the `EditorialContentEntityBase`, such as the Node entity, have a `published` entity key and a corresponding `isPublished()` method. So, for any other entity keys, do check the respective entity type if you can use them.

Here are some extra methods you can use to inspect entities of any type:

- `isNew()` checks whether the entity has been persisted already.
- `getEntityTypeId()` returns the machine name of the entity type of the entity.
- `getEntityType()` returns the `EntityTypeInterface` plugin of the given entity.
- `getTypedData()` returns the `EntityAdapter` DataType plugin instance that wraps the entity. It can be used for further inspection as well as validation.

Moreover, we can also check whether they are content or configuration entities:

```
$entity instanceof ContentEntityInterface
$entity instanceof ConfigEntityInterface
```

Similarly, we can also check whether they are a specific type of entity:

```
$entity instanceof NodeInterface
```

This is similar to using `$entity->getEntityTypeId === 'node'` but it is much more explicit, plus the IDE can benefit from the information in many cases.

Now, let's turn to content entities and see how we can read their field data.

Like configuration entity types, many content entity types can have helper methods on their classes (or parent classes) to make accessing certain fields easier. For example, the Node entity type has the `getTitle()` method, which gets the first primitive value of its title field. However, let's see how we can apply what we learned in the TypedData section and navigate through the field values like a pro. To exemplify this, we will examine a simple article node.

Content entities also have the `get()` method, but unlike configuration entities, it doesn't return the raw field value. Instead, it returns an instance of `FieldItemList`:

```
/** @var \Drupal\node\NodeInterface $node */
$node = Node::load(1);
/** @var \Drupal\Core\Field\FieldItemListInterface
  $title */
$title = $node->get('title');
```

For quick prototyping, in this example, I used the static `load()` method on the content entity class to load an entity by ID. Under the hood, this will delegate to the relevant storage class. This is a quick alternative to using the entity type manager, but you should only rely on it wherever you cannot inject dependencies.

Here are some of the things we can learn about the title `FieldItemList`:

```
$parent = $title->getParent();
```

This is its parent (the DataType plugin it belongs to; in this case, the `EntityAdapter`):

```
$definition = $title->getFieldDefinition();
```

This is the `DataDefinitionInterface` of the list. In this case, it's a `BaseFieldDefinition` instance, but can be a `BaseFieldOverride` or a `FieldConfig` for fully configurable fields:

```
$item_definition = $title->getItemDefinition();
```

This is the `DataDefinitionInterface` for the individual items in the list, typically a `FieldItemDataDefinition`:

```
$total = $title->count();
$empty = $title->isEmpty();
$exists = $title->offsetExists(1);
```

These are some handy methods for inspecting the list. We can see how many items there are in it, whether it's empty, and whether there are any values at a given offset. Do keep in mind that value keys start at 0, so if the cardinality of the field is 1, the value will be at key 0.

To retrieve values from the list, we have several options. The most common thing you'll end up doing is the following:

```
$value = $title->value;
```

This is a magic property pointing to the first primitive value in the list. However, it's very important to note that, although most fields use the `value` property, some fields have a different property name. For example, entity reference fields use `target_id`:

```
$id = $field->target_id;
```

This returns the ID of the referenced entity. As a bonus, if you use the magic `entity` property, you get the fully loaded entity object:

```
$entity = $field->entity;
```

But enough of this magic way of doing things; let's see what other options we have:

```
$value = $title->getValue();
```

The `getValue()` method is present on all `TypedData` objects and returns the raw values that it stores. In our case, it will return an array with one item (since we only have one item in the list) that contains the individual item's raw values. So, an array with one element keyed `value` and the title string as its actual value. We will see in a moment why this is keyed `value`.

In some cases, we might want this to be returned and can find it useful. In other cases, though, we might just want the one field value. For this, we can ask for a given item in the list:

```
$item = $title->get(0);
$item = $title->offsetGet(0);
```

Both do the same thing and return a `FieldType` plugin which, as we saw, extends `FieldItemBase`, which is nothing more than a fancy Map DataType plugin. Once we have this, we again have a few choices:

```
$value = $item->getValue();
```

This again returns an array of the raw values, in this case, with one key called `value` and the string title as the actual value. So, just like when we called `getValue()` on the list, but this time, returning the raw values of only one item instead of an array of raw values of multiple items.

The reason why we have the actual title string keyed by `value` is that we are requesting the raw value from the `StringItem` field type plugin, which in this case happens to define the value column as `value`. Others might differ (for example, the entity reference field that stores a `target_id` named value).

Alternatively, again, we can navigate a bit further down:

```
$data = $item->get('value');
```

We know that this field uses the name `value` for its property, so we can use the `get()` method from the `Map` DataType (which, if you remember, is subclassed by the `StringItem` field type) to retrieve its own property by name. This is the same as what we did with the license plate map when we requested the `number` or `state` code. In the case of `StringItem` field types, this is going to be a `StringData` DataType plugin.

And as we did before, we can ask this final plugin for its value:

```
$value = $data->getValue();
```

Now we have the final string for the title. Of course, all the way down from the top, we can inspect the definitions of each of these plugins and learn more information about them.

Typically, day to day, you will use two methods for retrieving values from fields, depending on the cardinality. If the field has only one value, you will end up using something like this:

```
$title = $node->get('title')->value;
$id = $node->get('field_referencing_some_entity')->
    target_id;
$entity = $node->get('field_referencing_some_entity')->
    entity;
```

If the field can have multiple values, you will end up using something like this:

```
$names = $node->get('field_names')->getValue();
$tags = $node->get('field_tags')->referencedEntities();
```

The `referencedEntities()` method is a helper one provided by `EntityReferenceFieldItemList` (which is a subclass of `FieldItemList`) that loads all the referenced entities and returns them in an array keyed by the position in the field (the delta).

Manipulating entities

Now that we know how we can read field data programmatically, let's see how we can change this data and persist it to the storage. So, let's look at the same Node title field and update its value programmatically.

The most common way you can change a field value on a content entity is this:

```
$node->set('title', 'new title');
```

This works well with fields that have only one value (cardinality = 1) and, behind the scenes, this happens:

```
$node->get('title')->setValue('new title');
```

This one value gets transformed into a raw array of one value because we are dealing with a list of items and the first item receives the changed value. If the field has a higher cardinality and we pass only one value as such, we essentially remove all of them and replace them with only one. So, if we want to make sure we are not deleting items but instead adding to the list, we can do this:

```
$values = $node->get('field_multiple')->getValue();
$values[] = ['value' => 'extra value'];
$node->set('field_multiple', $values);
```

If we want to change a specific item in the list, we can do this:

```
$node->get('field_multiple')->get(1)->setValue('changed
    value');
```

This will change the value of the second item in the list. You just have to make sure it is set first:

```
$node->get('field_test')->offsetExists(1);
```

All these modifications we make to field values are, however, kept in memory (they are not persisted). To save them to a database, we just have to save the entity:

```
$node->save();
```

That's it. We can achieve the same thing via the entity type manager as well:

```
\Drupal::entityTypeManager()->getStorage('node')->
    save($node);
```

Since we are talking about saving, deleting entities can be done in the exact same way, except by using the delete() method on the entity object. We also have this method on the storage handler. However, it accepts an array of entities to delete, so you can use that to delete more entities at once.

Configuration entities have it a bit easier. This is how we can easily change the value of a configuration entity field:

```
/** @var \Drupal\node\Entity\NodeType $type */
$type = \Drupal::entityTypeManager()->
   getStorage('node_type')->load('article');
$type->set('name', 'News');
$type->save();
```

Nothing too complex going on here. We load the entity, set a property value, and save it using the same API.

Creating entities

Programmatically creating new entities is also not rocket science and, again, we use the entity type storage handler to do so:

```
$values = [
   'type' => 'article',
   'title' => 'My title'
];
/** @var \Drupal\node\NodeInterface $node */
$node = \Drupal::entityTypeManager()->getStorage('node')
   ->create($values);
$node->set('field_custom', 'some text');
$node->save();
```

The storage handler has the `create()` method, which takes one argument in the form of an associative array of field values. The keys represent the field names and the values represent the values. This is where you can initially set some simpler values, and for more complex fields, you still have the API we covered earlier.

If the entity type has bundles, such as the Node example above, the bundle needs to be specified in the `create()` method. The key it corresponds to is the entity key for the bundle. If you remember the Node entity type plugin, that is `type`.

That is pretty much it. Again, we need to save it in order to persist it in our storage.

Rendering content entities

Now, let's see what we can do with an entity to render it on the page. In doing so, we will stick to the existing view modes and try not to break it up into pieces for rendering in a custom template through our own theme hook. If you want to do that, you can. You should have all the knowledge for that already:

- Defining a theme hook with variables

- Querying and loading entities

- Reading the values of an entity

- Creating a render array that uses the theme hook

Instead, we will rely on the entity's default building methodology, which allows us to render it according to the display mode configured in the UI, so, for example, as a teaser or as the full display mode. As always, we will continue with the Node as an example.

The first thing we need to do is get our hands on the `view_builder` handler of the entity type. Remember this from the entity type plugin definition? Just like the storage handler, we can request it from the `EntityTypeManager`:

```
/** @var \Drupal\node\NodeViewBuilder $builder */
$builder = \Drupal::entityTypeManager()->
  getViewBuilder('node');
```

Now that we have that, the simplest way of turning our entity into a render array is to use the `view()` method:

```
$build = $builder->view($node);
```

By default, this will use the full view mode, but we can pass a second parameter and specify another, such as teaser or whatever we have configured. A third optional parameter is the langcode of the translation (if we have it) we want to render in.

The `$build` variable is now a render array that uses the `node` theme hook defined by the Node module. You will also notice a `#pre_render` theme property, which specifies a callable to be run before the rendering of this array. That is a reference back to the `NodeViewBuilder` (the node entity type view builder), which is responsible for preparing all the field values and all sorts of other processing that we are not going to cover now. But the `node.twig.html` template file, preprocessed by the `*_preprocess_node()` preprocessors, also plays a big role in providing some extra variables to be used or rendered in the template.

If we want, we can also build render arrays for multiple entities at once:

```
$build = $builder->viewMultiple($node);
```

This will still return a render array that contains multiple children for each entity being rendered. The `#pre_render` property I mentioned earlier, however, will stay at the top level and, this time, be responsible for building multiple entities.

Essentially, it is that simple to get from loading an entity to turning it into a render array. You have many different places where you can take control of the output. As I said, you can write your own theme hook and break up the entity into variables. You can also implement the preprocessor for its default theme functions and change some variables in there. You can even change the theme hook used and append a suggestion to it and then take it from there, as we saw in the chapter on theming:

```
$build = $builder->view($node);
$build['#theme'] = $build['#theme'] . '__my_suggestion';
```

Another important way in which we can control the output is by implementing a hook that gets fired when the entity is being built for rendering: `hook_entity_view()` or `hook_ENTITY_TYPE_view()`. So, let's see an example by which we want to append a disclaimer message at the bottom of all our Node entities when they are displayed in their `full` view mode. We can do something like this:

```
function hello_world_entity_view(array &$build,
\Drupal\Core\Entity\EntityInterface $entity,
\Drupal\Core\Entity\Display\EntityViewDisplayInterface
$display, $view_mode) {
  if ($entity->getEntityTypeId() === 'node' && $view_mode
    === 'full') {
    $build['disclaimer'] = [
      '#markup' => t('The content provided is for general
        information purposes only.'),
      '#weight' => 100
    ];
  }
}
```

The three important arguments we work with are the `$build` array passed by reference, which contains the render array for the entire entity, the `$entity` object itself, and the `$view_mode` the latter is being rendered in. So, all we have to do is add our own render bits inside the `$build` array. As a bonus, we try to ensure that the message gets printed at the bottom by using the `#weight` property on the render array.

Pseudo-fields

Drawing from our example on implementing `hook_entity_view()`, there's a neat little technique we can use to empower our site builders further with respect to that disclaimer message. This is by turning it into a *pseudo-field*. By doing this, site builders will be able to choose the bundles it should show on, as well as its position relative to the other fields, all through the UI in the **Manage display** section:

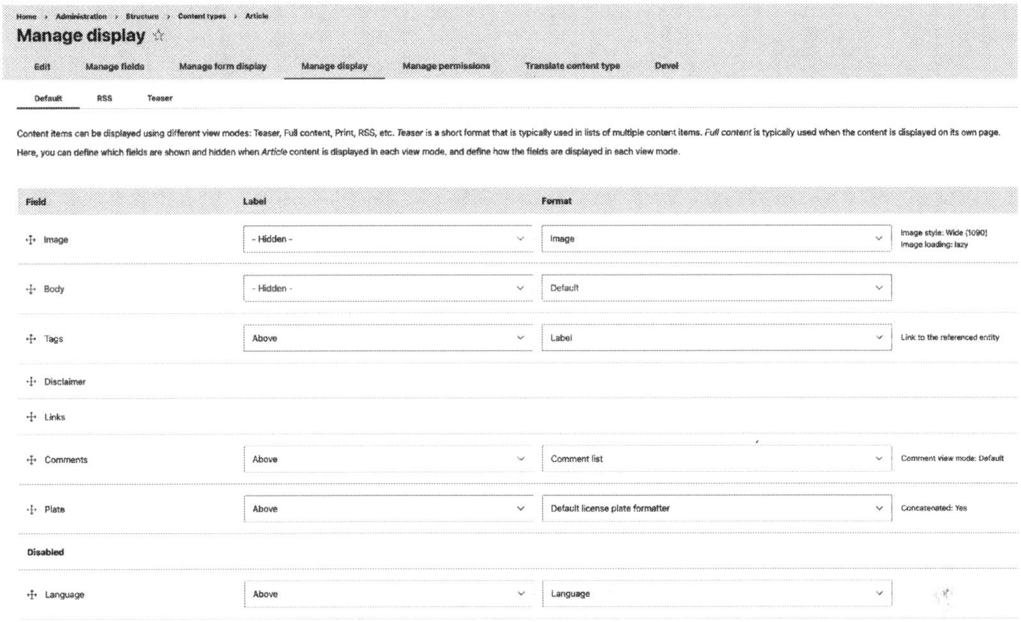

Figure 6.4: Pseudo-fields

So, there are two things we need to do for this. First, we need to implement `hook_entity_extra_field_info()` and define our *pseudo-field*:

```
/**
 * Implements hook_entity_extra_field_info().
 */
function hello_world_entity_extra_field_info() {
  $extra = [];

  foreach (NodeType::loadMultiple() as $bundle) {
    $extra['node'][$bundle->id()]['display']['disclaimer']
      = [
```

```
            'label' => t('Disclaimer'),
            'description' => t('A general disclaimer'),
            'weight' => 100,
            'visible' => TRUE,
        ];
    }


    return $extra;
}
```

As you can see, we loop through all the available node types, and for the node entity display, we add our disclaimer definition with some defaults to use. The weight and visibility will, of course, be overridable by the user, per node bundle.

Next, we need to go back to our hook_entity_view() implementation and make some changes. Because we know we want this applied to Node entities only, we can implement the more specific hook instead:

```
/**
 * Implements hook_ENTITY_TYPE_view().
 */
function hello_world_entity_view(array &$build,
\Drupal\Core\Entity\EntityInterface $entity,
\Drupal\Core\Entity\Display\EntityViewDisplayInterface
$display, $view_mode) {
  if ($display->getComponent('disclaimer')) {
    $build['disclaimer'] = [
      '#markup' => t('The content provided is for general
        information purposes only.'),
    ];
  }
}
```

In this case, we don't need to check for view modes or entity types, but rather use the entity view display configuration object to check for the existence of this extra disclaimer field (technically called a *component*). If found, we simply add our markup to the $build array. Drupal will take care of things like weight and visibility to match whatever the user has set through the UI, and that's it. Clearing the cache, we should still see our disclaimer message, but we can now control it a bit from the UI.

Entity validation

The last thing we are going to talk about in this chapter is entity validation and how we can make sure that entities and their fields contain valid data. When I say valid, I don't mean whether it complies with the strict TypedData definition but whether, within that, it complies with certain restrictions (constraints) we impose on it. As such, most of the time, entity validation applies to content entities. However, we can also run validation on configuration entities but only insofar as to ensure that the field values are of the correct data type as described in the configuration schema. And in this respect, we are talking about TypedData definitions under the hood.

Drupal uses the Symfony Validator component for applying constraints and then validating entities, fields, and any other data against those constraints. I do recommend that you check out the Symfony documentation page on this component to better understand its principles. For now, let's quickly see how it is applied in Drupal.

There are three main parts to validation: a constraint plugin, a validator class, and potential violations. The first is mainly responsible for defining what kind of data it can be applied to, the error message it should show, and which validator class is responsible for validating it. If it omits the latter, the validator class name defaults to the name of the constraint class with the word `Validator` appended to it. The validator, on the other hand, is called by the validation service to validate the constraint and build a list of violations. Finally, the violations are data objects that provide helpful information about what went wrong in the validation: things like the error message from the constraint, the offending value, and the path to the property that failed.

To better understand things, let's go back to the TypedData and see some simple examples because that is the level at which the validation happens:

```
$definition = DataDefinition::create('string');
$definition->addConstraint('Length', ['max' => 20]);
```

The data definitions have methods for applying and reading constraints. If you remember, one of the reasons why we need this API is to be able to enrich data with meta information. Constraints are such information. In this example, we are applying a constraint called `Length` (the plugin ID of the constraint) with some arbitrary parameters expected by that constraint (in this case, a maximum length, but a minimum would also work). Having applied this constraint, we are essentially saying that this piece of string data is only valid if it's shorter than 20 characters. And we can use it like so:

```
/** @var \Drupal\Core\TypedData\TypedDataInterface $data */
$data = \Drupal::typedDataManager()->create($definition,
  'my value that is too long');
$violations = $data->validate();
```

DataType plugins have a `validate()` method on them that uses the validation service to validate their underlying data definition against any of the constraints applied to it. The result is an instance of the `ConstraintViolationList` iterator, which contains a `ConstraintViolationInterface` instance for each validation failure. In this example, we should have a violation from which we can get some information like so:

```
/** @var \Symfony\Component\Validator\
   ConstraintViolationInterface
   $violation */
foreach ($violations as $violation) {
   $message = $violation->getMessage();
   $value = $violation->getInvalidValue();
   $path = $violation->getPropertyPath();
}
```

The `$message` is the error message that comes from the failing constraint, the `$value` is the actual incorrect value, and `$path` is a string representation of the hierarchical path down to the value that has failed. If you remember our license plate example or the content entity fields, TypedData can be nested, which means you can have all sorts of values at different levels. In our previous example, `$path` is, however, going to be " " (an empty string) because the data definition has only one level.

Let's revisit our license plate example and see how such a constraint would work there. Imagine we wanted to add a similar constraint to the state code definition:

```
$state_code_definition = DataDefinition::create('string');
$state_code_definition->addConstraint('Length', array('max'
   => 2));

// The rest of the setup code we saw earlier.

/** @var \Drupal\Core\TypedData\Plugin\DataType\Map $plate
*/
$plate = \Drupal::typedDataManager()->create
   ($plate_definition, ['state' => 'NYC', 'number' =>
      '405-307']);
$violations = $plate->validate();
```

If you look closely, I instantiated the plate with a `state` code longer than two characters. Now, if we ask our individual violations for the property path, we get `state`, because that is what we called the state definition property within the bigger map definition.

Content entities

Let's now see an example of validating constraints on entities. First of all, we can run the `validate()` method on an entire entity, which will then use its TypedData wrapper (`EntityAdapter`) to run a validation on all the fields on the entity, plus any of the entity-level constraints. The latter can be added via the `EntityType` plugin definition (the annotation). For example, the `Comment` entity type has this bit:

```
 *     constraints = {
 *       "CommentName" = {}
 *     }
```

This means that the constraint plugin ID is `CommentName` and it takes no parameters (since the braces are empty). We can even add constraints to entity types that do not "belong" to us by implementing `hook_entity_type_alter()`, for example:

```
function my_module_entity_type_alter(array &$entity_types)
{
  $node = $entity_types['node'];
  $node->addConstraint('ConstraintPluginID', ['option']);
}
```

Going one level below and knowing that content entity fields are built on top of the TypedData API, it follows that all those levels can have constraints. We can add the constraints regularly to the field definitions or, in the case of fields that are either not "ours" or are configurable fields, we can use hooks to add constraints. Using `hook_entity_base_field_info_alter()`, we can add constraints to base fields while with `hook_entity_bundle_field_info_alter()`, we can add constraints to configurable fields (and overridden base fields). Let's see an example of how we can add constraints to the Node ID field:

```
function my_module_entity_base_field_info_alter(&$fields,
  \Drupal\Core\Entity\EntityTypeInterface $entity_type) {
  if ($entity_type->id() === 'node') {
    $nid = $fields['nid'];
    $nid->addPropertyConstraints('value', ['Range' =>
      ['min' => 5, 'max' => 10]]);
  }
}
```

As you can see, we are still just working with data definitions. One thing to note, however, is that when it comes to base fields and configurable fields (which are lists of items), we also have the `addPropertyConstraints()` method available. This simply makes sure that whatever constraint we add is targeted to the actual items in the list (specifying which property) rather than the entire list, as would have happened had we used the main `addConstraint()` method. Another difference with this method is that constraints get wrapped into a `ComplexDataConstraint` plugin. However, you don't have to worry too much about that; just be aware when you see it.

We can even inspect the constraints found on a data definition object. For example, this is how we can read the constraints found on the Node ID field:

```
$nid = $node->get('nid');
$constraints = $nid->getConstraints();
$item_constraints = $nid->getItemDefinition()->
  getConstraints();
```

Where the `getConstraints()` method returns an array of constraint plugin instances.

Now, let's see how we can validate entities:

```
$node_violations = $node->validate();
$nid = $node->get('nid');
$nid_list_violations = $nid->validate();
$nid_item_violations = $nid->get(0)->validate();
```

The entity-level `validate()` method returns an instance of `EntityConstraintViolationList`, which is a more specific version of the `ConstraintViolationList` we talked about earlier. The latter is, however, returned by the `validate()` method of the other cases in the example above. But for all of them, inside, we have a collection of `ConstraintViolationInterface` instances from which we can learn some things about what was not validated.

The entity-level validation goes through all the fields and validates them all. Next, the list will contain violations of any of the items in the list, while the item will contain only the violations on that individual item in the list. The property path is something interesting to observe. The following is the result of calling `getPropertyPath()` on a violation found in all three of the resulting violation lists from the example above:

```
nid.0.value
0.value
value
```

As you can see, this reflects the TypedData hierarchy. When we validate the entire entity, it gives us a property path all the way down to the value: field name -> delta (the position in the list) -> property name. Once we validate the field, we already know what field we are validating, so that is omitted. And the same goes for the individual item (we also know the delta of the item).

A word of warning about base fields that can be overridden per bundle such as the Node title field. As I mentioned earlier, the base definition for these fields uses an instance of BaseFieldOverride, which allows certain changes to be made to the definition via the UI. In this respect, they are very close to configurable fields. The "problem" with this is that, if we tried to apply a constraint like we just did with the nid to, say, the Node title field, we wouldn't have gotten any violations when validating. This is because the validator performs the validation on the BaseFieldOverride definition rather than the BaseFieldDefinition.

This is no problem, though, as we can use hook_entity_bundle_field_info_alter() and do the same thing as we did before, which will then apply the constraint to the overridden definition. In doing so, we can also account for the bundle we want this applied to. This is the same way you apply constraints to a configurable field you create in the UI.

Configuration entities

Configuration entity fields are not exposed to the TypedData API in terms of data definition. If you remember, though, we do have the configuration schema, which describes the type of data that is considered valid in an entity. And in that schema, we can have a constraints option, which references the constraint plugin the value should be validated against. For example, here is the schema for the uuid field (found in core.data_types.schema.yml):

```
uuid:
  type: string
  label: 'UUID'
  constraints:
    Uuid: {}
```

Now, let's quickly see how we can validate a configuration entity. Here is a quick example:

```
$config_entity = \Drupal\views\Entity\
  View::load('content');
$config_entity->set(uuid, 'not a correct uuid');
$typed_config_entity =
\Drupal\Core\Entity\Plugin\DataType\ConfigEntityAdapter::
  createFromEntity($config_entity);
$violations = $typed_config_entity->validate();
```

The first thing we do is load a configuration entity. In this case, it's a View, but it doesn't matter as it's backed by a schema definition (found in `views.schema.yml`). By default, the entity is valid, so in this example, I change the `uuid` field to a string (not a correct UUID value). Then, for the actual validation, we create a new `ConfigEntityAdapter` instance (which is like the `EntityAdapter` we saw earlier for content entities). And we can now call `validate()` on that like before. The result will be a list of violations, which in the case of this example, will contain one that says we are using an invalid UUID value for the `uuid` field. And that is pretty much it.

Validation recap

As we've seen, Drupal applies the Symfony Validator component to its very own TypedData and Plugin API both for discoverability and data validation handling. In doing so, we get a low-level API for applying constraints to any kind of data, ranging from simple primitive data definitions all the way to complex entities and fields. We have not covered this here, but we can also easily create our own constraints and validators if the ones provided are not enough.

Summary

You didn't think you were ever going to see this heading, did you? This chapter has been very long and highly theoretical. We haven't built anything fun and the only code we saw was to exemplify most of the things we talked about. It was a difficult chapter, as it covered many complex aspects of data storage and handling. But trust me, these things are important to know, and this chapter can serve both as a starting point to dig deeper into the code and a reference to go back to when unsure of certain aspects.

We saw what the main options for storing data in Drupal are. Ranging from the State API all the way to entities, you have a host of alternatives. After covering the simpler ways, such as the State API, the private and shared tempstores, and the UserData API, we dove a bit deeper into the configuration system, which is a very important one to understand. There, we saw what kinds of configuration types we have, how to work with simple configuration, how it's managed and stored, and so on. Finally, in what was arguably the most complex part of the chapter, we looked at entities, both content and configuration. Just as you were recovering from reading all about how entity types are plugins with so many options, I hit you with the TypedData API. But right after that, we put it to good use and saw how we can interact with entities: querying, loading, manipulating, and validating data based on TypedData.

In the next chapter, we will apply in a very practical way a lot of the knowledge we learned in this one, especially related to content and configuration entities, but also plugin types and so on. So, that should be much more enjoyable, as we are going to create a new module that actually does something useful.

7

Your Own Custom Entity and Plugin Types

I am sure that you are looking forward to applying some of the knowledge gained from the previous chapters and doing something practical and fun. As promised, in this chapter, we will do just that. Also, apart from implementing our own entity types, we will cover some new things as well. So, here's the game plan.

The premise is that we want to have products on our site that hold some basic information, such as an ID, a name, and a product number. However, these products need to somehow get onto our site. One way will be manual entry. Another, more important way, will be through an import from multiple external sources (such as a JSON endpoint). Now, things will be kept simple. For all intents and purposes, these products aren't going to do much, so don't expect an e-commerce solution being laid out in front of you. Instead, we will practice modeling data and functionality in Drupal.

First, we will create a simple content entity type to represent our products. In doing so, we will make sure that we can use the UI to create, edit, and delete these products with ease by taking advantage of many Entity API benefits available out of the box.

Second, we will model our importing functionality. One side of the coin will be a simple configuration entity type to represent the configuration needed for our various importers. Again, we will make use of the Entity API for quick scaffolding and entity management. The other side will be a custom plugin type whose plugins will actually perform the import based on the configuration found in the entities. As such, these will be linked from the direction of the config entities, which will choose to use one plugin or another.

So these are the highlights. In building all this, we will see much of what is needed to define a content and configuration entity type with fields to hold data and configuration, as well as a plugin type to encapsulate logic.

The code we write in this chapter will go inside a new module called products. Since we have learned how to create a module from scratch, I will not cover the initial steps needed for getting started with this.

The main topics we will cover in this chapter are as follows:

- Creating our own custom entity type
- Creating our own custom plugin type
- Writing a custom Drush command

Our custom content entity type

As we saw in the previous chapter, when looking at the Node and NodeType entity types, entity type definitions belong inside the Entity folder of our module's namespace. In there, we will create a class called Product, which will have an annotation at the top to tell Drupal that this is a content entity type. This is the most important part of defining a new entity type:

```
namespace Drupal\products\Entity;

use Drupal\Core\Entity\ContentEntityBase;

/**
 * Defines the Product entity.
 *
 * @ContentEntityType(
 *   id = "product",
 *   label = @Translation("Product"),
 *   handlers = {
 *     "view_builder" = "Drupal\Core\Entity\
 *       EntityViewBuilder",
 *     "list_builder" = "Drupal\products\
 *       ProductListBuilder",
 *
 *     "form" = {
 *       "default" = "Drupal\products\Form\ProductForm",
 *       "add" = "Drupal\products\Form\ProductForm",
 *       "edit" = "Drupal\products\Form\ProductForm",
 *       "delete" = "Drupal\Core\Entity\
 *         ContentEntityDeleteForm",
```

```
 *       },
 *     "route_provider" = {
 *       "html" = "Drupal\Core\Entity\Routing\
 *           AdminHtmlRouteProvider"
 *     }
 *   },
 *   base_table = "product",
 *   admin_permission = "administer site configuration",
 *   entity_keys = {
 *     "id" = "id",
 *     "label" = "name",
 *     "uuid" = "uuid",
 *   },
 *   links = {
 *     "canonical" = "/admin/structure/product/{product}",
 *     "add-form" = "/admin/structure/product/add",
 *     "edit-form" = "/admin/structure/product/{product}/
 *         edit",
 *     "delete-form" = "/admin/structure/product/{product}/
 *         delete",
 *     "collection" = "/admin/structure/product",
 *   }
 * )
 */
class Product extends ContentEntityBase implements
  ProductInterface {}
```

In the above code block, I omitted the actual contents of the class to first focus on the annotation and some other aspects. We will see the rest of it shortly. However, the entire working code can be found in the accompanying repository.

If you remember the previous chapter, we have the ContentEntityType annotation with the entity type plugin definition. Our example is relatively barebones compared to Node, for example, because I wanted to keep things simple. It has no bundles and is not revisionable, nor translatable. Also, for some of its handlers, we fall back to the Entity API defaults.

The entity type ID and label are immediately visible, so no need to explain that; we can instead skip to the *handlers* section.

For the view builder handler, we choose to default to the basic `EntityViewBuilder` because there is nothing specific our products need to be rendered. Most of the time, this will be enough, but you can also extend this class and create your own.

For the list builder, although we are still keeping things simple, we need our own implementation in order to take care of things such as the list headers. We will see this class soon. The form handler for creating and editing products is our own implementation found inside the `Form` namespace of our module, and we will see it soon to get a better understanding. We rely on Drupal to help us out with the delete form, though.

Finally, for the route provider, we used the default `AdminHtmlRouteProvider`, which takes care of all the routes necessary for an entity type to be managed in the admin UI. This means that we no longer need to do anything for routing the links referenced in the `links` section of the annotation. Speaking of links, it makes sense to place them under the `admin/structure` section of our administration for our example, but you can choose another place if you want.

The database table our products will be stored in is `products`, and the permission needed for users to manage them is `administer site configuration`. I have deliberately omitted to create permissions specific to this entity type because we will cover this topic in a chapter dedicated to access. So, we will use this permission that comes with Drupal core.

Finally, we also have some basic entity keys to map to the respective fields.

Our `Product` class extends the `ContentEntityBase` class (since we don't need any "editorial" features such as Node, for example) and implements our very own `ProductInterface`, which will contain all the methods used to access relevant field values. Let's create this interface in the same `Entity` folder:

```
namespace Drupal\products\Entity;

use Drupal\Core\Entity\ContentEntityInterface;
use Drupal\Core\Entity\EntityChangedInterface;

/**
 * Represents a Product entity.
 */
interface ProductInterface extends ContentEntityInterface,
  EntityChangedInterface {

  /**
   * Gets the Product name.
   *
```

```php
 * @return string
 */
public function getName();

/**
 * Sets the Product name.
 *
 * @param string $name
 *
 * @return \Drupal\products\Entity\ProductInterface
 *   The called Product entity.
 */
public function setName($name);

/**
 * Gets the Product number.
 *
 * @return int
 */
public function getProductNumber();

/**
 * Sets the Product number.
 *
 * @param int $number
 *
 * @return \Drupal\products\Entity\ProductInterface
 *   The called Product entity.
 */
public function setProductNumber($number);

/**
 * Gets the Product remote ID.
 *
 * @return string
 */
```

```php
public function getRemoteId();

/**
 * Sets the Product remote ID.
 *
 * @param string $id
 *
 * @return \Drupal\products\Entity\ProductInterface
 *    The called Product entity.
 */
public function setRemoteId($id);

/**
 * Gets the Product source.
 *
 * @return string
 */
public function getSource();

/**
 * Sets the Product source.
 *
 *
 * @param string $source
 *
 * @return \Drupal\products\Entity\ProductInterface
 *    The called Product entity.
 */
public function setSource($source);

/**
 * Gets the Product creation timestamp.
 *
 * @return int
 */
```

```
   public function getCreatedTime();


   /**
     * Sets the Product creation timestamp.
     *
     * @param int $timestamp
     *
     * @return \Drupal\products\Entity\ProductInterface
     *    The called Product entity.
     */
   public function setCreatedTime($timestamp);
}
```

As you can see, we are extending not only the obligatory ContentEntityInterface but also the EntityChangedInterface, which provides some handy methods to manage the last changed date of the entities. Those method implementations will be added to our Product class via the EntityChangedTrait:

```
use EntityChangedTrait;
```

The methods on the ProductInterface are relatively self-explanatory. We will have a product name, number, remote ID, and source field, so it's nice to have getters and setters for those. If you remember, the Entity API provides the get() and set() methods with which we can consistently access and store field values across all entity types. However, I find that using an interface with well-defined methods makes code much clearer, not to mention that IDE autocompletion is a great time-saver. We also have a getter and setter for the created date field, which is a typical field that content entities have.

Now, we can take a look at the baseFieldDefinitions() method of our Product entity type and see how we can actually define our fields:

```
public static function baseFieldDefinitions
   (EntityTypeInterface $entity_type) {
   $fields = parent::baseFieldDefinitions($entity_type);

   $fields['name'] = BaseFieldDefinition::create('string')
     ->setLabel(t('Name'))
     ->setDescription(t('The name of the Product.'))
     ->setSettings([
       'max_length' => 255,
```

```php
    'text_processing' => 0,
  ])
  ->setDefaultValue('')
  ->setDisplayOptions('view', [
    'label' => 'hidden',
    'type' => 'string',
    'weight' => -4,
  ])
  ->setDisplayOptions('form', [
    'type' => 'string_textfield',
    'weight' => -4,
  ])
  ->setDisplayConfigurable('form', TRUE)
  ->setDisplayConfigurable('view', TRUE);

$fields['number'] = BaseFieldDefinition::
  create('integer')
  ->setLabel(t('Number'))
  ->setDescription(t('The Product number.'))
  ->setSettings([
    'min' => 1,
    'max' => 10000
  ])
  ->setDisplayOptions('view', [
    'label' => 'above',
    'type' => 'number_unformatted',
    'weight' => -4,
  ])
  ->setDisplayOptions('form', [
    'type' => 'number',
    'weight' => -4,
  ])
  ->setDisplayConfigurable('form', TRUE)
  ->setDisplayConfigurable('view', TRUE);
```

```php
$fields['remote_id'] = BaseFieldDefinition::create
  ('string')
  ->setLabel(t('Remote ID'))
  ->setDescription(t('The remote ID of the Product.'))
  ->setSettings([
    'max_length' => 255,
    'text_processing' => 0,
  ])
  ->setDefaultValue('');

$fields['source'] = BaseFieldDefinition::create('string')
  ->setLabel(t('Source'))
  ->setDescription(t('The source of the Product.'))
  ->setSettings([
    'max_length' => 255,
    'text_processing' => 0,
  ])
  ->setDefaultValue('');

$fields['created'] = BaseFieldDefinition::create
  ('created')
  ->setLabel(t('Created'))
  ->setDescription(t('The time that the entity was
    created.'));

$fields['changed'] = BaseFieldDefinition::create
('changed')
  ->setLabel(t('Changed'))
  ->setDescription(t('The time that the entity was last
    edited.'));

  return $fields;
}
```

First and foremost, we will need to inherit the base fields of the parent class. This includes things such as the ID and UUID fields.

Second, we define our own fields, starting with the product name field, which is of the `string` type. This `string` type is nothing more than a `FieldType` plugin, which I mentioned in the previous chapter. If you remember, this plugin extends a `TypedData` class itself. Apart from the obvious label and description, it has some settings, most notably a maximum length for the value, which is 255 characters. The `view` and `form` display options reference the `FieldFormatter` and `FieldWidget` plugins, respectively, responsible for how the field values should be rendered and input. Lastly, with the `setDisplayConfigurable()` method, we specify that some of the options on this field should be configurable through the UI.

Then, we have the `number` field, which is of the `integer` type and, for this example, is restricted to a number between 1 and 10,000. This restriction setting turns into a constraint under the hood. The rest of the options are similar to the name field.

Next, we have the `remote_id` string field, but it doesn't have any widget or display settings because we don't want to display or edit this value. It is mostly for internal use to keep track of the product ID of the remote source it came from. Similarly, the `source` string field is not displayed or configurable either because we want to use it to store the source of the product, where it has been imported from, and also to keep track of it programmatically.

Finally, the `created` and `changed` fields are special fields that store the timestamps for when the entity is created and modified. Not much more than that needs to be done because these field types automatically set the current timestamps as the field values.

By now, we can also see the rest of the class content, which is mostly made up of the methods required by our `ProductInterface`:

```
use EntityChangedTrait;

/**
 * {@inheritdoc}
 */
public function getName() {
  return $this->get('name')->value;
}


/**
 * {@inheritdoc}
 */
public function setName($name) {
  $this->set('name', $name);
  return $this;
```

```
}

/**
 * {@inheritdoc}
 */
public function getProductNumber() {
  return $this->get('number')->value;
}

/**
 * {@inheritdoc}
 */
public function setProductNumber($number) {
  $this->set('number', $number);
  return $this;
}

/**
 * {@inheritdoc}
 */
public function getRemoteId() {
  return $this->get('remote_id')->value;
}

/**
 * {@inheritdoc}
 */
public function setRemoteId($id) {
  $this->set('remote_id', $id);
  return $this;
}

/**
 * {@inheritdoc}
 */
public function getSource() {
```

```
    return $this->get('source')->value;
  }


  /**
   * {@inheritdoc}
   */
  public function setSource($source) {
    $this->set('source', $source);
    return $this;
  }


  /**
   * {@inheritdoc}
   */
  public function getCreatedTime() {
    return $this->get('created')->value;
  }


  /**
   * {@inheritdoc}
   */
  public function setCreatedTime($timestamp) {
    $this->set('created', $timestamp);
    return $this;
  }
```

As promised, we are making use of the `EntityChangedTrait` to handle the `changed` field and implement simple getters and setters for the values found in the fields we defined as base fields. If you remember the `TypedData` section, the way we access a value (since the cardinality is always 1 for these fields) is by running the following:

```
$this->get('field_name')->value
```

Before we finish off with our Product entity class, let's ensure we *use* all the remaining classes at the top:

```
use Drupal\Core\Entity\EntityChangedTrait;
use Drupal\Core\Entity\EntityTypeInterface;
use Drupal\Core\Field\BaseFieldDefinition;
```

Let's now move through the entity type plugin annotation and create the handlers we've been referencing there. We can start with the list builder, which we can place at the root of our namespace:

```php
namespace Drupal\products;

use Drupal\Core\Entity\EntityInterface;
use Drupal\Core\Entity\EntityListBuilder;

/**
 * EntityListBuilderInterface implementation for the
 *    Product entities.
 */
class ProductListBuilder extends EntityListBuilder {

  /**
   * {@inheritdoc}
   */
  public function buildHeader() {
    $header['id'] = $this->t('Product ID');
    $header['name'] = $this->t('Name');
    return $header + parent::buildHeader();
  }

  /**
   * {@inheritdoc}
   */
  public function buildRow(EntityInterface $entity) {
    /* @var $entity \Drupal\products\Entity\Product */
    $row['id'] = $entity->id();
    $row['name'] = $entity->toLink();
    return $row + parent::buildRow($entity);
  }

}
```

The purpose of this handler is to build the administration page that lists the available entities. On this page, we will then have some info about them, as well as operation links to edit and delete and whatever else we might need. For our products, we simply extend from the default `EntityListBuilder` class, but override the `buildHeader()` and `builderRow()` methods to add some information specific to our products. The names of these methods are self-explanatory, but one thing to keep in mind is that the keys from the `$header` array we return need to match the keys from the `$row` array we return. Also, of course, the arrays need to have the same number of records so that the table header matches the individual rows. If you look inside `EntityListBuilder`, you can note some other handy methods you might want to override, such as the one that builds the query and the one that loads the entities. For us, this is enough.

Our products list builder will have, for now, only two columns: the ID and the name. For the latter, each row will actually be a link to the product's canonical URL (the main URL for this entity in Drupal). The way we built the link to the entity is by using the shorthand `toLink()` method, which does nothing more than create a `Link` object with the label and canonical URL of the entity.

> **Note**
>
> The construct for the entity canonical route is in the `entity.[entity_type].canonical` format. Other useful entity links can be built by replacing the word `canonical` with the keys from the `links` definition of the `EntityType` plugin annotation.

That is pretty much it for the list builder, and we can move on to the form handler.

Since creating and editing an entity share so much in terms of what we need in the form, we use the same `ProductForm` for both of those operations. Let's create that form class now inside the *Form* directory of the module namespace:

```
namespace Drupal\products\Form;

use Drupal\Core\Entity\ContentEntityForm;
use Drupal\Core\Form\FormStateInterface;

/**
 * Form for creating/editing Product entities.
 */
class ProductForm extends ContentEntityForm {

  /**
   * {@inheritdoc}
   */
```

```php
public function save(array $form, FormStateInterface
  $form_state) {
  $entity = $this->entity;

  $status = parent::save($form, $form_state);

  switch ($status) {
    case SAVED_NEW:
      $this->messenger()->addMessage($this->t('Created
        the %label Product.', [
        '%label' => $entity->label(),
      ]));
      break;

    default:
      $this->messenger()->addMessage($this->t('Saved the
        %label Product.', [
        '%label' => $entity->label(),
      ]));
  }
  $form_state->setRedirect('entity.product.canonical',
    ['product' => $entity->id()]);
}

}
```

We extend ContentEntityForm, which is a specialized form class for content entities. It itself extends EntityForm, which then subclasses the FormBase we've already encountered in *Chapter 2, Creating Your First Module*. However, the former two give us a lot of the functionality needed to manage our entities without writing much code ourselves.

The only thing we actually want to do is override the save() method in order to write a message to the user, informing them that the product has either been created or updated. We know what happened because the EntityInterface::save() method returns a specific constant to denote the type of operation that occurred.

We also want to redirect to the canonical URL of the product entity when the save happens. This we do with a very handy method on the FormStateInterface object with which we can specify a route (and any necessary parameters), and it will make sure that when the form is submitted, the user will be redirected to that route. Neat, isn't it?

> **Note**
> You can see I used the helper `messenger()` method from the parent class to print the message to the user. I did this on purpose to keep things short, but it is in fact used statically as it's not been injected. As we saw in *Chapter 2, Creating Your First Module*, you should instead inject the `Messenger` service. Do refer back to that chapter for a recap on how to inject services if you are unsure.

As I mentioned, for the delete operation, we just use the `ContentEntityDeleteForm`, which does all we need: it presents a confirmation form where we submit and trigger the delete operation. This is a typical flow for deleting resources in Drupal. As we will see a bit later, for configuration entities, there will be some methods we will need to write ourselves for this same process to happen.

All our handlers are done now, and our product entity type is operational. However, in order to be able to work with it, let's create some links in the admin menu to be able to easily manage them.

First, create the `products.links.menu.yml` file:

```yaml
entity.product.collection:
  title: 'Product list'
  route_name: entity.product.collection
  description: 'List Product entities'
  parent: system.admin_structure
  weight: 100
```

This defines a menu link under the **Structure** link for the product list (the page built with our list builder handler, located at the `entity.product.collection` route).

Next, let's create some local tasks (tabs) so that we get handy links on the product page to edit and delete the product entity. So, inside a `products.links.task.yml` file:

```yaml
entity.product.canonical:
  route_name: entity.product.canonical
  base_route: entity.product.canonical
  title: 'View'

entity.product.edit_form:
  route_name: entity.product.edit_form
  base_route: entity.product.canonical
  title: 'Edit'
```

```
entity.product.delete_form:
  route_name: entity.product.delete_form
  base_route: entity.product.canonical
  title: Delete
  weight: 10
```

You remember this from *Chapter 5, Menus and Menu Links*, don't you? The base route is always the canonical route for the entity, which essentially groups the tabs together. Then, the routes we use for the other two tasks are the `edit_form` and `delete_form` links of the entity type. You can refer to the *links* section of the Entity type plugin annotation to understand where these come from. The reason we don't need to specify any parameters here (since those routes do require a product ID) is because the base route has that parameter in the URL already. So, the tasks will use that one. And this is very handy.

Finally, we also want an action link to create a new product entity, which will be on the product list page. So, inside the `products.links.action.yml` file:

```
entity.product.add_form:
  route_name: entity.product.add_form
  title: 'Add Product'
  appears_on:
    - entity.product.collection
```

Again, none of this should be new, as we covered it in detail in *Chapter 5, Menus and Menu Links*. We are finally done. Enable the module and you can play with the products.

If the `products` module was enabled on your site before writing all the entity code, please read the next subsection on performing entity updates.

To play with the products, we can go to `admin/structure/product` and take a look at our (empty) product entity list:

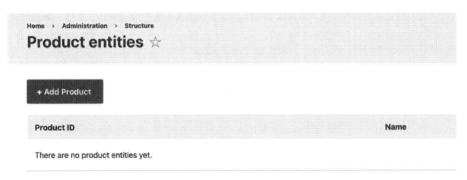

Figure 7.1: Our product entity list

We can create new products, edit them, and finally, delete them. Remember, due to our field configuration, the manual product creation/edit does not permit the remote_id and source fields to be managed. For our purpose, we want those to only be programmatically available since any manual products will be considered as not needing that data. For example, if we wanted to make the source field show up as a form widget, all we would have to do is change its base field definition to this:

```
$fields['source'] = BaseFieldDefinition::create('string')
  ->setLabel(t('Source'))
  ->setDescription(t('The source of the Product.'))
  ->setSettings([
    'max_length' => 255,
    'text_processing' => 0,
  ])
  ->setDefaultValue('')
  ->setDisplayOptions('form', [
    'type' => 'string_textfield',
    'weight' => -4,
  ]);
```

Also, we'd need to clear the cache. This would make the form element for the source field show up, but the value would still not be displayed on the canonical page of the entity because we have not set any view display options. In other words, we have not chosen a formatter.

However, in our case, the product entity is ready to store data, and all the TypedData APIs we practiced in the previous chapter with the Node entity type will work just as well with this one. So, we can now turn to writing our importer logic to get some remote products onto our website. But not before talking for a bit about entity updates.

Entity updates

Whenever we create an entity type or add a base field to an existing one, we need Drupal to run some updates so that the relevant database tables get created. The only way we can get away with not doing this is if the module where we define these is not yet installed. Because all tables get created upon module installation.

Otherwise, there are two ways to do this.

Development

The first way is intended solely for development. This means that you should only use it when iterating over your work locally, before deploying your application somewhere else. And the way to do it is by using the entity-updates command of the devel_entity_updates contributed module.

This command will compare the entity type definitions (the plugin) to the state of the database tables and perform the updates. Do keep in mind that it won't always work, depending on what kind of data you have already stored. For example, if you have entities, it won't delete the tables.

Production

The second way is to write the updates ourselves inside `hook_update_N()`. We will talk more about this hook later, but inside such a hook we can instruct Drupal to update the tables in order to match the definitions. And we can do so quite granularly. We are not going to get into details on all the types of updates that can be made because there are plenty. Instead, we will cover a simple example of how we could have installed our Product entity type using this approach:

```
function products_update_10000(&$sandbox) {
  \Drupal::entityTypeManager()->clearCachedDefinitions();

  $entity_type = \Drupal::entityTypeManager()->
    getDefinition('product');
  \Drupal::entityDefinitionUpdateManager()->
    installEntityType($entity_type);
}
```

For the time being, don't worry too much about the function this goes into. We will get back to this. But essentially this is the code that would install the Product entity type had our module been already installed on the site before us creating its definition in code. So, what happens here?

We first clear the cached definitions of the entity types defined in code to ensure our new Product definition is picked up. Then, we load this definition (the plugin basically) and pass that to the entity definition update manager. This is the service that has all the methods we need in order to perform updates to the entity type definitions: install, uninstall, create/update fields, and so on. I encourage you to check it out for more information: `Drupal\Core\Entity\EntityDefinitionUpdateManagerInterface`.

For now, since we are still developing, we will use the development approach because it's much faster and we do not have our site installed anywhere else.

Our custom plugin type

Since pretty much the second page of this book, you've been reading about how important plugins are and how widely they are used in Drupal. I have backed that claim with references to "this or that" being a plugin in basically every chapter. However, I have not really explained how you can create your own custom plugin type. Now, since our importer logic is a perfect candidate for plugins, I will do so here, and to exemplify the theory, we will implement an `Importer` plugin type.

The very first thing a plugin type needs is a manager service. This is responsible for bringing together two critical aspects of plugins (but not only): discovery and factory (instantiation). For these two tasks, it delegates to specialized objects. The most common method of discovery is through annotations (AnnotatedClassDiscovery), and the most common factory is the container-aware one—ContainerFactory. So, essentially, the manager is the central player that finds and processes all the plugin definitions and instantiates plugins. Also, it does so with the help of those other guys.

Many plugin types in Drupal, since they follow the defaults I mentioned before, use the DefaultPluginManager, or I should say, they extend this class. It provides them with the annotated discovery and container-aware factory. So, that is what we will do as well and see how simple it is to create a plugin type manager.

Typically, it lives in the Plugin namespace of the module, so ours can look like this:

```
namespace Drupal\products\Plugin;


use Drupal\Core\Plugin\DefaultPluginManager;
use Drupal\Core\Cache\CacheBackendInterface;
use Drupal\Core\Extension\ModuleHandlerInterface;


/**
 * Provides the Importer plugin manager.
 */
class ImporterManager extends DefaultPluginManager {

  /**
   * ImporterManager constructor.
   *
   * @param \Traversable $namespaces
   *    An object that implements \Traversable which
   *       contains the root paths
   *    keyed by the corresponding namespace to look for
   *       plugin implementations.
   * @param \Drupal\Core\Cache\CacheBackendInterface
   *    $cache_backend
   *    Cache backend instance to use.
   * @param \Drupal\Core\Extension\ModuleHandlerInterface
   *    $module_handler
   *    The module handler to invoke the alter hook with.
```

```
    */
  public function __construct(\Traversable $namespaces,
    CacheBackendInterface $cache_backend,
      ModuleHandlerInterface $module_handler) {
    parent::__construct('Plugin/Importer', $namespaces,
      $module_handler, 'Drupal\products\Plugin\
        ImporterPluginInterface', 'Drupal\products\
          Annotation\Importer');

    $this->alterInfo('products_importer_info');
    $this->setCacheBackend($cache_backend,
      'products_importer_plugins');
  }
}
```

Aside from extending the `DefaultPluginManager`, we will need to override the constructor and re-call the parent constructor with some parameters specific to our plugins. This is the most important part, and in order, these are the following (omitting the ones that are simply passed through):

- The relative namespace where plugins of this type will be found—in this case, in the `Plugin/ Importer` folder

- The interface each plugin of this type needs to implement—in our case, `Drupal\products\ Plugin\ImporterPluginInterface` (which we have to create)

- The `annotation` class used by our plugin type (the one whose class properties map to the possible annotation properties found in the DocBlock above the plugin class)—in our case, `Drupal\products\Annotation\Importer` (which we have to create)

In addition to calling the parent constructor with these options, we will need to provide the "alter" hook for the available definitions. This will make it possible for other modules to implement this hook and alter the found plugin definitions. The resulting hook in our case is `hook_products_ importer_info_alter`.

Lastly, we also provide a specific cache key for the backend responsible for caching the plugin definitions. This is for increased performance: as you should already know by now, creating a new plugin requires clearing the cache.

That's it for our manager. However, since this is a service, we will need to register it as such inside the `products.services.yml` file:

```
services:
  products.importer_manager:
```

```
class: Drupal\products\Plugin\ImporterManager
parent: default_plugin_manager
```

As you can see, we inherit the dependencies (arguments) from the `default_plugin_manager` service instead of duplicating them here again. If you remember from *Chapter 3, Logging and Mailing*, this is a neat little trick we can do.

Now, since we referenced some classes in the manager, we will need to create them. Let's start with the annotation class:

```
namespace Drupal\products\Annotation;

use Drupal\Component\Annotation\Plugin;

/**
 * Defines an Importer item annotation object.
 *
 * @see \Drupal\products\Plugin\ImporterManager
 *
 * @Annotation
 */
class Importer extends Plugin {

  /**
   * The plugin ID.
   *
   * @var string
   */
  public $id;

  /**
   * The label of the plugin.
   *
   * @var \Drupal\Core\Annotation\Translation
   *
   * @ingroup plugin_translatable
   */
  public $label;
}
```

This class needs to extend `Drupal\Component\Annotation\Plugin`, which is the base class for annotations and already implements `AnnotationInterface`.

For our purpose, we keep it simple. All we need is a plugin ID and a label. If we wanted to, we could add more properties to this class and describe them. It's standard practice to do so because otherwise there is no clear way to know which properties a plugin annotation can contain.

Next, let's also write the interface the plugins are required to implement:

```
namespace Drupal\products\Plugin;

use Drupal\Component\Plugin\PluginInspectionInterface;

/**
 * Defines an interface for Importer plugins.
 */
interface ImporterPluginInterface extends
  PluginInspectionInterface {

  /**
   * Performs the import.
   *
   * Returns TRUE if the import was successful or FALSE
   *   otherwise.
   *
   * @return bool
   */
  public function import();
}
```

Again, we keep it simple. For now, our importer will have only one method specific to it: `import()`. However, it will have other methods specific to plugins, which can be found in the `PluginInspectionInterface` we are extending. These are `getPluginId()` and `getPluginDefinition()` and are also quite important as the system expects to be able to get this info from the plugins.

Next, plugins of any type need to extend `PluginBase` because it contains a host of mandatory implemented methods (such as the ones I mentioned before). However, it is also best practice for the module that introduces a plugin type to also provide a base plugin class that plugins can extend. Its goal is to extend `PluginBase` and also provide all the necessary logic needed by all the plugins of this type. For example, when we create a new block, we extend `BlockBase`, which, somewhere down the line, extends `PluginBase`.

In our case, this base (abstract) class can look something like this:

```
namespace Drupal\products\Plugin;

use Drupal\Component\Plugin\Exception\PluginException;
use Drupal\Component\Plugin\PluginBase;
use Drupal\Core\Entity\EntityTypeManager;
use Drupal\Core\Plugin\ContainerFactoryPluginInterface;
use Drupal\products\Entity\ImporterInterface;
use GuzzleHttp\Client;
use Symfony\Component\DependencyInjection\
  ContainerInterface;

/**
 * Base class for Importer plugins.
 */
abstract class ImporterBase extends PluginBase implements
  ImporterPluginInterface, ContainerFactoryPluginInterface {

  /**
   * @var \Drupal\Core\Entity\EntityTypeManager
   */
  protected $entityTypeManager;

  /**
   * @var \GuzzleHttp\Client
   */
  protected $httpClient;

  /**
   * {@inheritdoc}
   */
  public function __construct(array $configuration,
    $plugin_id, $plugin_definition, EntityTypeManager
      $entityTypeManager, Client $httpClient) {
    parent::__construct($configuration, $plugin_id,
      $plugin_definition);
```

```
    $this->entityTypeManager = $entityTypeManager;
    $this->httpClient = $httpClient;

    if (!isset($configuration['config'])) {
      throw new PluginException('Missing Importer
        configuration.');
    }

    if (!$configuration['config'] instanceof
      ImporterInterface) {
      throw new PluginException('Wrong Importer
        configuration.');
    }
  }

  /**
   * {@inheritdoc}
   */
  public static function create(ContainerInterface
    $container, array $configuration, $plugin_id,
      $plugin_definition) {
    return new static(
      $configuration,
      $plugin_id,
      $plugin_definition,
      $container->get('entity_type.manager'),
      $container->get('http_client')
    );
  }
}
```

We implement ImporterPluginInterface to require subclasses to have the import() method. However, we also make the plugins container aware and already inject some helpful services. One is the EntityTypeManager because we expect all importers to need it. The other is the Guzzle HTTP client that we use in Drupal to make PSR-7 requests to external resources.

Adding this here is a judgment call. We can imagine more than one plugin needing external requests, but if it turns out they don't, we should surely remove it and add it only to that specific plugin. The opposite also holds true. If in the third plugin implementation we identify another common service, we can remove it from the plugins and inject it here. All while watching out for backward compatibility.

Before talking about those exceptions we're throwing in the constructor, it's important to know how the plugin manager creates a new instance of a plugin. It uses its `createInstance()` method, which takes a plugin ID as the first parameter and an optional array of plugin configuration as a second parameter. The relevant factory then passes that array of configuration to the plugin constructor itself as the second parameter. Oftentimes, this is empty. However, for our plugin type, we will need configuration to be passed to the plugin in the form of a configuration entity (which we have to create next). Without such an entity, we want the plugins to fail because they cannot work without the instructions found in this entity. So, in the constructor, we check whether `$configuration['config']` is an instance of `Drupal\products\Entity\ImporterInterface`, which will be the interface our configuration entity will implement (we don't have it yet). Otherwise, we throw the exception because this plugin cannot work without it.

Our plugin type is complete for now. Obviously, we don't have any plugins yet, and before we create one, let's create the Importer configuration entity type.

Our custom configuration entity type

If you remember `NodeType` from the previous chapter, you know the essentials of creating custom configuration entity types. So, let's create our `Importer` type now. Like before, we start with the annotation part, which this time is a `ConfigEntityType`:

```
namespace Drupal\products\Entity;

use Drupal\Core\Config\Entity\ConfigEntityBase;

/**
 * Defines the Importer entity.
 *
 * @ConfigEntityType(
 *   id = "importer",
 *   label = @Translation("Importer"),
 *   handlers = {
 *     "list_builder" = "Drupal\products\
 *       ImporterListBuilder",
 *     "form" = {
 *       "add" = "Drupal\products\Form\ImporterForm",
```

```
 *        "edit" = "Drupal\products\Form\ImporterForm",
 *        "delete" = "Drupal\products\Form\
 *           ImporterDeleteForm"
 *      },
 *      "route_provider" = {
 *        "html" = "Drupal\Core\Entity\Routing\
 *           AdminHtmlRouteProvider",
 *      },
 *    },
 *    config_prefix = "importer",
 *    admin_permission = "administer site configuration",
 *    entity_keys = {
 *      "id" = "id",
 *      "label" = "label",
 *      "uuid" = "uuid"
 *    },
 *    links = {
 *      "add-form" = "/admin/structure/importer/add",
 *      "edit-form" = "/admin/structure/importer/{importer}/
 *         edit",
 *      "delete-form" = "/admin/structure/importer/
 *         {importer}/delete",
 *      "collection" = "/admin/structure/importer"
 *    },
 *    config_export = {
 *      "id",
 *      "label",
 *      "url",
 *      "plugin",
 *      "update_existing",
 *      "source"
 *    }
 * )
 */
class Importer extends ConfigEntityBase implements
  ImporterInterface {}
```

As with the Product entity, we will need to create a list builder handler, as well as form handlers. In this case, though, we also need to create a form handler for the delete operation—we will soon see why. Finally, since we have a configuration entity, we also specify the config_export and config_prefix keys to be used for exporting. If you remember from the previous chapter, the first one denotes the names of the fields that should be persisted (we'll see them in a minute), while the second denotes the prefix the configuration names should get when stored. One thing you'll note is that we don't have a canonical link because we don't really need one—our entities don't need a detail page, hence no canonical link to it needs to be defined.

Now, it's time to create the ImporterInterface that the entities implement:

```php
namespace Drupal\products\Entity;

use Drupal\Core\Config\Entity\ConfigEntityInterface;
use Drupal\Core\Url;

/**
 * Importer configuration entity.
 */
interface ImporterInterface extends ConfigEntityInterface {

  /**
   * Returns the Url where the import can get the data
     from.
   *
   * @return Url
   */
  public function getUrl();

  /**
   * Returns the Importer plugin ID to be used by this
     importer.
   *
   * @return string
   */
  public function getPluginId();
```

```
/**
 * Whether or not to update existing products if they
   have already been imported.
 *
 * @return bool
 */
public function updateExisting();

/**
 * Returns the source of the products.
 *
 * @return string
 */
public function getSource();
}
```

In these configuration entities, we want to store, for now, a URL to the resource where the products can be retrieved from, the ID of the importer plugin to use, whether we want existing products to be updated if they had already been imported, and the source of the products. For all these fields, we create some getter methods. You'll note that getUrl() needs to return a Url instance. Again, we create a well-defined interface for the public API of the entity type as we did with the product entity type.

And this is what the Importer class body that implements this interface looks like:

```
/**
 * The Importer ID.
 *
 * @var string
 */
protected $id;

/**
 * The Importer label.
 *
 * @var string
 */
protected $label;
```

```
/**
 * The URL from where the import file can be retrieved.
 *
 * @var string
 */
protected $url;

/**
 * The plugin ID of the plugin to be used for processing
   this import.
 *
 * @var string
 */
protected $plugin;

/**
 * Whether or not to update existing products if they have
   already been imported.
 *
 * @var bool
 */
protected $update_existing = TRUE;

/**
 * The source of the products.
 *
 * @var string
 */
protected $source;

/**
 * {@inheritdoc}
 */
public function getUrl() {
  return $this->url ? Url::fromUri($this->url) : NULL;
}
```

```
/**
 * {@inheritdoc}
 */
public function getPluginId() {
    return $this->plugin;
}


/**
 * {@inheritdoc}
 */
public function updateExisting() {
    return $this->update_existing;
}


/**
 * {@inheritdoc}
 */
public function getSource() {
    return $this->source;
}
```

If you remember from the previous chapter, defining fields on a configuration entity type is as simple as defining properties on the class itself. Then, the interface methods are implemented next, and there is no rocket science involved in that. The getUrl() method, as expected, will try to create an instance of Url from the value.

Let's not forget the *use* statement for it at the top:

```
use Drupal\Core\Url;
```

Since we are talking about configuration here, we need a schema, so let's define that as well. If you remember, it goes inside the config/schema folder of our module in a *.schema.yml file. This can be named after the module and contains the schema definitions of all configurations of the module. Alternatively, it can be named after the individual configuration entity type, so, in our case, importer.schema.yml (to keep things neatly organized):

```
products.importer.*:
    type: config_entity
    label: 'Importer config'
    mapping:
```

```
id:
  type: string
  label: 'ID'
label:
  type: label
  label: 'Label'
url:
  type: uri
  label: Uri
plugin:
  type: string
  label: Plugin ID
update_existing:
  type: boolean
  label: Whether to update existing products
source:
  type: string
  label: The source of the products
```

If you recall, the wildcard is used to apply the schema to all configuration items that match the prefix. So, in our case, it will match all the importer configuration entities. And the individual field definition should be easy to understand from the lessons of the previous chapter.

Now, let's go ahead and create the list builder handler that will take care of the admin entity listing:

```
namespace Drupal\products;

use Drupal\Core\Config\Entity\ConfigEntityListBuilder;
use Drupal\Core\Entity\EntityInterface;

/**
 * Provides a listing of Importer entities.
 */
class ImporterListBuilder extends ConfigEntityListBuilder {

  /**
   * {@inheritdoc}
   */
```

```
public function buildHeader() {
    $header['label'] = $this->t('Importer');
    $header['id'] = $this->t('Machine name');
    return $header + parent::buildHeader();
}

/**
 * {@inheritdoc}
 */
public function buildRow(EntityInterface $entity) {
    $row['label'] = $entity->label();
    $row['id'] = $entity->id();
    return $row + parent::buildRow($entity);
}
}
```

This time we are extending the `ConfigEntityListBuilder`, which provides some functionalities specific to configuration entities. However, we are essentially doing the same as with the products listing—setting up the table header and the individual row data, nothing major. I recommend that you inspect `ConfigEntityListBuilder` and see what else you can do in the subclass.

Now, we can finally take care of the form handler and start with the default create/edit form:

```
namespace Drupal\products\Form;

use Drupal\Core\Entity\EntityForm;
use Drupal\Core\Form\FormStateInterface;
use Drupal\Core\Messenger\MessengerInterface;
use Drupal\Core\Url;
use Drupal\products\Plugin\ImporterManager;
use Symfony\Component\DependencyInjection\
    ContainerInterface;

/**
 * Form for creating/editing Importer entities.
 */
class ImporterForm extends EntityForm {
```

```php
/**
 * @var \Drupal\products\Plugin\ImporterManager
 */
protected $importerManager;

/**
 * ImporterForm constructor.
 *
 * @param \Drupal\products\Plugin\ImporterManager
 *     $importerManager
 * @param \Drupal\Core\Messenger\MessengerInterface
 *     $messenger
 */
public function __construct(ImporterManager
  $importerManager, MessengerInterface $messenger) {
  $this->importerManager = $importerManager;
  $this->messenger = $messenger;
}

/**
 * {@inheritdoc}
 */
public static function create(ContainerInterface
  $container) {
  return new static(
    $container->get('products.importer_manager'),
    $container->get('messenger')
  );
}

/**
 * {@inheritdoc}
 */
public function form(array $form, FormStateInterface
  $form_state) {
  $form = parent::form($form, $form_state);
```

```php
/** @var \Drupal\products\Entity\ImporterInterface
  $importer */
$importer = $this->entity;

$form['label'] = [
  '#type' => 'textfield',
  '#title' => $this->t('Name'),
  '#maxlength' => 255,
  '#default_value' => $importer->label(),
  '#description' => $this->t('Name of the Importer.'),
  '#required' => TRUE,
];

$form['id'] = [
  '#type' => 'machine_name',
  '#default_value' => $importer->id(),
  '#machine_name' => [
    'exists' => '\Drupal\products\Entity\
      Importer::load',
  ],
  '#disabled' => !$importer->isNew(),
];

$form['url'] = [
  '#type' => 'url',
  '#default_value' => $importer->getUrl() instanceof
    Url ? $importer->getUrl()->toString() : '',
  '#title' => $this->t('Url'),
  '#description' => $this->t('The URL to the import
   resource'),
  '#required' => TRUE,
];

$definitions = $this->importerManager->
  getDefinitions();
$options = [];
```

```
    foreach ($definitions as $id => $definition) {
      $options[$id] = $definition['label'];
    }

    $form['plugin'] = [
      '#type' => 'select',
      '#title' => $this->t('Plugin'),
      '#default_value' => $importer->getPluginId(),
      '#options' => $options,
      '#description' => $this->t('The plugin to be used
        with this importer.'),
      '#required' => TRUE,
    ];

    $form['update_existing'] = [
      '#type' => 'checkbox',
      '#title' => $this->t('Update existing'),
      '#description' => $this->t('Whether to update
        existing products if already imported.'),
      '#default_value' => $importer->updateExisting(),
    ];

    $form['source'] = [
      '#type' => 'textfield',
      '#title' => $this->t('Source'),
      '#description' => $this->t('The source of the
        products.'),
      '#default_value' => $importer->getSource(),
    ];

    return $form;
  }

  /**
   * {@inheritdoc}
   */
```

```
public function save(array $form, FormStateInterface
  $form_state) {
  /** @var \Drupal\products\Entity\Importer $importer */
  $importer = $this->entity;
  $status = $importer->save();

  switch ($status) {
    case SAVED_NEW:
      $this->messenger->addMessage($this->t('Created the
        %label Importer.', [
        '%label' => $importer->label(),
      ]));
      break;

    default:
      $this->messenger->addMessage($this->t('Saved the
        %label Importer.', [
        '%label' => $importer->label(),
      ]));
  }

  $form_state->setRedirectUrl($importer->toUrl
    ('collection'));
}

}
```

We are directly extending EntityForm in this case because configuration entities don't have a specific form class like content entities do. For this reason, we also have to implement the form elements for all our fields inside the form() method.

But first things first. We know we want the configuration entity to select a plugin to use, so, for this reason, we inject the ImporterManager we created earlier. We will use it to get all the existing definitions. And we also inject the Messenger service to use it later for printing a message to the user.

Inside the form() method, we define all the form elements for the fields. We use a textfield for the label and a machine_name field for the ID of the entity. The latter is a special JavaScript-powered field that derives its value from a "source" field (which defaults to the field label if one is not specified). It is also disabled if we are editing the form, and is using a dynamic callback to try to load an entity by the provided ID, failing validation if it exists already. This is useful to ensure that IDs are not duplicated.

Next, we have a `url` form element, which does some URL-specific validation and handling to ensure that a proper URL is added. Then, we create an array of `select` element options of all the available importer plugin definitions. For this, we use the plugin manager's `getDefinitions()`, from which we can get the IDs and labels. A plugin definition is an array that primarily contains the data found in the annotation and some other data processed and added by the manager (in our case, only defaults). At this stage, our plugins are not yet instantiated. And we use those options on the select list.

Finally, we have the simple `checkbox` and `textfield` elements for the last two fields, as we want to store the `update_existing` field as a Boolean and the `source` as a string.

The `save()` method is pretty much like it was in the Product entity form; we are simply displaying a message and redirecting the user to the entity listing page (using the handy `toUrl()` method on the entity to build the URL). Since we named the form elements exactly the same as the fields, we don't need to do any mapping of the form values to the field names. That is taken care of.

Let's now write the delete form handler:

```
namespace Drupal\products\Form;

use Drupal\Core\Entity\EntityConfirmFormBase;
use Drupal\Core\Form\FormStateInterface;
use Drupal\Core\Messenger\MessengerInterface;
use Drupal\Core\Url;
use Symfony\Component\DependencyInjection\
  ContainerInterface;

/**
 * Form for deleting Importer entities.
 */
class ImporterDeleteForm extends EntityConfirmFormBase {

  /**
   * ImporterDeleteForm constructor.
   *
   * @param \Drupal\Core\Messenger\MessengerInterface
   *   $messenger
   */
```

```php
public function __construct(MessengerInterface
  $messenger) {
  $this->messenger = $messenger;
}

/**
 * {@inheritdoc}
 */
public static function create(ContainerInterface
  $container) {
  return new static(
    $container->get('messenger')
  );
}

/**
 * {@inheritdoc}
 */
public function getQuestion() {
  return $this->t('Are you sure you want to delete
    %name?', ['%name' => $this->entity->label()]);
}

/**
 * {@inheritdoc}
 */
public function getCancelUrl() {
  return new Url('entity.importer.collection');
}

/**
 * {@inheritdoc}
 */
public function getConfirmText() {
  return $this->t('Delete');
}
```

```
/**
 * {@inheritdoc}
 */
public function submitForm(array &$form,
  FormStateInterface $form_state) {
  $this->entity->delete();

  $this->messenger->addMessage($this->t('Deleted @entity
    importer.', ['@entity' => $this->entity->label()]));

  $form_state->setRedirectUrl($this->getCancelUrl());
  }

}
```

As I mentioned earlier, for configuration entities, we will need to implement this form handler ourselves. However, it's not a big deal because we can extend `EntityConfirmFormBase` and just implement some simple methods:

- In `getQuestion()` we return the string to be used for the question on the confirmation form.
- In `getConfirmText()` we return the label of the delete button.
- In `getCancelUrl()` we provide the redirect URL for the user after either a cancellation or a successful delete.
- In `submitForm()` we delete the entity, print a success message, and redirect to the URL we set in `getCancelUrl()`.

And with this, we are done with our configuration entity type. The last thing we might want to do is create some menu links to be able to navigate to the relevant pages (the same as we did for the product entity type). For the entity list page, we can have this in our `products.links.menu.yml` file:

```
entity.importer.collection:
  title: 'Importer list'
  route_name: entity.importer.collection
  description: 'List Importer entities'
  parent: system.admin_structure
  weight: 99
```

There's nothing new here. We can also create the action link to add a new entity inside the `products.links.action.yml` file:

```
entity.importer.add_form:
  route_name: 'entity.importer.add_form'
  title: 'Add Importer'
  appears_on:
    - entity.importer.collection
```

We do the same thing here as we did with the products. However, we won't create local tasks because we don't have a canonical route for the configuration entities, so we don't really need them.

Now, if we clear our cache and go to `admin/structure/importer`, we should see the empty importer entity listing:

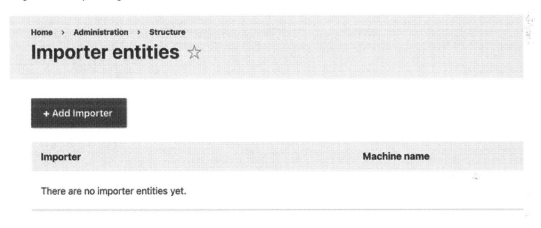

Figure 7.2: Importer Entity list

We can access the form to create a new Importer entity, but we cannot yet save it because there are no Importer plugins in the system for the Plugin field. We will deal with these next.

The Importer plugin

Alright, since all of our setup is in place, we can now go ahead and create our first importer plugin. As we defined it in the manager, these plugins need to go in the `Plugin/Importer` namespace of modules. So, let's start with a simple `JsonImporter`, which will use a remote URL resource to import products. This is an example JSON file that will be processed by this plugin, just for testing purposes:

```
{
    "products" : [
```

```
  {
     "id" : 1,
     "name": "TV",
     "number": 341
  },
  {
     "id" : 2,
     "name": "VCR",
     "number": 123
  },
  {
     "id" : 3,
     "name": "Stereo",
     "number": 234
  }
]
}
```

I know, VCR, right? We have an ID, a name, and a product number. This is all totally made-up information about products just to illustrate the process. So, let's create our `JsonImporter plugin`:

```php
namespace Drupal\products\Plugin\Importer;

use Drupal\products\Plugin\ImporterBase;

/**
 * Product importer from a JSON format.
 *
 * @Importer(
 *    id = "json",
 *    label = @Translation("JSON Importer")
 * )
 */
class JsonImporter extends ImporterBase {

  /**
    * {@inheritdoc}
```

```
 */
public function import() {
  $data = $this->getData();
  if (!$data) {
    return FALSE;
  }

  if (!isset($data->products)) {
    return FALSE;
  }

  $products = $data->products;
  foreach ($products as $product) {
    $this->persistProduct($product);
  }
  return TRUE;
}

/**
 * Loads the product data from the remote URL.
 *
 * @return object
 */
private function getData() {
  /** @var \Drupal\products\Entity\ImporterInterface
    $config */
  $config = $this->configuration['config'];
  $request = $this->httpClient->get($config->getUrl()->
    toString());
  $string = $request->getBody()->getContents();
  return json_decode($string);
}

/**
 * Saves a Product entity from the remote data.
 *
```

```php
   * @param object $data
   */
  private function persistProduct($data) {
    /** @var \Drupal\products\Entity\ImporterInterface
      $config */
    $config = $this->configuration['config'];

    $existing = $this->entityTypeManager->getStorage
      ('product')->loadByProperties(['remote_id' => $data
        ->id, 'source' => $config->getSource()]);
    if (!$existing) {
      $values = [
        'remote_id' => $data->id,
        'source' => $config->getSource()
      ];
      /** @var \Drupal\products\Entity\ProductInterface
        $product */
      $product = $this->entityTypeManager->getStorage
        ('product')->create($values);
      $product->setName($data->name);
      $product->setProductNumber($data->number);
      $product->save();
      return;
    }

    if (!$config->updateExisting()) {
      return;
    }

    /** @var \Drupal\products\Entity\ProductInterface
      $product */
    $product = reset($existing);
    $product->setName($data->name);
    $product->setProductNumber($data->number);
    $product->save();
  }
}
```

You can immediately spot the plugin annotation where we specify an ID and a label. Next, by extending `ImporterBase`, we inherit the dependent services and ensure that the required interface is implemented. Speaking of which, we basically only have to implement the `import()` method. So, let's break down what we are doing:

1. Inside the `getData()` method, we retrieve the product information from the remote resource. We do so by getting the URL from the `Importer` configuration entity and using Guzzle to make a request to that URL. We expect that to be JSON, so we just decode it as such. Of course, error handling is virtually nonexistent in this example, and that is not good.

2. We loop through the resulting product data and call the `persistProduct()` method on each item. In there, we first check whether we already have the product entity. We do so using the simple `loadByProperties()` method on the product entity storage and try to find products that have the specific source and remote ID. If one doesn't exist, we create it. This should all be familiar from the previous chapter when we looked at manipulating entities. If the product already exists, we first check whether, according to the configuration, we can update it, and only do so if that allows us to. The `loadByProperties()` method always returns an array of entities, but since we only expect to have a single product with the same remote ID and source combination, we simply reset this array to get to that one entity. Then, we just set the name and product number onto the entity.

As you can see, instead of using the Entity API/TypedData `set()` method to update the entity field values, we use our own interface methods. I find that this is a much cleaner, more modern, and IDE-friendly way because everything is very explicit.

One thing you might notice is the error handling in this import process, or more precisely, a lack thereof. This is because I kept things simple for the purpose of focusing on the current topic. Normally, you would want to maybe throw and catch some exceptions and definitely log some messages (both error and success). You know how to do the latter from *Chapter 3, Logging and Mailing*.

And that is pretty much it. We can now create our first importer entity and make it use this importer plugin (after clearing the cache of course):

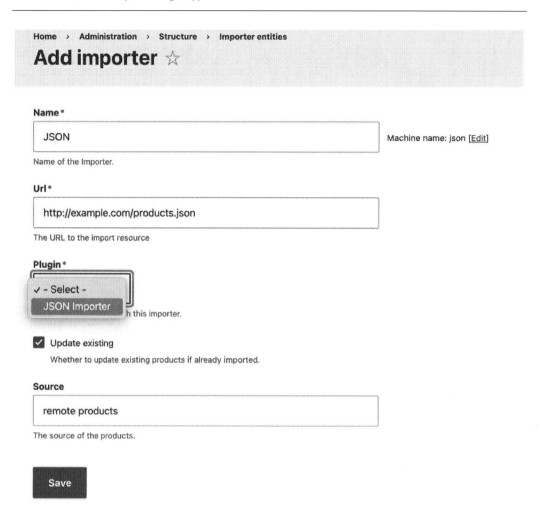

Figure 7.3: Creating an importer

The URL in the previous screenshot is a random URL where the example JSON file is found (you should use your own), and we can see the only plugin available to choose, as well as the other entity fields we created form elements for. By saving this new entity, we can make use of it programmatically (assuming that the products.json file referenced in the URL exists):

```
$config = \Drupal::entityTypeManager()->getStorage
  ('importer')->load('json');
$plugin = \Drupal::service('products.importer_manager')
  ->createInstance($config->getPluginId(), ['config' =>
    $config]);
$plugin->import();
```

We first load the importer entity by ID. Then, we use the `ImporterManager` service to create a new instance of a plugin using the `createInstance()` method. Only one parameter is required for it—the ID of the plugin—but as I said earlier, we want to pass the configuration entity to it because it depends on it. So we do just that. Then, we call the `import()` method on the plugin. After running this code, the product entity listing will show some shiny new products.

Let's, however, improve things a bit. Since the configuration entities and plugins are so tightly connected, let's use the plugin manager to do this entire thing rather than having to first load an entity and request the plugin from it. In other words, let's add a method to the plugin manager where we can pass the configuration entity ID, and it returns an instance of the relevant plugin; something like this:

```
public function createInstanceFromConfig($id) {
  $config = $this->entityTypeManager->getStorage
    ('importer')->load($id);
  if (!$config instanceof \Drupal\products\Entity\
    ImporterInterface) {
    return NULL;
  }

  return $this->createInstance($config->getPluginId(),
    ['config' => $config]);
}
```

Here, we essentially do the same thing as before, but we return NULL if there is no configuration entity found. You can choose to throw an exception if you want instead. However, as you may have correctly noticed, we also need to inject the `EntityTypeManager` into this class, so our constructor changes as well to take it as a last parameter and set it as a class property. You should be able to do that on your own. But we also need to alter the service definition for the plugin manager to add the `EntityTypeManager` as a dependency:

```
products.importer_manager:
  class: Drupal\products\Plugin\ImporterManager
  parent: default_plugin_manager
  arguments: ['@entity_type.manager']
```

As you can see, we keep the `parent` inheritance key so that all the parent arguments are taken in. On top, however, we add our own regular `arguments` key, which will append arguments to the ones that come from the parent.

And with this we have simplified things for the client code:

```
$plugin = \Drupal::service('products.importer_manager')
  ->createInstanceFromConfig('my_json_product_importer');
$plugin->import();
```

All we have to interact with is the plugin manager, and we can directly run the import. This is in some ways better because our configuration entities are not something we designed for being used by anyone else. They are simple configuration storage used by our importer plugins.

Content entity bundles

We have written a neat little piece of functionality. There are still improvements that we can and will make, but those are for later chapters when we cover other topics that we will need to learn about. Now, however, let's take a step back to our content entity type and extend our products a bit by enabling bundles. We want to have more than one type of product that can be imported. And this will be a bundle that will be an option to choose when creating an Importer configuration. However, first, let's make the product entity type "bundleable."

We start by adjusting our Product entity plugin annotation:

```
/**
 * Defines the Product entity.
 *
 * @ContentEntityType(
 *   ...
 *   label = @Translation("Product"),
 *   bundle_label = @Translation("Product type"),
 *   handlers = {
 *   ...
 *   entity_keys = {
 *      ...
 *     "bundle" = "type",
 *   },
 *   ...
 *   bundle_entity_type = "product_type",
 *   field_ui_base_route = "entity.product_type.edit_form"
 * )
 */
```

We add a `bundle_label` for our bundle, an entity key for it that will map to the `type` field, the `bundle_entity_type` reference to the configuration entity type that will act as a bundle for the products, and a `field_ui_base_route`. This latter option is something we could have added before but was not necessary. Now, we can (and should) add it because we need a route where we can configure our product entities from the point of view of managing UI fields and the bundles. We'll see these a bit later on.

Moreover, we also need to change something about the links. First, we will need to alter the `add-form` link:

```
"add-form" = "/admin/structure/product/add/
   {product_type}",
```

This will now take a product type in the URL to know which bundle we are creating. If you remember from the previous chapter when we were creating entities programmatically, the bundle is a required value from the beginning if the entity type has bundles.

Then, we add a new link, as follows:

```
"add-page" = "/admin/structure/product/add",
```

This will go to the initial `add-form` path but will list options of available bundles to select for creating a new product. Clicking on one of those will take us to the `add-form` link.

Since we made these changes, we also need to make a quick alteration to the product entity action link to use `add-page` instead of the `add-form` route:

```
entity.product.add_page:
   route_name: entity.product.add_page
   title: 'Add Product'
   appears_on:
     - entity.product.collection
```

This is required because, on the product entity list page (the collection URL), we don't have a product type in context, so we cannot build a path to `add-form`; nor would it be logical to do so as we don't know what type of product the user wants to create. As a quick bonus, if there is only one bundle, Drupal will redirect the user to the `add-form` link of that particular bundle.

The good thing is that since we specified an entity key for the bundle, we don't have to define the field that will reference the bundle configuration entity. It will be done for us by the parent, `ContentEntityType::baseFieldDefinitions()`. So, what is left to do is to create the `ProductType` configuration entity type that will serve as product bundles. We already know more or less how this works. Inside our `Entity` namespace, we start our class like so:

```
namespace Drupal\products\Entity;
```

```
use Drupal\Core\Config\Entity\ConfigEntityBundleBase;

/**
 * Product type configuration entity type.
 *
 * @ConfigEntityType(
 *   id = "product_type",
 *   label = @Translation("Product type"),
 *   handlers = {
 *     "list_builder" = "Drupal\products\
 *         ProductTypeListBuilder",
 *     "form" = {
 *       "add" = "Drupal\products\Form\ProductTypeForm",
 *       "edit" = "Drupal\products\Form\ProductTypeForm",
 *       "delete" = "Drupal\products\Form\
 *           ProductTypeDeleteForm"
 *     },
 *     "route_provider" = {
 *       "html" = "Drupal\Core\Entity\Routing\
 *           AdminHtmlRouteProvider",
 *     },
 *   },
 *   config_prefix = "product_type",
 *   admin_permission = "administer site configuration",
 *   bundle_of = "product",
 *   entity_keys = {
 *     "id" = "id",
 *     "label" = "label",
 *     "uuid" = "uuid"
 *   },
 *   links = {
 *     "canonical" = "/admin/structure/product_type/
 *         {product_type}",
 *     "add-form" = "/admin/structure/product_type/add",
 *     "edit-form" = "/admin/structure/product_type/
 *         {product_type}/edit",
```

```
 *      "delete-form" = "/admin/structure/product_type/
 *         {product_type}/delete",
 *      "collection" = "/admin/structure/product_type"
 *    },
 *    config_export = {
 *      "id",
 *      "label"
 *    }
 *  )
 */
class ProductType extends ConfigEntityBundleBase implements
  ProductTypeInterface  {

  /**
   * The Product type ID.
   *
   * @var string
   */
  protected $id;

  /**
   * The Product type label.
   *
   * @var string
   */
  protected $label;
}
```

Much of this is exactly the same as when we created the importer configuration entity type. The only difference is that we have the bundle_of key in the annotation, which denotes the content entity type this serves is a bundle for. Also, we don't really need any other fields. Because of that, the ProductTypeInterface can look as simple as this:

```
namespace Drupal\products\Entity;

use Drupal\Core\Config\Entity\ConfigEntityInterface;
```

```
/**
 * Product bundle interface.
 */
interface ProductTypeInterface extends
  ConfigEntityInterface {}
```

Let's quickly take a look at the individual handlers, which will seem very familiar by now as well. The list builder looks almost the same as for the Importer:

```
namespace Drupal\products;

use Drupal\Core\Config\Entity\ConfigEntityListBuilder;
use Drupal\Core\Entity\EntityInterface;

/**
 * List builder for ProductType entities.
 */
class ProductTypeListBuilder extends
  ConfigEntityListBuilder {

  /**
   * {@inheritdoc}
   */
  public function buildHeader() {
    $header['label'] = $this->t('Product type');
    $header['id'] = $this->t('Machine name');
    return $header + parent::buildHeader();
  }

  /**
   * {@inheritdoc}
   */
  public function buildRow(EntityInterface $entity) {
    $row['label'] = $entity->label();
    $row['id'] = $entity->id();
    return $row + parent::buildRow($entity);
  }
}
```

The create/edit form handler also looks very similar, albeit much simpler due to not having many fields on the configuration entity type:

```
namespace Drupal\products\Form;

use Drupal\Core\Entity\EntityForm;
use Drupal\Core\Form\FormStateInterface;
use Drupal\Core\Messenger\MessengerInterface;
use Symfony\Component\DependencyInjection\
  ContainerInterface;

/**
 * Form handler for creating/editing ProductType entities
 */
class ProductTypeForm extends EntityForm {

  /**
   * ProductTypeForm constructor.
   *
   * @param \Drupal\Core\Messenger\MessengerInterface
   *    $messenger
   */
  public function __construct(MessengerInterface
    $messenger) {
    $this->messenger = $messenger;
  }

  /**
   * {@inheritdoc}
   */
  public static function create(ContainerInterface
    $container) {
    return new static(
      $container->get('messenger')
    );
  }
```

```php
/**
 * {@inheritdoc}
 */
public function form(array $form, FormStateInterface
  $form_state) {
  $form = parent::form($form, $form_state);

  /** @var \Drupal\products\Entity\ProductTypeInterface
    $product_type */
  $product_type = $this->entity;
  $form['label'] = [
    '#type' => 'textfield',
    '#title' => $this->t('Label'),
    '#maxlength' => 255,
    '#default_value' => $product_type->label(),
    '#description' => $this->t('Label for the Product
      type.'),
    '#required' => TRUE,
  ];

  $form['id'] = [
    '#type' => 'machine_name',
    '#default_value' => $product_type->id(),
    '#machine_name' => [
      'exists' => '\Drupal\products\Entity\
        ProductType::load',
    ],
    '#disabled' => !$product_type->isNew(),
  ];

  return $form;
}

/**
 * {@inheritdoc}
 */
```

```
public function save(array $form, FormStateInterface
  $form_state) {
  $product_type = $this->entity;
  $status = $product_type->save();

  switch ($status) {
    case SAVED_NEW:
      $this->messenger->addMessage($this->t('Created the
        %label Product type.', [
        '%label' => $product_type->label(),
      ]));
      break;

    default:
      $this->messenger->addMessage($this->t('Saved the
        %label Product type.', [
        '%label' => $product_type->label(),
      ]));
  }
  $form_state->setRedirectUrl($product_type->
    toUrl('collection'));
  }
}
```

Since we created the form for saving field values, we mustn't forget about the configuration schema for this entity type:

```
products.product_type.*:
  type: config_entity
  label: 'Product type config'
  mapping:
    id:
      type: string
      label: 'ID'
    label:
      type: label
      label: 'Label'
```

Next, we should also quickly write the form handler for deleting product types:

```php
namespace Drupal\products\Form;

use Drupal\Core\Entity\EntityConfirmFormBase;
use Drupal\Core\Form\FormStateInterface;
use Drupal\Core\Messenger\MessengerInterface;
use Drupal\Core\Url;
use Symfony\Component\DependencyInjection\
  ContainerInterface;

/**
 * Form handler for deleting ProductType entities.
 */
class ProductTypeDeleteForm extends EntityConfirmFormBase {

  /**
   * ProductTypeDeleteForm constructor.
   *
   * @param \Drupal\Core\Messenger\MessengerInterface
   *    $messenger
   */
  public function __construct(MessengerInterface
    $messenger) {
    $this->messenger = $messenger;
  }

  /**
   * {@inheritdoc}
   */
  public static function create(ContainerInterface
    $container) {
    return new static(
      $container->get('messenger')
    );
  }
```

```php
/**
 * {@inheritdoc}
 */
public function getQuestion() {
  return $this->t('Are you sure you want to delete
    %name?', ['%name' => $this->entity->label()]);
}

/**
 * {@inheritdoc}
 */
public function getCancelUrl() {
  return new Url('entity.product_type.collection');
}

/**
 * {@inheritdoc}
 */
public function getConfirmText() {
  return $this->t('Delete');
}

/**
 * {@inheritdoc}
 */
public function submitForm(array &$form,
  FormStateInterface $form_state) {
  $this->entity->delete();

  $this->messenger->addMessage($this->t('Deleted @entity
    product type.', ['@entity' => $this->entity->
      label()]));

  $form_state->setRedirectUrl($this->getCancelUrl());
}

}
```

You should already be familiar with what we're doing here as it's the same as with the Importer entities.

Finally, we should create the menu link to the `ProductType` entity list URL, just like we did for the other two entity types inside `products.links.menu.yml`:

```
entity.product_type.collection:
  title: 'Product types'
  route_name: entity.product_type.collection
  description: 'List Product bundles'
  parent: system.admin_structure
  weight: 99
```

And the same for the action link used to create a new product bundle, inside `products.links.action.yml`:

```
entity.product_type.add_form:
  route_name: 'entity.product_type.add_form'
  title: 'Add Product type'
  appears_on:
    - entity.product_type.collection
```

Now, we are done. We can clear the caches and run the `drush entity-updates` development command because Drupal needs to create the `type` field on the product entities. Once that is done, we can go to the UI at `admin/structure/product_type` and see our changes.

> **Note**
>
> If when running the `entity-updates` command you encounter an error that says that the field storage definition for "type" could not be found, it means you've likely encountered a bug in Drupal. Either use the patch from the Drupal issue queue (#3126661) or simply uninstall the module and install it back to recreate the product entity type directly with the bundle field installed on it. Hopefully, this is temporary and you won't encounter this problem.

We now have a Product type entity listing where we can create Product bundles. Moreover, we also have some extra operations since this entity type is used as a bundle: we can manage fields and displays (both for viewing and the forms) for each individual bundle:

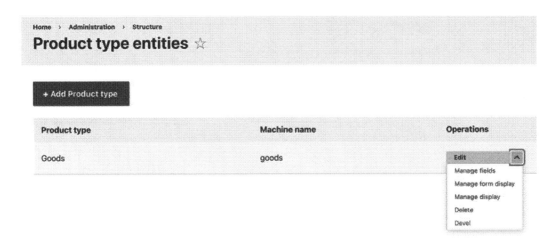

Figure 7.4: Managing our product type fields

Managing fields and displays would have been possible before creating the bundle had we provided the `field_ui_base_route` to the Product entity type and created a menu link for it.

Now we can add fields to our individual bundles and can distinguish between our product types—for example, we can have a bundle for goods and one for services. We can well imagine that the two types might require a different set of fields and/or they are being pulled from different external resources. So, let's just update our importing logic to allow the selection of a bundle because now it is actually mandatory to specify one when attempting to create a product.

We start by adding a new field to the Importer entity type. First, for the interface change:

```
/**
 * Returns the Product type that needs to be created.
 *
 * @return string
 */
public function getBundle();
```

Then, we will implement it in the class:

```
/**
 * The product bundle.
 *
 * @var string
 */
```

```
protected $bundle;
...
/**
 * {@inheritdoc}
 */
public function getBundle() {
  return $this->bundle;
}
```

Next, we must include the new field in the configuration schema:

```
...
bundle:
  type: string
  label: The product bundle
```

And add it to the list of fields that get exported with the entities:

```
*    config_export = {
*        "id",
...
*        "bundle"
*    }
```

The last thing we will need to do on the Importer entity type is to add the form element for choosing a bundle:

```
$form['bundle'] = [
  '#type' => 'entity_autocomplete',
  '#target_type' => 'product_type',
  '#title' => $this->t('Product type'),
  '#default_value' => $importer->getBundle() ? $this->
    entityTypeManager->getStorage('product_type')->
      load($importer->getBundle()) : NULL,
  '#description' => $this->t('The type of products that
    need to be created.'),
  '#required' => TRUE,
];
```

Here, we use an `entity_autocomplete` form element, which gives us the option to use an autocomplete text field to look up an existing entity and select one of the found ones. The ID of the selected entity will then be submitted in the form as the value. This field definition requires choosing a `#target_type`, which is the entity type we want to autocomplete. One thing to note is that even if the submitted value is only the ID (in our case, a string), the `#default_value` requires the full entity object itself (or an array of entity objects). This is because the field shows more information about the referenced entity than just the ID.

In order to load the referenced entity for the default value, we need to inject the `EntityTypeManager`. You should already know how to do this injection, so I'm not going to show it again here. We simply tack on the dependency to the `Messenger` service, which is already being injected.

That should be it for the Importer entity type alterations. The one last thing we need to do is handle the bundle inside the `JsonImporter` plugin we wrote. However, this is as simple as adding the `type` value when creating the product entity:

```
if (!$existing) {
  $values = [
    'remote_id' => $data->id,
    'source' => $config->getSource(),
    'type' => $config->getBundle(),
  ];
  /** @var \Drupal\products\Entity\ProductInterface
    $product */
  $product = $this->entityTypeManager->getStorage
    ('product')->create($values);
  ...
```

And there we have it. Running the import code will now create products of the bundle specified in the Importer configuration.

Our own Drush command

So, our logic is in place, but we will need to create a handy way we can trigger the imports. One option is to create an administration form where we go and press a button. However, a more typical example is a command that can be added to the crontab and that can be run at specific intervals automatically. So, that's what we are going to do now, and we will do so using Drush.

The Drush command we are going to write will take an optional parameter for the ID of the Importer configuration entity we want to process. This will allow the use of the command for more than just one importer. Alternatively, passing no options will process each importer (in case this is something we want to do later on).

One thing to note is that we won't focus on performance in this example. This means the command will work just fine for smaller sets of data, but it would be better to use a queue and/or batch processing for larger sets. We will have a chapter dedicated to these subsystems later on, but for now, let's get on with our example.

Before we actually write our new Drush command, let's make some alterations to our logic as they will make sense in the context of what we want to do.

First, let's add a getter method to the Importer plugins to retrieve the corresponding configuration entities. We start with the interface like so:

```
/**
 * Returns the Importer configuration entity.
 *
 * @return \Drupal\products\Entity\ImporterInterface
 */
public function getConfig();
```

Then, to the `ImporterBase` class, we can add the implementation (it will be the same for all individual plugin instances):

```
/**
 * {@inheritdoc}
 */
public function getConfig() {
  return $this->configuration['config'];
}
```

As you can see, it's not rocket science.

Second, let's add a `createInstanceFromAllConfigs()` method to the `ImporterManager`, which will return an array of plugin instances for each existing Importer configuration entity:

```
public function createInstanceFromAllConfigs() {
  $configs = $this->entityTypeManager->getStorage
    ('importer')->loadMultiple();
  if (!$configs) {
    return [];
  }
  $plugins = [];
  foreach ($configs as $config) {
```

```
    $plugin = $this->createInstanceFromConfig($config->
      id());
    if (!$plugin) {
      continue;
    }

    $plugins[] = $plugin;
  }

  return $plugins;
}
```

Here, we use the `loadMultiple()` method on the entity storage handler, which, if we use it without any arguments, will load all existing entities. If we get any results, we use our existing `createInstanceFromConfig()` method to instantiate the plugins based on each configuration entity. That's it; we can now go ahead and create our Drush command. There are a few steps we need to take.

We need to create a *composer.json* file for our module. It can look very barebones:

```
{
  "name": "drupal/products",
  "description": "Importing products like a boss.",
  "type": "drupal-module",
  "autoload": {
    "psr-4": {
      "Drupal\\products\\": "src/"
    }
  },
  "extra": {
    "drush": {
      "services": {
        "drush.services.yml": "^10"
      }
    }
  }
}
```

Apart from the normal boilerplate package and autoloader information, we have an `extras` section where we specify a YAML file where Drush can find the service definition that contains the commands.

Now that we have referenced the Drush-specific services file, let's go ahead and create it. It looks exactly like the other services files we're used to:

```yaml
services:
  products.commands:
    class: Drupal\products\Commands\ProductCommands
    arguments: [,@products.importer_manager']
    tags:
      - { name: drush.command }
```

As you can see, we have another tagged service (`drush.command`) whose class should contain some Drush commands. And I already know we will need the plugin manager, so we are already adding it as an argument.

So, let's see how we can start the command class, which should go in the `Commands` namespace of our module:

```php
namespace Drupal\products\Commands;

use Drush\Commands\DrushCommands;
use Symfony\Component\Console\Input\InputOption;
use Drupal\products\Plugin\ImporterManager;

/**
 * Drush commands for products.
 */
class ProductCommands extends DrushCommands {

  /**
   * @var \Drupal\products\Plugin\ImporterManager
   */
  protected $importerManager;

  /**
   * ProductCommands constructor.
   *
```

```
 * @param \Drupal\products\Plugin\ImporterManager
     $importerManager
 */
public function __construct(ImporterManager
  $importerManager) {
  $this->importerManager = $importerManager;
}

/**
 * Imports the Products
 *
 * @option importer
 *   The importer config ID to use.
 *
 * @command products-import-run
 * @aliases pir
 *
 * @param array $options
 *   The command options.
 */
public function import($options = ['importer' =>
  InputOption::VALUE_OPTIONAL]) {
  // ... add the logic here.
}

}
```

We are extending the DrushCommands base class to inherit all the things necessary or useful for Drush commands. And we have a single method that maps to a single command. What makes this an actual command is an annotation at the top, which describes all the things related to it:

- @command is the most important and specifies the actual Drush command name.

- @alias specifies other aliases for the command.

- @param is simple documentation of what input arguments the command takes. In our case, we don't have any mandatory arguments. We do have optional arguments though. If we wanted mandatory arguments, we could have simply added more method parameters without defaults.

- @option specifies the name of the option that can be passed; this is found inside the $options array parameter as one of its keys. And since it's optional, we use a constant to denote that.

With this definition, we can already use the command. After we clear the cache we can run the command as in the following examples:

```
drush products-import-run
drush products-import-run —importer=
  my_json_product_importer
```

Obviously, nothing will happen if we run these because the callback method is empty. So, let's flesh it out:

```
$importer = $options['importer'];

if (!is_null($importer)) {
  $plugin = $this->importerManager->
    createInstanceFromConfig($importer);
  if (is_null($plugin)) {
    $this->logger()->error(t('The specified importer does
      not exist.'));
    return;
  }


  $this->runPluginImport($plugin);
  return;
}

$plugins = $this->importerManager->createInstanceFrom
  AllConfigs();
if (!$plugins) {
  $this->logger()->error(t('There are no importers to
    run.'));
  return;
}

foreach ($plugins as $plugin) {
  $this->runPluginImport($plugin);
}
```

What is happening here? First, we check if an importer ID was passed as an option. If yes, we simply use our importer manager to create an instance of the corresponding plugin and delegate it to a helper method to run the import on that plugin. Otherwise, we use the built-in Drush logger to log an error. On the contrary, if no importer ID has been passed, we use our new `createInstanceFromAllConfigs()` method on the plugin manager to create plugin instances from all existing configuration entities. We then loop through each and, again, delegate to our helper method to run them.

Before we conclude, let's see the helper method as well:

```
protected function runPluginImport(\Drupal\products\Plugin\
   ImporterPluginInterface $plugin) {
   $result = $plugin->import();
   $message_values = ['@importer' => $plugin->getConfig()
     ->label()];
   if ($result) {
     $this->logger()->notice(t('The "@importer" importer has
       been run.', $message_values));
     return;
   }

   $this->logger()->error(t('There was a problem running the
     "@importer" importer.', $message_values));
}
```

This method is mostly used for logging the result of the plugin import: a different message depending on the success of the process. And in doing so, we use the actual Importer label rather than the ID that was passed, which makes it nicer to read.

Now if we clear the caches, we can run the command again (with or without an importer ID) and see that it correctly imports the products and prints the message to the terminal. Better yet, we can now add it to our crontab and have it run at specific intervals, once a day, for example.

Summary

In this chapter, we got to implement some fun stuff. We created our very own content and configuration entity types as well as a custom plugin type to handle our logic.

What we built was a Product entity type that holds some product-like data in various types of fields. We even created a bundle configuration entity type so that we can have multiple types of products with the possibility of different fields per bundle—a great data model.

We wanted to be able to import products from all sorts of external resources. For this reason, we created the Importer plugin type, which is responsible for doing the actual imports—a great functional model. However, these plugins only work based on a set of configurations, which we represented via a configuration entity type. These can then be created in the UI and exported into YAML files like any other configuration.

Finally, to use the importers, we created a Drush command, which can process either a single Importer or all the existing ones. This can be used inside a crontab for automatic imports.

There are still some shortcomings in the way we constructed the importing functionality. For example, we added the URL field on the Importer configuration entity as if all imports need to happen from an external resource. What if we want an import to be from a CSV file? The URL field would be superfluous, and we'd need a file upload field on the configuration entity. This very much points to the differences between generic Importer configuration values and plugin-specific ones. In future chapters, we'll come back to our module and make some adjustments in this respect.

In the next chapter, we will look at the Database API and how we can directly interact with the underlying storage engine.

8

The Database API

In the previous two chapters, we talked extensively about our options as Drupal module developers for modeling and storing data. We also saw some examples of how to use things such as the State, Configuration, and Entity APIs, going into greater detail about the latter by using it to build something useful. One of the key takeaways from those chapters is that the need for custom database tables and/ or direct queries against them and the database has become minimal.

The Entity system is flexible and robust, the combination of configuration and content entities providing much of the needs for storing data. Moreover, the Entity query and loading mechanisms have also made finding them easy. Odds are, this is enough for most of your use cases.

Furthermore, storage subsystems such as the State API (key/value) and UserData have also removed much of the need to create custom tables to store that kind of "one-off" data. Also, the Configuration API provides a unified way to model exportable data, leaving no need for anything else.

However, apart from these features, Drupal also has a strong Database API that actually powers them under the hood. This API is made available to us in case we need it. For example, we can create our own database tables and then run queries against them however we want, all through a secure layer that can work on top of multiple types of databases.

Creating custom database tables is not something you will do very often—maybe never—but in this chapter, you will still learn how the API works in order to do so. There are contributed modules out there that have legitimate uses for them, and who knows, you might also. So, it is still important to understand this system. However, even more pertinent is the API for running queries (particularly select queries), because you may need to run these, even against entities. There are times in which the entity query does not provide all you need, so looking up entities based on complex queries can, in fact, be more common. Hence, we will cover how to do that in this chapter, as well.

More concretely, in this chapter, we will start by creating a couple of database tables so that we can see how the Schema API works in Drupal. Then, we will see the various ways we can perform queries against these tables by using the database abstraction layer. We can create two different types of select queries, and we will practice both. For the others (`INSERT`, `UPDATE`, and `DELETE`), there is a standard way of doing it. Next, we will take a look at how queries can be altered and how we can tag them for better targeting. Finally, we will look at the database update hooks, the purpose of which is to make database updates once the tables have already been created. And if you remember, also to perform updates to the entity table schemas.

The topics we will cover in this chapter are the following:

- The Schema API
- Running and altering queries
- Database update hooks and post update hooks

The Schema API

The purpose of the Schema API is to allow the defining of database table structures in PHP and to have Drupal interact with the database engine and turn those definitions into a reality. Apart from the fact that we don't ever have to see things such as CREATE TABLE, we ensure that our table structures can be applied to multiple types of databases. If you remember, in *Chapter 1, Developing for Drupal 10*, I mentioned that Drupal can work with MySQL, PostgreSQL, SQLite, and others, if they support PDO, so the Schema API ensures this cross-compatibility.

The central component of the Schema API is hook_schema(). This is used to provide the initial table definitions of a given module. Implementations of this hook belong in the *.install file of the module and are fired when the module is first installed. If alterations need to be made to existing database tables, there are a number of methods that can be used inside update hooks to make these changes.

In this section, we will create a new module called sports in which we want to define two tables: players and teams. The records in the former can reference records in the latter, as each player can be part of only one team at a time. This is a simple example, and one which could, and should, be implemented using entities. However, for the purpose of demonstrating the database API, we will stick with the manual setup.

So, in our sports.install file; we can implement hook_schema() as follows:

```
/**
 * Implements hook_schema().
 */
function sports_schema() {
  $schema = [];

  $schema['teams'] = [
    'description' => 'The table that holds team data.',
    'fields' => [
      'id' => [
```

```php
      'description' => 'The primary identifier.',
      'type' => 'serial',
      'unsigned' => TRUE,
      'not null' => TRUE,
    ],
    'name' => [
      'description' => 'The team name.',
      'type' => 'varchar',
      'length' => 255,
      'not null' => TRUE,
    ],
    'description' => [
      'description' => 'The team description.',
      'type' => 'text',
      'size' => 'normal',
    ],
  ],
  'primary key' => ['id'],
];

$schema['players'] = [
  'description' => 'The table that holds player data.',
  'fields' => [
    'id' => [
      'description' => 'The primary identifier.',
      'type' => 'serial',
      'unsigned' => TRUE,
      'not null' => TRUE,
    ],
    'team_id' => [
      'description' => 'The ID of the team it belongs
        to.',
      'type' => 'int',
      'unsigned' => TRUE,
    ],
    'name' => [
```

```
        'description' => 'The player name.',
        'type' => 'varchar',
        'length' => 255,
        'not null' => TRUE,
      ],
      'data' => [
        'description' => 'Arbitrary data about the
         player.',
        'type' => 'blob',
        'size' => 'big',
      ],
    ],
    'primary key' => ['id'],
  ];

  return $schema;
}
```

Implementations of this hook need to return an associative array keyed by the table name whose values are an array that defines the respective table. The table definition consists of various types of information, particularly the individual column definitions (fields), and also things such as which fields represent the primary key, foreign keys (strictly for documentation purposes), unique keys, and indexes. For a full reference to all the available options, check out the Drupal.org (https://www.drupal.org/) documentation pages for the Schema API.

In our example, we defined the two tables we mentioned and defined their fields inside the fields array. The primary key indicates which of the fields will be used for that purpose, opting for the standard id field for both. Speaking of which, the latter is a field of the type serial, which means that it is an integer that has an auto-increment option to it. For number fields such as integer, float, and numeric, the unsigned option means that numbers cannot go below 0. Also, not null is pretty easy to understand—it prevents the column from ever being empty.

For the team and player name, we opted for a simple varchar field that takes a maximum of 255 characters (a pretty standard table column definition), and these, too, cannot be null. The description field, on the other hand, is of the text type with the normal size (as opposed to tiny, small, medium, or big). In here, we want to store strings that are longer than 255 characters.

Lastly, for the player table, we also have a team_id, which is a simple integer field, and a data column, in which we want to store some arbitrary serialized data. This is a blob type, which can also be big or normal.

That is pretty much all for our schema definitions. Installing the `sports` module will create these tables for us automatically, according to these definitions. Also, just as important, uninstalling the module will delete these tables, so we don't need to do any kind of handling. However, if our module is already enabled and we add this implementation afterward, it won't get fired. Instead, we will need to implement an update hook and use the `drupal_install_schema()` function, which will trigger it, like this:

```
drupal_install_schema('sports');
```

We will see more about update hooks soon.

Running queries

Now that we have some tables to work with, let's see how we can run queries against them. If you are following along for testing purposes, feel free to add some dummy data into the tables via the database management tool of your choice. We will look at `INSERT` statements soon, but before that, we will need to talk about the most common types of query you'll run—`SELECT`.

Queries using the Drupal database abstraction layer are run using a central database connection service—`database`. Statically, this can be accessed via a shortcut:

```
$database = \Drupal::database();
```

This service is a special one compared to the ones we saw before because it is actually created using a factory. This is its definition to better help you understand what I mean:

```
database:
    class: Drupal\Core\Database\Connection
    factory: Drupal\Core\Database\Database::getConnection
    arguments: [default]
```

This is a definition by which the responsibility for the instantiation is delegated to the factory instead of the container as we've seen before. So, the resulting class does not necessarily need to match the one specified for the `class` key. However, in this case, the `Drupal\Core\Database\Connection` is an abstract base class that the resulting service extends. Again, in this case, the `arguments` are responsible for specifying the type of connection that it has to create. The site-default type is used (MySQL, usually), which means that the resulting service will be an instance of `Drupal\Core\Database\Driver\mysql\Connection`.

From this connection service, we can then request the relevant object with which we can build queries. So, let's see how these work in practice.

Select queries

There are two ways we can run select queries in Drupal. One is by writing actual SQL query strings, and the other is by using a query builder object to do so. The second option is the recommended approach, as they can be deconstructed and altered by others before being executed.

The first type of select query is typically used for simpler queries, but if you are an SQL guru, it can actually be faster and easier to write a complex query using that method. Moreover, they rely on developers to ensure that the SQL statement is compatible with the underlying database. So, it is up to you which of the two types you choose, considering all of these factors.

Let's first take a look at how we can run a basic query against our tables using the first method. We'll then see how the same query can be run using the other way:

```
$database = \Drupal::database();
$result = $database->query("SELECT * FROM {players} WHERE
    [id] = :id", [':id' => 1]);
```

This is a simple SQL statement. We passed the query string as the first argument to the `query()` method of the connection object. The second argument is an array of placeholder values for this query string. These are found throughout the SQL string proceeded by a colon (`:id`) and are later replaced with the value that maps to the same key in the placeholder values array. Another thing to note is that the table name in the query is surrounded by curly braces. This is because, in reality, table names can be prefixed when the site is installed, and our code should not concern itself with that prefix. Drupal will prepend it automatically.

Now, let's take a look at how we can run the same query using the query builder:

```
$result = $database->select('players', 'p')
    ->fields('p')
    ->condition('id', 1)
    ->execute();
```

This time, we will use the `select()` method on the connection object to get our hands on a `SelectInterface` instance with which we can build our query. We need to pass the table we want to query, as well as an alias for that table. This is particularly important when performing joins. Then, we use the `fields()` method to specify which of the table columns we want to retrieve. The first parameter is the table alias, whereas the second (optional) is an array of column names. All columns will be included in this case (`*`). Next, we have a single condition being applied to the query for the `id` column and the value `1`. The third optional parameter is the operator that defaults to `=`. Lastly, we execute the query and get the same result as with the previous example.

You will immediately note, if you remember, that the structure of this query builder is very similar to the Entity Query, and the components are also chainable to a certain extent, as we will see.

Handling the result

Both of the previous queries return a `StatementInterface`, which is iterable. So, to access its data, we can do this:

```
foreach ($result as $record) {
  $id = $record->id;
  $team_id = $record->team_id;
  $name = $record->name;
  $data = $record->data;
}
```

Each item in the loop is a `stdClass`, and their property names are the actual names of the columns returned, while their values are the column values.

Alternatively, the `StatementInterface` also has some fetcher methods that can prepare the results for us in different ways. These mostly come from the parent `\PDOStatement` class, which is native PHP. The simplest is `fetchAll()`:

```
$records = $result->fetchAll();
```

This returns an array of `stdClass` objects, as we saw before, so it does all the looping to extract the records for us. If we want this array keyed by the value of a field in the record, we can perform the following:

```
$records = $result->fetchAllAssoc('id');
```

This will use the value in the `id` field to key the array.

If we're expecting single records, we can also use the `fetch()` method, which returns only one such object (the next one in the result set); `fetchObject()` does the same thing.

More complex select queries

Let's create a more complex query now, to join our team table and retrieve the team information in the same record as the player:

```
$result = $database->query("SELECT * FROM {players} p JOIN
  {teams} t ON t.[id] = p.[team_id] WHERE p.[id] = :id",
    [':id' => 1])->fetchAll();
```

This will return the same record as before, but inclusive of the values from the matching team record. Note that since we have a join, we had to use table aliases here as well. There is one problem with this query, though—since both tables have the `name` column, we cannot use * to include all of the fields, as they will get overridden. Instead, we need to include them manually:

```
$database->query("SELECT p.[id], p.[name] as player_name,
    t.[name] as team_name, t.[description] as
        team_description, p.[data] FROM {players} p JOIN
            {teams} t ON t.[id] = p.[team_id] WHERE p.[id] =
                :id", [':id' => 1])->fetchAll();
```

As you can see, we specified the fields from both tables we wanted to include, and we indicated different names as aliases where there was a name conflict. Now, let's write the same query using the query builder:

```
$query = $database->select('players', 'p');
$query->join('teams', 't');
$query->addField('p', 'name', 'player_name');
$query->addField('t', 'name', 'team_name');
$query->addField('t', 'description', 'team_description');
$result = $query
    ->fields('p', ['id', 'data'])
    ->condition('p.id', 1)
    ->execute();

$records = $result->fetchAll();
```

First of all, not all methods on the query builder are chainable. The `join()` method (and the other types of join methods, such as `innerJoin()`, `leftJoin()`, and `rightJoin()`), and the `addField()` method are prominent examples. The latter is a way we can add fields to the query by specifying an alias (we cannot do it via the `fields()` method). Moreover, the `condition()` field is also prefixed with the table alias it needs to be in (which was not necessary before when we didn't use a join).

For more information about all the other methods useful for building queries, check out the `SelectInterface` and `ConditionInterface`. They are typically well documented in there.

Range queries

Since limiting queries to a certain range depends on the underlying database engine, we also have the `queryRange()` method on our database connection service, which we can use to write queries that include ranges:

```
$result = $database->queryRange("SELECT * FROM {players}",
    0, 10);
```

In this example, we query for all the players and limit the result set to the first 10 records (from 0 to 10). So, with this method, the placeholder value array is the fourth parameter after `$from` and `$count`.

Alternatively, using the `SELECT` query builder, we have a method on the `SelectInterface` whereby we can specify a range. So, in that format, the previous query would look like this:

```
$result = $database->select('players', 'p')
    ->fields('p')
    ->range(0, 10)
    ->execute();
```

As you can see, we have the `range()` method, which takes those arguments and limits the query.

> **A note on running select queries on Entity tables:**
>
> If you can do so using the Entity Query, use that. If not, feel free to use the database API. And if you must, stick to using the query to figure out the IDs of the entities you need, but then use the entity storage handler to load those entities properly.

Pagers

Now that we have seen how to make `SELECT` queries of all kinds, let's see how we can use Drupal's built-in pagination capabilities and how pagers work in Drupal. We will illustrate these by running some queries and rendering the results inside a table. Refer to *Chapter 4, Theming*, if you don't remember the theming aspects of outputting a table.

Our playground will be inside a new controller method (`SportsController::players()`) which maps to the route with the `/players` path. Refer to *Chapter 2, Creating Your First Module*, for a refresher on how to create routes if you don't remember.

The first thing we'll do is create a simple query that loads all the players and outputs them inside a table. We'll stick to only showing the player names for simplicity:

```
/**
 * Renders a table of players.
```

```
 */
public function players() {
  $query = $this->database->select('players', 'p')->
    fields('p');
  $result = $query->execute()->fetchAll();
  $header = [$this->t('Name')];
  $rows = [];

  foreach ($result as $row) {
    $rows[] = [
      $row->name
    ];
  }

  $build = [];
  $build[] = [
    '#theme' => 'table',
    '#header' => $header,
    '#rows' => $rows,
  ];

  return $build;
}
```

All of this should already be familiar to you, including how to inject the database connection service. We are running the query and preparing the data for a table, using the `table` theme hook to render it. You'll note that we are creating a `$build` array so that we can include more things in the final output.

By navigating to `/players`, we should now already see a table with our player names. This will be our baseline from which to explore pagers.

Pagers work by storing some information regarding a query in the global state, namely the total number of items to be paged, the limit of items per page, and an identifier for the respective pager (so we can potentially have multiple pagers at once). All of this information is set using the following code (you don't have to add this anywhere now):

```
pager_default_initialize($total, $limit, $element = 0);
```

Moreover, the current page is determined by the query parameter in the URL, named `page`.

Once the pager is initialized, we have a `pager` render element we can use to easily render a themed pager that uses this information and builds all the necessary links to move between the pages. As query builders, we then have to read the current page and use that inside our query.

However, there is a much simpler way to work with pagers, and that is using *select extenders*. These are *decorator* classes for the SELECT query class we've seen before, and they allow us to decorate it with an extra piece of functionality, such as pagers or sorting; they encapsulate the necessary functionality for handling pagers in the query. So, let's see it in action.

Here is how our player query would look using the `PagerSelectExtender`:

```
$limit = 5; // The number of items per page.
$query = $this->database->select('players', 'p')
  ->fields('p')
  ->extend('\Drupal\Core\Database\Query\
    PagerSelectExtender')
  ->limit($limit);
$result = $query->execute()->fetchAll();
```

As you can see, we have an `extend()` method on the SELECT query builder, which allows us to pass the name of the class that will decorate the resulting SELECT query class. This also provides us with a new method called `limit()`, through which we specify the number of records to load per page. Under the hood, it uses the `range()` method we saw earlier. Moreover, when running the query, it initializes the pager for us using `pager_default_initialize()`, and even determines the current page all on its own. So typically, you'll use the extender directly.

> **The Decorator Pattern**
>
> The *Decorator Pattern* is an object-oriented programming design pattern that allows us to statically or dynamically add behavior to an existing object without altering how it, or other objects of the same class, behave inside. A decorator essentially wraps an existing object to provide extra functionality from the outside.

So, all we need to do now is render the following pager (below the table):

```
$build[] = [
  '#type' => 'pager'
];
```

Positively rocket science, right? Not really. If we refresh the page, we should now see only five players in the table, and also a pager below it.

The Pager render element (`https://api.drupal.org/api/drupal/core%21lib%21Drupal%21Core%21Render%21Element%21Pager.php/class/Pager/10.0.x`) has some interesting properties we can use to customize it further. We can append query elements to the resulting links, or even specify another route for the links if we want to. We can, of course, control the label of the pager links, and even the number of links being output. Check out the documentation of this element for more information.

Moreover, for full customization, we also have the option of preprocessing these variables by implementing our own preprocessor for the `pager` theme hook (such as `template_preprocess_page`) and/or overriding the `pager.twig.html` template file. We learned how to do these things in *Chapter 4, Theming*.

Insert queries

In order to get data into our custom database tables, we have an `INSERT` query builder that we can use. And, you guessed it, via the `insert()` method on the connection service to build our query with the `Insert` object that gets returned. So, let's see how we can add a record to our `players` table:

```
$database->insert('players');
$fields = ['name' => 'Diego M', 'data' => serialize(['known
  for' => 'Hand of God'])];
$id = $database->insert('players')
  ->fields($fields)
  ->execute();
```

The main thing about an insert query is the `fields()` method. It expects an array of key/value pairs, where the keys are the column names and the values are the data that needs to be added to the respective columns. Alternatively, the first argument can be an array of the column names and the second an array of the values in the same order as the column names from the first array.

We can also run an `INSERT` query with multiple sets of values (records):

```
$values = [
  ['name' => 'Novak D.', 'data' => serialize(['sport' =>
    'tennis'])],
  ['name' => 'Michael P.', 'data' => serialize(['sport' =>
    'swimming'])]
];
$fields = ['name', 'data'];
$query = $database->insert('players')
  ->fields($fields);
```

```
foreach ($values as $value) {
  $query->values($value);
}
$result = $query->execute();
```

In this example, the `fields()` method receives only an array of column names that need to be inserted, and we use `values()` method calls to add the individual values.

The `execute()` method typically returns the ID (primary key) of the last record to be inserted. This is handy, especially if you insert only one record. However, for multiple inserts, it can also be misleading. So, do experiment for yourself with different use cases.

Update queries

Now that we've seen INSERT queries, let's take a look at how we can update existing records. Say we wanted to update one of our player records; we will do so as follows:

```
$result = $database->update('players')
  ->fields(['data' => serialize([
    'sport' => 'swimming',
    'feature' => 'This guy can swim'
  ])])
  ->condition('name', 'Michael P.')
  ->execute();
```

UPDATE queries are like INSERT ones, except that they take a `condition()` to figure out which records to update (all that match the condition). Leaving this out will update all records, naturally. Using the `fields()` method, we will simply specify which columns are getting updated, and with what. If we leave out a column, it will stay untouched. Lastly, the result of this query is the total number of records affected.

Delete queries

Lastly, we can also get rid of our records using the DELETE query:

```
$result = $database->delete('players')
  ->condition('name', 'Michael P.')
  ->execute();
```

All records that match the condition will get removed. Be careful with this because, as with update queries, leaving out a condition will basically truncate your table. The query will return the number of records affected, that is, deleted.

> **Note**
>
> Although you can write SELECT queries against entity and field tables to find the IDs of the entities you want to load, you should never perform INSERT, UPDATE, or DELETE queries against these tables. You run a very high risk of corrupting your data.

Transactions

The Drupal database API also provides a way to represent and handle database transactions (for database types that support them). Transactions are a way in which database operations can be wrapped and grouped together with a view of committing them in an "all or none" type of fashion. For example, if you have multiple records that are related, it's possible you will not want them written if one fails its INSERT operation for some reason. It could leave you with corrupt or incomplete data that could throw your application into a spin.

Performing multiple database-changing operations after a transaction has been opened only finalizes (commits) those changes to the database when that transaction closes. If something goes wrong, it can also be rolled back, which will prevent the data from being committed.

In Drupal, a transaction is represented by a Transaction object (a specific subclass for each database type). As soon as the object is destroyed (it is no longer in scope), the operations get committed to the database. However, if we get an indication that something went wrong in our operations (usually via catching an exception), we can roll back the transaction, which will stop those operations from being committed. Moreover, transactions can be nested, so Drupal keeps track of transactions that have been opened within the scope of other transactions.

Let's see an example of how to use transactions:

```
$transaction = $database->startTransaction();
try {
  $database->update('players')
    ->fields(['data' => serialize(['sport' => 'tennis',
      'feature' => 'This guy can play tennis'])])
    ->condition('name', 'Novak D.')
    ->execute();
}
catch (\Exception $e) {
  $transaction->rollback();
  watchdog_exception('my_type', $e);
}
```

The first thing we did was start a transaction using our connection service. Then, we wrapped our operation in a *try/catch* block to catch any exceptions that might be thrown in performing it. If one does get thrown, we roll back the transaction because we don't want to commit anything to the database, as we don't know what failed and what shape our data is in. Finally, we used the `watchdog_exception()` helper to log the exception to the database log. Do note that logging this before the rollback would prevent the exception from being written to the database as well.

If there is no exception, the operation gets committed as soon as the `$transaction` variable gets removed and is no longer in scope (usually at the end of the function). It is also interesting to note that if, within this transaction, we call another function in which we perform database operations, those operations will be part of this same transaction by default. So they also get rolled back if we roll back or get committed if we don't. This is why the database watchdog log will not be saved if called before the rollback.

Query alters

Lots of things in Drupal are alterable using various hooks; queries are no different. This means that if a module writes a query such as we've seen before, other modules can alter it by implementing `hook_query_alter()`. So let's consider an example of how this may work.

Assume the following query, which simply returns all player records:

```
$result = $database->select('players', 'p')
    ->fields('p')
    ->execute();
```

Imagine that another module wants to alter this query and limit the results to find only the players in a specific team. There is one problem. Our query has no markers that can indicate to another module that this is the one that needs to be altered. As you can imagine, there are a bunch of queries that are run in any given request, so identifying queries becomes impossible. Enter *query tags*.

The previous query would not be alterable because it's not recognizable, and therefore, `hook_query_alter()` is not even fired on it. In order to make it alterable, we will need to add a query tag and make it identifiable. There is a simple method on the query builder for doing just that: `addTag()`:

```
$result = $database->select('players', 'p')
    ->fields('p')
    ->addTag('player_query')
    ->execute();
```

Query tags are simple strings that can be read from inside a `hook_query_alter()` implementation. So, we could alter the query like this:

```
/**
 * Implements hook_query_alter().
 */
function module_name_query_alter(Drupal\Core\Database\Query
  \AlterableInterface $query) {
  if (!$query->hasTag('player_query')) {
    return;
  }


  // Alter query
}
```

The only parameter of this hook is the query object onto which we can apply our changes. It also has methods for reading the tags, such as `hasTag()`, `hasAnyTag()`, or `hasAllTags()`. In the previous example, we took a defensive approach and simply exited if the query was not about our `player_query` tagged query. I'll come back to this later on.

Now, let's see how we can alter this query to achieve what we set out to do:

```
$query->join('teams', 't', 't.id = p.team_id');
$query->addField('t', 'name', 'team_name');
$query->condition('t.name', 'My Team');
```

As you can see, we are doing a similar thing to what we did before when we built our joined query. We join the team table, add its name field (as a bonus), and set a condition to only return the players in a certain team. Easy peasy.

Let's now return for a second to my remark about the defensive approach we took with this hook implementation. I personally prefer to keep methods short and return early, rather than have a bunch of unintelligible nested conditions. This is typically easy to do in an object-oriented setting. However, with procedural code, it becomes a bit more tedious as you need many private functions that are tricky to name, and even more so with hook implementations into which you might need to add more than one block of code. For example, in our `hook_query_alter()` implementation, we might need to add an alteration for another query later on. Also, since we return early, we need to add another condition for checking for two tags, and then some more conditions and *if* statements, and even more conditions (OK, rant over). From a PHP point of view, in this case, you'd delegate the actual logic to another function based on the tag of the query, either using a simple switch block or *if* conditionals. This way, if a new tag comes, a new function can be created for it specifically and called from the switch block. However, we can do one better in this case.

There are a few hooks, particularly *alter* ones, that have general targeting but also a more specific one. In this example, we also have a `hook_query_TAG_alter()` hook, which is specific to a given tag. So, instead of us delegating to other functions, we could implement the more specific hook variation:

```
/**
 * Implements hook_query_TAG_alter().
 */
function module_name_query_player_query_alter(Drupal\Core\
  Database\Query\AlterableInterface $query) {
  // Sure to alter only the "player_query" tagged queries.
}
```

So, essentially, the tag itself becomes part of the function name, and we don't need any extra functions.

Update hooks

At the beginning of this chapter, we defined two tables using `hook_schema()`, which got installed together with the module. To reiterate, if the module had already been installed, we could have triggered the schema installation using the `drupal_install_schema()` function. However, what if we needed to add another column later on, say to the `teams` table? Our module is installed, and so is the schema; we cannot exactly uninstall it on production just to trigger the schema creation again. Luckily, there is a system in place for this, namely, *update* hooks—`hook_update_N()`—where N represents the schema version. These are sequentially named hook implementations that go inside the module `*.install` file and that are triggered when running the updates, either by going to `/update.php` or by using the `drush updatedb` command.

The main purpose of these update hooks is to make schema alterations to existing database tables.

> **Note**
>
> If you remember, when we were talking about entities, this was the update hook I mentioned that entity definition updates go into when staging them between environments. The principles are the same, except here, we are updating our own table schemas rather than the Drupal core entity-specific ones.

As mentioned, these hook implementations go into the `*.install` file. Let's see an example:

```
/**
 * Update hook for performing an update task.
 */
function my_module_update_10001(&$sandbox) {
  // Do stuff
}
```

The DocBlock of this hook implementation should contain a description of what it does. It is displayed when running the updates (either via the UI or using Drush).

The name of the function is one of its most important aspects. It starts with the module name, followed by `update`, and finally, the module's schema version (the next one if we want this update hook to actually run); but what is a module's schema version?

When installed, Drupal sets each module a schema version: 10000. In Drupal 9, it was 9000, and in 8, it was 8000. You get the difference between the major versions of Drupal. When an update hook runs, Drupal sets that module's schema version to the number found in the update hook. So, in the previous example, it would be 9001. This is to keep track of all the update hooks and to not run them more than once.

Let's now see how we can alter our `teams` database table with an update hook and add a column to store a `location` string field. The first thing we want to do is update our `hook_schema()` implementation and add this information there as well. This won't do anything in our case; however, due to the way update hooks work, we need to add it there as well. What I mean by this is that if a module is first installed and it has update hooks in it already, those update hooks do not run, but the module's schema version gets set as the number of the last update hook found in it. So, if we do not add our new column inside `hook_schema()`, installing this module on another site (or even on the current one after an uninstall) will not get our new column in. So, we need to account for both situations.

In the field definition of our `teams` table schema, we can add the following column definition:

```
'location' => [
    'description' => 'The team location.',
    'type' => 'varchar',
    'length' => 255,
],
```

It's as simple as that. Next, we can implement an update hook and add this field to the table:

```
/**
 * Adds the "location" field to the teams table.
 */
function sports_update_10001(&$sandbox) {
  $field = [
    'description' => 'The team location.',
    'type' => 'varchar',
    'length' => 255,
  ];
  $schema = \Drupal::database()->schema();
```

```
    $schema->addField('teams', 'location', $field);
}
```

Here, we used the same field definition, loaded the database connection service, and used its schema object to add that field to the table. The code itself is pretty self-explanatory, but it's also worth mentioning that this is an example in which we cannot inject the service; hence we have to use it statically. So, don't feel bad about situations like this.

Next, we can use Drush to run the updates:

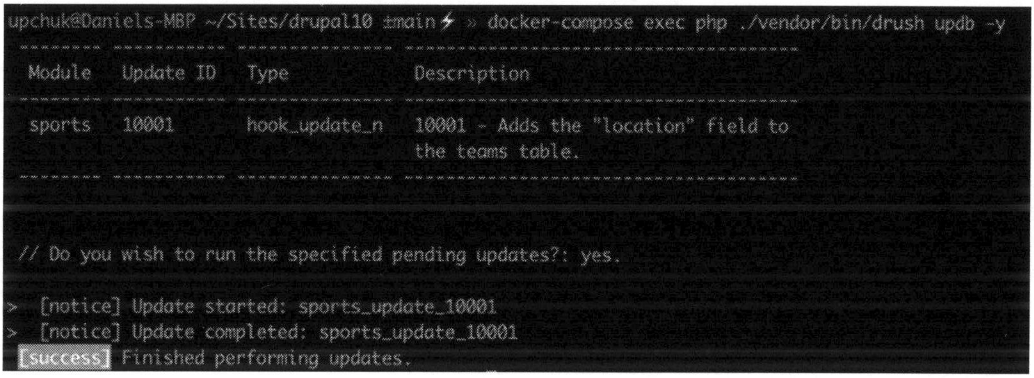

Figure 8.1: Using Drush to run the updates

Sure enough, the `teams` table now has a new column. If you try to run the updates again, you'll note that there are none to be run because Drupal has set the schema version of the `sports` module to 10001. So, the next one in line to be run has to have 10002 at the end.

In the previous example, we added a new field to an existing table. However, we might need to create a new table entirely or even delete one. The schema object on the database connection service has the relevant methods to do so. The following are a few examples, but I recommend that you check out the base `Drupal\Core\Database\Schema` class for the available methods:

```
$schema->createTable('new_table', $table_definition);
$schema->addField('teams', 'location', $field);
$schema->dropTable('table_name');
$schema->dropField('table_name', 'field_to_delete');
$schema->changeField('table_name', 'field_name_to_change',
    'new_field_name', $new_field_definition);
```

There are a few cautionary aspects you need to consider when using update hooks. For example, you cannot be sure of the state of the environment before the hooks run, so ensure that you account for this. I recommend you check out the documentation (`https://api.drupal.org/api/drupal/core%21lib%21Drupal%21Core%21Extension%21module.api.php/function/hook_update_N/10.0.x`) about `hook_update_N()` and carefully read the section about the function body.

Post update hooks

Partly due to the weak configuration management system in versions of Drupal (7 and before), the update hooks we just talked about have evolved—through developer creativity—into a mechanism for updating various types of configuration or performing tasks (even content-related) upon deployment to the next environment. Helping out with this is the `$sandbox` argument passed to the hook implementations, which can be used to batch these operations (to prevent an execution timeout). We will not cover the batching aspect here but rather as part of the standalone Batch API chapter.

Since Drupal 8, we no longer have to misuse the update hooks for performing tasks that are not strictly related to updating schemas: be that our own custom table schemas or content entity ones. Instead, we can use `hook_post_update_NAME()`.

Post update hooks are fired after update hooks have run and we are sure all the database tables have been brought to their correct state. They need to go inside the `*.post_update.php` file of the module and they are fired in the order they are declared inside this file—likewise only once. And instead of consecutive numbers, they can have any string name we choose. Do check out the documentation for a quick example of how to use them.

Summary

In this chapter, we looked at the basics of interacting with the database API. Although it's something that has taken a significant step back in importance in day-to-day Drupal module development, it's important to understand it and be able to work with it.

We started the chapter by creating our very own database tables to hold player and team information in a relational way. We did so using an API that transforms definitions into actual tables without us having to even understand much about MySQL. The SQL terminology and basic operations are, however, something that every developer should be familiar with, notwithstanding their actual day-to-day application in Drupal.

Then, we looked at some examples of how we can run SELECT, INSERT, UPDATE, and DELETE queries using both the more SQL-oriented way of writing statements and the query builder approach, which uses an OO representation of the queries. We've also seen how these queries can be wrapped into transactions (where supported) so that we can commit data changes while minimizing the potential for incomplete or corrupt data. Finally, we saw how these queries can be altered using query tags, allowing for yet another small extension point that other modules can contribute through. Regardless of how we build our queries, however, a key takeaway is that using this API is crucial for a secure interaction with the database. Moreover, it accounts for cross-compatibility with the different database types Drupal can work with.

Lastly, we looked at update hooks and how they can be used to perform changes to our database tables. And we also mentioned post update hooks that can be employed to perform some other tasks that might need to be coded and then deployed to the next environment to be run once.

In the next chapter, we will look at custom Drupal entity fields and see how we can define our own; yes, we'll be playing with some more plugins.

9
Custom Fields

In *Chapter 6, Data Modeling and Storage*, and *Chapter 7, Your Own Custom Entities and Plugin Types*, we talked quite extensively about content entities and how they use fields to store the actual data that they are supposed to represent. Then, we saw how these fields, apart from interacting with the storage layer for persisting it, extend TypedData API classes to organize this data better at the code level. For example, we saw that the `BaseFieldDefinition` instances used on entities are actually data definitions (and so are the `FieldConfig` ones). Moreover, we also saw the DataType plugins at play there, namely, the `FieldItemList` with their individual items, which, down the line, extend a basic DataType plugin (`Map` in most cases). Also, if you remember, when we were talking about these items, I mentioned how they are actually instances of yet another plugin—`FieldType`. So essentially, they are a plugin type whose plugins extend plugins of another type. I recommend that you revisit that section if you are fuzzy on the matter.

Most of these concepts are buried inside the Entity API and are only seen and understood by developers. However, the `FieldType` plugins (together with their corresponding `FieldWidget` and `FieldFormatter` plugins) break out and are one of the principal things site builders and content editors actually work with in the UI. They allow users to input structured data and save it to the database. If you recall, I mentioned them a few times in *Chapters 6* and *7*, and I promised you a chapter in which we will see how we can create field types that a site builder can then add to an entity type and use to input data. Well, this is that chapter, but first, let's do a quick recap on what we know about them.

The topics we will cover in this chapter are the following:

- Field type plugins
- Field widget plugins
- Field formatter plugins
- Various kinds of field settings

A recap of Field type plugins

Field type plugins extend the lower-level TypedData API to create a unique way of not only representing data (within the context of entities) but also storing it in the database (and other stuff as well). They are primarily known as the type of fields site builders can add to an entity type bundle. For example, a plain text field or a select list with multiple options. Nothing can be more common than that in a CMS.

However, they are also used as entity base fields. If you remember our product entity type's name field definition, we did use these plugin types:

```
$fields['name'] = BaseFieldDefinition::create('string')
  ->setLabel(t('Name'))
  ->setDescription(t('The name of the Product.'))
  ->setSettings([
    'max_length' => 255,
    'text_processing' => 0,
  ])
  ->setDefaultValue('')
  ->setDisplayOptions('view', [
    'label' => 'hidden',
    'type' => 'string',
    'weight' => -4,
  ])
  ->setDisplayOptions('form', [
    'type' => 'string_textfield',
    'weight' => -4,
  ])
  ->setDisplayConfigurable('form', TRUE)
  ->setDisplayConfigurable('view', TRUE);
```

The create() method of the definition class accepts a FieldType plugin ID. Also, the type of the view display option provided a bit below in the code is a FieldFormatter plugin ID, whereas the type of the form display option provided even lower in the code is a FieldWidget plugin ID.

A crucial lesson from this recap that I insist you retain is the following: when defining your custom entities, think about the types of fields you need. If there are bundles that need to have different sets of fields, configurable fields are your choice. Otherwise, base fields are perhaps more appropriate. They sit tightly with your entity type class and appear on all bundles (if that's something you need), and I encourage you to explore the Drupal code base and understand the existing field types, widgets, and formatters better (as well as relevant settings they come with).

Also, when you define base fields, think the same way as you would if adding them through the UI—which field type do I want (find a `FieldType` plugin), how do I want users to interact with it (find a `FieldWidget` plugin), and how do I want its values to be shown (find a `FieldFormatter` plugin)? Then, inspect the relevant classes to determine the right settings that will go with them.

In this chapter, we will take a look at how we can create our own custom field type with its own default widget and formatter. To provide a bit of continuity, I am going to ask you to think back to the more complex example we used when talking about the TypedData API—the license plate. We will create a field type designed specifically to store license plates in the following format: *CODE NUMBER* (just as we saw with the example New York plate). Why?

At the moment, there is no field type that can represent this accurately. Of course, we have the simple text field, but that implies having to add both pieces of data that make up a license plate into the same field, stripping them of their meaning. When we were discussing the TypedData API, we saw that one of its core principles is the ability to apply meaning to a piece of data so as to understand that `$license_plate` (for example) is actually a license plate from which we can ask its code and its number (as well as a general description if we want to). Similar to this (or actually building on top of this), fields are also about storing this data. So, apart from understanding it in code, we also need to persist it in the same way. That is, placing the individual pieces of data in separate meaningful table columns in order to also persist that meaning.

An example from Drupal core that does the same thing is the `Text (formatted)` field. Apart from its string value, this field also stores a format for each value, which is used upon rendering. Without that format, the string value loses its meaning, and Drupal is no longer able to reliably render it in the way it was intended upon creation. So you can now see that fields take the idea of *meaning* from TypedData and also apply it to storage as needed. So, in this chapter, you will learn how these three types of plugins work by creating your own license plate field type. Let's get started.

Field type

The primary plugin type for creating a field is, as we discussed, `FieldType`. It is responsible for defining the field structure, how it is stored in the database and various other settings. Moreover, it also defines a default widget and formatter plugin that will be autoselected when we create the field in the UI. You see, a single field type can work with more than one widget and formatter. If more exist, the site builder can choose one when creating the field and adding it to an entity type bundle.

Otherwise, it will be the default; each field needs one because without a widget, users can't add data, and without a formatter, they can't see it. Also, as you'd expect, widgets and formatters can also work with more than one field type.

The field we will create in this section is for the license plate data, which, as we saw, needs two individual pieces of information: a code (such as the state code) and the number. License plates around the world are more complex than this, but I chose this example to keep things simple.

Our new `FieldType` plugin needs to go inside the `Plugin/Field/FieldType` namespace of a new module we will create called `license_plate`. Although not mandatory, the class name should end with the word `Item`. It's a standard thing in Drupal core, and we will follow suit. So, let's take a look at our `LicensePlateItem` plugin implementation and then talk about the code:

```php
namespace Drupal\license_plate\Plugin\Field\FieldType;

use Drupal\Core\Field\FieldItemBase;
use Drupal\Core\StringTranslation\StringTranslationTrait;

/**
 * Plugin implementation of the 'license_plate' field type.
 *
 * @FieldType(
 *   id = "license_plate",
 *   label = @Translation("License plate"),
 *   description = @Translation("Field for storing license
 *     plates"),
 *   default_widget = "default_license_plate_widget",
 *   default_formatter = "default_license_plate_formatter"
 * )
 */
class LicensePlateItem extends FieldItemBase {
  use StringTranslationTrait;
}
```

I omitted the class contents, as we will be adding the methods one by one and discussing them individually. However, first, we have the plugin annotation, which is very important. We have the typical plugin metadata such as the ID, label, and description, as well as the plugin IDs for the widget and formatter that will be used by default with this field type. Make a note of those because we will create them soon.

Speaking from experience, often, when creating a field type, you'll extend the class of an already existing field type plugin, such as a text field or an entity reference. This is because Drupal core already comes with a great set of available types, and usually, all you need is to either make some tweaks to an existing one, maybe combine them, or add an extra piece of functionality. This makes things easier, and you don't have to copy and paste code or come up with it again yourself. Naturally, though, at some point, you'll be extending from `FieldItemBase` because that is the base class all field types need to extend from.

In our example, we will extend straight from the `FieldItemBase` abstract class because we want our field to stand on its own. Also, it's not super practical to extend from any existing ones in this case. That is not to say, though, that it doesn't have commonalities with other field types, such as `TextItem`, for example.

Let's now see the first method in our class:

```
/**
 * {@inheritdoc}
 */
public static function defaultStorageSettings() {
  return [
    'number_max_length' => 255,
    'code_max_length' => 5,
  ] + parent::defaultStorageSettings();
}
```

The first thing we do in our class is override the `defaultStorageSettings()` method. The parent class method returns an empty array; however, it's still a good idea to include whatever it returns to our own array. If the parent method changes and returns something later, we are a bit more robust.

The purpose of this method is two-fold: specifying what storage settings this field has and setting some defaults for them. Also, note that it is a static method, which means that we are not inside the plugin instance. However, what are storage settings, you may ask?

Storage settings are the configuration that applies to the field everywhere it's used. As you know, a field can be added to multiple bundles of an entity type. They usually deal with things related to the schema—how the database table columns are constructed for this field—but they also deal with a lot of other things. Also, even more important to know is that once there is data in the field tables, they cannot be changed. It makes sense as you cannot easily change database tables when there is data in them. This restriction is something we enforce, as we will see in a bit.

In our example, we only have two storage settings: `number_max_length` and `code_max_length`. These will be used when defining the schema for the two table columns where the license plate data will be stored (as the maximum length that can be stored in those table fields). By default, we will go with the ever-so-used 255-character maximum length on the number column and 5 for the code column, but these are just defaults. The user will be able to change them when creating the field or when editing, as long as there is no data yet.

Next, we can write our storage settings form, which allows users to provide the actual settings when creating a field in the UI:

```php
/**
 * {@inheritdoc}
 */
public function storageSettingsForm(array &$form,
  FormStateInterface $form_state, $has_data) {
  $elements = [];

  $elements['number_max_length'] = [
    '#type' => 'number',
    '#title' => $this->t('Plate number maximum length'),
    '#default_value' => $this->getSetting
    ('number_max_length'),
    '#required' => TRUE,
    '#description' => $this->t('Maximum length for the
      plate number in characters.'),
    '#min' => 1,
    '#disabled' => $has_data,
  ];

  $elements['code_max_length'] = [
    '#type' => 'number',
    '#title' => $this->t('Plate code maximum length'),
    '#default_value' => $this->getSetting
      ('code_max_length'),
    '#required' => TRUE,
    '#description' => $this->t('Maximum length for the
      plate code in characters.'),
    '#min' => 1,
    '#disabled' => $has_data,
  ];

  return $elements + parent::storageSettingsForm($form,
    $form_state, $has_data);
}
```

This method is called by the main field configuration form, and we need to return an array of form elements that can be used to set values to the storage settings we defined earlier. We have access to the main $form and $form_state of the form where this is embedded, as well as a handy Boolean, $has_data, which tells us whether there is already any data in this field. We use this to disable the elements we don't want to be changed if there is data in the field (in our case, both).

So basically, our form consists of two number form elements (both required) whose values default to the lengths we specified earlier. The number form element also comes with the #min and #max properties, which we can use to restrict the number to a range. Also, we obviously want our minimum lengths to be a positive number, that is, above 1. This method is relatively straightforward to understand if you get the basics of the Form API, which you should, by now.

Finally, for our storage handling, we will need to implement the schema method and define our table columns:

```
/**
 * {@inheritdoc}
 */
public static function schema(FieldStorageDefinition
    Interface $field_definition) {
    $schema = [
      'columns' => [
        'number' => [
          'type' => 'varchar',
          'length' => (int) $field_definition->getSetting
            ('number_max_length'),
        ],
        'code' => [
          'type' => 'varchar',
          'length' => (int) $field_definition->getSetting
            ('code_max_length'),
        ],
      ],
    ];

    return $schema;
}
```

This is another static method, but one that receives the current field's `FieldStorageDefinition-Interface` instance. From there, we can access the settings the user has saved when creating the field, and based on those, we define our schema. If you were paying attention in the previous chapter when we discussed `hook_schema()`, this should already be clear to you. What we need to return is an array of column definitions keyed by their name. So, we define two columns of the `varchar` type with the maximum lengths the user has configured. Of course, we could have had more storage settings and made this schema definition even more configurable if we wanted to.

With these three methods, our storage handling is complete; however, our field type is not quite so. We still have a couple more things to take care of.

Apart from storage, as we discussed, fields also deal with data representation at the code level with TypedData structures. So, our field type needs to define its individual properties for which we create storage. For this, we have two main methods: first, to actually define the properties, and then to set some potential constraints on them:

```
/**
 * {@inheritdoc}
 */
public static function propertyDefinitions
  (FieldStorageDefinitionInterface $field_definition) {
  $properties['number'] = DataDefinition::create('string')
    ->setLabel(t('Plate number'));

  $properties['code'] = DataDefinition::create('string')
    ->setLabel(t('Plate code'));

  return $properties;
}
```

The previous code will look very familiar to the one in *Chapter 6, Data Modeling and Storage*, when we talked about TypedData. Again, this is a static method that needs to return the `DataDefinitionInterface` instance for the individual properties. We choose to call them `number` and `code`, respectively, and set some sensible labels—nothing too complicated.

The previous code is enough to define the properties, but if you remember, our storage has some maximum lengths in place, meaning that the table columns are only so long. So, if the data that gets into our field is longer, the database engine will throw a fit in a not-so-graceful way. In other words, it will throw a big exception, and we can't have that. So, there are two things we can do to prevent that: put the same maximum length on the form widget to prevent users from inputting more than they should and add a constraint on our data definitions.

The second one is more important because it ensures that the data is valid in any case, whereas the first one only deals with forms. However, not to worry; we will also take care of the form, so our users can have a nicer experience and are aware of the maximum size of the values they need to input.

So, let's add the following constraints:

```
/**
 * {@inheritdoc}
 */
public function getConstraints() {
  $constraints = parent::getConstraints();
  $constraint_manager = \Drupal::typedDataManager()->
    getValidationConstraintManager();
  $number_max_length = $this->getSetting
    ('number_max_length');
  $code_max_length = $this->getSetting('code_max_length');
  $constraints[] = $constraint_manager->create
    ('ComplexData', [
    'number' => [
      'Length' => [
        'max' => $number_max_length,
        'maxMessage' => $this->t('%name: may not be longer
          than @max characters.', [
          '%name' => $this->getFieldDefinition()->
            getLabel() . ' (number)',
          '@max' => $number_max_length
        ]),
      ],
    ],
    'code' => [
      'Length' => [
        'max' => $code_max_length,
        'maxMessage' => $this->t('%name: may not be longer
          than @max characters.', [
          '%name' => $this->getFieldDefinition()->
            getLabel() . ' (code)',
          '@max' => $code_max_length
        ]),
```

```
        ],
      ],
    ]);

    return $constraints;
  }
```

Since our field class actually implements `TypedDataInterface`, it also has to implement the `getConstraints()` method (which the `TypedData` parent already starts up). However, we can override it and provide our own constraints based on our field values.

We are taking a slightly different approach here from adding constraints to what we saw in *Chapter 6, Data Modeling and Storage*. Instead of adding them straight to the data definitions, we will create them manually using the validation constraint manager (which is the plugin manager of the `Constraint` plugin type we saw in *Chapter 6, Data Modeling and Storage*). This is because fields use a specific `ComplexDataConstraint` plugin that can combine the constraints of multiple properties (data definitions). Do note that even if we had only one property in this field, we'd still be using this constraint plugin.

> **Note**
>
> There aren't many classes in Drupal in which you cannot inject dependencies, but the `FieldType` plugins are one of them. This is because these plugins are built on top of the `Map` TypedData plugin, and their manager doesn't use a container-aware factory for instantiation but instead delegates it to the `TypedDataManger` service, which, as we saw, is not container-aware either. For this reason, we have to request the services we need statically.

The data needed to create this constraint plugin is a multidimensional array keyed by the property name, which contains constraint definitions for each of them. So, we have a `Length` constraint for both properties, whose options denote a maximum length and a corresponding message if that length is exceeded. If we wanted, we could have had a minimum length in the same way as well: `min` and `minMessage`. As for the actual length, we will use the values chosen by the user when creating the field (the storage maximum). Now, regardless of the form widget, our field will not validate unless the maximum lengths are respected.

It's time to finish this class with the following two methods:

```
/**
 * {@inheritdoc}
 */
public static function generateSampleValue
  (FieldDefinitionInterface $field_definition) {
```

```
   $random = new Random();
   $values['number'] = $random->word(mt_rand(1,
     $field_definition->getSetting('number_max_length')));
   $values['code'] = $random->word(mt_rand(1,
     $field_definition->getSetting('code_max_length')));
   return $values;
}


/**
 * {@inheritdoc}
 */
public function isEmpty() {
  // We consider the field empty if either of the
    properties is left empty.
  $number = $this->get('number')->getValue();
  $code = $this->get('code')->getValue();
  return $number === NULL || $number === '' || $code ===
    NULL || $code === '';
}
```

With `generateSampleValue()`, we create some random values that fit within our field. That's it. This can be used when profiling or site building to populate the field with demo values. Arguably, this is not going to be your top priority, but it is good to know.

Finally, we have the `isEmpty()` method, which is used to determine whether the field has values or not. It may seem pretty obvious, but it's an important method, especially for us, and you can probably deduce from the implementation why. When creating the field in the UI, the user can specify whether it's required or not. However, typically, that applies (or should apply) to the entire set of values within the field. Also, if the field is not required, and the user only inputs a license plate code without a number, what kind of useful value is that to save? So, we want to make sure that both of them have something before even considering this field as having a value (not being empty), and that is what we are checking in this method.

Since we started writing the class, we made references to a bunch of classes that we should *use* at the top before moving on:

```
use Drupal\Component\Utility\Random;
use Drupal\Core\Field\FieldDefinitionInterface;
use Drupal\Core\Field\FieldStorageDefinitionInterface;
use Drupal\Core\Form\FormStateInterface;
use Drupal\Core\TypedData\DataDefinition;
```

Now that we are finished with the actual plugin class, there is one last thing that we need to take care of, something that we tend to forget, myself included: the configuration schema. Our new field is a configurable field whose settings are stored. Guess where? In configuration. Also, as you may remember, all configuration needs to be defined by a schema. Drupal already takes care of those storage settings that come from the parent. However, we need to include ours. So, let's create the typical `license_plate.schema.yml` (inside `config/schema`), where we will put all the schema definitions we need in this module:

```
field.storage_settings.license_plate:
  type: mapping
  label: 'License plate storage settings'
  mapping:
    number_max_length:
      type: integer
      label: 'Max length for the number'
    code_max_length:
      type: integer
      label: 'Max length for the code'
```

The actual definition will already be familiar, so the only thing that is interesting to explain is its actual naming. The pattern is `field.storage_settings.[field_type_plugin_id]`. Drupal will dynamically read the schema and apply it to the settings of the actual `FieldStorageConfig` entity being exported.

That's it for our `FieldType` plugin. When creating a new field of this type, we have the two storage settings we can configure (which will be disabled when editing if there is actual field data already in the database):

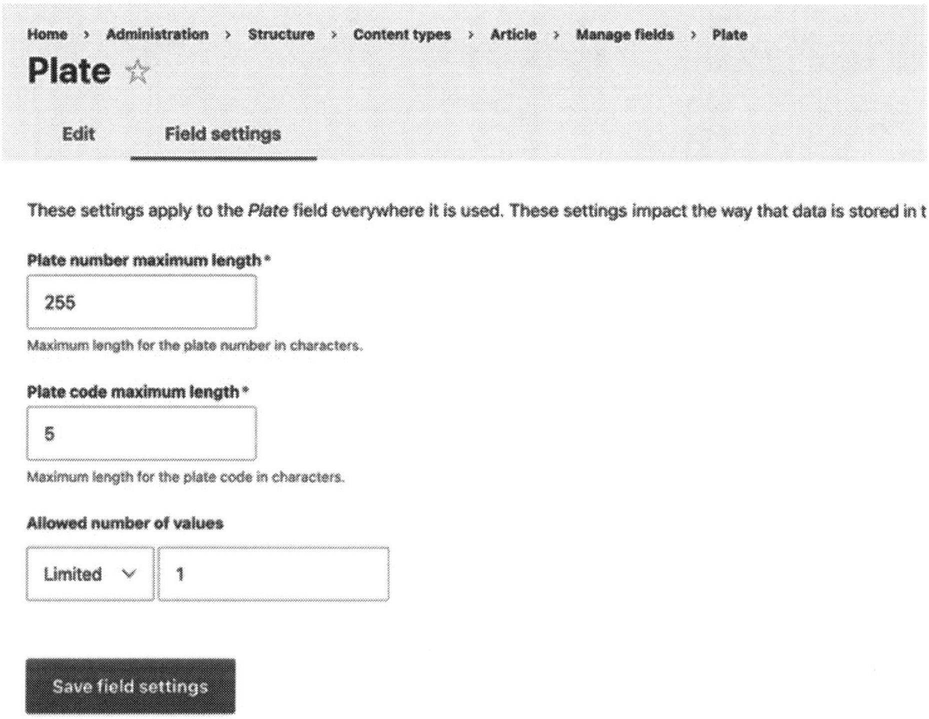

Figure 9.1: Configuring the field storage settings

Unfortunately, we won't be able to create the new field yet because the widget and formatter plugins we reference in the annotation don't exist yet. So, let's create those now.

Field widget

Let's now create that default license plate widget plugin we referenced in the annotation of the field type, which belongs in the `Plugin/Field/FieldWidget` namespace of our module:

```
namespace Drupal\license_plate\Plugin\Field\FieldWidget;

use Drupal\Core\StringTranslation\StringTranslationTrait;
use Drupal\Core\Field\WidgetBase;

/**
 * Plugin implementation of the
   'default_license_plate_widget' widget.
 *
```

```
 * @FieldWidget(
 *   id = "default_license_plate_widget",
 *   label = @Translation("Default license plate widget"),
 *   field_types = {
 *      "license_plate"
 *   }
 * )
 */
class DefaultLicensePlateWidget extends WidgetBase {

  use StringTranslationTrait;
}
```

Again, we start by examining the annotation and class parents for just a bit. You will notice nothing particularly complicated, except maybe the `field_types` key, which specifies the `FieldType` plugin IDs this widget can work with. Just as a field type can have more than one widget, a widget can work with more than one field type. Also, it's important that we specify it here; otherwise, site builders won't be able to use this widget with our license plate field type.

We extended `WidgetBase`, which implements the obligatory `WidgetInterface` and provides some common defaults for all its subclasses.

The first thing we can do inside the class is handle our settings. First, we will define what settings this widget has and set the default values for these settings:

```
/**
 * {@inheritdoc}
 */
public static function defaultSettings() {
  return [
    'number_size' => 60,
    'code_size' => 5,
    'fieldset_state' => 'open',
    'placeholder' => [
      'number' => '',
      'code' => '',
    ],
  ] + parent::defaultSettings();
}
```

We have some settings specific to how the form widget would be configured for our field. We will use the first two settings mentioned in the previous code to limit the size of the form element. It will not actually prevent users from filling in longer values but will be a good indication for them as to how long the values should be. Then, we have the `fieldset_state` setting, which we will use to indicate whether the form fieldset used to group the two license plate textfields is, by default, open or closed. We will see that in a minute. Lastly, each of these textfields can have a placeholder value (potentially). So, we have that setting as well. Do note that these are all settings we make up and that make sense for our field. You can add your own if you want.

Next, we have the form used to configure these settings (as part of the widget configuration):

```
/**
 * {@inheritdoc}
 */
public function settingsForm(array $form,
  FormStateInterface $form_state) {
  $elements = [];

  $elements['number_size'] = [
    '#type' => 'number',
    '#title' => $this->t('Size of plate number textfield'),
    '#default_value' => $this->getSetting('number_size'),
    '#required' => TRUE,
    '#min' => 1,
    '#max' => $this->getFieldSetting('number_max_length'),
  ];

  $elements['code_size'] = [
    '#type' => 'number',
    '#title' => $this->t('Size of plate code textfield'),
    '#default_value' => $this->getSetting('code_size'),
    '#required' => TRUE,
    '#min' => 1,
    '#max' => $this->getFieldSetting('code_max_length'),
  ];

  $elements['fieldset_state'] = [
    '#type' => 'select',
```

```
    '#title' => $this->t('Fieldset default state'),
    '#options' => [
      'open' => $this->t('Open'),
      'closed' => $this->t('Closed')
    ],
    '#default_value' => $this->getSetting
      ('fieldset_state'),
    '#description' => $this->t('The default state of the
        fieldset which contains the two plate fields: open
          or closed')
  ];

  $elements['placeholder'] = [
    '#type' => 'details',
    '#title' => $this->t('Placeholder'),
    '#description' => $this->t('Text that will be shown
      inside the field until a value is entered. This hint
        is usually a sample value or a brief description of
          the expected format.'),
  ];

  $placeholder_settings = $this->getSetting('placeholder');
  $elements['placeholder']['number'] = [
    '#type' => 'textfield',
    '#title' => $this->t('Number field'),
    '#default_value' => $placeholder_settings['number'],
  ];
  $elements['placeholder']['code'] = [
    '#type' => 'textfield',
    '#title' => $this->t('Code field'),
    '#default_value' => $placeholder_settings['code'],
  ];

  return $elements;
}
```

We have to return the elements for our widget settings, which will then be added to a bigger form (passed as an argument). There is nothing special about the first three form elements. We have two `number` fields and a `select` list to control the first three settings we saw in our defaults. For the first two settings, we want the numbers to be positive and max out at the same maximum length we have set in the storage. We don't want the widget exceeding that length. However, if we want, we can shorten the size of the element.

The textfields for the two placeholder values are wrapped inside a `details` form element. The latter is a fieldset that can be open or closed and can contain other form elements. We will use it to wrap the actual textfields with which users will input license plate data.

The previous form will look like this when users configure the widget:

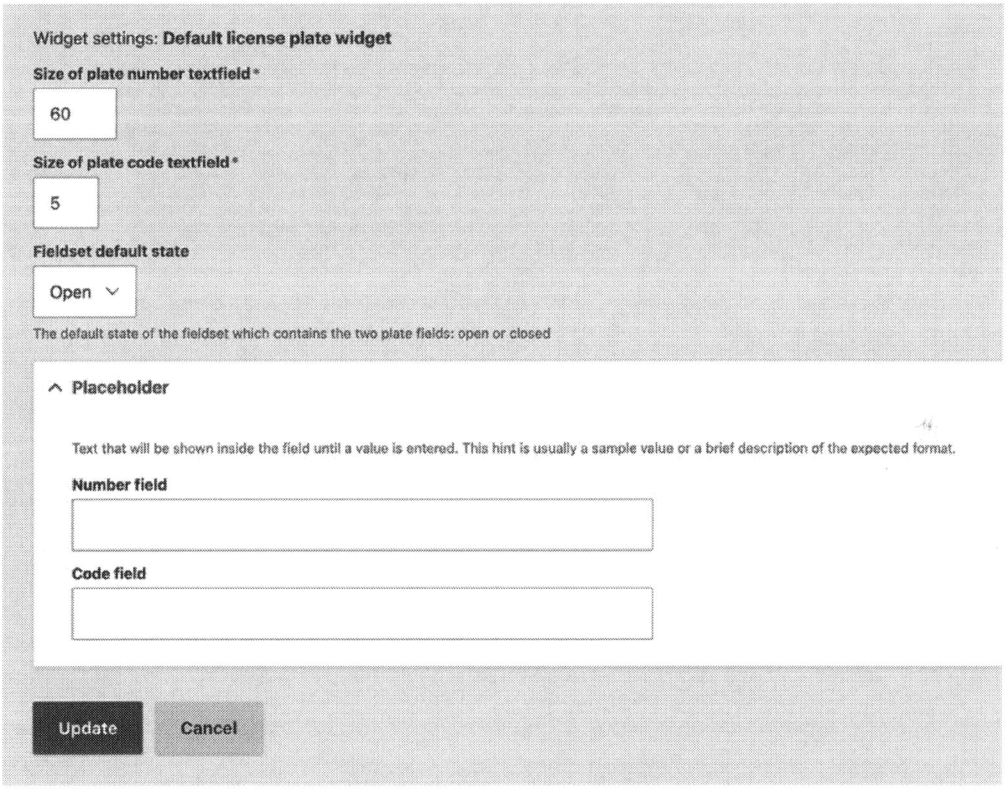

Figure 9.2: Configuring the field widget

Lastly, we have the summary of the widget settings, which will be displayed on the **Manage form display** page for our field:

```
/**
 * {@inheritdoc}
 */
public function settingsSummary() {
  $summary = [];

  $summary[] = $this->t('License plate size: @number (for
    number) and @code (for code)', ['@number' => $this->
      getSetting('number_size'), '@code' => $this >
        getSetting('code_size')]);
  $placeholder_settings = $this->getSetting('placeholder');
  if (!empty($placeholder_settings['number']) && !empty
    ($placeholder_settings['code'])) {
    $placeholder = $placeholder_settings['number'] . ' ' .
      $placeholder_settings['code'];
    $summary[] = $this->t('Placeholder: @placeholder',
      ['@placeholder' => $placeholder]);
  }
  $summary[] = $this->t('Fieldset state: @state', ['@state'
    => $this->getSetting('fieldset_state')]);

  return $summary;
}
```

This method needs to return an array of strings that will make up the settings summary. That is what we do now: read all our settings values and list them in a human-friendly way. The end result will look something like this:

Figure 9.3: The field widget summary

Next, we will have to implement the core of the field widget plugins—the actual form used for inputting the field data:

```
/**
 * {@inheritdoc}
 */
public function formElement(FieldItemListInterface $items,
  $delta, array $element, array &$form, FormStateInterface
    $form_state) {
  $element['details'] = [
    '#type' => 'details',
    '#title' => $element['#title'],
    '#open' => $this->getSetting('fieldset_state') ==
      'open' ? TRUE : FALSE,
    '#description' => $element['#description'],
  ] + $element;

  $placeholder_settings = $this->getSetting('placeholder');
  $element['details']['code'] = [
    '#type' => 'textfield',
    '#title' => $this->t('Plate code'),
    '#default_value' => isset($items[$delta]->code) ?
      $items[$delta]->code : NULL,
    '#size' => $this->getSetting('code_size'),
    '#placeholder' => $placeholder_settings['code'],
    '#maxlength' => $this->getFieldSetting
      ('code_max_length'),
    '#description' => '',
    '#required' => $element['#required'],
  ];

  $element['details']['number'] = [
    '#type' => 'textfield',
    '#title' => $this->t('Plate number'),
    '#default_value' => isset($items[$delta]->number) ?
      $items[$delta]->number : NULL,
    '#size' => $this->getSetting('number_size'),
```

```
    '#placeholder' => $placeholder_settings['number'],
    '#maxlength' => $this->getFieldSetting
      ('number_max_length'),
    '#description' => '',
    '#required' => $element['#required'],
  ];


  return $element;
}
```

This is a bit more complicated at first glance, but we'll break it down and you'll see that it makes sense with what you've been learning in the previous chapters.

The first argument passed to this method is the entire list of values for this field. Remember that each field can have multiple values, hence the usage of the `FieldItemListInterface` instance to hold them. So, from there, we can get the values of any of the items in the list. The second argument is the actual delta of the item in the list, which we can use to pinpoint the one for which the form is being built (to retrieve the default value). Then, we have an `$element` array that we should actually return, but which contains some pieces of data already prepared for us based on the field configuration. For example, when creating a field, if we set it to be required, then this `$element` already contains the form property, `#required => TRUE`. Likewise, it contains the weight of the field (compared to the others on the entity type), the `#title` property, and many others. I recommend that you debug that array and see what's in it. Also, you can look inside `WidgetBase::formMultipleElments()` and `WidgetBase::formSingleElement()` and see how this array is prepared. Lastly, we get the form definition and form state information of the larger form our field element gets embedded in.

So, what we are doing inside the method is getting a bit creative with the data that we have. The one-value (columns) fields would typically just add to the `$element` array and then simply return that. However, we have two values we want to wrap inside a nice collapsible fieldset, so we create a `details` element for that.

It is on this element that we copy over the field title and description the user has specified when creating the field, which is prepared for us in the `$element` array. This is because those relate to the entire field, not just one of the values. Moreover, we also set the default `#open` state to whatever was stored in the widget settings. Lastly, to all this, we add the rest of the values found in the `$elements` array because we want to inherit them as well.

> **Note**
>
> I could have left `#title` and `#description` to be inherited as well, but I overtly added them to make them more visible for you.

Next, within our details element, we can add the two textfields for the license plate code and number. For both, we use the widget settings to set the element size and placeholder value, as well as a maximum length value equal to the field item storage. This is what will prevent users from providing values that are longer than what the database columns can handle. The default value for the two form elements will be set to the actual field values of these properties, retrieved from the list of items using the current delta key. Finally, we set the `#required` property to whatever the user has configured for this field. This property would be useless on the parent `details` element, so we have to move it down to the actual text fields. And that's pretty much it.

The last method we can implement, and in our case, have to, is one that prepares the field values a bit when submitting:

```php
/**
 * {@inheritdoc}
 */
public function massageFormValues(array $values, array
  $form, FormStateInterface $form_state) {
  foreach ($values as &$value) {
    $value['number'] = $value['details']['number'];
    $value['code'] = $value['details']['code'];
    unset($value['details']);
  }

  return $values;
}
```

Here's what happens. From our property definitions, our field expects two properties: number and code. However, submitting this form will present only one property called "details" because that is what we arbitrarily named our fieldset form element (which contains the properties). Since we made this choice, we will need to now *massage* the submitted values a bit to match the expected properties. In other words, we have to bring the number and code properties to the top level of the `$values` array and unset the details element, as it's no longer needed upon submission. So, now, the field receives the array in the following format:

```php
$values = [
  'number' => 'My number',
  'code' => 'My code'
];
```

If you remember, this is incidentally also what we would pass to the `set()` method of the field if we wanted to set this value on the field. Look at the following example:

```
$node->set('field_license_plate', ['code' => 'NY', 'number'
    => '63676']);
```

With that, our widget is done; well, not quite. We should ensure we use all the newly referenced classes at the top:

```
use Drupal\Core\Field\FieldItemListInterface;
use Drupal\Core\Form\FormStateInterface;
```

Also, we again forgot about the configuration schema. Let's not do that again. In the same file as we wrote the field storage schema (`license_plate.schema.yml`), we can add the definition for the widget settings:

```
field.widget.settings.default_license_plate_widget:
  type: mapping
  label: 'Default license plate widget settings'
  mapping:
    number_size:
      type: integer
      label: 'Number size'
    code_size:
      type: integer
      label: 'Code size'
    fieldset_state:
      type: string
      label: 'The state of the fieldset which contains the
        two fields: open/closed'
    placeholder:
      type: mapping
      label: 'The placeholders for the two fields'
      mapping:
        number:
          type: string
          label: 'The placeholder for the number field'
        code:
          type: string
          label: 'The placeholder for the code field'
```

It works just like before: a dynamic schema name that starts with `field.widget.settings.` and has the actual plugin ID at the end; and inside, we have a property mapping, as we've seen before. With this, we really are done.

Alright, so our field now also has a widget that users can input data with. Let's create the default field formatter to make the field whole.

Field formatter

Before coding it, let's establish what we want our formatter to look and behave like. By default, we want the license plate data to be rendered like this:

```
<span class="license-plate—code">{{ code }}</span> <span
    class="license-plate—number">{{ number }}</span>
```

So, each component is wrapped inside its own span tag, and some handy classes are applied to them. Alternatively, we may want to concatenate the two values together into one single span tag:

```
<span class="license-plate">{{ code }} {{ number
    }}</span>
```

This could be a setting on the formatter, allowing the user to choose the preferred output. So, let's do it then.

Field formatters go inside the `Plugin/Field/FieldFormatter` namespace of our module, so let's go ahead and create our own:

```
namespace Drupal\license_plate\Plugin\Field\FieldFormatter;

use Drupal\Core\Field\FormatterBase;
use Drupal\Core\StringTranslation\StringTranslationTrait;

/**
 * Plugin implementation of the
 *   'default_license_plate_formatter' formatter.
 *
 * @FieldFormatter(
 *   id = "default_license_plate_formatter",
 *   label = @Translation("Default license plate
 *       formatter"),
 *   field_types = {
```

```
 *        "license_plate"
 *    }
 * )
 */
class DefaultLicensePlateFormatter extends FormatterBase {

  use StringTranslationTrait;
}
```

Again, we start by inspecting the annotation, which looks very unsurprising. It looks almost like the one for our widget earlier, as formatters can also be used on multiple field types.

The class extends `FormatterBase`, which itself implements the obligatory `FormatterInterface`. By now, you recognize the pattern used with plugins—they all have to implement an interface and typically extend a base class, which provides some helpful functionalities common to all plugins of those types. Fields are no different.

The first thing we do inside this formatter class is, again, deal with its own settings (if we need any). As it happens, we have a configurable setting for our formatter, so let's define it and provide a default value:

```
/**
 * {@inheritdoc}
 */
public static function defaultSettings() {
  return [
    'concatenated' => 1,
  ] + parent::defaultSettings();
}
```

This is just like with the previous plugins. The `concatenated` setting will be used to determine the output of this field according to the two options we talked about earlier.

Next, predictably, we will need the form to manage this setting:

```
/**
 * {@inheritdoc}
 */
public function settingsForm(array $form,
  FormStateInterface $form_state) {
  return [
    'concatenated' => [
```

```
        '#type' => 'checkbox',
        '#title' => $this->t('Concatenated'),
        '#description' => $this->t('Whether to concatenate
           the code and number into a single string separated
              by a space. Otherwise the two are broken up into
                 separate span tags.'),
        '#default_value' => $this->getSetting
           ('concatenated'),
     ]
   ] + parent::settingsForm($form, $form_state);
}
```

Again, nothing special; we have a checkbox, which we use to manage a Boolean value (represented by 1 or 0). Lastly, just like with the widget, we have a summary display for formatters as well that we can define:

```
/**
 * {@inheritdoc}
 */
public function settingsSummary() {
  $summary = [];
  $summary[] = $this->t('Concatenated: @value', ['@value'
    => (bool) $this->getSetting('concatenated') ? $this->
       t('Yes') : $this->t('No')]);
  return $summary;
}
```

Here, we just print in a human-readable name of whatever has been configured, and this will be displayed when managing the field display in the UI and will look just like it did with the widget. Consistency is nice.

Now, we've reached the most critical aspect of any field formatter—the actual display:

```
/**
 * {@inheritdoc}
 */
public function viewElements(FieldItemListInterface $items,
  $langcode) {
  $elements = [];
```

```
  foreach ($items as $delta => $item) {
    $elements[$delta] = $this->viewValue($item);
  }

  return $elements;
}


/**
 * Generate the output appropriate for one field item.
 *
 * @param \Drupal\Core\Field\FieldItemInterface $item
 *   One field item.
 *
 * @return array
 */
protected function viewValue(FieldItemInterface $item) {
  $code = $item->get('code')->getValue();
  $number = $item->get('number')->getValue();
  return [
    '#theme' => 'license_plate',
    '#code' => $code,
    '#number' => $number,
    '#concatenated' => $this->getSetting('concatenated')
  ];
}
```

The method used for this is `viewElements()`, but for each element in the list, we simply delegate the processing to a helper method because, as you remember, the field is itself a list of value items (depending on the field cardinality), even if there is only one value in the field. These are keyed by a delta, which we also use to key the array of `$elements` that we return from the method.

For each individual item in the list, we then retrieve the value of the license plate code and number using the TypedData accessors we saw earlier. Remember that at this point, we are working with `FieldItemInterface` whose `get()` method returns the DataType plugin that represents the actual value, which, in our case, is `StringData`. Because that is what our field property definitions were:

```
$properties['number'] = DataDefinition::create('string')
  ->setLabel(t('Plate number'));
```

Also, the actual values inside these plugins are the string representations the user provided. We use these values together with the setting to determine whether to concatenate and pass them to a custom theme function (we have yet to define this). The important thing to keep in mind is that we need to return, for each item, a render array. This can be anything; consider the following example:

```
return [
  '#markup' => $code . ' ' . $number,
];
```

However, that doesn't look nice, nor is it configurable or overridable. So, we opt for a clean new theme function that takes those three arguments (remember this from when we spoke about theming?):

```
/**
 * Implements hook_theme().
 */
function license_plate_theme($existing, $type, $theme,
  $path) {
  return [
    'license_plate' => [
      'variables' => ['code' => NULL, 'number' => NULL,
        'concatenated' => TRUE],
    ],
  ];
}
```

We default the value for `concatenated` to TRUE because that is what we used inside `defaultSettings()` as well. We have to be consistent. The template file that goes with this, `license-plate.html.twig`, is also very simple:

```
{% if concatenated %}
  <span class="license-plate">{{ code }} {{ number
    }}</span>
{% else %}
  <span class="license-plate--code">{{ code }}</span> <span
    class="license-plate--number">{{ number }}</span>
{% endif %}
```

Depending on our setting, we output the markup differently. Other modules and themes now have a host of options to alter this output:

- They can create a new formatter plugin altogether.
- They can override the template inside a theme.
- They can alter the template to be used by this theme hook.

That's it for the formatter plugin itself, but this time we're not forgetting about the configuration schema. Although we have a measly little Boolean value to define, it still needs to be done:

```
field.formatter.settings.default_license_plate_formatter:
  type: mapping
  label: 'Default license plate formatter settings'
  mapping:
    concatenated:
      type: boolean
      label: 'Whether to concatenate the two fields into
        one single span tag'
```

This works the same way as the other ones but with a different prefix: `field.formatter.settings`.

With that, we have our field formatter in the bag. We should not forget, however, the missing *use* statements at the top of the formatter plugin class:

```
use Drupal\Core\Field\FieldItemInterface;
use Drupal\Core\Field\FieldItemListInterface;
use Drupal\Core\Form\FormStateInterface;
```

Now after clearing the cache, the new field type can be used to create fields.

However, I still think we can do one better. Since we are working with license plates that deal with certain known formats, what if we make our field configurable to provide a list of license plate codes that can be used when inputting the data? This will have the added benefit of us learning something new about fields—field settings.

Field settings

When we created our field type, we specified some storage settings, and we saw that these are typically linked to underlying storage and cannot be changed once the field has data in it. This is because databases have a hard time making table column changes when there is data present in them. However, apart from storage settings, we also have something called field settings, which are specific to the field instance on a certain entity bundle. Even more, they can (or should) be changeable even after the field has been created and has data in it. An example of such a field setting, which is available from Drupal core on all field types, is the "required" option, which marks a field as required or not. So, let's see how we can add our own field settings to configure what we said we wanted to do.

Back in our `LicensePlateItem` plugin class, we start by adding the default field settings:

```
/**
 * {@inheritdoc}
 */
public static function defaultFieldSettings() {
  return [
      'codes' => '',
    ] + parent::defaultFieldSettings();
}
```

This is the same pattern we've been seeing by which we specify what the settings are and what are their relevant defaults. Then, as expected, we need the form, where users can input the setting values for each field instance:

```
/**
 * {@inheritdoc}
 */
public function fieldSettingsForm(array $form,
  FormStateInterface $form_state) {
  $element = [];

  $element['codes'] = [
    '#title' => $this->t('License plate codes'),
    '#type' => 'textarea',
    '#default_value' => $this->getSetting('codes'),
    '#description' => $this->t('If you want the field to be
      have a select list with license plate codes instead
        of a textfield, please provide the available codes.
          Each code on a new line.')
  ];

  return $element;
}
```

What we provide here is a `textarea` form element by which the administrator can add multiple license plate codes, one per line. In our widget, we will use these and turn them into a select list. However, before we do that, we need to provide the configuration schema for this new setting:

```
field.field_settings.license_plate_type:
  type: mapping
  label: 'License plate field settings'
  mapping:
    codes:
      type: string
      label: 'Codes'
```

With this in place, we can turn to our field widget and make the necessary changes.

Inside the `formElement()` method, let's replace the block where we defined the code form element with this:

```
$this->addCodeField($element, $items, $delta,
  $placeholder_settings);
```

Since the logic for determining that element depends on configuration, it's a bit more complicated, so it's best to refactor to its own method. Now let's write it up:

```
protected function addCodeField(&$element,
  FieldItemListInterface $items, $delta,
    $placeholder_settings) {
  $element['details']['code'] = [
    '#title' => $this->t('Plate code'),
    '#default_value' => isset($items[$delta]->code) ?
      $items[$delta]->code : NULL,
    '#description' => '',
    '#required' => $element['#required'],
  ];

  $codes = $this->getFieldSetting('codes');
  if (!$codes) {
    $element['details']['code'] += [
      '#type' => 'textfield',
      '#placeholder' => $placeholder_settings['code'],
      '#maxlength' => $this->getFieldSetting
```

```
        ('code_max_length'),
      '#size' => $this->getSetting('code_size'),
    ];
    return;
  }


  $codes = explode("\r\n", $codes);
  $element['details']['code'] += [
    '#type' => 'select',
    '#options' => array_combine($codes, $codes),
  ];
}
```

We start by defining the code form element defaults, such as title, default, and value. Then, we get the field settings for the `codes` setting we just created. Note that `getFieldSetting()` and `getFieldSettings()` delegate to the actual field type and return both storage and field settings combined. So, we don't need to use separate methods. However, one implication is that you should probably stick to different setting names for the two categories.

Then, if we don't have any codes configured in this field instance, we build up our textfield form element as we did before. Otherwise, we break them up into an array and use them in a select list form element. Also, note that in this latter case, we no longer need to apply any length limits because of the validation inherent to select lists. Values that are not present in the original options list will be considered invalid.

That's pretty much it. The field can now be configured to either default to the open textfield for adding a license plate code or to a select list of predefined ones. Also, the same field can be used in these two ways on two different bundles, which is neat.

Using our custom field type as a base field

At the beginning of this chapter, I stressed the importance of understanding the makeup of a field (type, widget, and formatter) so as to easily define base fields on custom entity types. This understanding allows you to navigate through Drupal core code, discover their settings, and use them on base fields. So, let's cement this understanding by seeing how our new field could be defined as a base field on a custom entity type.

Here is an example where we actually use all the available settings we defined for each of the three plugins. Note that any settings that are left out default to the values we specified in the relevant *defaults* method, as follows:

```php
$fields['plate'] = BaseFieldDefinition::create
  ('license_plate')
  ->setLabel(t('License plate'))
  ->setDescription(t('Please provide your license plate
    number.'))
  ->setSettings([
    'number_max_length' => 255,
    'code_max_length' => 5,
    'codes' => implode("\r\n", ['NY', 'FL', 'IL']),
  ])
  ->setDisplayOptions('view', [
    'label' => 'above',
    'type' => 'default_license_plate_formatter',
    'weight' => 5,
    'settings' => [
      'concatenated' => 0,
    ]
  ])
  ->setDisplayOptions('form', [
    'type' => 'default_license_plate_widget',
    'weight' => 5,
    'settings' => [
      'number_size' => 60,
      'code_size' => 5,
      'fieldset_state' => 'open',
      'placeholder' => [
        'number' => '',
        'code' => '',
      ],
    ]
  ])
  ->setDisplayConfigurable('form', TRUE)
  ->setDisplayConfigurable('view', TRUE);
```

This is very similar to what we've been seeing. For the `create()` method, we use the `FieldType` plugin ID. Inside the `setSettings()` method, we pass both storage and field settings. They will then be used appropriately. Note that since the `codes` setting is stored as a string with codes separated by line breaks, we will need to add it accordingly.

Similarly, for the `view` and `form` display options, we use the formatter and widget plugin IDs, respectively, and inside a `settings` array, we pass any of the settings we have defined. Lastly, `setDisplayConfigurable()` indicates that all these settings for the formatter and widget are also configurable through the UI. Doing so will turn `BaseFieldDefinition` into `BaseFieldOverride`, as it needs to store the configured overrides.

This should be a recap for you, as we covered all these concepts in earlier chapters.

Summary

In this chapter, we looked at how we can create custom fields that site builders (and developers) can add to entity types. This implied defining three plugin types: `FieldType`, `FieldWidget`, and `FieldFormatter`, each with its own responsibility. The first defined the actual field, its storage, and individual data properties, using the TypedData API. The second defined the form through which users can input field data when creating or editing entities that use the field. The third defined how the values inside this field can be displayed when viewing the entity.

We also saw that each of these plugins can have custom sets of configurable settings that can be used to make the field dynamic—both in how the widget works and in how the values are displayed. Moreover, these settings are part of the exported field configuration, so we saw how we can define their respective configuration schemas.

Lastly, we also saw how—aside from creating our new field through the UI—developers can add it to an entity type as a base field, making it available on all bundles of that entity type.

In the next chapter, we will talk about access control, a very important topic, as we need to ensure that our data and functionality are only exposed to the users we want when we want.

10
Access Control

We've already talked about quite a few topics in the previous chapters, but we have been purposefully omitting an important aspect in many of them—access control. Much of what we have covered deals in some way or another with access, but we have kept it out of our discussions to keep things more to the point. However, access control is an immensely important topic for Drupal development because it has implications in almost everything we do. So, for this purpose, we have a chapter dedicated to it in which we will cover the most important things you need to know in order to keep your application secure.

When I say secure, I don't mean writing code in a secure way to avoid your site getting hacked. For that, we'have an appendix at the end of the book to give you some pointers. Instead, I mean handling access control programmatically to ensure that your pages and any other resources are only accessible to the right users.

In this chapter, aside from introducing new concepts that stand on their own, we'll be revisiting some of the previous topics and seeing how we can apply access control in that context. We will start by talking about how Drupal sees access restrictions at a high level, but then dive deep into more specific and complex examples. Also, as usual, we will see code to better understand what we're talking about.

So, what exactly are we going to learn in this chapter?

- First, we will introduce the Drupal access system of roles and permissions and see how we can create them in our code. Even more importantly for us as module developers, we will see how we can check whether users have permissions programmatically. This is still while keeping things general.

- Next, we will dive into more exciting things by looking at route permissions. We have enormous flexibility here and we'll explore several approaches we can use to restrict access to custom and existing routes—ranging from simple permission-based access control to dynamic service-oriented access handlers.

- After covering routes, we will look at entities and how access control works with them. In doing so, we will work a bit on the Product entity type we created in *Chapter 7, Your Own Custom Entity and Plugin Types*. Moreover, we will also talk about the *Node Access Grants* system, which is a powerful way to control access specific to the Node entity type.

- Finally, we will also look at Block plugins and see how we can control access and ensure that they are rendered on the page. Blocks can have certain contextual rules that determine whether they are displayed on a certain page in the region they have been added to. So, we will talk about that a bit as well.

The purpose of this chapter is to bring together all aspects related to access control that you need to get started as a Drupal module developer. However, you can expect even more than that, and for this reason, this chapter can also serve as a resource for coming back and reading up on certain approaches to access control that you may want to use in your own project, rather than having them scattered across the book.

Introduction to the Drupal access system

If you've been doing some site building in Drupal or have experience with previous versions of Drupal, you may already know a thing or two about roles and permissions. If not, no need to worry, as we will talk a bit about how these work.

Essentially, one of the things that makes Drupal special is the flexible access system it has out of the box, based on user roles and permissions. Roles are attributes that can be given to a user. The latter can have multiple roles assigned but always has at least the default *Authenticated User* role. Permissions are the individual access indicators that can be assigned to roles. By the transitive property, users have all the permissions assigned to the roles they have been assigned. So, the result is a matrix of permissions by role, and that's actually how it is visualized in the UI at `admin/people/permissions`:

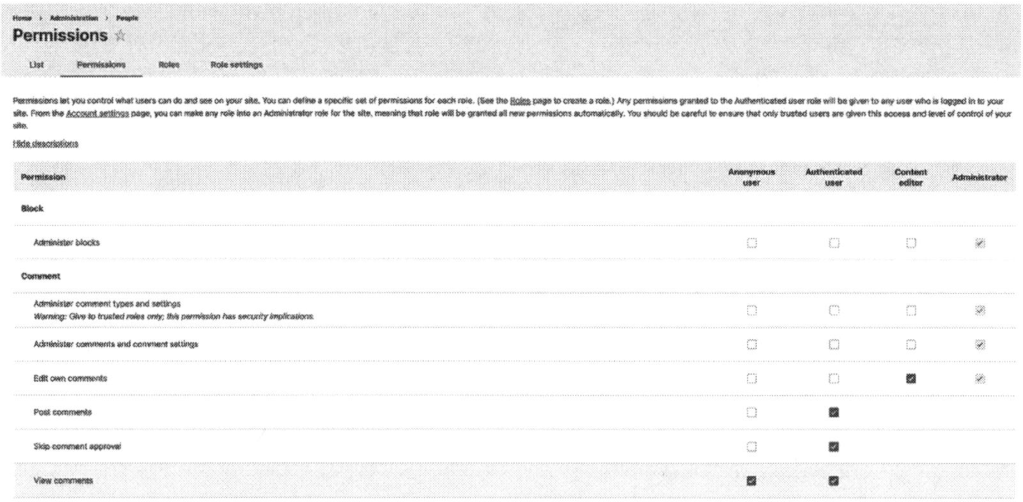

Figure 10.1: Configuring user permissions

Drupal core, by default, comes with three roles—**ANONYMOUS USER**, **AUTHENTICATED USER**, and **ADMINISTRATOR**. Also, by default, there are many permissions already defined by Drupal core (and contributed) modules, ready to be assigned to various roles.

The anonymous user role is pretty self-explanatory and can be used as a bucket for the permissions all anonymous users should have—that is, users who are not authenticated. Similarly, the authenticated user role is automatically assigned to all users upon logging in (and cannot be removed). So, it can be used as a bucket of permissions that all authenticated users should have.

The super admin user (the one with the ID = 1) actually has all the permissions on the site without having to explicitly assign roles or permissions. Most of the time, it bypasses most of the access control in any given subsystem.

Roles and permissions under the hood

Roles are configuration entities (`user_role`) represented by the `Role` entity type class. They can be created through the UI and exported as configuration to be available on all the environments. As such, there is not much you need to do in your code to define a role, but simply create them as needed in the UI and export them to configuration. As you remember, if you want your role to be provided by your module, add the exported YAML file to the `config/install` folder (and remove the UUID). Refer to *Chapter 6, Data Modeling and Storage*, for more information.

Permissions, on the other hand, are a custom construct. They are created using a YAML file (very similar to how we define menu links). The `PermissionHandler` service is responsible for reading all the YAML files and figuring out all the existing permissions on the site. This is not something you need to worry about, as you won't be interacting with this service. You'll mostly be interested in defining new permissions and checking whether a user has them or setting those permissions in various access contexts.

Defining permissions

The way to create permissions in a custom module is by creating a `*.permissions.yml` file and adding the definitions in there. Consider the following example:

```
administer my feature:
  title: 'Administer my feature'
  restrict access: true
```

In this example, `administer my feature` is the machine name of the permission and actually the most important part. This is what you will use in your code to reference it. Then, we have a title that shows up on the permissions management page we saw earlier. Finally, we have a `restrict access` key through which we can specify whether we need a warning to be output on the permissions management page regarding the security implications, as follows: *Warning: Give to trusted roles only; this permission has security implications:*

Comment

Administer comment types and settings
Warning: Give to trusted roles only; this permission has security implications.

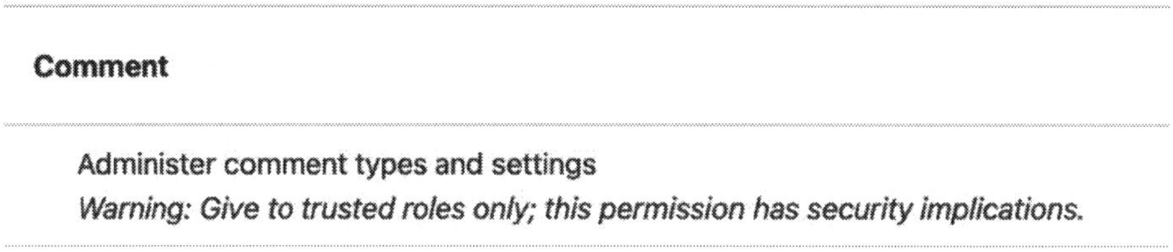

Figure 10.2: Secure permissions notice

This is to indicate that our permission is more sensitive and administrators should pay attention to who they assign it to. This option can, however, be left out (as you will see in most cases actually).

You may have noticed the static nature of this way of defining permissions. In other words, we hardcoded the permission name and only have one permission. In most cases, this will be fine. However, there can be times when you will need multiple permissions defined dynamically based on some other factors in your application. For this, we can use a permission callback.

For example, the Node module defines individual permissions to manage each of its bundles, and this makes sense. Some roles should have access to some bundles while other roles should have access to other bundles. However, there is no way it can know which bundles it will have at any given point. So, it uses a permission callback:

```
permission_callbacks:
  - \Drupal\node\NodePermissions::nodeTypePermissions
```

This is found in the `node.permissions.yml` file just like the statically defined ones, but it delegates the responsibility of getting the permissions to the `nodeTypePermissions` method of the `NodePermissions` class. This is the same notation we use to define controllers in the route. As a matter of fact, the same class resolver is used to instantiate it.

One last thing about defining permissions before we continue: they can have dependencies. We just said that permissions can be declared dynamically based on existing configuration, such as the available node types. Well, if that node type is deleted, the permission gets removed as well. However, permissions are configured in user roles so Drupal needs to know that when a dependency of a permission gets removed, it should also update all the roles where the permission is used. So, the permission definition can also have a `dependencies` key, such as this:

```
dependencies:
  config:
    - node.type.article
```

As you can see, it looks exactly like a regular configuration dependency.

Checking the user credentials

You can easily check whether a given user should access a certain resource if you have that user account at hand. Here, you can encounter two scenarios:

- You want to "interrogate" the current user
- You want to "interrogate" a given user, not necessarily the current one

As we saw in *Chapter 2*, *Creating Your First Module*, the current user is represented by a service that implements the `AccountProxyInterface` interface. This service can be accessed by the `current_user` key or statically with this shorthand:

```
$account_proxy = \Drupal::currentUser();
```

From this account proxy, we can request the `AccountInterface`, which represents the actual logged-in user account (the `UserSession` object). It holds a reference to the User entity, with some of its account-related data, but that is pretty much it. If we need to access its entity fields, we need to load the entity as we normally do:

```
$user = \Drupal::entityTypeManager()
  ->getStorage('user')
  ->load($account_proxy->id());
```

The resulting `UserInterface`, by the way, also implements the same `AccountInterface`, so these common methods can be used on both objects. In other words, the `User` entity type is essentially the storage facility for the `AccountInterface` that represents a user who is browsing the site. However, for the moment, the User entity is not so relevant, so we will get back to the account, which we can retrieve from the proxy, like so:

```
$account = $account_proxy->getAccount();
```

The methods on this interface allow us to "interrogate" the account (either the current user account or the one represented by a given User entity) for its credentials. Also, many of these methods are present in the AccountProxy, meaning that you can ask it directly for this information.

Two very general but often helpful methods are the following:

```
$account->isAnonymous();
$account->isAuthenticated();
```

These check whether the account is anonymous or not, without taking any roles or permissions into account. Sometimes, your access control is solely based on this distinction.

We can also get a list of roles the account has, as follows:

```
$account->getRoles();
```

Even more important, we can check whether the user has a given permission:

```
$account->hasPermission($permission)
```

Where $permission is a string (the machine name of the permission as we saw it defined earlier). This method is very helpful because it checks all the roles the user has for the specified permission.

You can use these methods anywhere in your code when you need to check whether a user should be accessing certain parts of your functionality.

Route access

Now that we've seen how the access system works in Drupal at a basic level and how we can define permissions and check user credentials, it's time to talk about routes.

As we saw from the very first time we wrote code in this book, routes are the entry points into your application. Also, as a developer, it is one of the main things you'll be dealing with, so controlling who can access these routes is the responsibility of the access system.

There are several ways we can ensure that routes are only accessible to the right users, so let's see what these are.

The simplest way is by checking for a permission. We actually did that in *Chapter 2, Creating Your First Module*, when we defined our hello_world.hello route:

```
hello_world.hello:
  path: '/hello'
  defaults:
    _controller: '\Drupal\hello_world\Controller\
      HelloWorldController::helloWorld'
    _title: 'Our first route'
  requirements:
    _permission: 'access content'
```

The requirements key in a route definition contains all the data that the request trying to reach this route must have. This contains mostly access-like information but also things such as the request format.

The requirement in the previous example is `_permission` (all these options typically start with an underscore). It is used to specify that the user accessing this route needs to have that permission, similar to how we checked whether a user has it earlier:

```
$account->hasPermission($permission).
```

The `access content` permission is something defined by Drupal core and is basically the one you'd use when the restrictions are very lax, meaning that all users should be able to access the resource. By default, this permission is also present on the *Anonymous* user role.

Speaking of lax restrictions, there is one option that is fully open:

```
_access: "TRUE"
```

This essentially opens up the route to basically everybody under any circumstance—not something you'll probably use often, but it's handy in some cases.

Returning to permissions, we can also include multiple permissions in this requirement. For example, to check whether a user has **either** of the two permissions, we separate them with a plus (+) sign:

```
_permission: "my custom permission+administer site
configuration"
```

For checking whether the user has **all** the given permissions, we separate them with a comma:

```
_permission: "my custom permission,my other permission"
```

So, we can already see quite some flexibility.

> **Note**
> `administer site configuration` is another staple permission from Drupal core that we can use to ensure that the user is an administrator; it is typically a sensitive permission given only to these users.

Next, we also have a requirement by which we can check whether the user has a given role. In a similar manner, we can include multiple roles to check, depending on whether we want to do AND or OR checking:

```
_role: "administrator"
_role: "editor,administrator"
_role: "editor+administrator"
```

This approach is not as flexible as using permissions and it's a little "hardcody". By this, I mean that you are hardcoding an access rule based on site configuration (as roles are configuration entities). If that configuration is removed, you may have broken code. Permissions, on the other hand, are also code, as they are defined in a module (or Drupal core). However, the option is there if you need it.

The next type of requirement we should be covering here is _entity_access. However, understanding this requires us to first know a bit about entity-level access, so we will skip it now; we'll come back to it later in the chapter. Instead, we will talk about the mother of all route access approaches—the custom one.

> **Note**
>
> Route access requirements can also be stacked, which means that we can add more than one access requirement to a route and access will be given if **all** of them grant access. If one denies it or has no opinion (neutral), access is denied to the route. This is done by simply adding multiple requirements to the route.

Custom route access

The previous ways of controlling routes are powerful and relatively flexible, but static. We are hardcoding the rules into a file and expect the incoming user to abide by them. However, what if things are more complicated than that, and we need a more dynamic approach? Trust me, things get complicated, fast. We can use the _custom_access option of the route requirements.

In this subsection, we will see how custom access checkers work, and how we can create our own; just something simple to demonstrate the process. Then, we will see a more advanced implementation that will have us work a bit with routes programmatically.

There are two ways custom access checkers can be created and used with a route, and they both involve creating a class. The way this class is used makes the distinction: we can either reference it directly (statically) or make it into a service and reference it like so. We will see an example of both later in this chapter.

To demonstrate, let's say that we want to make sure that our Hello World route is only accessible to users who don't have a specific role—editor. Doesn't make much sense, but it's a simple example we can run with.

Static approach

The static approach involves creating a method on our Controller (or somewhere else), usually called access(), and referencing it from the route definition. So, inside our controller we can have this:

```
/**
 * Handles the access checking.
 */
```

```
public function access(AccountInterface $account) {
  return in_array('editor', $account->getRoles()) ?
    AccessResult::forbidden() : AccessResult::allowed();
}
```

And the new *use* statements:

```
use Drupal\Core\Access\AccessResult;
use Drupal\Core\Session\AccountInterface;
```

This method receives the current user's `AccountInterface`, which we can use to determine the roles. Moreover, if we type-hint some extra parameters, Drupal will pass them to the method as well:

- `\Symfony\Component\Routing\Route $route`

- `\Drupal\Core\Routing\RouteMatch $route_match`

We've already discussed the `CurrentRouteMatch` service in *Chapter 2*, *Creating Your First Module*, and we saw that we can use it to find out things about the route that has just been accessed. In reality, that service simply uses `RouteMatch` objects underneath. So, in case our access rules for this route depend on something that relates to the route, this argument can be very important. Soon, I will demonstrate why that is in further detail.

Similarly, we can also type-hint the actual `Route` object that contains data about the route. This plays to the same point I just made, and we can also use it in our logic. But alas, for our use case, this won't be necessary, so we will stick with the `AccountInterface`.

What we are returning in this method is very important, as it needs to be an instance of `AccessResultInterface`. This is the standard interface the access system in Drupal works with. The following are the three main implementations of this interface you will often encounter:

- `AccessResultAllowed`

- `AccessResultNeutral`

- `AccessResultForbidden`

The gateway to these objects, however, is typically the `AccessResult` abstract base class (which all implementations extend as well) and its static methods. As you saw in the previous example, we used the `allowed()` and `forbidden()` methods to instantiate these objects. Of course, there is also the corresponding `neutral()` method we can use to indicate that we don't have a say in the matter. Typically, this is used when there are multiple actors involved in deciding access to a certain resource and one such actor encounters a resource for which they don't need to control access.

The neutral and forbidden access results also support a reason. This is typically used in REST scenarios to display a message as to why the access has been denied or skipped. So, for example, we can return something like this when denying access:

```
return AccessResult::forbidden('Editors are not allowed');
```

Some other built-in capabilities of the `AccessResult` base class are related to cacheability, but it also has convenience methods to achieve a bit more complex access logic. For example, the following methods can prove handy:

- `allowedIf($condition)`
- `forbiddenIf($condition)`

You simply pass a Boolean to these methods and they return the right access object. Do keep in mind that these methods return an `AccessResultNeutral` object if the condition evaluates to FALSE. So, you cannot use these methods if you need to map a Boolean to an explicitly allowed or explicitly denied result.

Additionally, we have methods like the following:

- `allowedIfHasPermission()`
- `allowedIfHasPermissions()`

These will check whether a given account has one or more permissions and returns the right access object depending on the case.

Finally, we also have the `orIf()` and `andIf()` methods with which we can build more complex access structures that combine multiple `AccessResultInterface` results.

Closing the parentheses on the `AccessResultInterface`, let's reference this method in our route in order to actually make use of it. This is what the route definition looks like now:

```
hello_world.hello:
  path: '/hello'
  defaults:
    _controller: Drupal\hello_world\Controller\
      HelloWorldController::helloWorld
    _title: 'Our first route'
  requirements:
    _custom_access: Drupal\hello_world\Controller\
      HelloWorldController::access
```

Instead of the `_permission` requirement, we use `_custom_access` with a reference to our Controller method. After clearing the cache, our new access checker will "kick out" those pesky `editor` users.

This static approach, as you can imagine, is slightly more powerful than using permission or roles-based access checking because it allows you to write PHP logic in order to determine the access. However, it falls short in several ways, and this is where the service-based approach can be used.

Service approach

The service approach involves creating a tagged service and referencing it in the route definition as a requirement. There are a few advantages to this method compared to the one we've just seen:

- Allows you to encapsulate complex access logic in its own class
- Allows you to inject dependencies and make use of them in calculating the access
- Allows you to reuse the access checker on multiple routes

Let's take a look at how we can implement this for our Hello World route. We will replace the previous approach but keep the goal of denying access to editors. However, to increase the complexity a bit, editors will be allowed if the Hello World salutation has not been overridden via the configuration form. If you recall, in *Chapter 2, Creating Your First Module*, we created a form where the salutation message can be overridden and stored in a configuration object.

First, let's create our class. Typically, access-related classes go inside the `Access` folder of the module namespace—it's not necessarily so, but it makes sense to put them there. Then, we can have something like this:

```
namespace Drupal\hello_world\Access;

use Drupal\Core\Access\AccessResult;
use Drupal\Core\Config\ConfigFactoryInterface;
use Drupal\Core\Routing\Access\AccessInterface;
use Drupal\Core\Session\AccountInterface;

/**
 * Access handler for the Hello World route.
 */
class HelloWorldAccess implements AccessInterface {

  /**
   * @var \Drupal\Core\Config\ConfigFactoryInterface
```

```
  */
  protected $configFactory;


  /**
   * HelloWorldAccess constructor.
   *
   * @param \Drupal\Core\Config\ConfigFactoryInterface
   *    $configFactory
   */
  public function __construct(ConfigFactoryInterface
    $configFactory) {
    $this->configFactory = $configFactory;
  }


  /**
   * Handles the access checking.
   *
   * @param AccountInterface $account
   *
   * @return AccessResult
   */
  public function access(AccountInterface $account) {
    $salutation = $this->configFactory->get
      ('hello_world.custom_salutation')->get('salutation');
    return in_array('editor', $account->getRoles()) &&
      $salutation != "" ? AccessResult::forbidden() :
        AccessResult::allowed();
  }
}
```

Right off the bat, I would like to mention that the `AccessInterface` we're implementing is at this point a bit up in the air. If you look inside, you'll see that it has no methods. This is because of the dynamic argument resolving we talked about earlier, by which we can get the route and route match if we type-hint them. There was an ongoing discussion at the time of writing this book on marking it deprecated and maybe eventually removing it completely (or finding another solution). So, it's something worth paying attention to in the long run.

Also, since there is no interface, the access() method naming is not enforced. However, we will need it because that is the name being looked for by the access system when using the service. As before, we get the user making the request from which we can get the roles. Moreover, we injected the configuration factory and checked whether the salutation text had been overridden. Only if that is the case will editors be denied access. It's nothing too complicated for us at this point.

Now, let's take a look at how we define this as a service to be used by our route as an access checker:

```
hello_world.access_checker:
  class: Drupal\hello_world\Access\HelloWorldAccess
  arguments: ['@config.factory']
  tags:
    - { name: access_check, applies_to:
      _hello_world_access_check }
```

As you can see, tagged services are very important in Drupal and are a great example of an extension point with which we can contribute our own code to an existing set of functionality. In this example, apart from tagging it for access checking, we also see another option for this tag: applies_to. The corresponding string is what we can now use in our route definition to target this particular access checker. So instead of the following line:

```
_custom_access: '\Drupal\hello_world\Controller\
  HelloWorldController::access'
```

We have this one:

```
_hello_world_access_check: 'TRUE'
```

The TRUE value we set doesn't make much of a difference. If we wanted, we could add a string value that could actually be used by the access checker internally. However, we'll use a different approach for that later. So, for now, the standard thing to do is just use TRUE.

After clearing the cache, our new access checker will kick in and that is pretty much it.

Programmatically checking access on routes

If we define routes and users go to those routes, Drupal checks access for us automatically (according to the requirements set forth in the route definition). However, we may often need to check access to a given route programmatically, for example, to know whether we should show a link to it to the current user.

In *Chapter 2, Creating Your First Module*, we saw how to work with `Url` objects to create links, and we can use these very `Url` objects to check access on a given route. Consider the following example:

```
$url = Url::fromRoute('hello_world.hello');
if ($url->access()) {
  // Do something.
}
```

The `access()` method on the `Url` object works only with *routed* URLs, those which have been determined to have a route behind them. It will obviously not work with things such as external URLs, so, in these cases, it will always return TRUE. Also, we can pass an `AccountInterface` to this method in case we want to check whether a specific user has access to that route. Without an argument, it defaults to the current user.

Under the hood, the `Url` class uses the `AccessManager` service to check the access of the route. This is done statically, so if you want, you can inject the service yourself (`access_manager`) and check the route access:

```
$access = $accessManager()->checkNamedRoute
  ('hello_world.hello', [], $account)
```

The empty array we pass as a second argument is an array of parameters that the route needs. You remember how route parameters work from *Chapter 2, Creating Your First Module*, right?

I mentioned earlier that it's very important to use the account, route, and route match that are being passed to the access checker as dynamic arguments if you need them for calculating the access logic, as opposed to injecting the current user or current route match services and using those. Maybe, now, you can start to understand why. Let me break it down.

One of my earlier points was that an advantage of the service-based access checking approach is that it allows us to use the same service on multiple routes. This means that we can have highly dynamic access rules by which we can check route options within the access checker and calculate access based on those, and this is quite powerful.

However, if you inject the current route match service and make use of that, your access rules will work only when that route is being requested in the browser, so, basically, when the user is trying to go to that path. This is because the current route just happens to be the same as the route the access checker is using (the injected one). However, if you programmatically check access on that route from another page (as we just saw), the current route match will be of that other page instead of the one you actually want to check access to.

You'll see this happen even if you don't manually check access on routes with menu links. If a given route is used in a menu link and printed on a page, Drupal will do the access checking automatically to ensure that users have access to that link. Moreover, recall from *Chapter 5, Menus and Menu Links*, that if you want to render menu links programmatically, one of the things you'll typically do is run the menu tree through a set of manipulators. An important manipulator is that which checks whether the current user has access to that route.

In these cases, you have the same problem. So, do remember to type-hint your access checker with the route and/or route match objects, and do not inject them. Of course, do not inject the current user service either (unless you have a very specific reason for doing so).

Bonus – dynamic route options for access control

We've seen how to create a service-based access checker that we can use on our routes. Using this technique, I want to demonstrate the flexibility of using the service on multiple routes. Imagine that we have multiple routes that display some user information. However, these routes are specific to a user type, and hence accessible only for that user type. In this example, a user type will be defined based on the value of a simple text field on the user entity, and we want to specify in the route definition for which user type it should be accessible. The code we write for this demonstration will go inside a new `user_types` module.

An alternative approach to checking the access inside a route for this example is to simply verify inside the Controller that the current user should access it. If not, throwing an `AccessDeniedHttpException` inside a `Controller` method will turn the request into a 403 (access denied). However, this is almost always the wrong approach because the route can no longer be verified for access, and we'll end up with links on our site that potentially lead to a 403 page. And we don't want that. For this reason, if the page has access rules, they belong in the access system and not in the Controller.

We'll go into this example with the assumption that the user entity has a field called `field_user_type` already on it; that we have users of three types: `board_member`, `manager`, and `employee`; and that we have the following four route definitions:

```
user_types.board_members:
  path: '/board-member'
  defaults:
    _controller: '\Drupal\user_types\Controller\
      UserTypesController::boardMember'
    _title: 'Board member'
user_types.manager:
  path: '/manager'
  defaults:
    _controller: '\Drupal\user_types\Controller\
      UserTypesController::manager'
    _title: 'Manager'
user_types.employee:
```

```
   path: '/employee'
   defaults:
     _controller: '\Drupal\user_types\Controller\
       UserTypesController::employee'
     _title: 'Employee'
 user_types.leadership:
   path: '/leadership'
   defaults:
     _controller: '\Drupal\user_types\Controller\
       UserTypesController::leadership'
     _title: 'Leadership'
```

These routes don't have any access requirements yet, as it is our job to create them now. However, you can already understand what kind of users should be able to access these routes. The user_types. board_members route is for board members, user_types.manager is for managers, user_ types.employee is for both employees and managers (since both are actual employees), and user_types.leadership is for the board members and managers. So, a bit of mix and match to highlight the need for flexibility in our access checker.

Obviously, we don't want to write a service for each combination of user types to handle the access here. Using the static approach is not suitable either because we need to inject a dependency, and we also don't want to duplicate the logic using different callables.

So, let's write the service definition for this access checker:

```
user_types.access_checker:
  class: Drupal\user_types\Access\UserTypesAccess
  arguments: [,@entity_type.manager']
  tags:
    - { name: access_check, applies_to: _user_types_access_
check }
```

We inject the entity type manager service so that we can load the user entity corresponding to the user whose access is being checked. As you remember, the AccountInterface is not enough to read field data from that user.

Now, we can update our route requirements (for all four routes) to make use of this access checker:

```
  requirements:
    _user_types_access_check: 'TRUE'
```

Note

Earlier, we saw the static access checker being referenced using the `_custom_access` requirement. This is the same as the one we are creating now but is provided by Drupal core and maps to the `CustomAccessCheck` service (instead of the custom one we are now writing). This, in turn, delegates the responsibility to the class method set in the definition.

Now, it's time to make the distinction between our four routes in terms of the types of users that should have access to them, and we can use *route options* for this. Options are a set of arbitrary pieces of data that we can put on a route definition and retrieve later programmatically. If you remember, in *Chapter 2*, *Creating Your First Module*, parameter converters are such an example that can be defined as an option in the route.

Let's take a look at just one of the routes as an example in full, and you'll extrapolate what the other routes will have to look like:

```
hello_world.employee:
  path: '/employee'
  defaults:
    _controller: '\Drupal\hello_world\Controller\
      UserTypesController::employee'
    _title: 'Employee'
  requirements:
    _user_types_access_check: 'TRUE'
  options:
    _user_types:
      - manager
      - employee
```

Route options are placed under the `options` key and are conventionally named with an underscore at the beginning (however, this is not mandatory). In a standard YAML notation, we have a sequence of string values underneath our `_user_types` option, which will be turned into a PHP array when read into the Route object.

Now, we can create our access checker service and make use of all this for controlling access:

```
namespace Drupal\user_types\Access;

use Drupal\Core\Access\AccessResult;
use Drupal\Core\Entity\EntityTypeManager;
use Drupal\Core\Routing\Access\AccessInterface;
```

```php
use Drupal\Core\Session\AccountInterface;
use Symfony\Component\Routing\Route;

/**
 * Access handler for the User Types routes.
 */
class UserTypesAccess implements AccessInterface {

  /**
   * @var \Drupal\Core\Entity\EntityTypeManager
   */
  protected $entityTypeManager;

  /**
   * UserTypesAccess constructor.
   *
   * @param \Drupal\Core\Entity\EntityTypeManager
   *     $entityTypeManager
   */
  public function __construct(EntityTypeManager
    $entityTypeManager) {
    $this->entityTypeManager = $entityTypeManager;
  }

  /**
   * Handles the access checking.
   *
   * @param AccountInterface $account
   * @param \Symfony\Component\Routing\Route $route
   *
   * @return \Drupal\Core\Access\AccessResult
   */
  public function access(AccountInterface $account, Route
    $route) {
    $user_types = $route->getOption('_user_types');
    if (!$user_types) {
```

```
      return AccessResult::forbidden();
    }
  if ($account->isAnonymous()) {
    return AccessResult::forbidden();
  }
  $user = $this->entityTypeManager->getStorage('user')
    ->load($account->id());
  $type = $user->get('field_user_type')->value;
  return in_array($type, $user_types) ?
    AccessResult::allowed() : AccessResult::forbidden();
  }
}
```

As per the service definition, we inject the entity type manager as a dependency. This is something we could not have done using the static approach. Then, in our `access()` method, we also type-hint the route on which this service is used for evaluating access. Now comes the fun part.

We inspect the route and try to retrieve our option by name. Just as a fail-safe, we deny access if the option is missing. This should never be the case, as we only use this access checker on routes that do have the option, but you never know. Additionally, we also deny access if the user is anonymous. Anonymous users are sure not to have any user type field value.

Then, we load the user entity of the current account and simply check that field value and return access according to whether it is within the allowed ones for the route. I recommend that you inspect the Route class and see what other handy data you can make use of.

This is it. Now we have a flexible access-checking service that we can use on any number of routes that need this *user type* access control.

A key takeaway from this bonus technique is that you can build incredibly flexible architectures using options on routes. In this example, we used them for access, but you can also use them for other functionalities that tie to, and can be controlled from, the route.

CSRF protection on routes

Cross-Site Request Forgery (CSRF) is an attack that forces an end user to execute unwanted actions on a web application in which they're currently authenticated.

— *(OWASP)*

Drupal comes equipped with various tools for handling CSRF protection.

One such tool is the ability to add a CSRF token to a route built using the Drupal API automatically. Let's take a look at an example.

Imagine that you have a route that is used as some sort of a callback. Hitting this route triggers a process (for logged-in users), so you need to make sure that users only end up on this route from the place they should (part of the flow that needs to trigger that process). Tokens can be used for this, and Drupal has this covered.

There are two things we need to do: add a requirement to the route for CSRF protection and then build that link using the regular Drupal API we saw in *Chapter 2, Creating Your First Module*. Here's the requirement:

```
_csrf_token: 'TRUE'
```

Also, note that this can go together with other access-based requirements such as the ones we've been talking about in this section.

Adding the CSRF token requirement now makes the route inaccessible if simply accessed by navigating to the path in the browser. To make it accessible, we will need to print a link to it somewhere using the Drupal API:

```
$url = Url::fromRoute('my_module.my_route');
$link = [
  '#type' => 'link',
  '#url' => $url,
  '#title' => 'Protected callback'
];
```

This is one way, but we can also use the LinkGenerator service or the Link class, as we've seen in *Chapter 2, Creating Your First Module*. They will all render the link with a token appended to the URL as a query parameter. Drupal will then evaluate that token as part of the access control and make sure that it is valid. As a matter of fact, the link building plays no role. It is the URL generator that handles it. So, if you get the string URL this way, you will have the token on it automatically:

```
$path = $url->toString();
```

Under the hood, to manage the creation and validation of the tokens, Drupal uses the CsrfTokenGenerator service, which we can also use if we need to. For example, after getting our hands on the service (csrf_token), we can create a token:

```
$token = $generator->get('my_value');
```

Here, `my_value` is an optional string that the generator can use to make the token unique. It also uses the current user session and the private site key. Keep in mind that if the user is anonymous and no session has been started, the token will be unique on each request.

We can then validate this token as follows:

```
$valid = $generator->validate($token, 'my_value');
```

Here, `$generator` is the same service we used for creating it.

Using the token generator manually can be handy, but as we saw, it is very easy to just put a requirement on the route, and let Drupal do the rest. Moreover, CSRF protection is embedded in the Form API, so we don't have to do anything at all when it comes to forms for additional protection.

Altering routes

We've seen so far how to create access rules on our own routes. However, it would not be Drupal if it wasn't also easy to alter existing routes and change their access rules to whatever we want. This is yet another small extension point with which our custom modules can contribute to existing functionality.

Altering route access is done by altering the routes themselves. Of course, access is not the only reason why routes may be altered, as you can change just about anything else on the definition. So, let's see how you can alter routes for any purpose you might need.

Routes can be altered by subscribing to an event, just as we've seen in *Chapter 2, Creating Your First Module*, when we subscribed to the `kernel.request` event. This event is dispatched the moment all the routes are being built and before they get cached. So, the alteration will not happen dynamically (upon someone accessing the route), but only when they all get rebuilt. Let's see how we can subscribe to that event.

Unlike most other subscribers, the `EventSubscriberInterface` class for routes typically goes in the `Routing` namespace of the module, so that's where we'll put it. Moreover, the event we're listening to is `RoutingEvents::ALTER`. However, the routing system provides us with a base subscriber class that we can extend and that contains all this boilerplate code, leaving us to do only the alterations themselves.

And these alterations can look like this:

```
namespace Drupal\hello_world\Routing;

use Drupal\Core\Routing\RouteSubscriberBase;
use Symfony\Component\Routing\RouteCollection;

/**
```

```php
 * Subscribes to route events for the Hello World module.
 */
class HelloWorldRouteSubscriber extends RouteSubscriberBase {

  /**
   * {@inheritdoc}
   */
  protected function alterRoutes(RouteCollection
    $collection) {
    $route = $collection->get('user.register');
    if (!$route) {
      return;
    }

    // Example 1:
    // We deny access to the Register page in all cases.
       With this requirement,
    // it doesn't matter anymore what other access
       requirements exist or if they
    // evaluate positively.
    $route->setRequirement('_access', 'FALSE');

    // Example 2:
    // We check for the presence of a specific access
       requirement and if it exists,
    // we clear all the access requirements on the route
       and set our own.
    if ($route->hasRequirement('_access_user_register')) {
      $route->setRequirements([]);
      $route->setRequirement('_user_types_access_check',
        'TRUE');
    }
  }
}
```

We extended `RouteSubscriberBase`, which subscribes to the event and provides us with the `alterRoutes()` method and a collection of all the routes on the site. I encourage you to look into the `RouteCollection` class as it's a very handy one to know when working with routes. One important feature is that we can retrieve routes based on their name, which we did in the previous example.

Then, we will work with `Route` objects like we did a bit earlier. We can see two examples, all with comments I will not repeat here. The second example does not make any sense in a real-world scenario, as we cannot have logged-in users register for new accounts anyway. However, it serves to illustrate how we can add our own access checker to an existing route.

Similar to how we manipulate access requirements, we can change a lot of other things: options, parameters, the controller, and even the actual route path. For this, I encourage you to familiarize yourself with the `Route` class methods and see what you can set on the new route. Couple this information with the documentation (`https://www.drupal.org/docs/drupal-apis/routing-system/structure-of-routes`) on all the things you can add to routes for a better understanding.

The only thing left for this to work is to register the subscriber as a tagged service, just like we did in *Chapter 2, Creating Your First Module*:

```
hello_world.route_subscriber:
  class: Drupal\hello_world\Routing\
    HelloWorldRouteSubscriber
  tags:
    - { name: event_subscriber }
```

And with this, we are done with altering our routes.

Now that we've covered how access control works on routes, let's dive into the entity access system and see how we can ensure that only the right users interact with our entities.

Entity access

To demonstrate the entity access system, we will work with the Product entity type we created in *Chapter 7, Your Own Custom Entity and Plugin Types*.

When we created the Product entity type, the annotation we wrote had an `admin_permission` property where we referenced the general permission to be used for any interaction with entities of this type. Since we didn't reference and implement an access control handler, this is the only access checking done on products. In many cases, this is enough. After all, entity types can be created for the sole purpose of structuring some data that nobody even needs to interact within the UI. However, many other cases require more granular access control on operating with the entities, especially the content-oriented ones, such as Node.

There are four operations for which we can control access when it comes to entities: `view`, `create`, `update`, and `delete`. The first one is clearly the most common one, but we always need to account for the rest as well. Let's first define permissions for all these operations (you remember how, right?):

```
view product entities:
  title: 'View Product entities'
edit product entities:
  title: 'Edit Product entities'
delete product entities:
  title: 'Delete Product entities'
add product entities:
  title: 'Create new Product entities'
```

These are four simple permissions that map to the operations that can be performed on Product entities.

Now, let's go ahead and create an access control handler for our Product entity type. You remember what these handlers are from *Chapter 6, Data Modeling and Storage*, don't you?

First, we will reference the class we build on the product annotation:

```
"access" = "Drupal\products\Access\
  ProductAccessControlHandler",
```

I choose to put this handler in the `Access` namespace of the module (this is common practice in core), but feel free to put it where you want.

Second, we will need the actual class:

```
namespace Drupal\products\Access;

use Drupal\Core\Entity\EntityAccessControlHandler;
use Drupal\Core\Entity\EntityInterface;
use Drupal\Core\Session\AccountInterface;
use Drupal\Core\Access\AccessResult;

/**
 * Access controller for the Product entity type.
 */
class ProductAccessControlHandler extends
  EntityAccessControlHandler {
```

```
/**
 * {@inheritdoc}
 */
protected function checkAccess(EntityInterface $entity,
  $operation, AccountInterface $account) {
  switch ($operation) {
    case 'view':
      return AccessResult::allowedIfHasPermission
        ($account, 'view product entities');

    case 'update':
      return AccessResult::allowedIfHasPermission
        ($account, 'edit product entities');

    case 'delete':
      return AccessResult::allowedIfHasPermission
        ($account, 'delete product entities');
  }

  return AccessResult::neutral();
}

/**
 * {@inheritdoc}
 */
protected function checkCreateAccess(AccountInterface
  $account, array $context, $entity_bundle = NULL) {
  return AccessResult::allowedIfHasPermission($account,
    'add product entities');
  }
}
```

As I mentioned in *Chapter 6, Data Modeling and Storage*, entity access control handlers need to extend the `EntityAccessControlHandler` base class. If one is not specifically provided, this is actually the handler the entity type defaults to. Also, there are two methods we will need to implement here (override):

- `checkAccess()`, which is used to control access on the `view`, `update` and `delete` operations
- `checkCreateAccess()`, which is used to control access on the `create` operation

The reason why these are separate is that for the `create` operation we don't have an entity we can inspect in the process.

Our access rules for the Product entity type are very simple. For each operation, we allow access if the user has the relevant permission; otherwise, access is neutral. However, what happens in this case?

It's worth looking into the `EntityAccessControlHandler` base class and understanding what is going on. The main access entry points are the `access()` and `createAccess()` methods. We should never override these because the logic happening in there is quite standardized and is expected behavior by everyone. Instead, our rules go inside the two methods we saw in our own handler subclass.

The `access()` and `createAccess()` methods invoke entity access hooks (we'll talk about those in a minute). If those do not come back with an access denied result, they call their respective access methods we are overriding in our own subclass, and the results of these are combined with the ones from the access hooks inside an `orIf()` access result. Remember earlier when we talked about the `AccessResult` base class and its handy `orIf()` and `andIf()` methods?

It's important to note how access is determined by all these factors. If at least one of the hook implementations grants access and none deny it, the user will have access, unless we deny access in our access handler. Neutral access plays no role in this equation, except if all hook implementations and the access handler return neutral access (so no specific access is being granted), then the access will be denied.

In our example, we defined permissions, and the handler simply checks for these. Already this is quite flexible because administrators can now assign these permissions to roles and control which users can perform any of these operations. However, there is nothing stopping us from adding more logic to these methods. For example, we can even inspect the entities (and/or the user account) and determine access based on some given values. Moreover, we can inject services into the access handler and make use of them in these calculations.

Injecting services into Entity handlers

One of the powers of using the access handler is that we can make it aware of the service container and inject whatever services we might need to determine access. However, it's not immediately clear how you can do this, so we'll break it down here.

The first thing we will need is to have our access handler implement the `\Drupal\core\Entity\EntityHandlerInterface`. Note that this applies in the same way to the other types of handlers, not just access-related. This interface has one method, which will receive the container and the entity type definition: `createInstance()`.

Knowing this, the rest is very similar to how we injected services into controllers and form classes using the create() method, which only takes the container as an argument, or into plugins, which also takes some plugin information:

```
/**
 * @var \Drupal\Core\Entity\EntityTypeManagerInterface
 */
protected $entityTypeManager;

/**
 * ProductAccessControlHandler constructor.
 *
 * @param \Drupal\Core\Entity\EntityTypeInterface
 *     $entity_type
 * @param \Drupal\Core\Entity\EntityTypeManager
 *     $entityTypeManager
 */
public function __construct(EntityTypeInterface
  $entity_type, EntityTypeManagerInterface
    $entityTypeManager) {
  parent::__construct($entity_type);
  $this->entityTypeManager = $entityTypeManager;
}

/**
 * {@inheritdoc}
 */
public static function createInstance(ContainerInterface
  $container, EntityTypeInterface $entity_type) {
  return new static(
    $entity_type,
    $container->get('entity_type.manager')
  );
}
```

And the new *use* statements:

```
use Drupal\Core\Entity\EntityTypeInterface;
use Drupal\Core\Entity\EntityTypeManagerInterface;
use Symfony\Component\DependencyInjection\
  ContainerInterface;
use Drupal\Core\Entity\EntityHandlerInterface;
```

With this, we have injected the entity type manager into the access handler, and if we want, we can use it. Of course, if we don't need it, we should not inject it in the first place.

Entity access hooks

As I mentioned, the core entity access handler invokes access hooks that modules that don't own the entity type can implement in order to have their say in the access to an entity. There are two sets of access hooks to speak of. The first set covers `create` operations, as follows:

- `hook_entity_create_access()`
- `hook_ENTITY_TYPE_create_access()`

The second set covers the `view`, `update`, and `delete` operations:

- `hook_entity_access()`
- `hook_ENTITY_TYPE_access()`

For each set, we have two hooks invoked at the same time that go from generic to entity type-specific. For example, when trying to view a node, the second hook that is invoked is `hook_node_access()`.

The entity access hook implementations, as you remember from our earlier discussion, also have to return an `AccessResultInterface`. This is because the result is used inside the `orIf()` combination with the access result of the access handler.

So, let's take a look at how we can implement these access hooks, especially their signatures. Hence, we begin with the first set:

```
/**
 * Implements hook_entity_create_access().
 */
function my_module_entity_create_access(\Drupal\Core\
  Session\AccountInterface $account, array $context,
    $entity_bundle) {
  // Perform access check and return an
```

```
      AccessResultInterface instance.
}
```

This is the generic entity create access hook. To make it specific to an entity type, we replace the word `entity` from the function name with the actual ID of the entity type. The parameters, however, remain the same—the user account being checked for access, a context (an array containing the entity type ID and the langcode of the entity being created), and the bundle of the entity being created.

The second set looks like this:

```
function
my_module_entity_access(\Drupal\Core\Entity\EntityInterface
   $entity, $operation, \Drupal\Core\Session\
     AccountInterface $account)
{

   // Perform access check and return an
     AccessResultInterface instance.
}
```

Again, to make it specific to an entity type, we can just replace the word `entity` with the ID of the entity type we want. Once again, the parameters remain, in essence, consistent—the entity being accessed (type-hinted with the relevant entity interface if implementing the more specific hook), the operation being attempted (one of three strings: `view`, `update`, and `delete`), and the user account being checked for access.

That's pretty much it. These hooks are invoked dynamically whenever access is being checked on an entity for the given operation. Let's talk about some examples of this.

First, the entity routes that come out of the box are checking access against these operations, so no need to worry there. So, if we navigate to the canonical, form, or delete URL, access will be checked.

Secondly, if we programmatically load an entity and render it as we saw in *Chapter 6, Data Modeling and Storage*, using the `view` builder handler, the entity access with the view operation gets invoked. However, if we load the entity and simply retrieve some data from it and print it within our own template, we bypass access control. If we are doing this, we will need to make sure that we always check access manually:

```
$access = $entity->access('view', $account);
```

This will return a Boolean, unless you specify a third argument as TRUE, which will return an `AccessResultInterface` object; your call, depending on the circumstances (such as cache metadata, as we will see later).

Thirdly, if we load an entity programmatically that we use inside a form builder and want to render the form, we again bypass the access check. So, we should perform it manually again using the `update` operation instead.

When it comes to programmatically dealing with URLs and menu links to pages that have CRUD connotations with regard to entities, we will need to perform access checking ourselves, but we will discuss entity access in routes in a minute; first, a word of caution.

Earlier, I made a note about extracting entity data and simply rendering field values. The same problem occurs when running entity queries—the results will contain entities that the current user may not have access to. So, we must be aware of this and handle it appropriately. This problem becomes even more prominent with Views, which makes custom database queries and will include potentially inaccessible entities in the result set. Compounded by the possibility of rendering field values with Views, this can cause quite unexpected behavior. So, keep in mind that for cases like this, the entity access hooks and access control handler do not fire. The Node module, however, has a complex grant system that takes care of all this, but, unfortunately, this is available only for node entities. We will talk about these soon as well.

Field access

We've seen so far how the entity-level access works. However, a very similar system also exists for the fields inside entities. If you look inside the `EntityAccessControlHandler`, you'll note that there is a `fieldAccess()` method. This is called whenever access needs to be checked on a given field. For example, the `FieldItemList::access()` method does just that and delegates to the entity handler. Inside that, a call is made to `checkFieldAccess()`, which is what we can implement in our access handler subclass to customize access rules if we need to.

In a similar way, we have multiple operations that access can be checked for, but `view` will be your most common one. For example, when manually rendering an entity using the entity builder handler, as we've seen before, each field is being checked for access to the `view` operation. The same goes, *this time*, when an entity form is being built for the entity to edit it. Each field that is being rendered in the form gets checked for access first using the `edit` operation.

Again, we also have access hooks that other modules can implement to have a say in whether fields should be accessible:

- `hook_entity_field_access()`
- `hook_entity_field_access_alter()`

In this case, we don't have an entity type or a field type-specific hook that we can implement. However, we have an alter hook that we can use to alter the access rules proposed by other modules.

Similar to the entity-level access handler, the field-level one takes its input from multiple sources—subclass and hook implementations. However, the order and combination of these are different. First, the access handler subclass is called (via the `checkFieldAccess()` method). Then, all the `hook_entity_field_access()` hooks are invoked to provide their input. Both of these in turn are then alterable by implementing `hook_entity_field_access_alter()`. Finally, the resulting access rules are combined into an `orIf()` and returned. So, the same principles are available as we saw at the entity level, but in a different order.

Entity access in routes

Now that we understand how entity-level access control works, let's return to routes for a moment. If you remember, I mentioned the `_entity_access` route requirement and how we would talk about it once we had covered entity access.

The `_entity_access` route requirement is nothing more than a service-based access checker, much like the one we wrote ourselves. However, it is created by the entity system in order to control access to routes based on dynamic entity parameters in those routes. Let's see a quick example of a route definition that can use the `_entity_access` requirement:

```
products.view_product:
  path: '/our-products/{product}'
  defaults:
    _controller: '\Drupal\products\Controller\
      ProductsController::showProduct'
  requirements:
    _entity_access: 'product.view'
  options:
    parameters:
      product:
        type: 'entity:product'
```

This route has a dynamic parameter called `product`. In the options, we map this parameter to the Product entity type, so that the Controller method (`showProduct()`) already receives the loaded product entity instead of just the ID. An added benefit of this is that if the product is not found, a 404 is thrown for us. Since this route is clearly dependent on that particular product, we also want to make sure that it can be accessible only if the user has access to view that product.

One way we can ensure access is to add a permission requirement that matches the one for viewing the Product entities. However, this is not a good idea for two reasons:

- If we change the permission used by the Product entity, we have to change it in this definition as well.

- Even more importantly, if the entity access logic depends on something more, such as dynamic data from the user or entity, this won't work anymore.

An alternative way to counter these problems is to implement an access checker service and check for access on the entity inside that service:

```
$access = $entity->access('view', $account);
```

However, there's a lot of boilerplate setup involved for just this line of code. We'd have to do so for all entity types and operations.

Instead, we use the built-in _entity_access access checker as in the example route definition. Instead of TRUE (what we've been using for our access checker), this one actually expects a value it will make use of, and that is a string with two parts separated by a period (.). The first part is the entity type, whereas the second is the operation. Under the hood, EntityAccessCheck will look in the route parameters and check for the found entity's access using the provided operation. Easy-peasy.

Node access grants

Earlier I warned that entity access controls are not being taken into account during queries (either written by us or Views). This is something to pay attention to. For example, if you make a listing of entities, you will need to ensure that users have access to these entities before printing the results out. The problem here occurs when using the built-in paging capabilities of either the entity query or database API. That's because the pager information will reflect all the query results. So, if you don't print the inaccessible entities, there will be a mismatch between the pager information and the visible results.

If you remember, in *Chapter 6*, *Data Modeling and Storage*, I mentioned that when it comes to nodes, the entity query takes access into account. If you want to avoid that, you should use the accessCheck(FALSE) method on the query builder. Let's elaborate a bit on this.

First, this method is available on all entity types, not just nodes. However, it is useful only for those that have defined a status field to denote that entities can be either published or unpublished (or/ off, enabled/disabled, however you prefer). The query will simply add a condition to that field and only return the ones with the status that equals 1. Passing FALSE to this method simply removes that condition.

Second, the Node entity type has a much more powerful built-in access system called *access grants*. Unfortunately, it is not there for other entity types. However, if you really need it, you could technically write it yourself.

The node access grants system is a granular way by which we can control access to any of the operations on a node. This is done using a combination of *realms* and *grants*. When a node is saved, we can create *access records* for that node that contain the following information:

- *realm* (string): A category for our access records. Typically, this is used to denote specific functionality under which the access control happens.

- *gid* (*grant ID*) (int): The ID of the grant by which we can verify the user trying to access the node. Typically, this will map to either a role or a custom-defined "group" that users belong to. For example, a *manager* user type (from the earlier example) can map to the grant ID 1. You'll understand this in a moment.

- *grant_view*, *grant_update*, and *grant_delete* (int): Boolean indicating whether this access record is for this operation.

- *langcode* (string): The language of the node this access record should apply to.

Then, we can return grant records for a given user when they try to access the node. For a given user, we can return multiple grants as part of multiple realms.

The node access records get stored inside the `node_access` table and it's a good idea to keep checking that table while you are developing and preparing your access records. By default, if there are no modules that provide access records, there will be only one row in that table referencing the Node ID 0 and the realm `all`. This means that basically the node access grants system is not used, and all nodes are accessible for viewing in all realms. In other words, default access rules apply. Once a module creates records, as we will see, this row is deleted.

To better understand how this system works, let's see a practical code example. For this, we'll get back to our User Types module and create some node access restrictions based on these user types. We'll start with an easy example and then expand on it to make it more complex (and more useful).

To begin with, we want to make sure that Article nodes are only viewable by users of all three types (so there are still some restrictions, as users need to have a type). Page nodes, on the other hand, are restricted to managers and board members. So, let's get it done.

All the work we will do now takes place inside the `.module` file of the module. First, let's create a rudimentary mapping function to which we can provide a user type string (as we've seen before) and that returns a corresponding grant ID. We will then use this consistently to get the grant ID of a given user type:

```
/**
 * Returns the access grant ID for a given user type.
 *
 * @param $type
 *
 * @return int
 */
function user_types_grant_mapping($type) {
```

```
    $map = [
       'employee' => 1,
       'manager' => 2,
       'board_member' => 3
    ];

    if (!isset($map[$type])) {
       throw new \InvalidArgumentException('Wrong user type
          provided');
    }

    return $map[$type];
}
```

It's nothing too complicated. We have our three user types that map to simple integers. Also, we throw an exception if a wrong user type is passed. Now comes the fun part.

Working with node access grants restrictions involves the implementation of two hooks: one for creating the access records for the nodes and one to provide the grants of the current user. Let's first implement hook_node_access_records():

```
/**
 * Implements hook_node_access_records().
 */
function user_types_node_access_records(\Drupal\node\
   NodeInterface $node) {
   $bundles = ['article', 'page'];
   if (!in_array($node->bundle(), $bundles)) {
      return [];
   }

   $map = [
      'article' => [
         'employee',
         'manager',
         'board_member',
      ],
      'page' => [
```

```
        'manager',
        'board_member'
    ]
];

$user_types = $map[$node->bundle()];
$grants = [];

foreach ($user_types as $user_type) {
  $grants[] = [
    'realm' => 'user_type',
    'gid' => user_types_grant_mapping($user_type),
    'grant_view' => 1,
    'grant_update' => 0,
    'grant_delete' => 0,
  ];
}

  return $grants;
}
```

This hook is invoked whenever a node is being saved and it needs to return an array of access records for that node. As expected, the parameter is the node entity.

The first thing we do is simply return an empty array if the node is not one of the ones we are interested in. If we return no access records, this node will be given one single record for the realm `all` with a grant ID of 1 for the `view` operation. This means that it is accessible in accordance with the default node access rules.

Then, we will create a simple map of the user types we want viewing our node bundles. Also, for each user type that corresponds to the current bundle, we create an access record for the `user_type` realm with the grant ID that maps to that user type, and with permission to view this node.

There are two ways we can trigger this hook and persist the access records. We can edit and save a node, which will create the records for that node, or we can rebuild the permissions that will do so for all the nodes on the site. The link to do this can be found on the status report page. Do note that it won't take any effect unless the module also implements `hook_node_grants()` in order to provide users with some grants as well.

It's a good idea to rebuild the permissions while developing to make sure that your changes get applied to all the nodes. Once we do this, our nodes now become inaccessible to basically anyone (except the super user with the ID of 1). That's because we need to specify the grants a given user should have by implementing hook_node_grants():

```php
/**
 * Implements hook_node_grants().
 */
function user_types_node_grants(\Drupal\Core\Session\
  AccountInterface $account, $op) {
  if ($account->isAnonymous()) {
    return [];
  }

  if ($op !== 'view') {
    return [];
  }

  $user = \Drupal::entityTypeManager()->getStorage('user')
    ->load($account->id());
  $user_type = $user->get('field_user_type')->value;
  if (!$user_type) {
    return [];
  }

  try {
    $gid = user_types_grant_mapping($user_type);
  }
  catch (InvalidArgumentException $e) {
    return [];
  }

  return ['user_type' => [$gid]];
}
```

This hook is invoked by the node access system every time access is being checked on a given node (for a given operation). Moreover, it is also invoked when running entity queries against the node entity type and the access check has not been disabled. Finally, it is also invoked in database API queries when the `node_access` tag is used. Remember the query alters based on tags that we talked about in *Chapter 8, The Database API*?

As an argument, it receives the user account for which access needs to be checked (the grants that it has within the node access grants system of the given operation). So, what we do here is start by returning an empty array (no grants) if the user is anonymous or the operation they are attempting to do is not `view`—they have not been granted access. The same thing happens if the user entity does not have any value in the `field_user_type` field. If they do, however, we get the corresponding grant ID and return an array of access grants keyed by the realm. For each realm, we can include more than one grant ID. In this case, though, it is only one since the user can only be of one type. We can also return multiple realms if needed, and, of course, other modules may do so as well, the results being centralized and used in the access logic.

With this in place, all our page nodes are now available for viewing only to board members and manager users, whereas articles are available for viewing to employees as well. If users don't have any type, they don't have access. The great thing is that these restrictions are now also being taken into account when running queries. So, we can automatically exclude from query results the nodes to which users don't have access. This works with Views as well.

Let's now enhance this solution with the following changes:

- Unpublished article nodes are only available to managers and board members.

- Managers also have access to update and delete articles and pages.

The first one is easy. After we define our internal map inside `user_types_node_access_records()`, we can unset the `employee` from the array in case the node is unpublished:

```
if (!$node->isPublished()) {
   unset($map['article'][0]);
}
```

This was a very simple example, but one meant to draw your attention to an important but often forgotten point. If you create access records for a node, you will need to account for the node status yourself. This means that if you grant access to someone to view a node, they will have access to view that node regardless of the status. Usually this is not something you want. So just make sure that you consider this point when implementing access grants.

Now, let's see how we can alter our logic to allow managers to update and delete nodes (both articles and pages). This is how user_types_node_access_records() looks like now:

```php
$bundles = ['article', 'page'];
if (!in_array($node->bundle(), $bundles)) {
  return [];
}

$view_map = [
  'article' => [
    'employee',
    'manager',
    'board_member',
  ],
  'page' => [
    'manager',
    'board_member'
  ]
];

if (!$node->isPublished()) {
  unset($view_map['article'][0]);
}

$manage_map = [
  'article' => [
    'manager',
  ],
  'page' => [
    'manager',
  ]
];

$user_types = $view_map[$node->bundle()];
$manage_user_types = $manage_map[$node->bundle()];
$grants = [];
```

```
foreach ($user_types as $user_type) {
  $grants[] = [
    'realm' => 'user_type',
    'gid' => user_types_grant_mapping($user_type),
    'grant_view' => 1,
    'grant_update' => in_array($user_type,
      $manage_user_types) ? 1 : 0,
    'grant_delete' => in_array($user_type,
      $manage_user_types) ? 1 : 0,
  ];
}

return $grants;
```

What we are doing differently is, first, we rename the $map variable to $view_map in order to reflect the actual grant associations. Then, we create a $manage_map to hold the user types that can edit and delete the nodes. Based on this map, we can then set the grant_update and grant_delete values to 1 for the user types that are allowed. Otherwise, they stay as they were.

All we need to do now is go back to the hook_node_grants() implementation and remove the following:

```
if ($op !== 'view') {
  return [];
}
```

We are now interested in all operations, so users should be provided with all the possible grants. After rebuilding the permissions, manager user types will be able to update and delete articles and pages, while the other user types won't have these permissions. This doesn't have many implications for queries because those use the view operation.

Before closing the topic on the node access grants, you should also know that there is an alter hook available that can be used to modify the access records created by other modules—hook_node_access_records_alter(). This is invoked after all the modules provide their records for a given node, and you can use it to alter whatever they provided before being stored.

The access grants system, as mentioned, is limited to the node entity type. It has been there since previous versions of Drupal and it didn't quite make it to become standard across the entity system.

To better understand how it works under the hood in case you want to write your own such system, I encourage you to explore the `NodeAccessControlHandler`. You'll note that its `checkAccess()` method delegates to the `NodeGrantDatabaseStorage` service responsible for invoking the grant hooks we've seen before. Moreover, you can also check out the `node_query_node_access_alter` implementation of `hook_query_QUERY_TAG_alter()` in which the Node module uses the same grant service to alter the query in order to take into account the access records. It's not the easiest system to dissect, especially if you are a beginner, but it's well worth going through to learn more.

Block access

Another major area where you will deal with access is when trying to control access to a custom block. If you remember, in *Chapter 2*, *Creating Your First Module*, we created the `HelloWorldSalutationBlock` plugin so that our salutation can also be rendered using a block. Now that block can be placed in a region and even configured to show up only on certain pages, for certain user roles, or even on node pages restricted by bundle. This is all done in the UI:

Figure 10.3: Configuring our custom block

However, this is oftentimes not enough, and you will want to have a block placed in a region and control under what circumstances it should show up yourself. Enter block access.

Inside the `BlockBase` plugin base class, there is the `blockAccess()` method, which always returns positively. This is because, by default, all blocks will be rendered once they are placed in a region. Unless, of course, they are configured to only show in certain cases, in which case a system of visibility based on the available contexts is used to control that. However, if we override this method in our block plugin class, we can control whether the block is shown. So, we can leave the visibility options empty when placing the block in a region and then handle everything we want regarding its visibility inside the `blockAccess()` method. Neat, isn't it?

Also, as expected, the method has one parameter, namely the account being checked, and needs to return an `AccessResultInterface`. Since we can inject services into our block plugin (by implementing the `ContainerFactoryPluginInterface` as we saw in *Chapter 2, Creating Your First Module*), we can use what we want to check whether the given user should see the block. If we deny access, the block is simply not rendered.

That is pretty much all there is to block access control.

Summary

In this chapter, we talked about many access-related topics and techniques. In doing so, we covered what you need to know when starting Drupal module development. Of course, as you progress, you'll dive deeper into the code and learn more subtle aspects and advanced concepts that you can employ in your modules. However, what we covered should set you well on your way. So, what exactly did we talk about?

We started by introducing the high-level Drupal access system, which is made up of the matrix between roles and permissions. In doing so, we not only saw how we can define permissions in code but also how we can check whether a user has those permissions. Of course, we looked at other ways we can check a user's credentials and saw how we can use the `AccountInterface` for this.

Then, we moved on to routes and saw all the various ways we can ensure access control on these. In doing so, we not only covered simple checks such as permissions and roles but also went into more advanced examples of using custom access checkers. We saw that these can be both static and service-based to make access checking fully dynamic. To demonstrate these concepts, we also looked at a case study of using route options to basically configure the access checker used on a group of similar routes.

Another major topic we covered was access on entities. We saw how we can create our own access control handler and check access for all the operations specific to entities. The access hooks invoked by the base access handler also go hand in hand with this, which allows other modules to have a say in the access to a given entity. Moreover, we also saw how we can use entity access checks on routes that have entity parameters.

Finally, we briefly covered block access, through which we can control the visibility of blocks based on whatever rules we want, including user credentials.

Apply these lessons in your code, and do not take access issues lightly. If there is one thing you should know a great deal about from the beginning, it is access. So, this chapter also serves as a reference point for when you are doing development; feel free to come back to it as many times as you need.

In the next chapter, we will look at caching and how to ensure that our application is performant.

11
Caching

Application performance has always been one of the pain points when developing with Drupal, and there are many reasons for this. For example, PHP is not the fastest language out there. Many beginner Drupal developers fall prey to the multitude of modules available and go a bit overboard with enabling more than needed. And indeed, Drupal architecture is simply not the most performant. In its defense though, a very complex architecture that does a lot out of the box will have some speed trade-offs.

One critical component in this game, however, is caching. For those of you not familiar with this term, caching is the application strategy of storing copies of processed code (or anything that results from it) in view of delivering it to the user more quickly when requested subsequent times. For example, when you go to a website, your browser will most likely cache (store) certain assets locally on your computer so that when you visit the site the next time, it can show them to you faster.

Although caching has been steadily improving with recent versions of Drupal, it has still been lacking significantly, particularly when it comes to serving registered users. Since Drupal 8, however, we are talking about a completely different ball game. The system has been totally revamped and brought into all aspects of the Drupal architecture. In this chapter, we will break it all down and see what we're dealing with, so that when you are doing module development in Drupal, your code will be more performant, your site will run faster, and ultimately your users will be happier.

So, what exactly are we going to talk about in this chapter?

First, we are going to cover some introductory notions about the caching system in Drupal and look at the main types of caching available. Here, we will also see how, during development, we can disable caching to increase our productivity.

Next, we are going to talk about cacheability metadata. This is one of the most important things you'll need to know as a Drupal module developer when it comes to caching. It has to do with declaring render arrays (and other objects) in a way in which Drupal can cache them properly (and invalidate caches accordingly). We will talk about things such as cache tags, contexts, and max-age, but also see how to apply them to render arrays, block plugins, and access results.

After that, we will look at how we can tackle highly dynamic components (render arrays) that cannot or should not be cached. Drupal has a powerful *auto-placeholdering* system that uses lazy builders to postpone rendering until a later stage, which can greatly improve both cacheability and perceived performance.

Lastly, we are going to look at how we can interact with the Cache API ourselves in order to create, read, and invalidate our own cache entries. Sometimes, we need to perform expensive calculations or show external data on our site, which can benefit from being cached.

The topics we will cover in this chapter are the following:

- Cache metadata and how it can be used

- Lazy building

- The Cache API

So, let's get to it!

Introduction to caching

The first thing I would like to mention before getting into the meat of the Cache API is that this subsystem is one of the best-documented ones (at the time of writing). You can check out the main entry page (`https://www.drupal.org/docs/8/api/cache-api/cache-api`) and I recommend keeping it close by when developing. At the time of writing, this was still under the Drupal 8 API section, but as you know, Drupal 10 is just an evolution from Drupal 8.

The cache system in Drupal provides the API needed to handle the creation, storage, and invalidation of cached data. From a storage perspective, it is extensible, allowing us to write our own custom cache *backends* (`CacheBackendInterface`). By default, however, cache data gets stored in the database and hence the default backend is `DatabaseBackend`. Going forward, we will focus only on this implementation since it is the most commonly used one, especially when starting a new project. Quite often though, once the site becomes more complex, alternative caching backends can be employed for better performance—such as Memcached or Redis.

The simplest type of cache in Drupal is the so-called *Internal Page Cache*, whose functionality resides inside the Page Cache core module. The goal of this cache layer is to serve anonymous users with responses that are cached in their entirety. The primary assumption is that certain pages can be cached once and served to all anonymous users just the same.

When it comes to serving authenticated users, however, we have the `Dynamic Page Cache` module, also enabled by default in a standard installation, which provides all the necessities for caching pages for all kinds of users. That is, pages that can depend on certain *cache contexts*. In a nutshell, the approach of this module is to cache together the bits of the page that can be served for all users and handle the dynamic content that depends on a context separately. It can do so because of the standardization of those bits into render arrays and other components that can provide *cacheability metadata*. The latter is collected and used to cache and invalidate the final result. We will talk about cache contexts and all this metadata in this chapter and get a better understanding of it.

Before continuing, I recommend you look back to the *Developer settings* section of *Chapter 1, Developing for Drupal 10*, where I recommended that you use the developer settings when doing development. One of the reasons is caching, primarily the dynamic page cache, which you can disable inside the `settings.php` file:

```
$settings['cache']['bins']['dynamic_page_cache'] =
   'cache.backend.null';
```

It is difficult to do actual development with caching enabled, but at the same time, it's important to often enable it and make sure your code still runs correctly. It is very easy to forget about certain bits of code that depend on a context or should be invalidated upon an action, and sometimes you will only spot these if you test with caching enabled.

That being said, let's talk about cacheability metadata and how this works with render arrays.

Cacheability metadata

Cacheability metadata is used to describe the *thing* that is rendered with respect to its *dynamism*. Most of the time, as Drupal module developers, we will be using this metadata when working with render arrays. We will see a bit later where else these come into play, but for now, let's see what the actual properties are and what they are used for in the context of render arrays.

When creating render arrays, there are a few things we need to think about when it comes to caching. And we **always** need to think about these things.

Cache tags

The first thing we need to think about is what our render array depends on. Are we rendering some entity data? Are we using some configuration values? Is anything that might be changed elsewhere, impacting what we have to render? If the answer is yes, we need to use *cache tags*. If we don't use them, our render array gets cached as it is, and if the underlying data changes, we end up showing our users stale content or data.

To look at this another way, imagine a simple Article node. This content can be shown on its main detail page, in a listing of article teasers, or even in a listing of article titles (and many other places potentially). And since there is no way of knowing where it will be used, it is the responsibility of the render array that displays this content to mark this node entity as a dependency using cache tags. This way, when the node gets updated, all the render arrays that depend on it get invalidated as well.

Cache tags are simple strings and we can declare many cache tags for a single render array. They do have a special form in the following pattern: `thing:identifier`, or, in some cases, just simply `thing` (if there is only one single element of that "thing"). For example, the cache tag for a given node would be in the format `node:1`, where the identifier is the actual node ID. Or, for a configuration object, it would be `config:hello_world.custom_salutation`.

To make life easier, all entities and configuration objects can be "interrogated" to provide their respective cache tags. For example:

```
$tags = $node->getCacheTags();
```

Where `$tags` will be an array containing one tag—`node:[nid]`.

Behind this is the generic `CacheableDependencyInterface` they implement, which defines the methods for retrieving the cache metadata properties. In fact, any value that needs to be a cache dependency can and should implement this interface. As you'll find, there are quite a few classes in Drupal core that do so.

> **Note**
>
> You will also encounter `RefinableCacheableDependencyInterface`, which is used in cases in which the cacheability of the underlying object can change at runtime. For example, an entity translation is added, which means that a new cache context needs to be added for that language.

As I mentioned, some node content can be present in a list, and therefore, by using the cache tags, we can ensure that the render array for that node gets updated when the node does. However, since render arrays are highly granular, this can present a small extra problem as the list itself can be a render array that may not even know which nodes it renders. Or even more so, it does not know when new nodes are created and should be included in it. To solve this issue, we have a special *list* cache tag we can use when rendering entities. For example, the `node_list` cache tag can be used for node entities, while the `product_list` cache tag can be used for product entities. These are automatically understood by the Drupal caching system, so all we have to do is use them appropriately.

We can also figure out the "list" cache tag specific to a given entity type. For example, instead of hardcoding the `product_list` tag, we can use the `getListCacheTags()` method on the `EntityTypeInterface`.

If your render array depends on something custom, you can use custom cache tags, but it will be your responsibility to also invalidate them when the underlying data is changed. We will see how this is done when we interact with the Cache API directly. It's always good to consistently use the `CacheableDependencyInterface` for any custom value objects.

Cache contexts

Once we've thought about the dependencies of the render array, the second most important thing to consider is what it differs by. In other words, is there any reason why this render array should be shown one way sometimes but another way some other time?

Let's take a simple example of a render array that prints out the name of the current user. Nothing could be less complicated. Ignoring the cache tags for now, we immediately realize that we cannot show the same username to all users, right? So, the user *Danny* should see "Hi Danny", while user *John* should see "Hi John". We are talking about the same render array but one that differs by context. In other words, a variation of this render array needs to get cached separately for each encountered context. This is where we use the aforementioned *cache contexts*.

Similar to cache tags, cache contexts are simple strings, and a render array can be defined with more than just one. For example, the `user` context will cache a variation of a given render array for each user.

Moreover, they are hierarchical in nature in the sense that some contexts can include others. For example, let's continue with our previous example. Let's assume that users with the `editor` role should see the greeting message but the ones with the `contributor` role should see a different, more complicated one. In this case, the cache context would be the role the user has. But since it already depends on the actual user due to the need to show its username, it doesn't make sense to even bother with the role context because the former encompasses the latter. Moreover, Drupal is smart enough to remove the superfluous one when combining the cache contexts from all the render arrays that make up a page. But if our render array differs, for example, only on the user roles and not necessarily the user itself, we should use the specific context—`user.roles`. As you may notice, the hierarchical nature is reflected in the dot (`.`) separation of the contexts.

There are a number of cache contexts already defined by Drupal core. Although you probably won't have to, at least in the beginning, you can define other contexts too. I recommend you check out the documentation page (`https://www.drupal.org/docs/8/api/cache-api/cache-contexts`) for the available cache contexts that come out of the box.

max-age

The last main thing we need to think about when creating render arrays is how long they should be stored in the cache, barring any changes in the underlying data that might invalidate them. This is something that you will probably rarely set and, by default, it will be permanent. More often, however, you will set this cache property to 0 in order to denote that this render array should never be cached. This is when you are rendering something highly dynamic that doesn't make sense to be cached at all.

Using the cache metadata

Now that we have looked at the three main cache properties, we need to consider creating render arrays, so let's revisit some of our previous work and apply this in practice as needed.

> **Note**
>
> Quite often, you'll see the `CacheableMetadata` object being used and passed around in Drupal core code. This is simply used to represent cache metadata and also provides some handy methods to apply that metadata to a render array, statically instantiate itself from one, or from a `CacheableDependencyInterface` object, as well as merge itself with another `CacheableMetadata` object.

The render array we will look at is inside the `HelloWorldSalutation::getSalutationComponent()` service and is used to render the salutation message. We are building it quite dynamically, but a simplified version looks like this (omitting some things):

```
$render = [
  '#theme' => 'hello_world_salutation',
  '#salutation' => [
    '#markup' => $salutation
  ]
];
```

Here, `$salutation` is either the message from the configuration object or the one generated based on the time of day.

Right off the bat, I will mention that this is one of those cases in which we cannot really cache the render array due to its highly dynamic nature. This is caused by the dependency on the time of day. Sure, we could set a maximum age of a few seconds or an hour, but is it even worth it? And we also run the risk of showing the wrong salutation.

So, in this case, what we can do is add a maximum age of `0`:

```
$render = [
  '#theme' => 'hello_world_salutation',
  '#salutation' => [
    '#markup' => $salutation
  ],
  '#cache' => [
    'max-age' => 0
  ]
];
```

The cache metadata goes under a `#cache` render array property as shown above.

Specifying the max-age basically tells Drupal not to ever cache this render array. Something important to know about this is that this declaration will bubble up to the top-level render array that makes the Controller response, preventing the entire thing from being cached. So, do not make the decision to prevent caching lightly. In our example, this is basically the entire Controller response and it is actually a very simple calculation, so we are good. Later in the chapter, we will talk about the ways this can be mitigated.

> **Note**
>
> There is still a problem with us setting the `max-age` to 0 in this example. Although it will work with dynamic page caching (`max-age` will bubble up), the internal page cache serving anonymous users will not get this information. So, anonymous users will see the same thing every time. Possibly in future Drupal releases, this will be fixed. We won't account for this issue yet because it's a great example of a bug that becomes apparent using automated tests, and we will see that in the final chapter of the book—as well as the solution, of course.

Let's, for a minute, assume that our salutation component is simply rendering the message stored in the configuration object and does not show time-specific content. If you remember:

```
$config = $this->configFactory->get
   ('hello_world.custom_salutation');
$salutation = $config->get('salutation');
```

In this case, we could cache the render array, but as we discussed earlier, we'd need to think about the dependencies as well as the potential variations it can have. It is already pretty obvious what the dependencies are—the configuration object. So, we would do the following:

```
$render = [
  '#theme' => 'hello_world_salutation',
  '#salutation' => [
    '#markup' => $salutation
  ],
  '#cache' => [
    'tags' => $config->getCacheTags()
  ]
];
```

Basically, we are requesting this particular configuration object's cache tags and setting those onto the render array. If we had more sets of cache tags to set from multiple objects, we would have to merge them. There is a tool we can use to ensure we do it right. For example:

```
$tags = Cache::mergeTags($config_one->getCacheTags(),
  $config_two->getCacheTags());
```

This will merge two arrays of cache tags, pure and simple. The `Drupal\Core\Cache\Cache` class also has static helper methods for merging cache contexts and max-ages (among other things, I encourage you to check this out as you progress).

Thankfully, our render array is simple and does not vary, and hence we don't need cache contexts. If, however, we had appended the current username to the salutation, we would have had to add the `user` context to the render array as follows:

```
'#cache' => [
  'tags' => $config->getCacheTags(),
  'contexts' => ['user']
]
```

This would have cached the render array differently for each user who visits the page and would serve them accordingly at subsequent visits.

Caching in block plugins

The render array we saw earlier was used as part of a Controller response. The latter is also known as the *main content* as it is the primary output of the page. In a normal Drupal installation, which uses the Block module, this is included inside the `Main page content` block. We also said that setting a max-age of 0 will bubble up to the top-level render array, causing the entire page to not be cached. This is true as far as the Controller response is concerned. Other blocks are still cached independently according to their own metadata.

In this book, you have already learned how we can create custom blocks, and we saw that they are also built using render arrays. Since this is the case, cache metadata can also be applied to those arrays for caching them properly. However, since we are extending from the `BlockBase` class when creating block plugins, we are essentially implementing the `CacheableDependencyInterface` because `BlockPluginInterface` extends it.

So instead of setting the metadata on the render array, we could use the methods on that interface by overriding the default parent implementations. For example:

```
/**
 * {@inheritdoc}
 */
```

```
public function getCacheContexts() {
  return Cache::mergeContexts(parent::getCacheContexts(),
    ['user']);
}
```

We should always merge our own values with the ones from the parent.

In some cases, though, especially when declaring cache tags, it makes more sense to set them inside the render array of the `build()` method. That is because you may have already done some work to get your hands on the dependent objects, and it doesn't make sense to repeat that inside another method. That is totally fine.

Caching access results

Another important place where cache metadata needs to be considered is on `AccessResultInterface` objects. If you remember from the previous chapter, objects implementing this interface are used consistently to represent access to a certain resource. On top of that, they can also contain cacheability metadata. This is because access may depend on certain data that can change with an impact on the access result itself. Since Drupal tries to cache access as well, we need to inform it of these dependencies.

A good example to see this in action is our `HelloWorldAccess` service, where we dynamically check access to our `hello_world.hello` route. So instead of simply returning the `AccessResultInterface`, we add cacheable dependencies to it before doing so. The rewritten `access()` method can now look like this:

```
$config = $this->configFactory->get
  ('hello_world.custom_salutation');
$salutation = $config->get('salutation');
$access = in_array('editor', $account->getRoles()) &&
  $salutation != "" ? AccessResult::forbidden() :
    AccessResult::allowed();
$access->addCacheableDependency($config);
$access->addCacheContexts(['user.roles']);
return $access;
```

The `addCacheableDependency()` method usually takes `CacheableDependencyInterface` objects to read their cache metadata. If something else is passed, the access result is deemed not cacheable. So, in our case, since access depends on the salutation configuration object, we add it as a cache dependency. Moreover, because the access varies by the current user roles, we add those as context as well.

Caching the Hello World redirect

In *Chapter 2, Creating Your First Module*, we learned about event subscribers by creating one with the purpose of redirecting the user to the homepage if they had a certain role. Back then, however, we didn't know about caching, so what we did was wrong. Kind of. Why? Because Drupal caches the redirect so if one user is redirected, all will be after that. And vice versa. If one is not, none will be after that. And this is a big deal. Let's go back to our `HelloWorldRedirectSubscriber` class and deal with this.

To fix it, we need to think about our questions: what does the redirect depend on, and by what does it vary?

The first thing we are checking is the route: we only want to redirect if the user reaches a certain route. So that is the first thing we have to vary by; hence, we need to add the `route` cache context.

The second thing we are checking is the current user and their roles. So again, we need the `user.roles` cache context.

And that's it. It seems we have no dependencies on anything, meaning we don't need any cache tags.

This is what the redirect could look like now:

```
$response = new LocalRedirectResponse($url->toString());
$cache = new CacheableMetadata();
$cache->addCacheContexts(['route']);
$cache->addCacheContexts(['user.roles']);
$response->addCacheableDependency($cache);
$event->setResponse($response);
```

What is happening here is that we create our own little cacheable object onto which we add the contexts we need. Then, we add that object as a dependency to the response, which, if you check, can support it because it extends `CacheableSecuredRedirectResponse`. And we are done. After, of course, adding the missing *use* statement:

```
use Drupal\Core\Cache\CacheableMetadata;
```

Now that we've seen a bit about how the cacheability metadata can be used in more common scenarios, let's shift gears and talk about those page components that have highly dynamic data.

Placeholders and lazy building

When we set the maximum age of our Hello World salutation to 0 seconds (don't cache), I mentioned that there are ways this can be improved in order to help performance. This involves postponing the rendering of the respective bit to the very last moment with the help of placeholders. But first, a bit of background.

Each of the cache properties we talked about can have values that make caching the render array pointless. We've already talked about the maximum age being set to 0, but you can also argue that very low expiration times have the same effect. Additionally, certain cache tags can be invalidated too frequently, again making the render arrays that depend on what they represent pointless to cache. Finally, certain cache contexts can provide many variations that significantly limit the effectiveness of the cache to the point that it may even be counterproductive (due to high storage costs).

Cache tags are something very specific to the application we are building, so there are no general assumptions that can be made as to which have a high invalidation rate. However, there are two cache contexts that, by default, are considered to have much too high cardinality to be effective: session and user. Yes, we talked about the user context earlier as a good example but in reality—by default—adding this context to a render array has pretty much the same effect as setting the max-age to 0—it will not be cached. The same goes for the session context because there can be so many sessions and users on the site, you probably won't want to have cache records for each individual one.

Since these are not rules that have to necessarily apply to all applications, Drupal configures these values as service parameters, making them changeable if needed. Inside the core.services.yml file (which lists most of the core services), we can find some parameter definitions as well, including this one:

```
renderer.config:
  auto_placeholder_conditions:
    max-age: 0
    contexts: ['session', 'user']
    tags: []
```

As you can see, the max-age value of 0 and the previously mentioned cache contexts are included, but no tags. We can also change these values. So, for example, if in our application, we know that we won't have too many users and it does, in fact, make sense to cache by user context, or we know of certain cache tags with high invalidation frequency, it makes sense to change this. There are two ways we can do it: either we use our site-wide services.yml file and copy these declarations (while making the appropriate changes) or we can use the services file of a given module in the same way. Both methods have the effect of overriding the default parameters set by Drupal core.

Now that we are clear on why certain things are not cacheable, let's see how this can be addressed using *auto-placeholdering*.

Auto-placeholdering is the process by which Drupal identifies the render arrays that cannot or should not be cached for the reasons we mentioned before, and replaces them with a placeholder. The latter is then replaced at the very last possible moment while allowing the rest of the page components to be cached. This is also called *lazy building*.

Drupal identifies the bits that need to be lazy-built by the cache metadata that fits the conditions we saw before and the presence of the #lazy_builder property on the render array. The latter maps to a callback that returns its own render array, which can also contain said cache metadata. And it doesn't matter which of the render arrays contains the latter.

Lazy builders

Lazy builders are nothing more than callbacks on a render array that Drupal can use to build the render array at a later stage. The callbacks can be static (a reference to a class and method) or dynamic (a reference to a service and method). Using the latter approach is more flexible as we can inject dependencies from the container as we do regularly with services. Moreover, the callback can take parameters, which means it can build the render array already, having at least part of the required data.

The best way to understand this is to see an example. Since we decided that our salutation component should have a cache lifetime of 0 seconds, it's a good opportunity to build it using a lazy builder.

To illustrate this, let's update our HelloWorldSalutationBlock and have it return a lazy-built component. To this end, the first thing we need to do is replace its build() method to only return this:

```
return [
  '#lazy_builder' => ['hello_world.lazy_builder:
    renderSalutation', []],
  '#create_placeholder' => TRUE,
];
```

Back in *Chapter 4, Theming*, when I said a render array needs to have at least one of the four properties (#type, #theme, #markup, or #plain_text), I lied. We can also use a lazy builder like this to defer the building of the render array to a later stage.

The #lazy_builder needs to be an array whose first item is the callback and the second is an array of arguments to pass to it. In our case, we don't need any of the latter. We could pass the salutation service, but instead, we will inject it into the new hello_world.lazy_builder service we will create in a minute. The callback reference is in the format of service_name:method (one colon used for separation) or, for static calls, class_name::method (two colons). We also explicitly declare #create_placeholder to make it clear that this render array should be replaced with a placeholder. Lastly, as I mentioned earlier, the cache metadata can be applied to this render array or it can also be on the resulting one from the lazy builder. So, we'll opt for the latter approach in this case.

Let's now define our service:

```
hello_world.lazy_builder:
  class: Drupal\hello_world\HelloWorldLazyBuilder
  arguments: ['@hello_world.salutation']
```

Nothing out of the ordinary here, but we are injecting the `HelloWorldSalutation` service as a dependency so that we can ask it for our salutation component. The actual service class looks like this:

```php
namespace Drupal\hello_world;

use Drupal\Core\Security\TrustedCallbackInterface;

/**
 * Lazy builder for the Hello World salutation.
 */
class HelloWorldLazyBuilder implements
  TrustedCallbackInterface {

  /**
   * @var \Drupal\hello_world\HelloWorldSalutation
   */
  protected $salutation;

  /**
   * HelloWorldLazyBuilder constructor.
   *
   * @param \Drupal\hello_world\HelloWorldSalutation
   *   $salutation
   */
  public function __construct(HelloWorldSalutation
    $salutation) {
    $this->salutation = $salutation;
  }

  /**
   * {@inheritdoc}
   */
  public static function trustedCallbacks() {
    return ['renderSalutation'];
  }

  /**
```

```
 * Renders the Hello World salutation message.
 */
public function renderSalutation() {
  return $this->salutation->getSalutationComponent();
}

}
```

What we do here is not a big deal. We implement the `TrustedCallbackInterface` to ensure Drupal knows that the callback of the lazy built render array can be trusted. This is an added security layer. Then, we implement the `renderSalutation()` method we referenced from the render array. That is all we have to do. But, what exactly happens with this?

When Drupal renders our block, it finds the lazy builder and registers it with a placeholder, which is then used instead of the actual final render array. Then, at a much later stage in the page-building process, the lazy builder is invoked and the actual output is rendered to replace the placeholder. There are a couple of advantages and implications of this.

First, it allows Drupal to bypass this highly dynamic bit of output and cache the rest of the components in the dynamic page cache. This is to prevent the lack of cacheability from infecting the entire page.

Second, there are two different strategies (so far) with which placeholders can be processed. By default, in using the so-called *Single Flush* method, the placeholder replacement is postponed until the last minute, but the response is not sent back to the browser before this is done. So, the dynamic page cache does improve things (caches what it can), but the response still depends on the placeholder processing finishing. Depending on how long that takes, the page load, in general, can suffer. However, when using the **BigPipe** approach, the response is sent back to the browser before the placeholders are replaced. And as the latter finishes as well, the replacements are streamed to the browser. This greatly improves the perceived performance of the site as users can already see most parts of the page before the slower bits appear.

The **BigPipe** technique was invented by Facebook as a way to deal with highly dynamic pages and was gradually brought into Drupal 8 as an experimental core module. With version 8.3, it has been marked stable and ready for use in production sites. I highly recommend you keep this module enabled as it comes with the Standard installation profile.

> **Note**
> As you've probably guessed by now, the lazy builder approach is only useful when it comes to Dynamic Page Caching. That is when we cache for authenticated users. It will not work with the Internal Page Cache, which is used for anonymous users.

Using the Cache API

So far in this chapter, we've mostly preoccupied ourselves with render arrays and how we can expose them to the Cache API for better performance. It's now time to talk a bit about how cache entries are stored by default in Drupal and how we can interact with them ourselves in our code.

As mentioned earlier, a central figure for the cache system is the `CacheBackendInterface`, which is the interface any caching system needs to implement. It basically provides the methods for creating, reading, and invalidating cache entries.

As we might expect, when we want to interact with the Cache API, we use a service to retrieve an instance of the `CacheBackendInterface`. However, the service name we use depends on the cache *bin* we want to work with. Cache bins are repositories that group together cache entries based on their type. So, the aforementioned implementation wraps a single cache bin, and each bin has a machine name. The service name will then be in the following format: `cache.[bin]`. This means that for each cache bin, we have a separate service.

The static shorthand for getting this service looks like this:

```
$cache = \Drupal::cache();
```

This will return the `default` bin represented by a `CacheBackendInterface` implementation. If we want to request a specific bin, we pass the name as an argument:

```
$cache = \Drupal::cache('render');
```

This will return the `render` cache bin.

And of course, if we need to inject a cache bin wrapper somewhere, we simply use the service machine name in the format I mentioned before.

Even though we have a separate service for each cache bin, they all basically do the same thing, that is, use the `CacheFactory` to instantiate the right type of cache backend for that bin. Individual cache backends can be registered and set as the default either globally or for specific bins.

As I mentioned at the beginning of the chapter, the default cache backend in Drupal—the one this factory will instantiate for all the bins—is the `DatabaseBackend`. And each bin is represented by a database table.

Now that we know how to load the cache backend service, let's see how we can use it to read and cache things. When it comes to this, your number one reference point is the `CacheBackendInterface`, which documents all the methods. However, since it does not reinforce return values, the examples we will see next are done with the database cache backend. They might differ from other cache backend implementations.

The first method we'll talk about is get(), which takes the ID of the cache entry we want to retrieve ($cid) and an optional $allow_invalid parameter. The first parameter is clear enough, but the second one is used in case we want to retrieve the entry even if it has expired or has been invalidated. This can be useful in those cases in which *stale* data is preferred over the recalculation costs of multiple concurrent requests:

```
$data = $cache->get('my_cache_entry_cid');
```

The resulting $data variable is a PHP standard class that contains the data key (the data that has been cached) and all sorts of metadata about the cache entry: its expiration, creation timestamp, tags, valid status, and so on.

Of course, there is also a getMultiple() method, which you can use to retrieve multiple entries at once.

More fun, though, is the set() method, which allows us to store something in the cache. There are four parameters to this method:

- $cid: The cache ID that can be used to retrieve the entry.

- $data: A serializable data structure such as an array or object (or simple scalar value).

- $expire: The Unix timestamp after which this entry is considered invalid, or CacheBackendInterface::CACHE_PERMANENT to indicate that this entry is never invalid unless specifically invalidated. The latter is the default.

- $tags: An array of cache tags that will be used to invalidate this entry if it depends on something else (cache metadata, basically).

So, to use it, we would do something like this:

```
$cache->set('my_cache_entry_cid', 'my_value');
```

With this statement, we are creating a simple non-serialized cache entry into our chosen bin that does not expire unless specifically invalidated (or deleted). Subsequent calls with the same cache ID will simply override the entry. If the cache value is an array or object, it will get serialized automatically.

When it comes to deleting, there are two easy methods, delete() and deleteMultiple(), which take the $cid (or an array of cache IDs, respectively) as an argument and remove the entries from the bin completely. If we want to delete all the items in the bin, we can use the deleteAll() method.

Instead of deleting entries, quite often, it's a good idea to invalidate them. We'll still be able to retrieve the data using the $allow_invalid parameter and can use the entry while the new one is being recalculated. This can be done almost exactly as deleting, but using the following methods instead: invalidate(), invalidateMultiple(), and invalidateAll().

OK, but what about those cache tags we can store with the entry? We already kind of know their purpose and that is to *tag* cache entries across multiple bins with certain data markers that can make them easy to invalidate when the data changes. Just like with render arrays. So, how can we do this?

Let's assume that we store the following cache entry:

```
$cache->set('my_cache_entry_cid', 'my_value',
  CacheBackendInterface::CACHE_PERMANENT, ['node:10']);
```

We essentially make it dependent on changes to the node with the ID of 10. This means that when that node changes, our entry (together with all other entries in all other bins that have the same tag) becomes invalid. Simple as that.

But we can also have our own tags that make it depend on something custom of ours like a data value (which, as we discussed earlier in the chapter, should implement the `CacheableDependencyInterface`) or a process of some kind. In that case, we would also have to take care of invalidating all the cache entries that have our tag. The simplest way we can do this is statically using the `Cache` class we encountered earlier when merging metadata together:

```
Cache::invalidateTags(['my_custom_tag']);
```

This will invalidate all cache entries that are *tagged* with any of the tags passed in the array. Under the hood, this method uses a static call to the cache invalidator service, so whenever possible, it's best to actually inject that service—`cache_tags.invalidator`.

Creating our own cache bin

Usually, the existing cache bins, particularly the default one, will be enough to store our own cache entries. However, there are times in which we need to create multiple entries for the same functionality, in which case, it would help to have a special bin for that. So, let's see how that can be created.

It's quite easy because all we have to do is define a service:

```
cache.my_bin:
  class: Drupal\Core\Cache\CacheBackendInterface
  tags:
    - { name: cache.bin }
  factory: cache_factory:get
  arguments: [my_bin]
```

The class used in this service definition is actually an interface. This is because we are using a factory to instantiate the service rather than the container directly. This means we don't know what class will be instantiated. In this case, the factory in question is the service with the name `cache_factory` and its `get()` method. In *Chapter 3, Logging and Mailing*, we saw an example in which something like this happened when we talked about logger channels.

The `cache.bin` tag is used so that Drupal can understand the function of this service, namely, that it is a cache bin. The responsibility of making sure this bin gets its storage belongs to the actual backend. So, in our example, the `DatabaseBackend` creates and removes the cache table as needed.

Lastly, the static argument is the name of the bin that gets passed to the factory and that is used to create the cache backend for this particular bin. That is pretty much it. If we clear the cache, we can already see a new cache table for our bin in the database.

Summary

In this chapter, we covered the main aspects of caching that any Drupal module developer needs to be familiar with. We introduced some key concepts and talked about the two main types of caching—Internal Page Cache (used for anonymous users) and Dynamic Page Cache (used for authenticated users).

We dug deeper into cacheability metadata, which is probably the most important and common thing we need to understand. It's imperative to use this properly so that all the render arrays we build are cached and invalidated correctly. We also saw how block plugins have specific methods we can use to define their cacheability metadata and how access results should also receive cacheability dependencies, as needed. Stemming from this, we also explored lazy builders and *auto-placeholdering* strategies, which allow us to handle highly dynamic components while maintaining good cacheability overall.

Lastly, we looked into using the Cache API ourselves in order to store, read, and invalidate our own cache entries. We even saw how to create our own custom cache bin.

In the next chapter, we are going to talk about JavaScript and how we can use it in a Drupal context, as well as the powerful Ajax API.

12
JavaScript and the Ajax API

In this chapter, we'll switch gears and talk a bit about *frontend development*, namely, how to work with JavaScript in a Drupal application. This is because there are many things developers can and should be doing in their modules that require frontend technologies. There are a few approaches and techniques specific to Drupal when it comes to adding and using JavaScript files, and we will talk about those here. Moreover, we will also prove how powerful Drupal is in allowing us to do quite a bit of JavaScript work without actually writing a single line of JavaScript code.

So, there are a few things we will cover in this chapter.

First, we will talk about the approach of writing JavaScript in Drupal. You already learned in *Chapter 4, Theming*, how you can create libraries and attach them to render arrays, elements, or pages. Basically, using libraries, we can get our JavaScript files loaded when we need. I recommend you check out the *Assets and libraries* section from *Chapter 4, Theming*, if you don't remember exactly how libraries work. In this chapter, we will continue from there and talk a bit about what actually goes inside those JavaScript files.

> **Note**
>
> A good resource to keep handy is the documentation page (`https://www.drupal.org/node/172169`), which lists the coding standards for JavaScript in Drupal that we should abide by.

We won't actually write a lot of JavaScript code in the first part—just enough to get you started. In the second part, we will not write any at all. Instead, we will talk about the robust Ajax API that comes with Drupal, which allows us to build some very dynamic functionalities that rely on JavaScript. To demonstrate how things work, we will revisit our importer functionality that we started in *Chapter 7, Your Own Custom Entity and Plugin Types*, and improve it using Ajax.

Finally, we will also talk about the States system of the Form API, which allows us to make our form elements dynamic and dependent on others in a declarative way. Again, we won't even have to know any JavaScript to do what is actually quite complex client-side behavior.

The major topics we will cover in this chapter are as follows:

- Getting familiar with JavaScript in Drupal

- The Ajax API

- The States (form) system

JavaScript in Drupal

Drupal relies on a few JavaScript libraries and plugins to perform some of its frontend tasks. For example, the ubiquitous *jQuery* library continues to be used in Drupal 10 as well. But of course, there are others.

Another thing I have already mentioned, but which is helpful to bring up again, is the fact that Drupal no longer loads things such as jQuery or its Ajax framework on all pages needlessly. For example, many pages serving anonymous users that do not require jQuery won't even load it. This can greatly improve performance. But it also means that when we define our libraries to include our own JavaScript files, we must always declare these as dependencies (if we need them). For example, jQuery is something you'll often depend on.

Drupal behaviors

One of the most important things you need to know when writing JavaScript files in Drupal is the concept of behaviors. But in order to understand that, let's get a bit of context.

When writing JavaScript code using jQuery, it's often standard to wrap our code inside a `ready()` method statement as follows:

```
$(document).ready(function () {
    // Essentially the entirety of your javascript code.
});
```

This ensures that your code runs only after the entire **Document Object Model** (**DOM**) has been loaded by the browser. Moreover, the use of jQuery for this helps a great deal with cross-browser compatibility and also allows us to place this code wherever we want on the page (header or footer).

In Drupal, however, we have a different solution that is better in the context of writing JavaScript that works with Drupal as well (not just with the DOM). That comes in the form of Drupal behaviors. In a nutshell, behaviors are methods we declare that get called when the DOM loads fully, that is, when the document is ready. However, on top of that, they also get called by the Ajax framework when new data is loaded onto the page. Even when using BigPipe and placeholder replacements are streamed.

Any Drupal site has a global `Drupal` object that is used for many things we won't go into right now. However, the `Drupal.behaviours` object is where we declare behaviors, and typically any JavaScript code that we want to run should go inside a behavior. So, let's see an example, as it will be much easier to understand.

What we want is to show a little dynamic JavaScript clock next to the **Hello World** salutation, if the message is not coming from the configuration but is dependent on the time of day. While writing the code for our functionality, we'll talk about Drupal behaviors and how they are used.

Our library

In order to get our JavaScript file loaded, it needs to be in a library and attached to *something*. As you learned in *Chapter 4, Theming*, the libraries file has the name `hello_world.libraries.yml` and is located in the root folder of our module:

```
hello_world_clock:
  version: 1.x
  js:
    js/hello_world_clock.js: {}
  dependencies:
    - core/jquery
    - core/drupal
    - core/once
```

We only have a single JavaScript file that is needed for our purpose, located in the `js` directory of our module. But we do have some dependencies. First, we want jQuery loaded because we will use it. Second, we want to have the general Drupal JavaScript library, which handles a bunch of things, including behaviors. The last dependency we will talk about soon, and it will make a bit more sense then.

Without these dependencies declared, in some cases (especially for anonymous users), Drupal would not have them loaded on the page, and our JavaScript functionality would not work.

Now, let's attach this library to our salutation component found inside the `HelloWorldSalutation` service.

Right after these two lines:

```
$time = new \DateTime();
$render['#target'] = $this->t('world');
```

We can add the following:

```
$render['#attached'] = [
  'library' => [
    'hello_world/hello_world_clock'
  ]
];
```

This is nothing new for us, but the point is that we are only attaching the library if the component is showing the dynamic salutation message that depends on the time of day. If this message has been overridden, we don't even want to load these libraries, and that is pretty much it. We can dive in and create our `hello_world_clock.js` file.

The JavaScript part

The first thing we need to do inside the JavaScript file is to wrap the entire code we write in the file in an **Immediately Invoked Function Expression (IIFE)**. In doing this, we protect the scope of what we write from the global one and even use global variables with more commonly associated names inside our own scope. This is how this looks:

```
(function (Drupal, $) {

  "use strict";

  // Our code here.

}) (Drupal, jQuery);
```

The most important thing here is that inside this function, we can now use the dollar sign (`$`) as a reference to the global jQuery object without interfering with other libraries that might use the same variable name. Also, we added the `use strict` declaration to ensure we write semantically correct code (and it's also part of the JavaScript coding standards for Drupal).

Let's now add the meat of our functionality and explain how it works. The following goes inside the IIFE block, where we indicated with the code comment:

```
Drupal.behaviors.helloWorldClock = {
  attach: function (context, settings) {
    function ticker() {
      var date = new Date();
      $(context).find('.clock').html
        (date.toLocaleTimeString());
    }

    var clock = '<div>The time is <span class="clock">
      </span></div>';

    $(document).find('.salutation').append(clock);
```

```
    setInterval(function() {
      ticker();
    }, 1000);
  }
};
```

First, we are defining a new behavior, which is an object on the Drupal.behaviors object and that has a unique name. You can look at a single behavior as one piece of functionality. We only need one function on this object called attach, which receives two parameters: context (the page or part of the page that is being loaded) and settings (the variable containing data passed from PHP).

This function gets invoked by Drupal whenever behaviors need to be attached—Drupal. attachBehaviors(). This happens when the page gets loaded for the first time (in which case context is the entire DOM) or after an Ajax request or BigPipe replacement (in which case context contains only the newly loaded parts of the page). Therefore, using the context instead of the entire document for looking up elements is sometimes more performant (especially after an Ajax request) and prevents other side effects.

Second, inside the attach function, we have our logic for creating a clock. First, we define a simple function that looks for the element with the .clock class and puts the current time into it. You'll notice that we used context to look for the element. Next, we create this element ourselves and append it to our salutation message element. In doing so, however, we use the entire document to look for the element because, depending on how this JS file is attached, the context may be the actual salutation div we are looking for. Since we are using BigPipe and lazy building, the context will be just that, as opposed to the entire DOM. Lastly, we set an interval every second to keep calling our ticker() function, essentially updating the time every second, giving the illusion of a clock. This is all pretty standard.

> **Note**
>
> Be aware that the strings we are printing to the user via JavaScript are not run through the translation system, and that is not good practice (even if the site is not multilingual). In *Chapter 13, Internationalization and Languages*, we will see how we need to handle it instead.

Clearing the cache and navigating to our /hello page, we can already see the new clock appearing (if we don't have the salutation message overridden). So, we're done, right? Well, not really.

If we open the browser's developer tools, namely the console, and try to attach the behaviors again:

```
Drupal.attachBehaviors();
```

We'll notice that our clock element gets appended again (it has been duplicated). In fact, even if we don't do this, we might see the clock appearing multiple times depending on other page conditions we may have (such as potential Ajax requests, BigPipe, etc.) This is where the once dependency comes in.

The once library allows us to track and make sure we are performing something only once. It's actually very simple to use. All we have to do is replace this line:

```
$(document).find('.salutation').append(clock);
```

With this:

```
$(once('helloWorldClock', '.salutation')).append(clock);
```

So what happens above? We use the once() function to find our .salutation element, wrap that in a jQuery selector, and call append() on it like before. Under the hood, once() ensures that the resulting elements are only going to be retrieved once to have our clock appended to them.

The third parameter to once() is an optional Element to restrict the search in, but by default, it looks in the entire document (same as we did before).

> **Note:**
> Before Drupal 10, the once library was a jQuery plugin widely used in Drupal code. However, it was deprecated and replaced with a standalone JavaScript library to decouple it from jQuery. You can read more about its API on the NPM documentation page here: https://www.npmjs.com/package/@drupal/once.

And with this, our clock is ready.

Drupal settings

Another powerful thing we can do (and something we often need to do) is pass values from our PHP code to the JavaScript layer. In custom PHP applications, this can get messy, but Drupal has a robust API that transforms PHP arrays into JavaScript objects. These can be found inside the settings object passed to the behavior's attach() function.

Again, the easiest way to understand this is through an example. So let's say we want to print an extra message after the salutation if it is the afternoon. Of course, we can use JavaScript to determine that as well, but so far, it has been the responsibility of our PHP code, so let's keep it that way. So then we need a way to tell our JavaScript that it is afternoon, and we can do this by setting a flag if that is the case, as follows:

```
if ((int) $time->format('G') >= 12 && (int) $time->
    format('G') < 18) {
```

```
$render['#salutation']['#markup'] = $this->t('Good
  afternoon');
$render['#attached']['drupalSettings']['hello_world']
  ['hello_world_clock']['afternoon'] = TRUE;
return $render;
}
```

New here is the second line from within the *if conditional*, namely the one where we attach something to the render array. In this case, though, it's not a library but `drupalSettings` in a big multidimensional array. The best practice is to *namespace* our settings hierarchically like so: our module name -> the functionality the setting belongs to -> the setting name. In JavaScript, this array will be transformed into an object.

> **Note**
>
> To get the `drupalSettings` to work, we need to make sure the `core/drupalSettings` library is loaded. In our case, this happens because the `core/drupal` library lists it as a dependency.

Now that we pass this flag (which could be much more complex if needed), we can make use of it in JavaScript:

```
if (settings.hello_world !== undefined &&
  settings.hello_world.hello_world_clock.afternoon !==
    undefined) {
  clock += 'Are you having a nice day?';
}
```

That is pretty much it. We managed to easily pass values from PHP into JavaScript and use them in client-side logic.

Now that you are on your way and ready to write whatever JavaScript you need for your application, and you are able to integrate this with the Drupal backend APIs, let's take a look at the Ajax framework.

The Ajax API

There's a lot we can do on the client side without having to write a single line of JavaScript code.

The Drupal Ajax API is a robust system that allows us to define client-side interactions via PHP. We most commonly use Ajax when we interact with forms—triggering certain actions that change the DOM without having to reload the page. We will demonstrate how all this works by expanding a bit more on the importer functionality we built in *Chapter 7, Your Own Custom Entity and Plugin Types*. Before that, though, let's take a quick look at a simpler use case of Ajax in Drupal.

Ajax links

The simplest way to interact with Drupal's Ajax API is to add the use-ajax class to any link. This will cause the link to make an Ajax request to the path of the link rather than moving the browser to it. A similar thing can be done with the submit button of a form using the use-ajax-submit class. This makes the form submit via Ajax to the path defined in the form's action.

The most important thing, however, is what we do on the other end of the process. Clicking a link that triggers an Ajax request won't do anything if we don't handle that request accordingly. What we have to do is return an AjaxResponse object with some jQuery *commands* that instruct the browser on the changes it needs to make to the DOM. So, let's see an example.

Remember in *Chapter 2, Creating Your First Module*, when we created our first block, which rendered the salutation message from the service? Let's say we want to add a link after the message that if the user clicks on it, the block gets hidden entirely. There are a few easy steps we need to take to achieve this.

First, we need to alter the renderSalutation() method of our HelloWorldLazyBuilder to get something like this:

```php
public function renderSalutation() {
  $build = [];

  $build[] = [
    '#theme' => 'container',
    '#children' => [
      '#markup' => $this->salutation->getSalutation(),
    ]
  ];

  $url = Url::fromRoute('hello_world.hide_block');
  $url->setOption('attributes', ['class' => 'use-ajax']);
  $build[] = [
    '#type' => 'link',
    '#url' => $url,
    '#title' => $this->t('Remove'),
  ];

  return $build;
}
```

And the new *use* statement:

```
use Drupal\Core\Url;
```

The first thing we do is wrap our original simple string in a Drupal core `container` theme hook (using a `#markup`-based array), just so that it gets some divs around and we don't have to create our own theme hook. After all, we are doing proof-of-concept work here. Next, below the message, we print a link to a new route we have to define. And as we talked about, to that link we add the `use-ajax` class. You'll notice that we can add attributes (refer back to *Chapter 4, Theming*, for more info on those) straight to the `Url` object, and they will be added to the rendered link element.

Second, we need to define this new route. Nothing could be simpler:

```
hello_world.hide_block:
  path: '/hide-block'
  defaults:
    _controller: Drupal\hello_world\Controller\
      HelloWorldController::hideBlock
  requirements:
    _permission: 'access content'
```

We map it to a new method on the same controller class we've been using and allow all users access to it.

Third (and last), we need to define the controller method:

```
public function hideBlock(Request $request) {
  if (!$request->isXmlHttpRequest()) {
    throw new NotFoundHttpException();
  }

  $response = new AjaxResponse();
  $command = new RemoveCommand('.block-hello-world');
  $response->addCommand($command);
  return $response;
}
```

Also, since we use the `$this->t()` method to ensure the translation of the strings, we should use the `StringTranslationTrait` as well:

```
use StringTranslationTrait;
```

And the new *use* statements at the top:

```
use Drupal\Core\Ajax\AjaxResponse;
use Drupal\Core\Ajax\RemoveCommand;
use Symfony\Component\HttpFoundation\Request;
use Symfony\Component\HttpKernel\Exception\
   NotFoundHttpException;
use Drupal\Core\StringTranslation\StringTranslationTrait;
```

The first thing you'll notice is the `$request` parameter of this method, and you may be wondering where it's coming from. Drupal passes the current request object to any controller method that simply type hints a parameter with that class. So, we don't have to inject it into our controller. The reason we need it is so that we can check whether the request to this route was made via Ajax. Because if not, we don't want to handle it. That is, we throw a `NotFoundHttpException`, which results in a regular 404.

Then comes the fun stuff relating to the Ajax API, namely, the building of an `AjaxResponse` full of commands back to the browser. In our example, there is only one command, which instructs it to run the jQuery `remove()` method on the elements that match the selector that is passed to it. In our case, this is the class of the block wrapper. And with this, our functionality is in place. We can clear our cache, and the block should now print a link that removes the block via Ajax.

You may be thinking: why do we need a trip back to the server for a job that can be done on the client-side alone? And the answer is—we actually don't. However, it serves as a good example of how Ajax responses work. And I encourage you to check out the documentation page (`https://api.drupal.org/api/drupal/core%21core.api.php/group/ajax/10.0.x`) for the Ajax API, where you can find a list of all the available commands. For example, we could have used the `ReplaceCommand` to replace the block with something else that comes back from the server, or the `HtmlCommand` to insert some data into an element on the page, or even an `AlertCommand` to trigger a JavaScript alert with some data coming from the server. The cool thing is that the response can process multiple commands, so we are not restricted to only using one.

Ajax in forms

The most common use of Ajax in Drupal is through the Form API, where we can create dynamic interactions between the server and client with ease. To demonstrate how this works, we will go through an example. This will be a rework of the Importer configuration entity form we created in *Chapter 7, Your Own Custom Entity and Plugin Types*.

If you remember, we said that tying certain configuration values to the generic entity does not make sense, as Importer plugins might be different. The first Importer we wrote loads a JSON file from a remote URL. So, it stands to reason that the configuration value for the URL is tied to the plugin and not the configuration entity (even if the latter actually stores it). Because if we want to create a CSV importer, for example, we don't need the URL. So, let's refactor our work to make this happen.

Here is an outline of the steps we need to take for this refactoring:

1. Importer plugins need to provide their own configuration form elements.

2. The Importer configuration form needs to read these elements depending on which plugin is selected (this is where the Ajax API comes into play).

3. We need to alter the storage and configuration schema of the values that are specific to plugins.

Let's start by making our plugins configurable and embeddable into forms. Luckily, Drupal provides us with two handy interfaces meant for plugins to implement just for this reason. So, let's have our `ImporterPluginInterface` extend from these:

```
interface ImporterPluginInterface extends
   PluginInspectionInterface, PluginFormInterface,
     ConfigurableInterface
```

And we use the two new interfaces at the top:

```
use Drupal\Core\Plugin\PluginFormInterface;
use Drupal\Component\Plugin\ConfigurableInterface;
```

Let's see what these interfaces provide.

The `PluginFormInterface` provides methods that are meant for embedding a plugin-specific form into another one as a subform. Let's implement the methods with sensible defaults in our base plugin class since not all plugins necessarily need to have any forms:

```
/**
 * {@inheritdoc}
 */
public function getConfig() {
  return $this->configuration['config'];
}


/**
 * {@inheritdoc}
 */
public function buildConfigurationForm(array $form,
  FormStateInterface $form_state) {
```

```
    return [];
  }


  /**
   * {@inheritdoc}
   */
  public function validateConfigurationForm(array &$form,
    FormStateInterface $form_state) {
  // Do nothing by default.
  }


  /**
   * {@inheritdoc}
   */
  public function submitConfigurationForm(array &$form,
    FormStateInterface $form_state) {
    // Do nothing by default.
  }
```

These methods should be quite self-explanatory as they mirror the regular Form API.

The `ConfigurableInterface` provides methods that make the plugin have some specific configuration, and it typically works hand in hand with the `PluginFormInterface`. And in the same way, let's add the default implementations in the base plugin class, as not all plugins may need configuration:

```
  /**
   * @inheritDoc
   */
  public function getConfiguration() {
    return $this->configuration;
  }


  /**
   * {@inheritdoc}
   */
  public function setConfiguration(array $configuration) {
    $this->configuration = $configuration + $this->
```

```
      defaultConfiguration();
}


/**
 * {@inheritdoc}
 */
public function buildConfigurationForm(array $form,
  FormStateInterface $form_state) {
  return [];
}
```

These are also quite straightforward to understand. The `defaultConfiguration()` method, just like we've seen with Field plugins, ensures that we have default values for certain configuration keys.

But if you remember, our plugins already receive the entire Importer configuration entity, so we need to make some adjustments to the constructor of the base plugin class to accommodate the extra configuration values we will be adding now (the default ones). So let's add this line at the end of the constructor, which would ensure default configuration values are included:

```
$this->setConfiguration($configuration);
```

Next, since we now have plugin-specific configuration methods, let's also rename the `getConfig()` method on the plugin base class and interface to `getImporterEntity()` for better clarity. Ensure you also update it everywhere it's used in the code (namely in the Drush command).

I believe we are missing a *use* statement at the top of the `ImporterBase` class, so let's add it:

```
use Drupal\Core\Form\FormStateInterface;
```

Next, on the `ImporterInterface` of the configuration entity, we need to remove the `getUrl()` method (since that is specific to the `JsonImporter` plugin) and replace it with generic methods for setting and retrieving all the configuration values pertaining to the plugin selected for the entity:

```
/**
 * Returns the configuration specific to the chosen plugin.
 *
 * @return array
 */
public function getPluginConfiguration();


/**
```

```
 * Sets the plugin configuration.
 *
 * @param array $configuration
 *   The plugin configuration.
 */
public function setPluginConfiguration($configuration);
```

And, of course, in the importer entity class, we reflect this change as well (by replacing the $url property):

```
/**
 * The configuration specific to the plugin.
 *
 * @var array
 */
protected $plugin_configuration = [];
```

And the actual methods, in line with the interface:

```
/**
 * {@inheritdoc}
 */
public function getPluginConfiguration() {
  return $this->plugin_configuration;
}

/**
 * {@inheritdoc}
 */
public function setPluginConfiguration($configuration) {
  $this->plugin_configuration = $configuration;
}
```

So far so good – nothing complicated going on. We are replacing the plugin-specific configuration values with a generic one in which values specific to the selected plugin will be stored. However, since our entity type no longer has the $url field but a $plugin_configuration one, we need to also adjust the config_export key in the annotation to reflect this change:

```
 *   config_export = {
 *     "id",
```

```
 *       "label",
 *       "plugin",
 *       "plugin_configuration",
 *       "update_existing",
 *       "source",
 *       "bundle"
 *     }
```

Before we adjust the `ImporterForm` and make all the adjustments there, we need to move the form element for the `url` field into the `JsonImporter`, where we have to implement some new methods from the interfaces we added.

First, the default configuration, which for our plugin is a URL value:

```
/**
 * {@inheritdoc}
 */
public function defaultConfiguration() {
  return [
    'url' => '',
  ];
}
```

Second, we have the `buildConfigurationForm()` method, where we move the URL form element:

```
/**
 * {@inheritdoc}
 */
public function buildConfigurationForm(array $form,
  FormStateInterface $form_state) {
  $form['url'] = [
    '#type' => 'url',
    '#default_value' => $this->configuration['url'],
    '#title' => $this->t('Url'),
    '#description' => $this->t('The URL to the import
      resource'),
    '#required' => TRUE,
  ];
```

```
    return $form;
}
```

You'll notice some differences in getting the default value. Instead of calling the now-removed getUrl()
method on the configuration entity, we use the local plugin configuration where we should always have
the url key. Also, since we use the $this->t() method to ensure the translation of the strings, we
should use the StringTranslationTrait as well (which can go inside the parent base class):

```
use StringTranslationTrait;
```

Don't forget the use statement:

```
use Drupal\Core\StringTranslation\StringTranslationTrait;
```

Third, we should also implement the form submit method, which will save the URL value into the
plugin configuration:

```
/**
 * {@inheritdoc}
 */
public function submitConfigurationForm(array &$form,
    FormStateInterface $form_state) {
    $this->configuration['url'] = $form_state->
        getValue('url');
}
```

This is a very simple method that just puts the submitted URL value that pertains to this plugin into
the array of plugin configuration values. The parent form will extract it from there as we will see soon.

Let's not forget that we are actually using the URL in the import, so we need to make some adjustments
to the getData() method as well:

```
protected function getData() {
    $request = $this->httpClient->get($this->
        configuration['url']);
    $string = $request->getBody()->getContents();
    return json_decode($string);
}
```

Much simpler now. But before moving on, let's add the missing *use* statement to the top of our JSON importer class:

```
use Drupal\Core\Form\FormStateInterface;
```

With this in place, we can go ahead and adjust our `ImporterForm` (where we need to remove the form element for the URL field).

There are two main things we need to do:

- Expose the plugin selection element to Ajax, that is, trigger an Ajax request when the user makes a selection
- Remove the `url` form element
- Add the extra elements to the form depending on the chosen plugin

This is what the new `plugin` element looks like:

```
$form['plugin'] = [
  '#type' => 'select',
  '#title' => $this->t('Plugin'),
  '#default_value' => $importer->getPluginId(),
  '#options' => $options,
  '#description' => $this->t('The plugin to be used with
    this importer.'),
  '#required' => TRUE,
  '#empty_option' => $this->t('Please select a plugin'),
  '#ajax' => [
    'callback' => [$this, 'pluginConfigAjaxCallback'],
    'wrapper' => 'plugin-configuration-wrapper'
  ],
];
```

There are two noticeable changes: we've added an `#empty_option` key (to be used as the option shown if the user has not made a choice) and the `#ajax` key (which we will discuss in a bit more detail).

What we did is pretty simple. We declared a callback method to be triggered when a user makes a change to this form element, and we declared the HTML ID of the element that should be replaced with the result of the Ajax callback. And in the latter (which is a simple method on the same class), all we have to do is this:

```
public function pluginConfigAjaxCallback($form,
  FormStateInterface $form_state) {
```

```
    return $form['plugin_configuration'];
}
```

We return a form element (which we still have to define). An important lesson here is that Ajax responses in forms can return content as well (in the form of render arrays or even strings), which will be used to replace the HTML found by the ID specified in the `wrapper` key of the Ajax declaration. Alternatively, an `AjaxResponse` full of commands can also be returned to do more complex things, as we saw in the previous section.

Before we look at this new `plugin_configuration` form element, let's briefly talk about some of the other options that can be used inside the `#ajax` array:

- `method`: This indicates the jQuery method to use when interacting with the `wrapper` element (if specified). The default is `replaceWith()`, but you can also use `append()`, `html()`, and others.

- `event`: This shows which event should be used to trigger the Ajax call. By default, the form element in question decides that. For example, when selecting an option in a select element or when typing something into a textfield.

- `progress`: This defines the indicator to be used while the Ajax request is taking place.

- `url`: A URL to trigger the Ajax request in case the `callback` was not specified. Typically, using the latter is more powerful as the entire `$form` and `$form_state` are passed as parameters and can be used in processing.

With that out of the way, we can go back to our form definition and add our missing parts, right after the `plugin` element:

```
$plugin_id = NULL;
if ($importer->getPluginId()) {
  $plugin_id = $importer->getPluginId();
}
if ($form_state->getValue('plugin') && $plugin_id !==
  $form_state->getValue('plugin')) {
  $plugin_id = $form_state->getValue('plugin');
}

if ($plugin_id) {
  $existing_config = [
    'config' => $importer
  ] + $importer->getPluginConfiguration();
  $plugin = $this->importerManager->
```

```
   createInstance($plugin_id, $existing_config);

 $form['plugin_configuration']['#type'] = 'details';
 $form['plugin_configuration']['#title'] = $this->
   t('Plugin configuration for <em>@plugin</em>',
     ['@plugin' => $plugin->getPluginDefinition()
       ['label']]);
 $form['plugin_configuration'][$plugin_id] = [
   '#process' => [[get_class($this),
     'processPluginConfiguration']],
   '#plugin' => $plugin,
 ];
}
```

First, we define the `plugin_configuration` form element as a `hidden` type. This means it will not be visible to users when the page loads for the first time. However, we do use the `#prefix` and `#suffix` options (a common practice with the Drupal Form API) to wrap this element with a div that has the ID we indicated as the `wrapper` in our Ajax declaration. So, the goal is to have this element replaced each time an Ajax request is made, that is, each time a plugin is selected. Moreover, we use the `#tree` property to indicate that when the form is submitted, the values of the elements are sent and stored in a tree that reflects the form element (a multidimensional array, basically). Otherwise, the form state values that are submitted get flattened, and we lose their connection to the `plugin_configuration` element.

Next, we try to get the ID of the chosen plugin. First, we load it from the configuration entity in case we are looking at an edit form. However, we also check in the form state to see if one has been selected (and is different from the one in the entity). And if you are wondering how we can have the plugin in the form state, the answer is that after an Ajax call is made (triggered by the user selecting a plugin), the form gets rebuilt. And we can see what's in the form state and retrieve the plugin ID that was chosen.

Even more than that, if we get our hands on a plugin ID, we can completely change the `plugin_configuration` element, which in turn then gets returned by the Ajax callback to be used to replace our wrapper. So, to sum up:

1. The page loads for the first time (on a new form). The element is hidden.

2. The user selects a plugin, and an Ajax request is triggered, which rebuilds the form.

3. As the form is rebuilt, we check for the selected plugin and alter the `plugin_configuration` element to reflect the selected plugin.

4. The Ajax response replaces the old element with the new, potentially changed one.

The new `plugin_configuration` element becomes a `details` one (a collapsible container for multiple elements), open by default, and which has one key, called `plugin`, onto which we add all the elements coming from the plugin. But what is that `#process` key? Using this key, we defer the building of the plugin subform to a process callback, which takes place whenever the form is being processed. So let's write that callback and see how we can build an embedded subform for our selected plugin:

```
public static function processPluginConfiguration(array
    &$element, FormStateInterface $form_state) {
    /** @var \Drupal\products\Plugin\ImporterPluginInterface
        $plugin */
    $plugin = $element['#plugin'];
    $subform_state = SubformState::createForSubform($element,
        $form_state->getCompleteForm(), $form_state);
    return $plugin->buildConfigurationForm($element,
        $subform_state);
}
```

In this callback, we first retrieve the plugin that we stored on the element array to make use of now, just to know what the user selected (or what was selected in the current *Importer*). Then, we build a `SubformState`, which is meant to be passed as the form state to the embedded form. And finally, we call the configuration form of the plugin, passing only the current element (that *details* element we created) as the form and the subform state.

And since we used a new class:

```
use Drupal\Core\Form\SubformState;
```

Moreover, since we set the plugin instance onto the form element, we need to ensure that importer plugins can be serialized properly (including their dependencies). So we should use the `DependencySerializationTrait` on the base plugin class:

```
use DependencySerializationTrait;
```

And its *use* statement:

```
use Drupal\Core\DependencyInjection\
    DependencySerializationTrait;
```

We are almost there, but we still have one problem. We are not calling the submit handler of the individual plugin and storing its resulting configuration on our Importer entity.

Whenever an entity form is being built either for validation or submission (save) or even when making Ajax callbacks, there is a `buildEntity()` method being called, responsible for hydrating the entity object with values found in the form state. So this is a perfect place to massage our submissions so that the entity `plugin_configuration` field only gets the actual values found in the plugin configuration. We can have something like this:

```
/**
 * {@inheritdoc}
 */
public function buildEntity(array $form, FormStateInterface
  $form_state) {
  if ($form_state->getValue('plugin_configuration') == "") {
    $form_state->setValue('plugin_configuration', []);
  }

  /** @var \Drupal\products\Entity\ImporterInterface
    $entity */
  $entity = parent::buildEntity($form, $form_state);

  $plugin_id = $form_state->getValue('plugin');
  if ($plugin_id) {
    $configuration = ['config' => $entity];
    $plugin_configuration = $form_state->getValue
      (['plugin_configuration', $plugin_id]);
    if ($plugin_configuration) {
      $configuration += $plugin_configuration;
    }
    /** @var \Drupal\Core\Plugin\PluginFormInterface
      $plugin */
    $plugin = $this->importerManager->createInstance
      ($plugin_id, $configuration);

    if (isset($form['plugin_configuration'][$plugin_id])) {
      $subform_state = SubformState::createForSubform
        ($form['plugin_configuration'][$plugin_id],
          $form_state->getCompleteForm(), $form_state);
      $plugin->submitConfigurationForm($form
```

```
            ['plugin_configuration'] [$plugin_id],
                $subform_state);
        }


    $configuration = $plugin->getConfiguration();
    unset($configuration['config']);
    $entity->setPluginConfiguration($configuration);
    }


    return $entity;
}
```

First, we need to ensure that the `plugin_configuration` form state submission value is always an array. This is because of the trick we did when making that element a `hidden` type. Then we simply call the parent to have it build the entity as it normally would. Next comes the interesting stuff. We again instantiate the plugin (passing the correct configuration values to it), create a `SubformState` like we did before, and call the submit handler on the plugin. We don't need to know what that does; we simply then just ask for its configuration and set it on the entity. But, of course, before we set it on the Importer, we need to remove the actual Importer object as it doesn't make sense to be included.

You'll notice that now when we instantiate an importer plugin, we also pass this extra configuration, which is plugin specific. So we need to adapt our other place where we instantiate these plugins, namely the plugin manager's `createInstanceFromConfig()` method. The method body will now look like this:

```
$config = $this->entityTypeManager->getStorage('importer')
    ->load($id);
if (!$config instanceof ImporterInterface) {
    return NULL;
}


$configuration = ['config' => $config] + $config->
    getPluginConfiguration();
return $this->createInstance($config->getPluginId(),
    $configuration);
```

With this, we are done. Well, not really, as we still need to handle the configuration schema aspect. Yes, remember those from *Chapter 6, Data Modeling and Storage*, and *Chapter 7, Your Own Custom Entity and Plugin Types*? We are now going to see how we can work with our own dynamic configuration schema, similar to how we did with the ones needed for the field plugins in *Chapter 9, Custom Fields*. But why do we need a dynamic configuration schema?

Before this refactoring, we knew the exact fields of the importer configuration entity, and we could declare the schema for each easily (as we did). However, now plugins can come with their own individual fields, so we need to make sure they can provide their own schema definitions for the respective data. So, how can we do this?

First, inside our `products.schema.yml` file, we need to remove the `url` field schema definition as it no longer exists. We replace it, however, with one for the new field we created, namely the `plugin_configuration` array of values that came from the plugin:

```yaml
plugin_configuration:
  type: products.importer.plugin.[%parent.plugin]
```

Here is where things become interesting. We don't know what fields there will be inside, so we instead reference another type (our own). Moreover, the name of the type is dynamic. We have a prefix (`products.importer.plugin.`) followed by a variable name given by the value of the plugin field of the parent (the main configuration entity). So basically, if a given configuration entity uses the `json` plugin, the type of schema definition will be `products.importer.plugin.json`. So now, it's the responsibility of whoever creates new plugins to also provide their own schema definitions (like we did in *Chapter 9, Custom Fields*, when we defined field plugins).

But before that can happen, we need to define this new type we created:

```yaml
products.importer.plugin.*:
  type: mapping
  label: 'Plugin configuration'
```

So essentially, our new type extends from `mapping` and has a simple label. Of course, it applies to all that start with that name (hence the wildcard we encountered before).

Now, we can add the schema definition for our single `json` Importer plugin:

```yaml
products.importer.plugin.json:
  type: mapping
  label: Plugin configuration for the Json importer plugin
  mapping:
    url:
      type: uri
      label: Uri
```

As you can see, we now have our first instance of the `products.importer.plugin` type, which contains the `url` field and which is inside the `plugin_configuration` field of the configuration entity—reflecting a simple array hierarchy.

But the point of this dynamic declaration is that other modules that define new plugins can now also define their own instances of the `products.importer.plugin.*` schema definitions to map their own fields. It is not the responsibility of the configuration entity (schema) to "guess" what field types are being used on each plugin.

With this, our refactoring is complete. Drupal is well aware of the type of data the configuration entity is saving, even if it is in part related to external input (the selected plugin). So, that means we can create (if we want) another importer plugin that uses a CSV file for the product data. But we'll see how to do that in *Chapter 16, Working with Files and Images*, when we talk about file handling.

The States (Form) system

The last thing we are going to look at in this chapter is the States system of the Form API (not to be confused with the State API we covered in *Chapter 6, Data Modeling and Storage*). This allows us to define our form elements to behave somewhat dynamically based on the user interaction with the form. It doesn't use Ajax but relies on JavaScript to handle the manipulations. This is another great example of client-side behavior where we don't have to write a single line of JavaScript. So, let's see what this is.

The `#states` are simple properties we can add to form elements, which have the role of changing them depending on the *state* of other elements. The best way to understand this is through some examples. Imagine these two form elements:

```
$form['kids'] = [
  '#type' => 'checkbox',
  '#title' => $this->t('Do you have kids?'),
];


$form['kid_number'] = [
  '#type' => 'textfield',
  '#title' => $this->t('How many kids do you have?'),
];
```

In the first, we ask the user if they have kids (using a simple checkbox), while in the second, we ask them how many kids they have. But why should the user actually see the second element if they don't have kids? This is where the `#states` property comes into play, and its role is to manipulate an element depending on the *state* of another. So instead, we can have this:

```
$form['kid_number'] = [
  '#type' => 'textfield',
```

```
  '#title' => $this->t('How many kids do you have?'),
  '#states' => [
    'visible' => [
      'input[name="kids"]' => ['checked' => TRUE],
    ],
  ],
];
```

Now the element for specifying the number of kids is only going to be visible if the *state* of the kid element is checked.

The #states property is an array whose key is the actual *state* that needs to be applied to the current element if the conditions inside are met. And the conditions can vary, but they all depend on a CSS selector (in our case input[name="kids"] matching another element).

Our example can also be written with this reverse logic:

```
'#states' => [
  'invisible' => [
    'input[name="kids"]' => ['checked' => FALSE],
  ],
],
```

Apart from visible and invisible, the following *states* can also be applied to form elements: enabled, disabled, required, optional, checked, unchecked, expanded and collapsed. As for the conditions that can "trigger" these *states*, we can have the following (apart from checked, which we already saw): empty, filled, unchecked, expanded, collapsed and value.

So, for example, we can even control the *state* of an element depending on the value the user selected on another. Combining these possibilities can greatly improve our forms when it comes to user experience, decluttering, and even building logical form trees.

Summary

In this chapter, we took on the client side and talked about JavaScript and client-side capabilities in Drupal. We started with the approach we need to take when writing JavaScript in a Drupal context. We learned about behaviors, why they are important, and how to use them. We also saw how we can pass around data from the server (Drupal) to the client side and make use of it in JavaScript.

Funnily enough, we then switched to a no-JavaScript-allowed policy for the rest of the chapter. We did this to prove how powerful the Drupal Ajax API is, with which we can perform complex server-to-client interactions even if we are not frontend developers that can write JavaScript code. And to demonstrate the API, we first looked at how simple links can be turned into Ajax requests. We followed that up with an important refactor of our earlier product importer functionality, which relied on Ajax to make the Importer configuration entity form dynamic (dependent on the selected plugin). And let's not forget another nugget of information—dynamic configuration schema—which allows us to decouple the configuration entity data definitions from that of their selected plugins.

Finally, we finished by looking at the States system of the Form API, which allows us to declaratively code client-side manipulations onto our form elements, essentially making them dependent on the user's interaction with the form.

In the next chapter, we are going to talk about internationalization and translations to make sure our applications can be used anywhere around the globe.

13
Internationalization and Languages

In this chapter, we are going to talk about internationalization and multilingual features in Drupal from the point of view of a module developer. Many of the built-in capabilities of this system are oriented toward site builders—enabling languages and translating content and configuration entities, as well as the Drupal interface (for administrators and visitors alike). Our focus will be on what we, as module developers, need to do programmatically to ensure that site builders and editors can use the aforementioned features. To that end, this chapter will be more of a reference guide with various tips, techniques, and even rules we need to follow when writing our code. Notwithstanding, we will also talk a bit about how we can work with languages programmatically.

First, however, we will start with an introduction to the multilingual ecosystem that comes out of the box and the modules responsible for various parts of it.

The main topics we will cover in this short chapter are as follows:

- The multilingual ecosystem
- Internationalization
- Translating the interface and content

Introduction to the multilingual ecosystem

The multilingual and internationalization system is based on four Drupal core modules. Let's quickly go through them and see what they do:

- Language
- Content translation
- Configuration translation
- Interface translation

Language

The *Language* module is responsible for dealing with the available languages on the site. Site builders can choose to install one or more languages from a wide selection. They can even create their own custom language if necessary. The installed languages can then be added to things such as entities and menu links in order to control their visibility, depending on the current language. Apart from the installed ones, Drupal comes with two extra special languages as well: *Not Specified* and *Not Applicable*.

The module also handles the contextual language selection based on various criteria, as well as provides a language switcher to change the current language of the site:

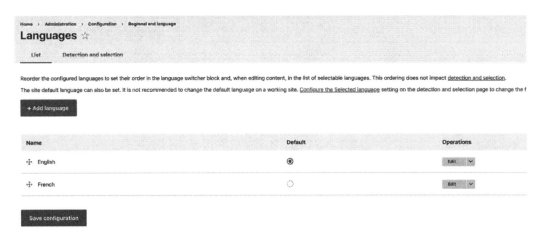

Figure 13.1: Language configuration page

Content translation

The *Content translation* module is responsible for the functionality that allows users to translate content. Content entities are the principal vehicle for content, and with this module, the data inside can be translated (and granularly configured for it at the field level). In other words, users can control which fields and which entity type bundles should be translatable:

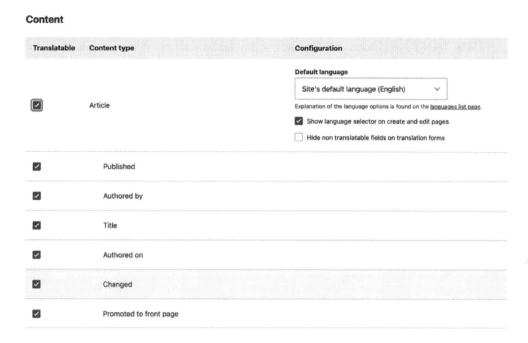

Figure 13.2: Enabling content translation

Configuration translation

The *Configuration translation* module is responsible for providing the interface via which users can translate configuration values. These can be from simple configuration objects or configuration entities. We've already seen how we can ensure that our configuration values can be translated in previous chapters, so we won't dive into that again here.

I recommend you reference the section on configuration schemas from *Chapter 6, Data Modeling and Storage*:

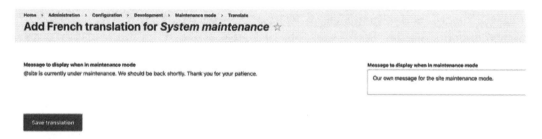

Figure 13.3: Configuration translation page

Interface translation

The *Interface translation* module is responsible for providing a system that allows users to translate any string or text output on the website in all the languages that are installed. Moreover, it provides a connection to the `localize.drupal.org` platform from which it can download translations for many languages of the more common interface strings that come with Drupal:

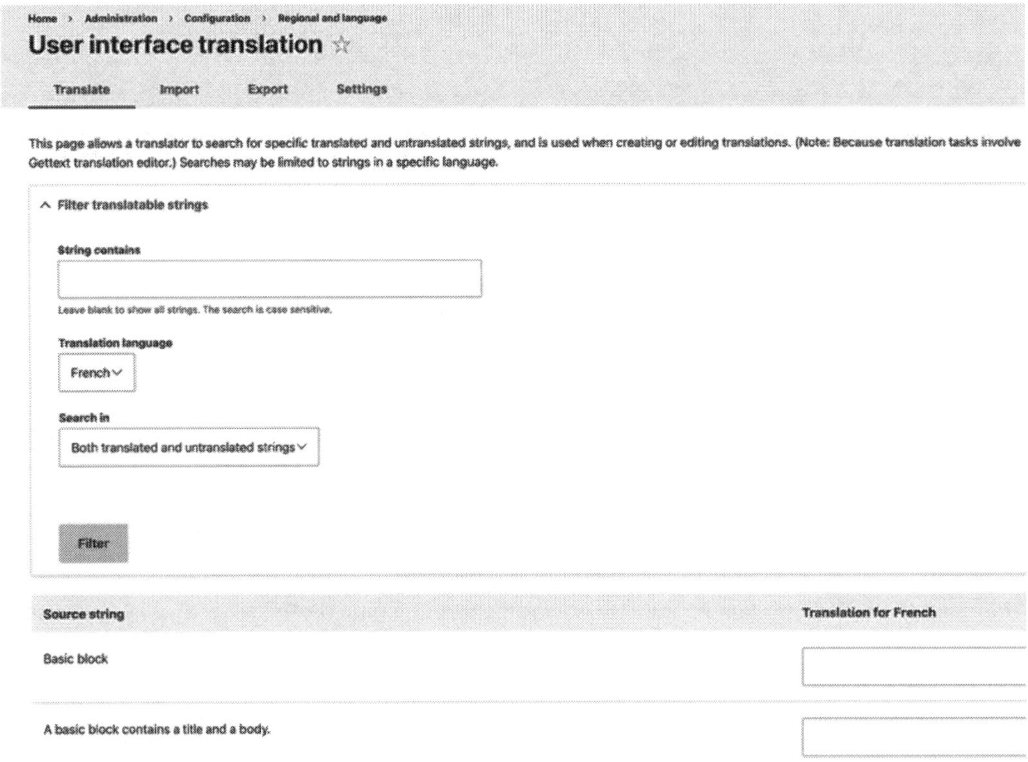

Figure 13.4: Interface translation page

These four modules are not alone in the multilingual system but rely on a cross-application standard of ensuring that all the written code works well with it. In other words, the entire Drupal code base is intertwined with the multilingual system at various levels and is written in such a way that anything that should be translatable or localizable can be. This means that all the code we write needs to respect the same standard.

Internationalization

The idea behind internationalization is to ensure that everything that gets output on the site can be translated into the enabled languages through a common mechanism. This refers to content, visible configuration values, and the strings and text that come out of modules and themes. But there are different ways this can happen, so let's see how in each of these cases we would ensure that our information can be translated.

A principal *rule* when writing Drupal modules or themes is to always use English as the code language. This is to ensure consistency and keep open the possibility that other developers will work on the same code base, who may not speak a particular language. This is also the case for text used to be displayed in the UI. It should not be the responsibility of the code to output the translated text, but rather to always keep it consistent, that is, in English.

Of course, this is dependent on it being done right in order to allow it to be translated via interface translation. There are multiple ways this can be ensured, depending on the circumstances.

The most common scenario we need to be aware of is when we print out to the user a PHP string of text. This is where the `t()` function comes into play, through which these strings are run. This function should be used whenever we are not inside a class context:

```
return t('The quick brown fox');
```

However, when we are inside a class, we should check whether any of the parents are using the `StringTranslationTrait`. If not, we should use it in our class and then we'll be able to do this instead:

```
return $this->t('The quick brown fox');
```

None of the examples given before should be new to us, as we've been using these throughout the code we've been writing in this book. But what actually happens behind the scenes?

The `t()` and `StringTranslationTrait::t()` functions both create and return an instance of `TranslatableMarkup` (essentially delegating to its constructor), which, upon rendering (being cast to a string), will return the formatted and translated string. The responsibility of the actual translation is delegated to the `TranslationManager` service. This process has two parts. Static analyzers pick up on these text strings and add them to the database in the list of strings that need to be localized. These can then be translated by editors via the user interface. Second, at runtime, the strings get formatted and the translated version is shown, depending on the current language context. And because of the first part, we should never do something like this:

```
return $this->t($my_text);
```

The reason is that static analyzers can no longer pick up on the strings that need to be translated. Moreover, if the text is coming from user input, it can lead to XSS attacks if not properly sanitized before.

That being said, we can still have dynamic, that is, formatted, text output using this method, and we've seen this in action as well:

```
$count = 5;
return $this->t('The quick brown fox jumped @count times',
    ['@count' => $count]);
```

In this case, we have a dynamic variable that will be used to replace the @count placeholder from the text. Drupal takes care of sanitizing the variable before outputting the string to the user. Alternatively, we can also use the % prefix to define a placeholder we want Drupal to wrap with <em class="placeholder">. The cool thing is that when performing translations, users can shift the placeholder in the sentence to accommodate for language specificity.

One of the intended consequences of the static analyzer picking out and storing the strings that need to be translated is that, by default, each individual string is only translated once. This is good in many cases but also poses some problems when the same English string has different meanings (which map to different translations in other languages). To counter this issue, we can specify a context to the string that needs to be translated so that we can identify which meaning we actually want to translate. This is where the third parameter of the t() function (and method) we saw in the previous paragraphs comes into play.

For example, let's consider the word *Book*, which is translated by default according to its meaning as a noun. But we may have a submit button on a form that has the value Book, which clearly has a different meaning as a call to action. So, in the latter case, we could do it like this:

```
t('Book', [], ['context' => 'The verb "to book"']);
```

Now in the interface translation, we will have both versions available:

Source string	Translation for French
Book	Livre
Book In Context: The verb "to book"	Réserver

Save translations

Figure 13.5: Interface translation page with translation context

Another helpful tip is that we can also account for plurals in string translations. The `StringTranslationTrait::formatPlural()` method helps with this by creating a `PluralTranslatableMarkup` object similar to `TranslatableMarkup`, but with some extra parameters to account for differences when it comes to plurals. This comes in very handy in our previous example with the brown fox jumping a number of times, because if the fox jumps only once, the resulting string would no longer be grammatically correct. So instead, we can do the following:

```
$count = 5;
return $this->formatPlural($count, 'The quick brown fox
  jumped 1 time', 'The quick brown fox jumped @count
  times')];
```

The first parameter is the actual count (the differentiator between singular and plural). The second and third parameters are the singular and plural versions, respectively. You'll also notice that since we specified the count already, we don't have to specify it again in the arguments array. It's important to note that the placeholder name inside the string needs to be @count if we want the renderer to understand its purpose.

The string translation techniques we discussed so far also work in other places—not just in PHP code. For example, in JavaScript, we would do something like this:

```
Drupal.t('The quick brown fox jumped @count times',
  {'@count': 5});
Drupal.formatPlural(5, 'The quick brown fox jumped 1 time',
  'The quick brown fox jumped @count times');
```

So, based on this knowledge, I encourage you to go back and fix our incorrect use of the string output in JavaScript in the previous chapter.

In Twig, we'd have something like this (for simple translations):

```
{{ 'Hello World.'|trans }}
{{ 'Hello World.'|t }}
```

Both lines do the same thing. To handle plurals (and placeholders), we can use the `{% trans %}` block:

```
{% set count = 5 %}
{% trans %}
  The quick brown fox jumped 1 time.
{% plural count %}
  The quick brown fox jumped {{ count }} times.
{% endtrans %}
```

Finally, the string context is also possible like so:

```
{% trans with {'context': 'The verb "to book"'} %}
  Book
{% endtrans %}
```

In annotations, we have the @Translation() wrapper, as we've seen already a few times when creating plugins or defining entity types.

Finally, in YAML files, some of the strings are translatable by default (so we don't have to do anything):

- Module names and descriptions in .info.yml files

- The _title (together with the optional _title_context) key values under the defaults section of .routing.yml files

- The title (together with the optional title_context) key values in the .links. action.yml, .links.task.yml, and .links.contextual.yml files

Dates are also potentially problematic when it comes to localization, as different locales show dates differently. Luckily, Drupal provides the DateFormatter service, which handles this for us. For example:

```
\Drupal::service('date.formatter')->format(time(),
  'medium');
```

The first parameter of this formatter is the Unix timestamp of the date we want to format. The second parameter indicates the format to use (either one of the existing formats or custom). Drupal comes with a few predefined date formats, but site builders can define others as well, which can be used here. However, if the format is custom, the third parameter is a PHP date format string suitable for input to date(). The fourth parameter is a timezone identifier we want to format the date in, and the final parameter can be used to specify the language to localize to directly (regardless of the current language of the site).

Content entities and the translation API

So far in this chapter, we've mostly talked about how to ensure that our modules only output text that can also be translated. The Drupal best practice is to always use these techniques regardless of whether the site is multilingual. You never know whether you'll ever need to add a new language.

In this section, we are going to talk a bit about how we can interact with the language system programmatically and work with entity translations.

A potentially important thing you'll often want to do is check the current language of the site. Depending on the language negotiation in place, this can either be determined by the browser language, a domain, a URL prefix, or something else. The `LanguageManager` is the service we use to figure this out. We can inject it using the `language_manager` key or use it via the static shorthand:

```
$manager = \Drupal::languageManager();
```

To get the current language, we do this:

```
$language = $manager->getCurrentLanguage();
```

Where `$language` is an instance of the `Language` class that holds some information about the given language (such as the language code and name). The language code is probably the most important, as it is used everywhere to indicate what language a given *thing* is.

There are other useful methods with this service that you can use. For example, we can get a list of all the installed languages with `getLanguages()` or the site default language with `getDefaultLanguage()`. I encourage you to check out the `LanguageManager` for all the available API methods.

When it comes to content entities, there is an API we can use to interact with the data inside them in different languages. So, for example, we have figured out the current language with the previous method, so we can now get some field values in that language. The way this works is that we ask for a *copy* of the entity in the respective language:

```
$translation = $node->getTranslation($language->getId());
```

`$translation` is now almost the same as `$node`, but with the default language set to the one we requested. From there, we can access field values normally. However, not all nodes have to have a translation, so it's better to first check whether a translation exists:

```
if ($node->hasTranslation($language->getId())) {
   $translation = $node->getTranslation($language->getId());
}
```

Since we can configure entity translatability at the field level (allowing only the fields that make sense to be translated), we can also check which of these fields can have translated values:

```
$fields = $node->getTranslatableFields();
```

Finally, we can also check which languages there are translations for:

```
$languages = $node->getTranslationLanguages();
```

Since it's up to the editors to add translations to an entity, we cannot guarantee in code that one exists.

Programmatically, we can also create a translation to an entity. For example, let's imagine we want to translate a Node entity and specify its title to be in French:

```
$node->addTranslation('fr', ['title' => 'The title fr']);
```

The second parameter is an array of values that needs to map to the entity fields just like when creating a new entity. Now, the respective node has the original language (let's say EN) but also a French translation. It should be noted that the values of all the other fields apart from the title, even in the French translation, remain in the original language because we did not pass any translated values when creating the translation.

And just as we add a translation, we can also remove one:

```
$node->removeTranslation('fr');
```

If we want to persist the addition or removal of a translation, we need to save the entity as we are used to. Otherwise, it's stored only in memory. Content entities implement the Drupal\Core\ TypedData\TranslationStatusInterface, which allows us to inspect the status of the translations. So, for example, we can do this:

```
$status = $node->getTranslationStatus('fr');
```

Where $status is the value of one of three constants from the TranslationStatusInterface class:

- TRANSLATION_REMOVED

- TRANSLATION_EXISTING

- TRANSLATION_CREATED

Summary

In this short chapter, we talked about the Drupal multilingual and internationalization system from a module developer perspective. We started with an introduction to the four main modules responsible for languages and translating content, configuration entities, and interface text.

Then, we focused on the rules and techniques we need to respect to ensure that our output text can be translated. We saw how we can do this in PHP code, Twig, and YAML files, and even in JavaScript. Finally, we looked a bit at the language manager and the Translation API to see how we can work with content entities that have been translated.

The main takeaway from this chapter should be that languages are important in Drupal even if our site is only in one language. So, in developing modules, especially if we want to contribute them back to the community, we need to ensure that our functionality can be translated as needed.

In the next chapter, we are going to talk about data processing using batches and queues, as well as the cron system that comes with Drupal.

14

Batches, Queues, and Cron

If in the previous chapter, we kept things a bit more theoretical with me throwing "rules" at you, in this chapter, I am going to make up for it and we are going to have some fun. This means we are going to write some code that demonstrates concepts related to data processing, especially larger amounts of it. And in doing so, we are going to cover a few topics.

First, we are going to look back at the `hook_post_update_NAME()` hook we saw in *Chapter 8, The Database API*. More specifically, we are going to see how the `&$sandbox` parameter can be used to handle updates that need to process some data that may take a bit longer and should be split across multiple requests. Next up, we are going to look at standalone *batches* (which basically use the same system) to process data in batches across multiple requests. And what better example to illustrate this technique than our Importer, which needs to process an undefined number of products?

We will explore a related subsystem that allows us to queue *things* for later processing (either in batches, during cron, or in simple requests). And since we are talking about cron, we will also go into a bit of detail and see how this system works in Drupal. Finally, we will finish this chapter by taking a look at the Lock API, an API that allows us to ensure multiple requests don't run a process at the same time.

The main topics we will cover in this chapter are as follows:

- Batch-powered update hooks
- Batch operations
- Cron
- The Queue API
- The Lock API

By the end of this chapter, you will be a lean, mean, data-processing machine. So, let's get to it.

Batch-powered update hooks

The first thing we are going to look at is post update hooks, revisiting our previous Sports module created in *Chapter 8*, *The Database API*. We will focus on the &$sandbox, which is present in both the update hooks (hook_update_N()) and the post update hooks (hook_post_update_NAME()). The goal is to run an update on each of our records in the players table and mark them as retired. The point is to illustrate how we can process each of these records one at a time in individual requests to prevent a PHP timeout. This is handy if we have many records.

So, to get us going, here is all the code, and we'll see right after what everything means. If you remember, this will go in the sports.post_update.php file of our module:

```php
/**
 * Update all the players to mark them as retired.
 */
function sports_post_update_retire_players(&$sandbox) {
  $database = \Drupal::database();

  if (empty($sandbox)) {
    $results = $database->query("SELECT [id] FROM
      {players}")->fetchAllAssoc('id');
    $sandbox['progress'] = 0;
    $sandbox['ids'] = array_keys($results);
    $sandbox['max'] = count($results);
  }

  $id = $sandbox['ids'] ? array_shift($sandbox['ids']) :
    NULL;

  $player = $database->query("SELECT * FROM {players} WHERE
    [id] = :id", [':id' => $id])->fetch();
  $data = $player->data ? unserialize($player->data) : [];
  $data['retired'] = TRUE;
  $database->update('players')
   ->fields(['data' => serialize($data)])
   ->condition('id', $id)
   ->execute();
  $sandbox['progress']++;
```

```
    $sandbox['#finished'] = $sandbox['progress'] /
        $sandbox['max'];
}
```

When this hook is fired, the $sandbox argument (passed by reference) is empty. Its goal is to act as temporary storage between the requests needed to process everything inside the function. We can use it to store arbitrary data, but we should be mindful of the size, as it must fit inside a LONGBLOB table column.

The first thing we are doing is getting our hands on the database service to make queries to our players table. But more importantly, we are checking whether the $sandbox variable is empty, which indicates that this is the start of the process. If it is, we add some data to it that is specific to our process. In this case, we want to store the progress (this is quite common), the IDs of the players that need to be updated, and the total number of records (also quite common). To do this, we make a simple query.

Once the sandbox is set, we can get the first ID in the list while also removing it so that iteratively, we have fewer records to process. Based on that ID, we load the relevant player, add our data to it, and update it back in the database. Once that is done, we increment the progress by 1 (as we have processed one record). Finally, the #finished key in the sandbox is what Drupal looks at to determine whether the process is finished. It expects an integer between 0 and 1, the latter signifying that we are done. If anything below 1 is found, the function gets called again and the $sandbox array will contain the data as we left it (incremented progress and one less ID to process). In this case, the main body of the function runs again, processing the next record, and so on, until the progress divided by the maximum number of records is equal to 1. If we have 100 records, when the progress reaches 100, the following is true: 100/100 = 1. Then, Drupal knows to finish the process and not call the function again.

This process is also called batching in Drupal terms and is very useful because Drupal will make as many requests as needed to finish it. We can control the workload each request needs to make in one request. The previous example might be a bit of overkill in the sense that a request is perfectly capable of processing more than one player. We are actually losing time because, like this, Drupal needs to bootstrap itself again and again for each request. So, it's up to us to find that sweet spot. In our previous example, what we could have done was break up the array of IDs into chunks of maybe five and allowed a request to process five records instead of one. That would have surely increased the speed, so I encourage you to go ahead and try that on your own now that you understand the principles behind using $sandbox for batching.

Now that we have a basic understanding of Drupal's capabilities of doing multi-request processing, let's switch gears and look at the Batch API.

Batch operations

To demonstrate how batching works, we are going to rebuild the way our product `JsonImporter` plugin processes the data it retrieves. Currently, we simply load all the values into an array of objects and loop through each, saving them to the database. So, if there are 100,000 products in the JSON response, we might get into trouble with this approach. To be fair, if the remote provider has so many products, it usually provides a paginated way of requesting them by passing an offset and a limit. This keeps the payloads smaller (which is good for both communicating servers) and makes processing easier. For now, we'll go with the assumption that the number of returned products is large, but not so large as to pose problems with communication or with the ability of PHP to store them in memory.

Moreover, while illustrating the Batch API, we will also perform an operation we "forgot" in *Chapter 7, Your Own Custom Entity and Plugin Types*. During the import, we also want to delete any products that have been previously imported but that are no longer in the JSON response. It is a kind of synchronization between the two data sources if you will. So, let's get to it.

Creating the batch

Inside the `JsonImporter::import()` method, once we get our hands on the `$products` array, let's replace the loop with the following:

```
$batch_builder = (new BatchBuilder())
  ->setTitle($this->t('Importing products'))
  ->setFinishCallback([$this, 'importProductsFinished']);

$batch_builder->addOperation([$this, 'clearMissing'],
  [$products]);
$batch_builder->addOperation([$this, 'importProducts'],
  [$products]);
batch_set($batch_builder->toArray());
```

And the new *use* statement at the top:

```
use Drupal\Core\Batch\BatchBuilder;
```

Creating a batch involves a few steps, the first one being the creation of a batch definition using the `BatchBuilder`.

The batch can have a title (used on the progress page). Similarly, it can also have an optional init, progress, and error message that can be set with corresponding methods, but which also come with sensible defaults. For more information as to what exactly you can do with them and what other options you have, make sure you check out the `BatchBuilder` class and the `batch_set` global function.

The most important part of the batch definition is the list of operations in which we specify what needs to take place in the batch. These are defined as any kind of valid PHP callback and an array of arguments to pass to these callbacks. If the latter resides in a file that has not been loaded, the `setFile()` method can be used to specify a file path to include. Each operation runs on its own PHP request, in the sequence in which they are defined. Moreover, each operation can also run across multiple requests, similar to how we wrote our post update hook earlier.

Our first operation will be responsible for removing from Drupal the products that no longer exist in the JSON response, while the latter will do the import. Both receive only one parameter—the array of products.

The `finished` key in the definition (set using the `setFinishCallback()` method) is another callback that gets fired at the end of the batch processing after all the operations are done.

Finally, we call the global `batch_set()` method, which statically sets the batch definition and marks it as ready to be run. There is just one more step to trigger the batch, and that is a call to `batch_process()`. But the reason we have not used it is that if the import runs as part of a form submission, the Form API triggers it automatically. So, it won't work if we trigger it here as well. The reason why the Form API does it for us is that most of the time, we want batches to run only because an action is taken. And usually, this is done via forms. However, the other common possibility is to trigger the batch via a Drush command. In this case, we need to use the `drush_backend_batch_process()` function instead.

So, what we will do first is check that we are in a command-line environment (aka Drush) and trigger it only in that case:

```
if (PHP_SAPI == 'cli') {
    drush_backend_batch_process();
}
```

Otherwise, we leave it up to the Form API. In doing this, we can trigger the import both from a Form submit handler and via Drush.

Batch operations

Now that we have our batch definition in place, we are missing those three callback methods we are referencing in it. So, let's see the first one:

```
public function clearMissing($products, &$context) {
    if (!isset($context['results']['cleared'])) {
        $context['results']['cleared'] = [];
    }
```

```
if (!$products) {
  return;
}

$ids = [];
foreach ($products as $product) {
  $ids[] = $product->id;
}

$ids = $this->entityTypeManager->getStorage('product')
  ->getQuery()
  ->condition('remote_id', $ids, 'NOT IN')
  ->accessCheck(FALSE)
  ->execute();
if (!$ids) {
  $context['results']['cleared'] = [];
  return;
}

$entities = $this->entityTypeManager->
  getStorage('product')->loadMultiple($ids);

/** @var \Drupal\products\Entity\ProductInterface $entity
*/
foreach ($entities as $entity) {
  $context['results']['cleared'][] = $entity->getName();
}
$context['message'] = $this->t('Removing @count
  products', ['@count' => count($entities)]);
$this->entityTypeManager->getStorage('product')->
  delete($entities);
}
```

This is the first operation in the batch process. As an argument, it receives all the variables we defined in the batch definition (in our case, the products array). But it also gets a $context array variable passed by reference, which we can use in a similar way to how we used $sandbox in the post update hook (with some extra capabilities).

The task at hand is simple. We prepare a list of IDs of all the products in the JSON and, based on those, we query our product entities for those that are NOT IN that list. If any are found, we delete them. You'll notice already that in this operation, we are not relying on the actual multi-request capabilities of Drupal's Batch API because we expect the workload to be minimal. After all, how many products could be missing at any given time and would need to be deleted? We'll assume not many for our use case.

But while we are doing all this, we are interacting somewhat with the batch processing. You'll notice that the $context array has a results key. This is used to store information related to the outcome of each operation in the batch. We are not supposed to use it for managing progress but instead for keeping track of what was done so that at the end, we can present the user with some useful information as to what has happened. So, in our example, we create an array keyed by cleared (to namespace the data for this particular operation), to which we add the names of each product that has been deleted.

Moreover, we also have a message key that we use to print a message as the action is happening. This gets printed out in real time to indicate to the user what is currently being processed. If the batch is run via the UI through a form, it very well might be that you won't see all the messages due to the speed of the processing. However, if triggered by Drush (as it will be in our case), each of these messages will be printed on the terminal screen.

With this, our first operation is done. It's time to look at the second, more complex one:

```
public function importProducts($products, &$context) {
  if (!isset($context['results']['imported'])) {
    $context['results']['imported'] = [];
  }


  if (!$products) {
    return;
  }


  $sandbox = &$context['sandbox'];
  if (!$sandbox) {
    $sandbox['progress'] = 0;
    $sandbox['max'] = count($products);
    $sandbox['products'] = $products;
  }


  $slice = array_splice($sandbox['products'], 0, 3);
  foreach ($slice as $product) {
    $context['message'] = $this->t('Importing product
```

```
      @name', ['@name' => $product->name]);
    $this->persistProduct($product);
    $context['results']['imported'][] = $product->name;
    $sandbox['progress']++;
  }

  $context['finished'] = $sandbox['progress'] /
    $sandbox['max'];
}
```

The arguments it receives are the same as with our previous operation since we defined them in the same way.

Here, again, we ensure we have some products and start up our results array, this time to keep track of the imported records. But we also work with the sandbox key of the $context array to use the multi-request processing capabilities. The approach is similar to what we did in the post update hook—we keep a progress count, store the maximum number of products, and then we calculate the $context['finished'] key based on the division between the two. However, in this case, we opt to process three products at a time instead of one. Again, as with our previous operation, we are using the message key to inform the user as to what is going on and the results key to compile a list of products that have been imported.

Before moving on, let's talk a bit about the way we are importing the products. Had the JSON resource been able to return paginated results, we would have had to change our approach. First, we could not have deleted the missing products in the same way. Instead, we would have had to keep track of the IDs of the imported products and only afterward delete the missing ones. Hence, the order of the two operations would have been reversed. Second, the retrieval of the products would have been done from inside the importProducts operation using an offset and a limit stored in the sandbox. So, each Drupal batch request would have made a new request to the JSON resource. Of course, we would have had to keep track of all the processed products so that we would know which ones were able to be deleted.

Finally, let's see the callback used when the batch processing finishes:

```
public function importProductsFinished($success, $results,
  $operations) {
  if (!$success) {
    $this->messenger->addStatus($this->t('There was a
      problem with the batch'), 'error');
    return;
  }
```

```
$cleared = count($results['cleared']);
if ($cleared == 0) {
  $this->messenger->addStatus($this->t('No products had
    to be deleted.'));
}
else {
  $this->messenger->addStatus($this->formatPlural
    ($cleared, '1 product had to be deleted.', '@count
      products had to be deleted.'));
}

$imported = count($results['imported']);
if ($imported == 0) {
  $this->messenger->addStatus($this->t('No products found
    to be imported.'));
}
else {
  $this->messenger->addStatus($this->formatPlural
    ($imported, '1 product imported.', '@count products
      imported.'));
}
}
```

This callback receives three parameters: a Boolean indicating whether the processing was successful or not, the results array we used inside our $context to keep track of what has been done, and the array of operations. What we are doing is pretty simple. We first print a generic message if the batch has failed. In this case, we also return early. Otherwise, we print relevant messages to the operations we have done, using the $results array. Note the use of the t() and formatPlural() methods you learned about in the previous chapter. Moreover, note the use of the local $messenger service used for printing the messages. We did not yet inject it but by now, you should know how to do this, so I will let you do it on your own.

Our reworked JSON Importer now uses batching to make the process more stable in case the number of records it needs to process gets too big. So, now if we run the Drush command we wrote in *Chapter 7, Your Own Custom Entity and Plugin Types*, to trigger our importer, we get an output similar to this:

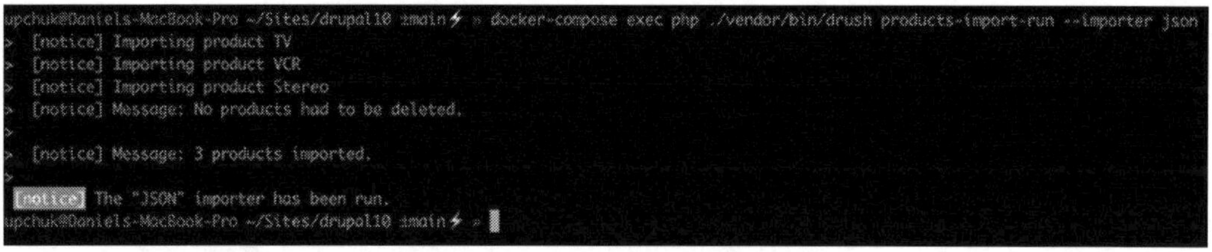

Figure 14.1: Drush command output

Note the messages set when importing each record, as well as the messages we set at the end of the process, which provides a kind of summary of what went down.

> **Note**
>
> When calling `batch_process()`, we can also pass in a URL to redirect to when the processing has finished. However, a better way is to return a `RedirectResponse` inside the `finished` callback. And it goes without saying that if we trigger the batch from Drush, there will be no actual redirect. However, it will work just fine in a form context.

Cron

In the previous section, we created an awesome multi-request batch processing of our JSON product import. In the next section, we'll jump into the Queue API and see how we can plan the processing of multiple items at a later stage. However, before we dive into that, let's talk a bit about how the Drupal cron works and what we can do with it. This is because our discussion about the Queue API is closely related to it.

Drupal doesn't actually have a fully-fledged cron system. That is because it's an application and not a server capable of scheduling tasks that run at specified times of the day. However, what it does have is a cron-like system, which can come very close, especially on busy websites. Often, it is affectionately referred to as the *poor man's cron*. Why? Since Drupal cannot by itself do anything without any sort of input, it relies on visitors coming to the website to trigger the cron tasks. So, even if we can configure the frequency of Drupal's cron, we are relying on visitors coming to the website and triggering it inadvertently. Drupal then keeps track of when the cron ran and ensures that the next time it runs is only after the configured amount of time has elapsed. So, in essence, if the cron is set to run every hour but the next visitor only comes in three hours, it will only run then:

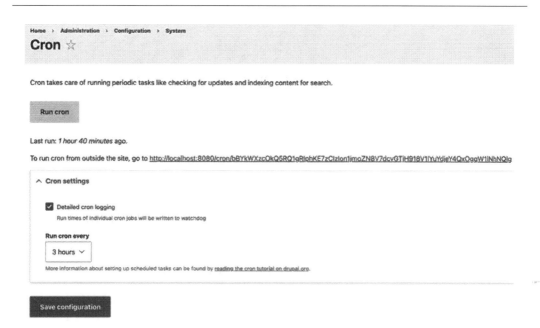

Figure 14.2: Cron management page

The Drupal cron is very useful for maintenance tasks and relatively small jobs that don't take too many resources away from the site visitors. Moreover, it can be triggered manually from the UI, from an outside script, or even with Drush, by using the following command:

```
drush cron
```

There are many Drupal core and contributed modules that rely on this system to perform various tasks, and we, as module developers, can do the same by implementing hook_cron(). The latter gets fired every time the cron runs, so basically, Drupal's cron is a collection of function calls to various modules. For this reason, we must avoid overloading the request with heavy processing; otherwise, the request might crash. But as we will see in the next section, we can do something to control this if we have such jobs to run.

First, though, let's look at an example implementation and see how it works. What we want to accomplish is that whenever cron runs, we delete all the records in the teams table (which we created in *Chapter 8, The Database API*) that are no longer referenced by any player. Essentially, if the teams don't have any players, they need to go. So, we could do something simple like this:

```
/**
 * Implements hook_cron().
 */
function sports_cron() {
```

```
$database = \Drupal::database();
$result = $database->query("SELECT [id] FROM {teams}
  WHERE [id] NOT IN (SELECT [team_id] FROM {players}
    WHERE [team_id] IS NOT NULL)")->fetchAllAssoc('id');
if (!$result) {
  return;
}

$ids = array_keys($result);
$database->delete('teams')
  ->condition('id', $ids, 'IN')
  ->execute();
}
```

We are implementing hook_cron(), and inside, we basically figure out which teams have no players and delete them. You'll notice that the query to do the former is a more complex one, as we are using a subquery, but it is still not rocket science. Feel free to check *Chapter 8, The Database API*, for a refresher on the Drupal database API.

This function will then be fired every time our Drupal cron runs, and we could argue that doing this task is not such a big strain on our resources. However, in the next section, we will see how we can handle cases like those. Moreover, we'll see why that approach might even be better than this one, regardless of resource intensiveness.

Queues

It's finally time to talk a bit about the Queue API, how it works, and what its main components are; the theory, basically. We will do this before diving into code examples, which we all thoroughly enjoy.

Introduction to the Queue API

The main purpose of the Queue API is to provide a way for us to add items to a *queue* to have them processed at a later time. In charge of processing these items are the *queue worker* plugins, which can be enlisted either automatically by the Drupal cron, manually (programmatically) by us, or by Drush. We will look at examples of all three.

The central player in this API is an implementation of the `QueueInterface`, which is the actual queue into which we put items. There are two types of queues Drupal can handle: reliable and unreliable. The first preserves the order in which the items are processed (first in, first out) and guarantees that each item gets processed at least once. In this chapter, we will focus only on this type of queue. But there is also the possibility of working with unreliable queues, which give their best effort when maintaining the item order but do not guarantee that all items get processed.

By default, when we are working with queues in Drupal, we use a reliable queue that is based on a database table to store the items. This is represented by the `DatabaseQueue` implementation. The Batch API in fact uses a type of queue that extends from the default one Drupal comes with. Okay, but what does a queue do?

A queue has three main roles:

- It creates items (adds *stuff* to a list that needs processing at some point).
- It claims items (puts a hold on them while a worker does the processing).
- It deletes items (removes the items from the queue once they have finished processing). Alternatively, it can also release them if another worker needs to process them, or if something went wrong, and they should be retrieved later.

We will soon see a practical example of how this works. But first, let's look at how a queue comes about.

The `QueueInterface` implementation is created with the help of the `QueueFactory` service, named `queue`. The factory delegates to another factory service specific to the type of queue being created. By default, this is the `QueueDatabaseFactory` service (named `queue.database`), which expectedly returns an instance of the `DatabaseQueue` class. The table used by the latter is simply called `queue`.

Finally, the crux of the Queue API for us module developers is the system of `QueueWorker` plugins that are responsible for processing a single item in the queue. These can be written in two ways. The simplest approach is to have them triggered by cron. In this case, the plugin ID needs to match the name of the queue it needs to process items for. This way, we don't have to worry about claiming, releasing, or deleting items. The cron system does it for us. However, a more flexible approach is the one in which we actually do that. We don't rely on cron but process the items ourselves whenever we want. Moreover, both types of queue workers can be enlisted via Drush using a command that triggers the processing of a queue with a given name.

Cron-based queues

In the previous section, we wrote the `sports_cron()` implementation, which, at each run, looks for teams that no longer have players and deletes them from the database. However, if we run the Drupal cron every hour, we keep running that query even if we are pretty certain that teams don't lose all their players so often. Moreover, we also go by the simple assumption (a functionality we have not written so far) that there is some code responsible for removing a player from a team. This would actually be the ideal place to check whether that team has lost all its players. The idea, then, is to check whether the team has been left empty and add it to a queue to be deleted later (whenever the cron runs).

We won't go into the code specific to player and team management, but instead, focus on the part that adds the team that needs to be deleted to the queue.

The first thing we need to do is get our hands on the `QueueFactory` service:

```
/** @var \Drupal\Core\Queue\QueueFactory $queue_factory */
$queue_factory = \Drupal::service('queue');
```

Then, we need to create an instance of the default `QueueInterface` (database) with the name of our future worker plugin ID:

```
/** @var \Drupal\Core\Queue\QueueInterface $queue */
$queue = $queue_factory->get('team_cleaner');
```

This is obviously the static approach to loading services, and you should be injecting them instead whenever possible. But if you cannot, there is also the following shorthand, which can achieve the same thing in one line:

```
$queue = \Drupal::queue('team_cleaner');
```

`$queue` is an instance of `DatabaseQueue` with the name `team_cleaner`.

The next thing we need to do is add items to it (assuming that we've identified a team without players):

```
$item = new \stdClass();
$item->id = $team_id;
$queue->createItem($item);
```

It's standard practice to create a PHP object to wrap the data for the queue item. Inside, we can put anything we want that can serialize properly, and that's all. We can now turn to our `TeamCleaner` worker plugin, which naturally goes into the `Plugin/QueueWorker` namespace of our module:

```php
namespace Drupal\sports\Plugin\QueueWorker;


use Drupal\Core\Database\Connection;
use Drupal\Core\Plugin\ContainerFactoryPluginInterface;
use Drupal\Core\Queue\QueueWorkerBase;
use Symfony\Component\DependencyInjection\
  ContainerInterface;


/**
 * A worker plugin that removes a team from the database.
 *
 * @QueueWorker(
 *   id = "team_cleaner",
 *   title = @Translation("Team Cleaner"),
 *   cron = {"time" = 10}
 * )
 */
class TeamCleaner extends QueueWorkerBase implements
  ContainerFactoryPluginInterface {

  /**
   * @var \Drupal\Core\Database\Connection
   */
  protected $database;

  /**
   * Constructs a TeamCleaner worker.
   *
   * @param array $configuration
   * @param string $plugin_id
   * @param mixed $plugin_definition
   * @param \Drupal\Core\Database\Connection $database
   */
```

```php
  public function __construct(array $configuration,
    $plugin_id, $plugin_definition, Connection $database) {
    parent::__construct($configuration, $plugin_id,
      $plugin_definition);
    $this->database = $database;
  }


  /**
   * {@inheritdoc}
   */
  public static function create(ContainerInterface
    $container, array $configuration, $plugin_id,
      $plugin_definition) {
    return new static(
      $configuration,
      $plugin_id,
      $plugin_definition,
      $container->get('database')
    );
  }


  /**
   * {@inheritdoc}
   */
  public function processItem($data) {
    $id = isset($data->id) && $data->id ? $data->id : NULL;
    if (!$id) {
      throw new \Exception('Missing team ID');
      return;
    }

    $this->database->delete('teams')
      ->condition('id', $id)
      ->execute();
  }
}
```

As we're already used to it, our plugin extends the base plugin class of its type to inherit any potential base functionality. In our case, this is limited to the implementation of the `QueueWorkerInterface`, which has one method whose name easily describes its responsibility: `processItem($data)`. Also, not new to us is the implementation of `ContainerFactoryPluginInterface`, which allows us to inject the `database` service into our plugin. We use that to delete the queued team.

All the action in fact happens in the `processItem()` method, where we simply look into the `$data` object and delete the team with the specified ID. We also throw a simple exception if something goes wrong. We'll talk about exceptions in queue processing shortly.

Somewhat more interesting for the Queue API, however, is the plugin annotation. Apart from the standard expected plugin definition, we also encounter the following:

```
cron = {"time" = 10}
```

This simply indicates that this plugin should be used by the cron system. In other words, when the Drupal cron runs, it loads all the worker plugin definitions, and whichever plugin has this information gets processed. And the key here is the `time` information, which we have set to 10 seconds. This essentially means that when the cron runs, we are saying: *go ahead and process as many queue items as you can within 10 seconds; once that time limit is up, stop and continue with the rest of the cron tasks.* This is actually very powerful because we allocated an amount of time from the PHP request and dedicated it to our queue. This means that we don't have to guess how many items to allocate for a request (as we did with the batching). However, it also means that the rest of the time left needs to be enough for everything else. So, we need to adjust this carefully. As for the queue items that don't fit into those 10 seconds, they will simply be processed at the next cron run.

This approach is better than our previous one, in which we ourselves implemented `hook_cron()`, because we don't want to always keep checking teams for players, but can instead create queue items and defer the deletion until a later time, as needed.

Very similarly, we could refactor our JSON product importer. When calling the `import()` method, the products would get queued, and then a separate worker plugin would handle the product data creation/update whenever cron runs. This of course depends on whether we are okay with splitting the import functionality into two classes, which is not a big deal. We are actually fine with the way things are at the moment, so to illustrate the programmatic processing of the queue, we will use another example.

Processing a queue programmatically

Now that we have our queue worker that deletes teams (for all it knows, the teams don't even have to be without any players), we can explore how we can process this queue ourselves if we don't want the cron option. If we wanted it to be processed using a Drush command, we would not have to write that ourselves. Drush comes with one, and it would work like this:

```
drush queue-run team_cleaner
```

However, we may want to create an admin interface, a form of some kind, which allows the user to trigger the queue processing. In that case, we could do something like this:

```
$queue = \Drupal::queue('team_cleaner');
/** @var \Drupal\Core\Queue\QueueWorkerInterface
  $queue_worker */
$queue_worker = \Drupal::service('plugin.manager
  .queue_worker')->createInstance('team_cleaner');

while($item = $queue->claimItem()) {
  try {
    $queue_worker->processItem($item->data);
    $queue->deleteItem($item);
  }
  catch (SuspendQueueException $e) {
    $queue->releaseItem($item);
    break;
  }
  catch (\Exception $e) {
    // Log the exception.
  }
}
```

In this example, we get our `QueueInterface` object just like we did before. But then, we also create an instance of our own `QueueWorker` plugin. Next, we use the `claimItem()` method inside a *while* loop, which returns an object that contains the data to be passed to the queue worker. Additionally, it blocks the item from being usable by another worker for a period of (lease) time (by default, an hour).

Then, we try to use the worker to process the item, and if no exception is thrown, we delete the item. It's done! However, if we catch a `SuspendQueueException`, that means we expect the entire queue to be problematic. This exception type is thrown when there is the expectation that all other items are also likely to fail, in which case we release the item and break out of the loop. Releasing the item means that other workers are now free to process it using the `claimItem()` method. Or even better, our own worker can try it later. Finally, we also catch any other exceptions, in which case we simply log the error but do not release the item to prevent an infinite loop. For the moment, that particular item cannot be processed, so we need to skip to the next one; it needs to stay blocked until our loop finishes. The latter can only happen when `$queue->claimItem()` no longer returns anything.

And that is pretty much the logic behind processing a queue ourselves: we claim an item, throw it to a worker, and delete it. If something goes wrong, we work with exceptions to determine whether the queue can be continued or whether it should be skipped altogether.

The Lock API

Whenever we process data on a regular basis, especially if it takes a while to complete, we might run into a situation in which parallel requests want to trigger that process again while the first is still running. Most of the time, this is not a good thing, as it can lead to conflicts and/or data corruption. A good example from Drupal core in which this can happen is the cron. If we start it, the process can end up taking a few seconds. Remember, it needs to pull together the `hook_cron()` implementations and run them all. So, while that is happening, if we trigger another cron run, it will give us a nice message asking us to chill because the cron is already running. It does this with the help of the Lock API.

The Lock API is a low-level Drupal solution for ensuring that processes don't trample each other. Since in this chapter we are talking about things such as batch operations, queues, and other kinds of potentially time-consuming processes, let's look at the Lock API to see how we can leverage it for our custom code. But first, let's get an understanding of how this locking works.

The concept is very simple. Before starting a process, we *acquire* a lock based on a given name. This means we check if, by any chance, this process has not already been started. If we get the green light (we *acquired* the lock), we go ahead and start the process. The API at this point locks down this named process so that other requests cannot *acquire* it again until the initial one has *released* it. This normally happens when the process is finished and other requests may then start it up again. Before that, though, we get a red light which tells us we cannot start it—to maintain the analogy of traffic lights. Speaking of which, the main Lock API implementation in Drupal, namely the one using the database, takes this analogy to heart, as it names the table where the locks are being stored `semaphore`.

The API is actually pretty simple. We have a `Lock` service, which is an implementation of `LockBackendInterface`. By default, Drupal comes with two: `DatabaseLockBackend` and `PersistentDatabaseLockBackend`. Usually, the former is used. The difference between the two is that the latter can be used to keep a lock across multiple requests. The former in fact releases all the locks at the end of the request. We'll be using this one to demonstrate how the API works, as that is what Drupal core uses mostly as well.

If you remember from *Chapter 7, Your Own Custom Entity and Plugin Types*, we created a Drush command that would run all of our Product importers. Of course, we so far have only created one plugin. But what we want to do is ensure that if this Drush command is executed multiple times at more or less the same time (before the actual import finishes), we don't run the imports simultaneously. It's probably not the most realistic example, as Drush commands must be run by someone so there is good control over their timing. However, the same approach, as we will see, can be applied to processes triggered by unpredictable requests.

We defined the `ProductCommands::runPluginImport()` helper method, which runs the import for a specific plugin. We can wrap this trigger with a *lock block*. First, though, we need to inject the service, and we can get to it using the `lock` key (or the static shorthand if we cannot inject it: `\Drupal::lock()`). By now, you should know how to inject a new service, so I will not repeat that step here.

So instead of just running the `import()` method on the plugin, we can first have this (make sure you use the `StringTranslationTrait` if you haven't already):

```
if (!$this->lock->acquire($plugin->getPluginId())) {
  $this->logger()->log('notice', $this->t('The plugin
    @plugin is already running.', ['@plugin' => $plugin->
      getPluginDefinition()['label']]));
  return;
}
```

We try to *acquire* the lock by passing an arbitrary name (in this case, our plugin ID). We are sticking to one plugin at a time here, so multiple plugins should in fact be able to run at the same time. If the `acquire()` method returns `FALSE`, that means we have a red light; a lock has already been acquired. In this case, we print a message to that effect and get out of there. However, if not, it means we have a green light and we can proceed with the rest of our code as it was. The `acquire()` method has locked it down, and other requests can no longer acquire it until we *release* it. Speaking of which, there is one thing we need to add at the end (after the import):

```
$this->lock->release($plugin->getPluginId());
```

We need to *release* the lock so other requests can run it again if they like. That is pretty much it. If we run our Drush command twice, more or less simultaneously, we will have something like this in the terminal:

Figure 14.3: The Lock API preventing parallel processes

As you can see, only one call to the Drush command actually went through. As expected.

But we can also do it a bit differently. Let's say that we want to wait with the second request until the first one is finished, and then still run it. After all, we don't want to miss out on any updates. We can do this using the `wait()` method of `LockBackendInterface`. The rework is minor:

```
if (!$this->lock->acquire($plugin->getPluginId())) {
  $this->logger()->log('notice', t('The plugin @plugin is
    already running. Waiting for it to finish.', ['@plugin'
      => $plugin->getPluginDefinition()['label']]));
  if ($this->lock->wait($plugin->getPluginId())) {
    $this->logger()->log('notice', t('The wait is killing
      me. Giving up.'));
    return;
  }
}
```

So basically, if we don't *acquire* a lock, we print a message that we are waiting for the go-ahead. Then, we use the `wait()` method, which puts the request to sleep for a maximum of 30 seconds. Within that time frame, it will continuously check every 25 milliseconds (until it reaches 500 milliseconds when it starts checking every 500 milliseconds) if the lock has become available. If it has, it breaks out of the loop and returns FALSE (meaning that we can go ahead, as the lock has become available). Otherwise, if the 30 seconds have passed, it returns TRUE, which means that we still need to wait. At this point, we give up. Guess what: the second parameter of the `wait()` method is the number of maximum seconds to wait, so we can control that as well. I recommend you check out the code to better understand what it does.

Like this, we can run our two Drush commands in parallel and ensure that the second one that was requested only runs after the first finishes. If it takes longer than 30 seconds, we give up, because something probably went wrong. And there we have the Lock API.

Summary

In this chapter, we looked at some of the ways we, as module developers, can set up simple and complex data-processing tasks that can run at any time we want.

We started by looking into using the multi-request capabilities of the post update hooks. This was a continuation from *Chapter 8*, *The Database API*, where we introduced them for the first time, and we have now seen how we can expand on their capabilities. Then, we turned to the more complex Batch API, which uses similar, albeit more complex, techniques. This system allowed us to construct a series of operations that leveraged Drupal's multi-request capabilities. Our playground was the JSON products importer, which can now handle large amounts of data without the worry of PHP memory timeouts. Next, we looked at how Drupal's cron system works and why it is there, and even saw an example of how, as module developers, we can hook into it and process our own tasks whenever it runs. But then, we took things to the next level with the introduction of the Queue API, which allowed us to add items to a queue so that they can get processed at a later stage. This processing, as we saw, can be triggered by cron or we can take matters into our own hands and handle them one by one. Not to mention the Drush option, which can also make things easy. Finally, we looked at the Lock API, which allows us to get control over the triggering of certain processes that take longer to complete. All this is done to prevent them from being run multiple times simultaneously, causing errors or data corruption.

In the next chapter, we are going to talk about Views and how we can programmatically interact with them as module developers.

15
Views

Before Drupal 8, Views has always been a staple module for any Drupal site. It was so popular and needed that it ended up being incorporated into Drupal core. So now, each new Drupal site ships with Views out of the box, fully integrated with the rest of the system and powering a great number of core features.

Essentially, Views is a tool for creating and displaying lists of data. This data can be almost anything, but we mostly use Drupal entities as they are now so robust. It provides the architecture to build and manipulate complex queries through the UI as well as many different ways of outputting the resulting data. From a module developer's point of *View* (yes, pun intended), much of this power has been broken down into multiple layers of building blocks, abstracted as plugins. Moreover, in keeping with tradition, there are also a multitude of hooks that are fired at different stages with which we can programmatically contribute to, or influence, Views.

In this chapter, we will look at the Views ecosystem from a module developer's perspective. As such, we won't be spending that much time with its site-building capabilities as you can argue an entire book could be dedicated just to that. Instead, we will focus on what we, as module developers, can do to empower site builders to have even more capabilities at their fingertips, as well as manipulating Views to behave the way our functionality needs it to.

So, what will we do in this chapter? We will first start with integrating our Product entity type with Views. The entity system and Views can work very closely together, and all we need to do is point them to one another. Then, we will switch gears and expose our own custom player and team data (from *Chapter 8, The Database API*) to Views so that our site builders can build Views that list this information, complete with filters, sorts, arguments, and the *whole shebang*. From there, we will look at how we can also alter data that has been exposed to Views by other modules, such as entity data such as Nodes.

Next, we will learn how to create our own `ViewsField`, `ViewsFilter`, and `ViewsArgument` plugins to account for those occasional requirements for which the existing ones are a bit lacking. Finally, we will talk a little bit about theming Views and the main components that play a role in this, just to get you going in the right direction, and apply the lessons from *Chapter 4, Theming*.

By the end of this chapter, you will get a pretty good understanding of how to leverage Views on top of your own data, as well as modify or contribute to how other modules leverage it. You should also get a pretty good understanding of the Views plugin ecosystem, even if quite a bit of work will have to be done on your own, studying the available plugins of all types.

So, let's get to it.

The major topics we will cover in this chapter are as follows:

- Exposing entity data to Views
- Exposing custom data to Views
- Creating custom Views plugins
- Theming Views

Entities in Views

Views and entities are very closely linked and it's a breeze to expose new content entities to Views. If you've followed along with *Chapter 7, Your Own Custom Entity and Plugin Types,* and have the Product entity type set up, you'll notice that if you try to create a View, you will have no option to make it based on products. That is because, in the entity type definition, we did not specify that it should be exposed to Views. That's all there is to it, actually. We just have to reference a new handler:

```
"views_data" = "Drupal\views\EntityViewsData"
```

That's it. Clearing the cache, we are now able to create Views with products that can show any of the fields, can filter and sort by them, and can even render them using view modes. All of them work consistently with the other entity types (at least fundamentally, as we will see in a moment).

You'll notice that we referenced the `EntityViewsData` data handler, which ensures basic logic for entities of all types. If we want to, we can extend this class and add some of our own specificities to the data that is being exposed to Views (or alter the existing one). This is done inside the `getViewsData()` method, and we will see an example later on. But if you already want to see an example, check out the `NodeViewsData` handler for the Node entity type, as it has quite a lot of extra stuff in there. Much of it probably won't make a lot of sense quite yet, so let's slowly get into how Views works by exposing our own custom data to it.

Exposing custom data to Views

To get a better understanding of how Views works, we are going to look at an example of totally custom data and how we can expose it to Views. Based on that, we will begin to understand the role of various plugins and can begin to create our own. Additionally, we'll be able to expand on our product entity type data to enrich its Views interaction.

To exemplify all of this, we are going to revisit our sports module where we declared the `players` and `teams` tables of data and that we will now be exposing to Views. The goal is to allow site builders to create dynamic listings of this data as they see fit. The lessons learned from this example can be applied to other data sources as well, even things such as remote APIs (with some extra work).

Views data

Whenever we want to expose data to Views, we need to define this data in a way Views can understand. That is actually what `EntityViewsData::getViewsData()` does for content entities. However, since we are dealing with something custom, we can do so by implementing `hook_views_data()`. A lot can go into it, but we'll start things simple.

Let's implement this hook and simply describe our first table (that of the players) and only one field, namely, the player ID, to start with.

> **Note**
>
> In Views lingo, the term `field` does not have to relate necessarily to entity fields or anything like that, but rather to an individual piece of data from a data source (real or not). A typical example to consider is a column in a table, but it can also be something such as a property from a remote API resource. Moreover, the same term is used to describe the *responsibility* of that piece of data of being somehow output. Other such responsibilities it can have are `filter`, `sort`, `relationship`, and more. Each of these responsibilities is handled by a specific type of Views plugin (also known as a handler in older versions of Views).

So, the basic implementation can look like this:

```
/**
 * Implements hook_views_data().
 */
function sports_views_data() {
  $data = [];

  // Players table
  $data['players'] = [];
  $data['players']['table']['group'] = t('Sports');
  $data['players']['table']['base'] = [
    'field' => 'id',
    'title' => t('Players'),
    'help' => t('Holds player data.'),
  ];
```

```
    // Player fields
    $data['players']['id'] = [
      'title' => t('ID'),
      'help' => t('The unique player ID.'),
      'field' => [
        'id' => 'numeric',
      ],
    ];

    return $data;
  }
```

This hook needs to return a multi-dimensional associative array that describes various things, the most important being the table and its fields. The table doesn't have to be an actual database table but can also mean something similar to an external resource. Of course, Views already knows how to query the database table, which makes things easy for us. Otherwise, we'd also have to create the logic for querying that external resource (by implementing a ViewsQuery plugin).

So, we start by defining the players table, which goes into the Sports group. This label can be found in the Views admin as the prefix to the fields we want to add. Next, we define our first *base* table, called players (mapping to the actual database table with the same name). The *base* table is the one used for *basing* a View on when creating it. In other words, whatever you select in the following screen text:

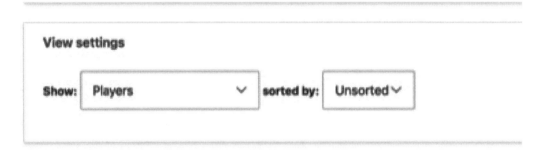

Figure 15.1: Creating a View with a custom data source

The base table definition contains some information, such as the field that refers to the column that contains the unique identifier for the records. title and help, both mandatory, are used in the UI. Moreover, it can also contain query_id, which references the plugin ID of a ViewsQuery plugin responsible for returning the data from the source in an intelligible way. Since we are using the database (hence SQL), omitting this property will make it default to that `views_query` plugin (the `Sql` class if you want to check it out).

Views fields

To actually use this table, we need to define one or more fields that can output some of its data. So, we start with a simple one: the player IDs. Anything that comes under the `$data['table_name']` array (that is not keyed by `table`, as we've seen) is responsible for defining Views fields. The keys are their machine names. The `title` and `help` values are there again to be used in the UI when we try to add the respective fields:

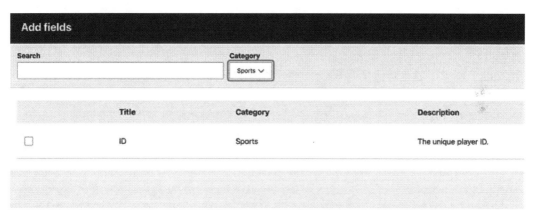

Figure 15.2: Selecting a Views field

The most important part of this definition, however, is the `field` key, which basically says that, for this piece of data, we want a Views field that uses the `ViewsField` plugin with the ID `numeric` (`NumericField`). So, we don't actually have to write our own plugin because Views already has a good one for us and it will treat our IDs according to the type of data they are. Of course, when defining Views fields (or any other types of data responsibilities, that is, plugins or handlers), we can have more options than just the ID of the plugin to use.

> **Note**
>
> You can check out all of the existing Views plugins defined by the module itself by looking at the `Drupal\views\Plugin\views` namespace. There are many plugin types that handle different responsibilities, but it's good to know where you can look because, more often than not, one will already exist for your needs.

With this, we are done. Clearing the cache, we can now go into the Views UI and create our first View that shows player data. To it, we can add the ID field, which will then naturally just show a list of IDs. Nothing else, as we haven't defined anything else. So, let's go ahead and expose the player name in the same way:

```
$data['players']['name'] = [
  'title' => t('Name'),
  'help' => t('The name of the player.'),
  'field' => [
    'id' => 'standard',
  ],
];
```

This time, we are using the standard plugin, which is the simplest one we can use. It essentially just outputs the data as it is found in the data source (with the proper sanitization in place). In the case of our player names, that is enough. Now we can add this new field to the View as well.

If you remember, the other column on our players table is one that can store arbitrary data in a serialized way. Obviously, this cannot be used for filtering or sorting, but we can still output some of that data as a field. There are two ways we can go about doing this, depending on our data and what we want to be accomplished. First, we can use the existing Serialized plugin, which allows us to display the serialized data or even a given key from the resulting array (depending on the field configuration). But for more complex situations (especially when the data is arbitrary), we can write our own field plugin.

Let's start by creating a simple data field that can output a printed version of our serialized data since we cannot rely on the actual data being stored:

```
$data['players']['data'] = [
  'title' => t('Data'),
  'help' => t('The player data.'),
  'field' => [
    'id' => 'serialized',
  ],
];
```

In the field configuration, we then have these options to choose from:

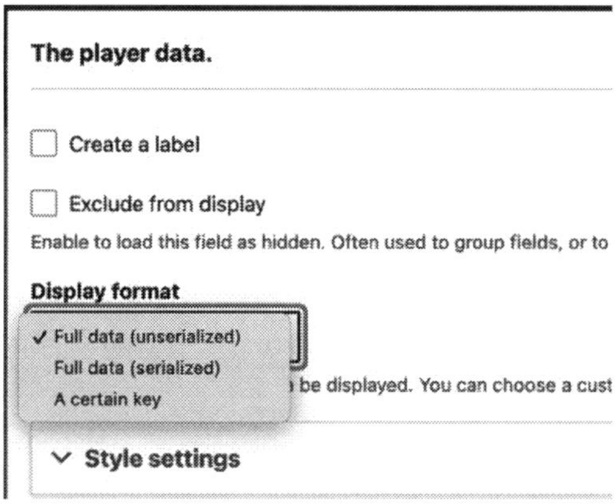

The player data.

☐ Create a label

☐ Exclude from display
Enable to load this field as hidden. Often used to group fields, or to

Display format

✓ Full data (unserialized)
Full data (serialized)
A certain key

be displayed. You can choose a cust

˅ **Style settings**

Figure 15.3: Serialized Views field configuration

With this, you should already get a picture of how to define fields for output in Views. Let's now see how we can bring our teams into the loop and show some data about the teams the players belong to.

Views relationships

The data about the teams our players belong to is stored in a different table. This means that, at a database level, a join will have to be created to pull them together. In Views lingo, this is a *relationship* in the sense that one table relates to another and the way these are declared is directional from one field to another field from the joined table. So, let's see how we can define the `team_id` field from the `players` table to join with the `teams` table on its `id` field:

```
$data['players']['team_id'] = [
  'title' => t('Team ID'),
  'help' => t('The unique team ID of the player.'),
  'field' => [
    'id' => 'numeric',
  ],
  'relationship' => [
    'base' => 'teams',
    'base field' => 'id',
    'id' => 'standard',
    'label' => t('Player team'),
  ],
];
```

First, we define it to Views as a field. Second, because we also might want to display the team ID, we can define its `field` responsibility as well using the `numeric` plugin, the same way we defined the ID of the player records themselves. Third, here comes another *responsibility* of this field in the form of a `relationship`, which requires four pieces of information:

- `base`: The name of the table we are joining
- `base field`: The name of the field on the table we are joining that will be used to join
- `id`: The `ViewsRelationship` plugin ID to use for the relationship
- `label`: How this relationship will be labeled in the UI

Usually, the `standard` relationship plugin will suffice, but we can always create one ourselves if we need to. It's doubtful you will ever need to though.

This definition now allows us to add a relationship to the `teams` table in Views. However, even if the database engine joins the two tables, we haven't achieved anything as we also want to output some fields from the new table. So, for that, we first have to define the table itself, as we did for the players:

```
// Teams table
$data['teams'] = [];
$data['teams']['table']['group'] = t('Sports');
```

Note that it is not mandatory to define it as a `base` table if we don't want to create Views that are basing themselves on this table. In our case, it can be secondary to the player information. Then, just as we did before, we can define a couple of team fields:

```
// Teams fields
$data['teams']['name'] = [
  'title' => t('Name'),
  'help' => t('The name of the team.'),
  'field' => [
    'id' => 'standard',
  ],
];

$data['teams']['description'] = [
  'title' => t('Description'),
  'help' => t('The description of the team.'),
  'field' => [
    'id' => 'standard',
  ],
];
```

There is nothing new here, just the basic data output for our two columns. But now, we can go to the View in the UI, add a relationship to the teams table, and then include the name and description of the teams our players belong to. Neat.

Views sorts and filters

Let's go ahead and enrich the *responsibilities* of the team name field by making our list of players filterable and sortable by it; for example, to only show the players of a given team or sort the players alphabetically by the team name. It could not be easier. We just have to add these to the team name field definition (like we added the `relationship` to the players' `team_id` field):

```
'sort' => [
  'id' => 'standard',
],
'filter' => [
  'id' => string,
],
```

So, we are using the `Standard` sort plugin for sorting (which basically defaults to whatever MySQL can do). As for the filter, we are using the `StringFilter` plugin, which is quite configurable from the Views UI. It even allows us various filtering possibilities, such as partial matching. With this, we can now sort and filter by the team name.

Views arguments

The last type of *responsibility* a Views field can have is to be used as an argument (or a contextual filter, for Drupal veterans). In other words, configuring the View to be filterable by a parameter that is dynamically passed to it. Let's face it; most of the time, if we want to filter by a team, we won't rely on the actual string name as that can change. Instead, we tie everything to the record (by its ID). So, that means we'll add the `argument` key to the `team_id` field of the `players` table (which also means that the query won't require a join, so it will be more performant):

```
'argument' => [
  'id' => 'numeric',
],
```

In this case, we use the `NumericArgument` plugin, which does pretty much all we need for our data type—it filters by what is expected to be a numerical data type. And we are finished with that as well. We can now dynamically filter our players view by the ID of the teams they belong to.

Altering Views data

We saw how we can expose to Views our own data that is totally custom. However, we can also alter existing data definitions provided by Drupal core or other modules by implementing hook_views_data_alter(). The $data parameter passed by reference will contain everything that has been defined and can be changed as needed.

Moreover, we can also use this implementation to create some new Views fields or filters on other tables that do not "belong" to us. This is actually more common than exposing totally custom tables or other kinds of resources. For example, we may want to create a new Views field that shows something related to the Node in the results. So, let's look at an example.

Do you remember in *Chapter 6, Data Modeling and Storage*, we saw how to create a *pseudo field*, which outputs a disclaimer message at the bottom of each Node? If our View is configured to render Node entities, that will work. However, if it's using fields, it cannot do that. So, let's see how we could expose this message also as a Views field. We won't include this in the final code, but let's just see how we could get it done if we wanted to.

First, we'd need to implement hook_views_data_alter() and define a new field on the Node entity type data table:

```
/**
 * Implements hook_views_data_alter().
 */
function module_name_views_data_alter(&$data) {
  $data['node_field_data']['disclaimer'] = [
    'title' => t('Disclaimer'),
    'help' => t('Shows a disclaimer message'),
    'field' => [
      'id' => 'custom',
    ],
  ];
}
```

In this example, we are adding our new Views field onto the Node data table (node_field_data). But then, we have a choice as to what plugin to use to render our message. We can, of course, create one ourselves (as we will do in the next section). This is actually very simple, especially since it doesn't even need to use any of the information from the resulting nodes. However, if that's the case, we might as well use the existing Custom plugin, which has two main advantages. For one, we don't have to write any more code. Second, it allows the site builder to specify (and modify as needed) the disclaimer message through the UI. Because basically, this plugin exposes a configuration form that we can use to add the text we want to be displayed for each row:

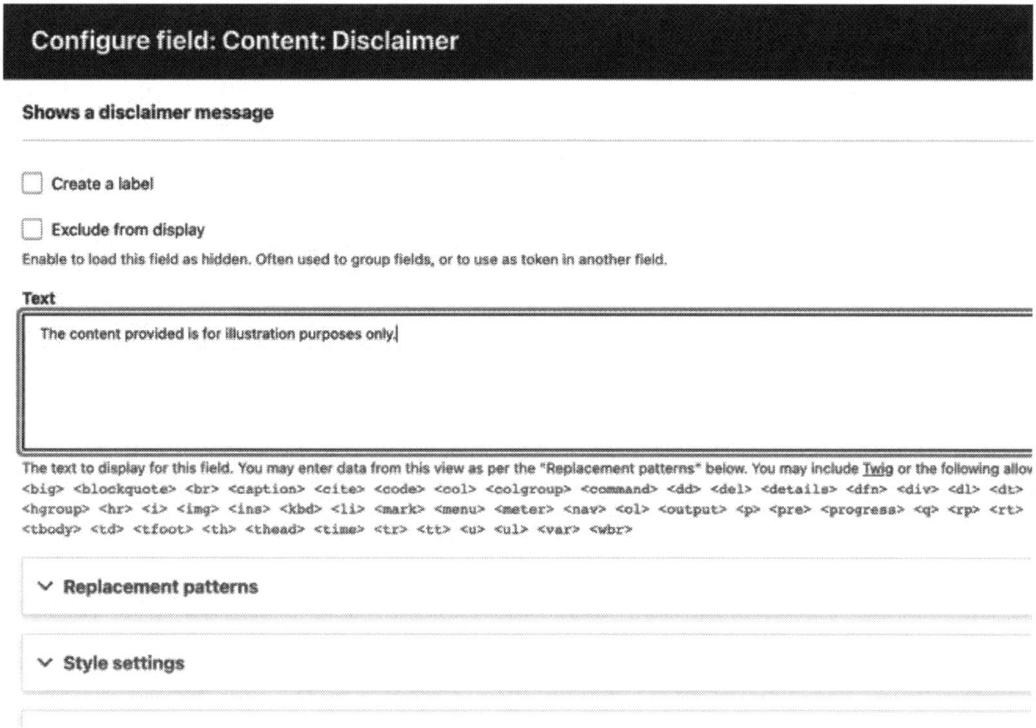

Configure field: Content: Disclaimer

Shows a disclaimer message

☐ Create a label

☐ Exclude from display
Enable to load this field as hidden. Often used to group fields, or to use as token in another field.

Text

The content provided is for illustration purposes only.

The text to display for this field. You may enter data from this view as per the "Replacement patterns" below. You may include Twig or the following allov
`<big> <blockquote> <br> <caption> <cite> <code> <col> <colgroup> <command> <dd> <del> <details> <dfn> <div> <dl> <dt>`
`<hgroup> <hr> <i> <img> <ins> <kbd> <li> <mark> <menu> <meter> <nav> <ol> <output> <p> <pre> <progress> <q> <rp> <rt>`
`<tbody> <td> <tfoot> <th> <thead> <time> <tr> <tt> <u> <ul> <var> <wbr>`

⌄ **Replacement patterns**

⌄ **Style settings**

Figure 15.4: Custom Views field configuration

Of course, there are some drawbacks to this approach as well. If we wanted to ensure consistency between the message here and the one we used in the pseudo field, we would probably want to write our own plugin and get the message from this unique place. The same applies if we wanted the message to be strictly in code, especially if we needed some sort of data from the node in the View results. So, the choice depends on the actual use case, but it's good to look into the existing Views plugins and see what already exists before creating your own.

Custom Views field

Now that we have seen how data is exposed to Views, we can start understanding the `NodeViewsData` handler I mentioned earlier (even if not quite everything) a bit better. But this also provides a good segue back to our Product entity type's `views_data` handler, where we can now see what the responsibility of `getViewsData()` is. It needs to return the definition for all of the tables and fields, as well as what they can do. Luckily for us, the base class already provides everything we need to turn our product data into Views fields, filters, sorts, arguments, and potentially relationships, all out of the box.

But let's say we want to add some more Views fields that make sense to us in the context of our product-related functionality. For example, each product has a `source` field that is populated by the Importer entity from its own `source` field. This is just to keep track of where they come from. So, we may want to create a Views field that simply renders the name of the Importer that has imported the product.

You'll be quick to ask: *but hey, that is not a column on the products table! What gives?* As we will see, we can define Views fields that render whatever data we want (that can relate to the record or not). Of course, this also means that the resulting data cannot be used inside a sort or filter because MySQL doesn't have access to it when building the query. So we are a bit less flexible there, but it makes sense.

In this section, we will learn two things. First, we'll see how to create our own `views_data` handler for our Product entity type. By now, you should be quite familiar with this process. More importantly, though, we'll use this handler to create a new Views field for our products that renders something no existing `ViewsField` plugin can offer: the name of the related Importer entity. That means our own custom plugin. How exciting, so let's get going!

There are two quick steps to create our own `views_data` handler. First, we need the class:

```
namespace Drupal\products\Entity;

use Drupal\views\EntityViewsData;

/**
 * Provides Views data for Product entities.
 */
class ProductViewsData extends EntityViewsData {

  /**
   * {@inheritdoc}
   */
  public function getViewsData() {
    $data = parent::getViewsData();
    // Add stuff.
    return $data;
  }
}
```

As you can see, we are extending the base `EntityViewsData` class we had been referencing in the Product entity type annotation before. Inside, we are overriding the `getViewsData()` method to add our own definitions (which will go where you can see the comment).

Second, we need to change the handler reference to this new class in the entity type annotation:

```
"views_data" = "Drupal\products\Entity\ProductViewsData",
```

That's it. We can now define our own custom fields and we can start with the views data definition:

```
$data['product']['importer'] = [
  'title' => $this->t('Importer'),
  'help' => $this->t('Information about the Product
    importer.'),
  'field' => [
    'id' => 'product_importer',
  ],
];
```

Simple stuff, as we did with the players. Except in this case, we are adding it to the `product` table and we are using a `ViewsField` plugin that doesn't exist. Yet. So, let's create it.

As you may have noticed if you checked some of the existing ones, Views plugins go in the `Plugin\views\[plugin_type]` namespace of the modules, where `[plugin_type]` in this case is `field`, as we are creating a `ViewsField` plugin. So, we can start with the plugin class scaffolding:

```
namespace Drupal\products\Plugin\views\field;

use Drupal\views\Plugin\views\field\FieldPluginBase;
use Drupal\views\ResultRow;

/**
 * Field plugin that renders data about the Importer that
   imported the Product.
 *
 * @ViewsField("product_importer")
 */
class ProductImporter extends FieldPluginBase {

  /**
   * {@inheritdoc}
   */
  public function render(ResultRow $values) {
```

```
    // Render something more meaningful.
    return '';
  }
}
```

Just like any other field plugin, we are extending the `FieldPluginBase` class, which provides all the common defaults and base functionalities the fields need. Of course, you will notice the admittedly small annotation, which simply contains the plugin ID. Our main job is to work in the `render()` method and output something, preferably using the `$values` object that contains all the data in the respective row.

> **Note**
>
> Inside the `ResultRow` object, we can find the values from the Views row, which can contain multiple fields. If it's a View that lists entities, we also have an `_entity` key that references the entity object itself.

Clearing the cache, we will now be able to add the new *Product Importer* field to a View for products. But if we do, we will notice an error. Views is trying to add to the query the `product_importer` field we defined, but it doesn't actually exist on the table. That isn't right! This happens because, even though Views can be made to work with any data source, it still has a preference for the SQL database, so we can encounter these issues every once in a while. Not to worry though, as we can simply tell our plugin not to include the field in any query—it will show totally custom data. We do so by overriding the `query()` method:

```
/**
 * {@inheritdoc}
 */
public function query() {
  // Leave empty to avoid a query on this field.
}
```

That's it. Now, our field is going to render an empty string: `''`. Let's change it to look for the related Importer entity and show its label. But in order to do that, we'll need the `EntityTypeManager` service to use for querying, so make sure you inject it in the plugin (you should know by now how to do this).

We can now proceed with the `render()` method:

```
public function render(ResultRow $values) {
  /** @var \Drupal\products\Entity\ProductInterface
    $product */
```

```
$product = $this->getEntity($values);
$source = $product->getSource();
$importers = $this->entityTypeManager->getStorage
  ('importer')->loadByProperties(['source' => $source]);
if (!$importers) {
  return NULL;
}

// We'll assume one importer per source.
/** @var \Drupal\products\Entity\ImporterInterface
  $importer */
$importer = reset($importers);
return $this->sanitizeValue($importer->label());
}
```

We start by getting the Product entity of the current row. We do so with the help of the parent class's getEntity() helper method, which allows us to extract robustly the current entity from the record.

Next, we query for the Importer configuration entities that have the source referenced on the product. We assume there is only one (even if we did not do a proper job ensuring this is the case) and simply return its label. We also pass it through the helper sanitizeValue() method, which takes care of ensuring that the output is safe against XSS attacks and such. So, now our products View can show, for each product, the name of the importer that brought them into the application.

> **Note**
>
> If we take a step back and try to understand what is going on, a word of caution becomes evident. Views performs one big query that returns a list of product entities and some data. But then, when that data is output, we perform a query for the Importer entity corresponding to each product in the result set (and we load those entities). So, if we have 100 products returned, that means 100 more queries. Try to keep this in mind when creating custom fields to ensure you are not getting a huge performance hit, which might often not even be worth it.

Field configuration

We got our field working, but let's say we want to make it a bit more dynamic. Now it's called *Product Importer* and we are showing the title of the Importer entity. But let's make it configurable so that we can choose which title to show—that of the entity or that of the actual Importer plugin—in the UI.

There are a few simple steps for making the field plugin configurable. These work similarly to other Views plugin types. They are also quite similar in concept to what we did in *Chapter 9, Custom Fields*, when we made the entity fields configurable. And, if you remember, to what we did when we made our Importer plugins support individual configurations.

First, we need to define some default options by overriding a method:

```
/**
 * {@inheritdoc}
 */
protected function defineOptions() {
  $options = parent::defineOptions();
  $options['importer'] = ['default' => 'entity'];


  return $options;
}
```

As you can see, we are adding to the options defined by the parent class (which are quite a few) our own `importer` one. And we set its default to the string `entity`. Our choice.

Second, we need to define the form element for our new option, and we can do this with another method override:

```
/**
 * {@inheritdoc}
 */
public function buildOptionsForm(&$form, FormStateInterface
  $form_state) {

  $form['importer'] = [
    '#type' => 'select',
    '#title' => $this->t('Importer'),
    '#description' => $this->t('Which importer label to
      use?'),
    '#options' => [
      'entity' => $this->t('Entity'),
      'plugin' => $this->t('Plugin')
    ],
    '#default_value' => $this->options['importer'],
```

```
    ];

    parent::buildOptionsForm($form, $form_state);
}
```

And the *use* statement:

```
use Drupal\Core\Form\FormStateInterface;
```

Nothing special here; we are simply defining a select list form element on the main options form. We can see that the $options class property contains all the plugin options, and there we can check for the default value of our importer one. Finally, we of course add to the form all the other elements from the parent definition.

Next, inside the render() method, once we get our hands on the importer entity, we can make a change to this effect:

```
// If we want to show the entity label.
if ($this->options['importer'] == 'entity') {
    return $this->sanitizeValue($importer->label());
}

// Otherwise we show the plugin label.
$definition = $this->importerManager->getDefinition
    ($importer->getPluginId());
return $this->sanitizeValue($definition['label']);
```

Pretty simple. We either show the entity label or that of the plugin. But of course—and we skipped this—the Importer plugin manager also needs to be injected into the class. I'll let you handle that on your own as you already know how to do this.

Finally, one last thing we need to do is define the configuration schema. Since our View (which is a configuration entity) is now being saved with an extra option, we need to define the schema for the latter. We can do this inside the products.schema.yml file:

```
views.field.product_importer:
  type: views_field
  label: 'Product Importer'
  mapping:
    importer:
```

```
type: string
label: 'Which importer label to use: entity or
  plugin'
```

This should already be familiar to you, including the dynamic nature of defining configuration schemas. We pretty much did the same in *Chapter 9, Custom Fields*, for the options on our field type, widget, and formatter plugins. This time, though, the type is `views_field`, from which we basically inherit a bunch of definitions and to which we add our own (the `importer` string). That's it. If we configure our new Views field, we should see this new option:

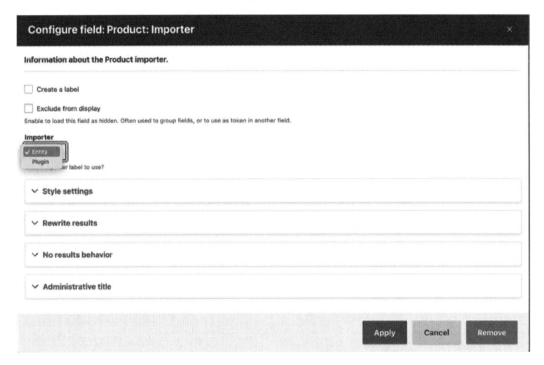

Figure 15.5: Configuring the Product importer field

Custom Views filter

In a previous section, we exposed our `players` and `teams` tables to Views, as well as made the team name a possible string filter to limit the resulting players by team. But this was not the best way we could have accomplished this because site builders may not necessarily know all the teams that are in the database, nor their exact names. So, we can create our own `ViewsFilter` to turn it into a selection of teams the user can choose from. Kind of like a taxonomy term filter. So, let's see how it's done.

First, we need to alter our data definition for the team name field to change the plugin ID that will be used for the filtering (inside `hook_views_data()`):

```
'filter' => [
  'id' => 'team_filter',
],
```

Now we just have to create that plugin. And naturally, it goes in the `Plugin/views/filter` namespace of our module:

```php
namespace Drupal\sports\Plugin\views\filter;

use Drupal\Core\Database\Connection;
use Drupal\views\Plugin\views\filter\InOperator;
use Drupal\views\ViewExecutable;
use Drupal\views\Plugin\views\display\DisplayPluginBase;
use Symfony\Component\DependencyInjection\
  ContainerInterface;

/**
 * Filter class which filters by the available teams.
 *
 * @ViewsFilter("team_filter")
 */
class TeamFilter extends InOperator {

  /**
   * @var \Drupal\Core\Database\Connection
   */
  protected $database;

  /**
   * Constructs a TeamFilter plugin object.
   *
   * @param array $configuration
   *   A configuration array containing information about
   *   the plugin instance.
```

```
 * @param string $plugin_id
 *    The plugin_id for the plugin instance.
 * @param mixed $plugin_definition
 *    The plugin implementation definition.
 * @param \Drupal\Core\Database\Connection $database
 *    The database connection.
 */
public function __construct(array $configuration,
  $plugin_id, $plugin_definition, Connection $database) {
  parent::__construct($configuration, $plugin_id,
    $plugin_definition);
  $this->database = $database;
}


/**
 * {@inheritdoc}
 */
public static function create(ContainerInterface
  $container, array $configuration, $plugin_id,
    $plugin_definition) {
  return new static(
    $configuration,
    $plugin_id,
    $plugin_definition,
    $container->get('database')
  );
}


/**
 * {@inheritdoc}
 */
public function init(ViewExecutable $view,
  DisplayPluginBase $display, array &$options = NULL) {
```

```
    parent::init($view, $display, $options);
    $this->valueTitle = $this->t('Teams');
    $this->definition['options callback'] = [$this,
      'getTeams'];
  }


  /**
   * Generates the list of teams that can be used in the
     filter.
   */
  public function getTeams() {
    $result = $this->database->query("SELECT [name] FROM
      {teams}")->fetchAllAssoc('name');
    if (!$result) {
      return [];
    }

    $teams = array_keys($result);
    return array_combine($teams, $teams);
  }
}
```

First and foremost, we see the annotation is in place to make this a plugin, like the Views fields. Then, we use dependency injection to get our hands on the database connection service. Nothing new so far. However, you will notice that we extend from the InOperator class, which provides the base functionality for a Views filter that allows an IN type of filter. For example, ... WHERE name IN(name1, name2). So, we extend from there to inherit much of this logic that applies to Views.

Then, we override the init() method (which initializes the plugin) in order to set the available values that site builders can choose from (the team names) and a title for the resulting form element. But we do so by specifying an options callback that will be used to retrieve the options at the right moment. This callback is a method on our class called getTeams(), which returns an array of all the team names. This array needs to be keyed by the value to be used in the query filter. And that is pretty much it. We don't need to worry about the options form or anything like that. The base class does it all for us.

Now, site builders can add this filter and choose a team (or more) to filter by in an inclusive way. For example, to show the players that belong to a respective team:

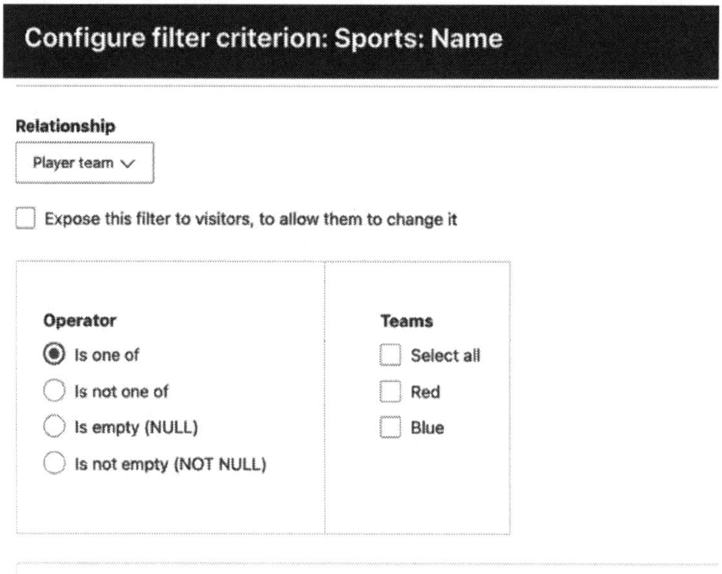

Figure 15.6: Player filter configuration

> **Note**
>
> Instead of using the options callback, we could have also directly overridden the getValueOptions() method of the parent (which in fact calls the options callback itself). The only caution here is that to prevent performance leaks, the values should be stored in the local valueOptions class property. Like this, they can be read multiple times.

Even if it's not that obvious, one last thing we need to do is define the configuration schema for our filter. You may be wondering why we are not creating any custom options. The answer is that when the user adds the filter and chooses a team to filter by, Drupal doesn't know what data type that value is. So, we need to tell it that it's a string. Inside our sports.schema.yml file, we can have this:

```
views.filter.team_filter:
  type: views_filter
  label: 'The teams to filter by'
  mapping:
    value:
      type: sequence
      label: 'Teams'
```

```
      sequence:
        type: string
        label: 'Team'
```

Like the Views field, we have a dynamic schema definition for the filter, of the type `views_filter`. In the mapping, we override the `value` field (which has already been defined by the `views_filter` data type). In our case, this is a sequence (an array with unimportant keys) whose individual values are strings.

Another way we can achieve the same (or similar) is like this:

```
views.filter_value.team_filter:
  type: sequence
  label: 'Teams'
  sequence:
    type: string
    label: 'Team'
```

This is because, in the definition of the `value` key found in the `views_filter` schema, the type is set to `views.filter_value.[%parent.plugin_id]`. This means that we can simply define the `views.filter_value.team_filter` data type ourselves for it to use. If you remember, this is very similar to what we did ourselves in *Chapter 12, JavaScript and Ajax API*. So, we can just define that missing bit as our sequence, rather than overriding the entire thing to change one small bit.

The existing Views filter classes provide a great deal of capability for either using them directly for custom data or extending to complement with our own specificities. So I recommend you check out all the existent filter plugins. However, the main concept of a filter is the alteration of the query being run by Views, which can be done inside the `query()` method of the plugin class. There, we can add extra conditions to the query based on what we need. You can check out this method on the `FilterPluginBase` class, which simply adds a condition (using the `addWhere()` method on the query object) based on the configured value and operator.

Custom Views argument

When we first exposed the player and team data to Views, we used an argument plugin so that we could have a contextual filter on the team ID a player belongs to. To do this, we used the existing `numeric` plugin on the actual `team_id` field of the `players` table. But what if we wanted an argument that works on more levels? For example, we don't exactly know what kind of data we'll receive, but we want to be able to handle nicely both a numeric one (team ID) and a textual one (team name). All in one argument. To achieve this, we can create a simple `ViewsArgument` plugin to handle this for us.

The first thing, like always, is to define this field. We don't want to mess with the `team_id` field onto which we added the earlier argument as that can still be used. Instead, we'll create a new field, this time on the `teams` table, which we will simply call `team`:

```
$data['teams']['team'] = [
  'title' => t('Team'),
  'help' => t('The team (either an ID or a team name).'),
  'argument' => [
    'id' => 'team',
  ],
];
```

This time, though, we don't create a *field* for it as we don't need this to display anything. Rather, we stick to the `argument` responsibility, which will be handled by our new `team` plugin. You may also note that the `team` column doesn't actually exist in the database table.

So, let's see the plugin:

```
namespace Drupal\sports\Plugin\views\argument;

use Drupal\views\Plugin\views\argument\ArgumentPluginBase;

/**
 * Argument for filtering by a team.
 *
 * @ViewsArgument("team")
 */
class Team extends ArgumentPluginBase {

  /**
   * {@inheritdoc}
   */
  public function query($group_by = FALSE) {
    $this->ensureMyTable();
    $field = is_numeric($this->argument) ? 'id' : 'name';
    $this->query->addWhere(0, "$this->tableAlias.$field",
      $this->argument);
  }
}
```

As usual, we are extending from the base plugin class of its type and adding the proper annotation. Inside, we only deal with the `query()` method, which we override. Arguments are very similar to filters in the sense that they aim to restrict the result set via the query. The main difference is the actual value used to filter, which, in this case, is dynamic and can be found on the `$argument` property of the (parent) class. And what we do is simply add a query condition to the right field on the `teams` table (since that is the base table), depending on the type of data we are dealing with. But before we do that, we call the `ensureMyTable()` method, which simply ensures that the table our plugin needs is included in the query by Views.

That's it. We can now add our newly created argument to the View and, regardless of what we passed as a contextual filter (ID or name), it will filter accordingly. Of course, we can also have options like most other Views plugin types, but I'll let you explore those on your own. There is also a lot more we can override from the parent class in order to integrate with Views. But that's a bit more advanced and it's unlikely you'll need to deal with that for a good while.

Views theming

Views is very complex and is made up of many pluggable layers. A View has a *display* (such as a Page or Block), which can render its content using a given *style* (such as an Unformatted list or Table). Styles can decide whether to control the rendering of a given result item (row) themselves or delegate this to a *row* plugin (such as Fields or Entity). Most, in fact, do the latter. The two most common scenarios for using *row* plugins are either using the `EntityRow` one, which renders the resulting entities using a specified view mode, or the `Fields` plugin, which uses individual `ViewField` plugins to render each field that is added to the View.

If we wanted to theme a View, there are all these points we can look at. Want the View to output a slideshow? Perhaps create a new *style* plugin. Want to do something crazy with each entity in the result set? Maybe create a new *row* plugin, or even just create a new *field* plugin (as we did) to render one piece of data in any way you want. These techniques are more oriented toward module developers taking control over Views. But we also have the theming aspects we can play with.

Again, from the top, *style* plugins are nothing more than glorified wrappers over a theme hook. For example, the *Unformatted list* plugin uses the `views_view_unformatted` theme hook, which means a few things: it can be overridden by a theme (or even module) and it can be preprocessed by a theme or module. Take a look at the default `template_preprocess_views_view_unformatted()` preprocessor and the `views-view-unformatted.html.twig` template file for more information. Don't forget about the theme hook suggestions, as Views defines quite a lot of them. All you need to do is enable theme (Twig) debugging and you'll see for each View *layer* which template is being used.

The *style* theme, however, only gets us to the wrapper around all the results. To go a bit deeper, we need to know what kind of *row* plugin it uses. If entities are being rendered, it's the same thing as controlling how entities are built. See *Chapter 6, Data Modeling and Storage*, for a refresher on that. If the *row* plugin uses *field* plugins, we have some options. This is a wrapper over a theme hook, namely `views_view_fields`, which renders together all the *field* plugins added to the View. So we can override that using the already-known theming methods.

But we can also override the default theme hook for each `field` plugin itself, namely `views_view_field`, responsible for wrapping the output of the plugin. This takes us to the *field* plugins themselves and whatever they end up rendering, which can differ from one plugin to another. So, make sure you check that.

Views hooks

Views also comes with a lot of hooks. We've already seen an important one that allowed us to expose our own data to Views. But there are many more, and you should check out the `views.api.php` file for more information.

Quite a few exist for altering plugin information for all sorts of plugin types. But there are also some important ones that deal with Views execution at runtime. The most notable of these is `hook_views_query_alter()`, which allows us to make alterations to the final query that is going to be run. There is also `hook_views_post_render()` and `hook_views_pre_render()`, which allow us to make alterations to the View results. For example, to change the order of the items or something like that.

I recommend you check out their respective documentation and make yourself aware of what you can do with these hooks. At times they can be helpful, even if most of the action happens in plugins, and you can now easily write your own to handle your specific requirements. This is why we won't be going into great detail about these.

Summary

In this chapter, we looked at Views from all sorts of module developer-oriented angles. We saw how we can expose our product entity type to Views. That was a breeze. But then, we also saw how our custom player and team data from *Chapter 8, The Database API*, can be exposed to Views. Even if we did have to write some code for that, much of it was definition, as we were able to leverage the existing Views plugin ecosystem for almost everything we wanted. However, since these are all plugins, we also saw how we can create our own field, filter, and argument plugins to handle those exceptional cases in which what exists may not be enough.

Closely tied to this, we also talked a bit about altering the way other modules expose their data to Views. The most notable example here was the ability to easily add more fields (and plugins) to entity-based Views in order to enrich them with custom functionalities.

Finally, we talked a bit about how we can approach the theming aspect of Views. We saw the different layers that make one up, starting from the display all the way down to the *field*. We closed the chapter with a shoutout to the existing hooks the Views module invokes at various times, via which we can also make changes to its normal operation.

In the next chapter, we are going to see how we can work with files and images.

16

Working with Files and Images

In this chapter, we will look at how we can work with files and images in Drupal, supported by the core features. Although the Media module allows developers to provide new source plugins to expose media entities to all sorts of types of media, we won't be going into this quite an advanced topic. Instead, we'll focus on lower-level tools that can be used for working with files. And we will see some examples along the way. So, what are we going to discuss?

First, we are going to get an understanding of the Drupal *filesystems*. Related to this, we're going to talk about *stream wrappers* and how Drupal handles native PHP file operations. We will even create our own custom stream wrapper a bit later in the chapter.

Then, we will talk a bit about the different ways to handle files in Drupal, namely, *managed* (tracked) and *unmanaged* files. While working with *managed* files, we will add an image field to our Product entity type and have images imported from a fictional remote environment. We will also create a brand-new CSV-based importer by which the product data is imported from a CSV file that we read. In this process, we will note the Entity CRUD hooks, a very important extension point in Drupal, and see how we can use them in our example context.

We will end the chapter by seeing how we can work with various APIs that deal specifically with images, especially for manipulating them via image toolkits and working with image styles. So, let's get to it.

The main topics we will cover in this chapter are as follows:

- Understanding the different types of files
- Stream wrappers
- Working with managed files
- The Private file system
- Images in the Drupal world

The filesystem

Drupal defines four main types of file storage for any given site: the *public*, the *private*, the *temporary*, and the *translation* filesystems. When installing Drupal, the folders that map to these filesystems are created automatically. In case that fails—most likely due to permission issues—we have to create them ourselves and give them the correct permissions. Drupal takes care of the rest (for example, adds the relevant `.htaccess` files for security reasons). Make sure you check out the documentation on `Drupal.org` to see how to successfully install Drupal if you are unsure how this works.

Public files are available to the world at large for viewing or downloading. This is where things such as image content, logos, and anything that can be downloaded are stored. Your public file directory must exist somewhere under Drupal's root, and it must be readable and writeable by whatever *user* your web server is running under. Public files have no access restrictions. Anyone, at any time, can navigate directly to a public file and view or download it. This also means that accessing these files does not require Drupal to bootstrap.

We can configure the path to the public filesystem in our `settings.php` file:

```
$settings['file_public_path'] = 'sites/default/files';
```

Private files, on the other hand, are not available to the world for general download. Therefore, the private files directory must not be accessible via the web. However, it still has to be writeable by the web server user. Isolating private files in this way allows developers to control who can and can't access them. For instance, we could write a module that only allows users who have a specific role to access PDFs in the private filesystem.

We can configure the path to the private filesystem in our `settings.php` file:

```
$settings['file_private_path'] = 'sites/default/private';
```

Temporary file storage is typically only used by Drupal for internal operations. When files are first saved by Drupal, they are initially written into the temporary filesystem so they can be checked for security issues. After they have been deemed safe, they are written to their final location.

We can configure the path to the temporary filesystem in our `settings.php` file:

```
$settings['file_temp_path'] = '/tmp';
```

Finally, the translation file storage is used by Drupal for storing the `.po` files that contain string translation values that can be imported into the system in bulk. We can configure the location of translation files through the UI:

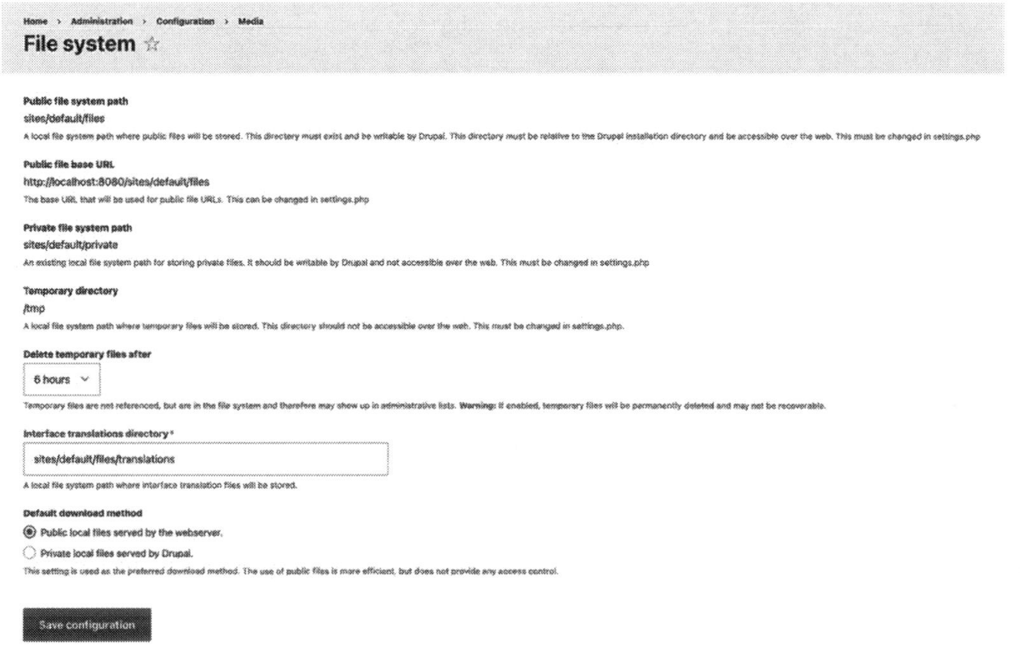

Figure 16.1: Filesystem configuration UI

Stream wrappers

If you've been writing PHP for a long time, you may have needed to work with local or remote files at some point. The following PHP code is a common way to read a file into a variable that you can do something with:

```
$contents = '';
$handle = fopen("/local/path/to/file/image.jpg", "rb");
while (!feof($handle)) {
 $contents .= fread($handle, 8192);
}
fclose($handle);
```

This is pretty straightforward. We get a handle to a local file using `fopen()` and read 8 KB chunks of the file using `fread()` until `feof()` indicates that we've reached the end of the file. At that point, we use `fclose()` to close the handle. The contents of the file are now in the `$contents` variable.

In addition to local files, we can also access remote ones through `fopen()` in the exact same way but by specifying the actual remote path instead of the local one we saw before (starting with `http(s)://`).

Data that we can access this way is streamable, meaning we can open it, close it, or seek to a specific place in it.

Stream wrappers are an abstraction layer on top of these streams that tell PHP how to handle specific types of data. When using a stream wrapper, we refer to the file just like a traditional URL—`scheme://target`. As a matter of fact, the previous example uses one of PHP's built-in stream wrappers: the `file://` wrapper for accessing files on local storage. It is actually the default scheme when none is specified, so that is why we got away with omitting it and just adding the file path. Had the file been in a remote location, we would have used something like `http://example.com/file/path/image.jpg`. That is another PHP built-in stream wrapper: `http://` (for the HTTP protocol).

If that's not enough, PHP also allows us to define our own wrappers for schemes that PHP does not handle out of the box; the Drupal File API was built to take advantage of this. This is where we link back to the different types of file storage we talked about earlier, as they all have their own stream wrappers defined by Drupal.

The public filesystem uses the rather known `public://` stream wrapper, the private one uses `private://`, the temporary one uses `temporary://`, and the translation one uses `translations://`. These map to the local file paths that we defined in `settings.php` (or the UI). Later in the chapter, we will see how we can define our own stream wrapper and what some of the things that go into it are. First, though, let's talk a bit about the different ways we can manage files in Drupal.

Managed versus unmanaged files

The Drupal File API allows us to handle files in two different ways. Files essentially boil down to two categories: they are either *managed* or *unmanaged*. The difference between the two lies in the way the files are used.

Managed files work hand-in-hand with the Entity system and are, in fact, tied to File entities. So, whenever we create a *managed* file, an entity gets created for it as well, which we can use in all sorts of ways. And the table where these records are stored is called `file_managed`. Moreover, a key aspect of *managed* files is the fact that their usage is tracked. This means that if we reference them on an entity or even manually indicate that we use them, this usage is tracked in a secondary table called `file_usage`. This way, we can see where each file is used and how many times, and Drupal even provides a way to delete "orphaned" files after a specific time if they are no longer needed.

A notable example of using *managed* files is the simple `Image` field type that we can add to an entity type. Using these fields, we can upload a file and *attach* it to the respective entity. This attachment is nothing more than a special (tracked) entity reference between the two entities.

By understanding how *managed* files are used, it's not difficult to anticipate what *unmanaged* files are. The latter are the files we upload to make use of for various reasons but that, of course, do not need to be *attached* to any entity or have their usage tracked.

Using the File and Image fields

In order to demonstrate how to work with *managed* files, we will go back to our product entity importer and bring in some images for each product. However, in order to store them, we need to create a field on the Product entity. This will be an `Image` field.

Instead of creating this field through the UI and attaching it to a bundle, let's do it the programmatic way and make it a base field (available on all bundles). We won't need to do anything complex; for now, we are only interested in a basic field that we can use to store the images we bring in from the remote API. It can look something like this:

```
$fields['image'] = BaseFieldDefinition::create('image')
  ->setLabel(t('Image'))
  ->setDescription(t('The product image.'))
  ->setDisplayOptions('form', array(
    'type' => 'image_image',
    'weight' => 5,
  ));
```

If you remember from *Chapter 6, Data Modeling and Storage*, and *Chapter 7, Your Own Custom Entity and Plugin Types*, we are creating a base field definition that, in this case, is of the type `image`. This is the `FieldType` plugin ID of the `ImageItem` field type. That is where we need to look and see what kind of field and storage options we may have. For example, we can have a file extension limitation (which by default contains `png`, `gif`, `jpg`, and `jpeg`) and things like `alt` and `title` attributes, as well as image dimension configuration. Do check out `ImageItem` to get an idea of the possible storage and field settings. However, we are fine with the defaults in this case, so we don't even have any field settings.

Another interesting thing to notice is that `ImageItem` extends the `FileItem` field type, which is a standalone `FieldType` plugin that we can use. However, it is more generic and lends itself for use with any kind of file upload situation. Since we are dealing with images, we might as well take advantage of the specific field type.

For the moment, we do not configure our image field to have any kind of display. We'll look into that a bit later. However, we do specify the widget it should use on the entity form, namely the `FieldWidget` plugin with the ID of `image_image`. This maps to the default `ImageWidget` field widget. But again, we are fine with the setting defaults, so we don't specify anything extra.

With this, our field definition is done. To have Drupal create the necessary database tables, we need to run the *Devel entity updates* contrib module's `Drush` command (or use `EntityDefinitionUpdateManager` if we need to deploy this change to production):

```
drush entity-update
```

Now let's create the interface methods for easily accessing and setting the images:

```
/**
 * Gets the Product image.
 *
 * @return \Drupal\file\FileInterface|null
 */
public function getImage();

/**
 * Sets the Product image.
 *
 * @param int $image
 *
 * @return \Drupal\products\Entity\ProductInterface
 *    The called Product entity.
 */
public function setImage($image);
```

The getter method is supposed to return a `FileInterface` object (which is the actual File entity) or NULL, while the setter is supposed to receive the ID (`fid`) of the File entity to save. As for the implementations, it should not be anything new to us:

```
/**
 * {@inheritdoc}
 */
public function getImage() {
  return $this->get('image')->entity;
}

/**
 * {@inheritdoc}
 */
public function setImage($image) {
  $this->set('image', $image);
  return $this;
}
```

With this, we are ready to proceed with the import of images from the remote API.

To take advantage of the media management power in Drupal, instead of Image or File fields, you'd create entity reference fields to Media entities, and you'd create these fields on the latter. As such, Media entities basically wrap the File entities to provide some additional functionality and expose them to all the goodies of media management. For now, we will work directly with these field types to learn about low-level file handling without the overhead of Media entities.

Working with managed files

In this section, we will look at two examples of working with managed files. First, we will see how we can import product images from our fictional remote JSON-based API. Second, we will see how to create a custom form element that allows us to upload a file and use it in a brand-new CSV-based importer.

Attaching managed files to entities

Now that we have our product image field in place and we can store images, let's revisit our JSON response that contains the product data and assume it looks something like this now:

```json
{
    "products" : [
        {
            "id" : 1,
            "name": "TV",
            "number": 341,
            "image": "tv.jpg"
        },
        {
            "id" : 2,
            "name": "VCR",
            "number": 123,
            "image": "vcr.jpg"
        }
    ]
}
```

What's new is the addition of the image key for each product, which simply references a filename for the image that goes with the respective product. The actual location of the images is at some other path we need to include in the code.

Going back to our `JsonImporter::persistProduct()` method, let's delegate the handling of the image import to a helper method called `handleProductImage()`. We need to call this method both if we are creating a new Product entity and if we are updating an existing one (right before saving):

```
$this->handleProductImage($data, $product);
```

And this is what the actual method looks like:

```
protected function handleProductImage($data,
  ProductInterface $product) {
  $name = $data->image;
  // This needs to be hardcoded for the moment.
  $image_path = '';
  $image = file_get_contents($image_path . '/' . $name);
  if (!$image) {
    // Perhaps log something.
    return;
  }

  /** @var \Drupal\file\FileInterface $file */
  $file = $this->fileRepository->writeData($image,
    'public://product_images/' . $name,
      FileSystemInterface::EXISTS_REPLACE);
  if (!$file) {
    // Something went wrong, perhaps log it.
    return;
  }

  $product->setImage($file->id());
}
```

And the new *use* statement at the top:

```
use Drupal\products\Entity\ProductInterface;
use Drupal\Core\File\FileSystemInterface;
```

First, we get the name of the image. Then we construct the path to where the product images are stored. In this example, it's left blank, but if the example were to work, we'd have to add a real path there. I leave that up to you for now. If you want to test it out, create a local folder with some images and reference that.

Using the native `file_get_contents()` function, we load the data of the image from the remote environment into a string. We then pass this string to the `FileRepository::writeData()` method (which I will let you inject into our plugin), which saves a new *managed* file to the public filesystem. This method takes three parameters: the data to be saved, the URI of the destination, and a flag indicating what to do if a file with the same name already exists. You'll notice that we used the Drupal `public://` stream wrapper to build the URI, and we already know which folder this maps to.

As for the third parameter, we chose to replace the file in case one already exists. The alternative would have been to either use the `EXISTS_RENAME` or `EXISTS_ERROR` constants of the same interface. The first would have created a new file whose name would have gotten a number appended until the name became unique. The second would have simply not done anything and returned `FALSE`.

If all goes well, this function returns a `File` entity (that implements `FileInterface`) whose ID we can use in the Product image setter method. With that in place, we can also synchronize the individual product images.

If you run into issues after this, make sure you create the destination folder and have all the permissions in order in the public filesystem to allow the copy to take place properly. In the next section, you'll learn about some helper functions you can use to better prepare the destination folder.

Moreover, in our database, a record is created in the `file_usage` table to indicate that this file is being used on the respective Product entity.

Helpful functions for dealing with managed files

Apart from the staple `FileRepositoryInterface::writeData()` method, we have a few other ones that can come in handy if we are dealing with *managed* files. Here are a few of them.

If we want to copy a file from one place to another while making sure a new database record is created, we can use `copy()` method on the same service. It takes three parameters:

- The `FileInterface` entity that needs to be copied
- The destination URI of where it should go
- The flag indicating what to do if a file with the same name exists

The parameters are the same as for `writeData()`.

Apart from the actual copying, this function also invokes `hook_file_copy()`, which allows modules to respond to files being copied.

Very similar to `copy()`, we also have `move()`, which takes the same set of parameters but instead performs a file move. The database entry of the File entity gets updated to reflect the new file path. And `hook_file_move()` is invoked to allow modules to respond to this action.

Not strictly related to *managed* files, but rather useful in all cases, we also have the `\Drupal\Core\File\FileSystem` service (accessible via the `file_system` service name), which contains all sorts of useful methods for dealing with files. We'll see some of them when we talk about *unmanaged* files. But one that is useful also for *managed* files is `::prepareDirectory()`, which we can use to ensure the file destination is correct. It takes two arguments: the directory (a string representation of the path or stream URI) and a flag indicating what to do about the folder (constants on the interface):

- `FileSystemInterface::CREATE_DIRECTORY` will create the directory if it doesn't already exist

- `FileSystemInterface::MODIFY_PERMISSION` will make the directory writable if it is found to be read-only

This function returns `TRUE` if the folder is good to go as a destination or `FALSE` if something went wrong or the folder doesn't exist.

> **Note**
>
> If you are upgrading from Drupal 9, please be aware that the `FileRepository` service with the three methods we mentioned (`writeData()`, `copy()`, and `move()`) are actually replacements for the old `file_save_data()`, `file_copy()`, and `file_move()` respectively, which have been deprecated in Drupal 9.3 and completely removed in Drupal 10.

Managed file uploads

Next, we are going to look at how we can work with *managed* files using a custom form element. And to demonstrate this, we are finally going to create another Product importer plugin. This time, instead of a remote JSON resource, we will allow users to upload a CSV file that contains product data, and imports that into Product entities. This is what the example CSV data looks like:

```
id,name,number
1,Car,45345
2,Motorbike,54534
```

It basically has the same kind of data as the JSON resource we've been looking at so far but without the image reference. So, let's get going with our new plugin class.

Here is our starting point:

```
namespace Drupal\products\Plugin\Importer;

use Drupal\Core\StringTranslation\StringTranslationTrait;
use Drupal\products\Plugin\ImporterBase;
```

```
/**
 * Product importer from a CSV format.
 *
 * @Importer(
 *   id = "csv",
 *   label = @Translation("CSV Importer")
 * )
 */
class CsvImporter extends ImporterBase {

  use StringTranslationTrait;

  /**
   * {@inheritdoc}
   */
  public function import() {
    $products = $this->getData();
    if (!$products) {
      return FALSE;
    }

    foreach ($products as $product) {
      $this->persistProduct($product);
    }

    return TRUE;
  }
}
```

We start by extending from the `ImporterBase` class and implementing the obligatory `import()` method. Like before, we delegate to `getData()` to retrieve the product information, but in this case, we simply loop over the resulting records and use the `persistProduct()` method to save the Product entities. So no batch operations. Apart from no longer saving images, this latter method looks exactly like the one from the `JsonImporter`, so I won't be copying it over again. But it makes for a good homework assignment to try to move it to the base class and abstract away the dynamic portions.

Managed file form element

Now, we need to handle the form and we have a few methods for this.

First, we have to define the default configurations of this plugin:

```php
/**
 * {@inheritdoc}
 */
public function defaultConfiguration() {
  return [
    'file' => [],
  ];
}
```

Like we did with the `JsonImporter` but this time we keep track of a file reference. We default to an empty array because we will store an array of file IDs (with one value).

Second, we have the form definition for uploading the file:

```php
/**
 * {@inheritdoc}
 */
public function buildConfigurationForm(array $form,
  FormStateInterface $form_state) {
  $form['file'] = [
    '#type' => 'managed_file',
    '#default_value' => $this->configuration['file'],
    '#title' => $this->t('File'),
    '#description' => $this->t('The CSV file containing the
      product records.'),
    '#required' => TRUE,
  ];

  return $form;
}
```

And the *use* statement at the top:

```
use Drupal\Core\Form\FormStateInterface;
```

The form element type is called `managed_file` (implemented by the `ManagedFile` form element class). The rest of the definition is straightforward. However, there are a couple of problems.

First, by default, using this form element, files are uploaded to the `temporary://` filesystem of Drupal. Since we don't want that, we need to specify an upload location:

```
'#upload_location' => 'public://'
```

The root of our public files folder will suffice for this example as we assume the file does not contain any sensitive information. If so, we could upload it to the `private://` one and control who gets access. We'll talk about how that works later in the chapter.

Second, by default, using this form element, the *allowed* file extensions for upload are limited to `jpg`, `jpeg`, `gif`, `png`, `txt`, `doc`, `xls`, `pdf`, `ppt`, `pps`, `odt`, `ods`, and `odp`. So if we want to allow CSV files, we need to specify the extension in a list of allowed upload extensions. And we do this by overriding the default upload validators:

```
'#upload_validators' => [
  'file_validate_extensions' => ['csv'],
],
```

This is an array of validator callbacks we want Drupal to run when the file is uploaded. And allowing only CSV files is enough for our purposes. But another handy validator we could use is `file_validate_size()`. Moreover, we can implement `hook_file_validate()` ourselves and perform any custom validation of the files being uploaded. So that's also something to keep in mind when dealing with validating files that don't belong to your modules.

With this, our plugin configuration form is in place; it looks something like this:

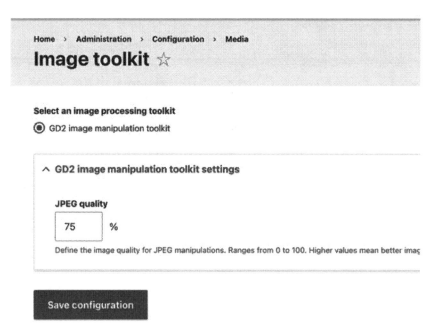

Figure 16.2: Plugin configuration form

But let's not forget about the form submit handler that stores the uploaded file ID into the plugin configuration:

```
/**
 * {@inheritdoc}
 */
public function submitConfigurationForm(array &$form,
    FormStateInterface $form_state) {
    $this->configuration['file'] = $form_state->getValue
        ('file');
}
```

However, there is still something we need to do in order for the uploaded file to be *managed* properly. When using this form element, the file gets correctly uploaded and a record is added to the file_ managed table. So we get our File entity. However, its status is not permanent because it doesn't have any usages. There are no records for it in the file_usage table. How could there be? So what we need to do is handle that ourselves and basically tell Drupal that the file uploaded in this form is *used* by the respective Importer configuration entity. And to do this, we need to know when the file is saved onto the entity, changed, and deleted.

With this, we can also learn about something very important that we skipped in *Chapter 6, Data Modeling and Storage*, and *Chapter 7, Your Own Custom Entity and Plugin Types:* entity CRUD hooks. But right before we jump into that, let's not forget about the configuration schema of this new configuration item—the `file` key of the plugin configuration:

```
products.importer.plugin.csv:
  type: mapping
  label: Plugin configuration for the CSV importer plugin
  mapping:
    file:
      type: sequence
      label: File IDs
      sequence:
        type: integer
        label: CSV File ID
```

We are doing the same as we did for the `url` key of the JSON importer but, in this case, we need to account for the fact that `file` is actually an array. So we define it as a sequence whose individual items are integers. Feel free to check *Chapter 6, Data Modeling and Storage*, for more information on configuration schemas whenever you need a reminder.

Entity CRUD hooks

Whenever entities are created, updated, or deleted, a set of hooks are fired that allow us to act on this information. We can use these hooks simply to perform some actions whenever this happens or even make changes to the entity being saved. So let's see what we have.

A very useful one is `hook_entity_presave()`, which gets fired during the saving process of an entity (both content and configuration). This applies to both when the entity is first created, as well as when it is being updated. Moreover, it allows us to inspect the original entity and detect changes made to it. And finally, since the entity has not yet been persisted, it allows us to make changes to it ourselves. So, very powerful stuff.

Since Drupal is very flexible, we also have the `hook_ENTITY_TYPE_presave()` version, which allows us to specifically target any entity type we want. We've already discussed the benefit of using more specific hooks to keep our code more organized as well as a little bit more performant. And this applies to all the entity CRUD hooks we are going to talk about next.

Next, we have `hook_entity_insert()` and `hook_entity_update()`, which get fired after an entity is created for the first time and after an entity is updated, respectively. We cannot make changes to the entity itself as it has already been saved, but they can come in handy at other times. The latter also gives us access to the original entity if we want to compare any changes. And similarly, we have `hook_entity_delete()`, which gets fired when an entity is deleted.

Finally, we also have `hook_entity_load()`, which allows us to perform actions whenever an entity is loaded. For example, we can tack on additional information if we want. So keep in mind these hooks, as they are going to be a very important tool in your module developer arsenal.

Now that we have an idea of the available entity CRUD hooks, we can implement three of them to handle our *managed* file problem. Because, if you remember, *managed* files are actually represented by the `File` entity type, so the Entity CRUD hooks get fired for these as well.

Managed file usage service

To mark a file as being used by *something*, we can use the `DatabaseFileUsageBackend` service (`file.usage`), which is an implementation of the `FileUsageInterface`. This has a few handy methods that allow us to add a usage or delete it. That is actually what we are going to do next.

What we want to do first is add a file usage whenever a new Importer entity gets created (and a file uploaded with it):

```
/**
 * Implements hook_ENTITY_TYPE_insert() for the Importer
   config entity type.
 */
function products_importer_insert(\Drupal\Core\Entity\
  EntityInterface $entity) {
  if ($entity->getPluginId() !== 'csv') {
    return;
  }

  // Mark the current File as being used.
  $fid = _products_importer_get_fid_from_entity($entity);
  $file = Drupal::entityTypeManager()->getStorage('file')
    ->load($fid);
  \Drupal::service('file.usage')->add($file, 'products',
    'config:importer', $entity->id());
}
```

We are implementing the specific version of `hook_entity_insert()` for our own entity type, and the first thing we are checking is whether we are looking at one using the CSV plugin. We're not interested in any importers that don't have a CSV file upload. If we are, we get the File entity ID from the importer using a private helper function:

```
function _products_importer_get_fid_from_entity(
   \Drupal\Core\Entity\EntityInterface $entity) {
   $fids = $entity->getPluginConfiguration()['file'];
   $fid = reset($fids);
   return $fid;
}
```

You'll notice that the `file` key in our plugin configuration array is an array of `File` IDs, even if we only uploaded one single file. That is just something we need to account for here (we also did so in our configuration schema earlier on).

Then, we load the File entity based on this ID and use the `file.usage` service to add a usage to it. The first parameter of the `add()` method is the File entity itself, the second is the module name that marks this usage, the third is the type of *thing* the file is used by, while the fourth is the ID of this *thing*. The latter two depend on the use case; we choose to go with our own notation (`config:importer`) to make it clear that we are talking about a configuration entity of the type `importer`. Of course, we used the ID of the entity.

With this, a new record will get created in the `file_usage` table whenever we save such an Importer entity for the first time. Now let's handle the case in which we delete this entity—we don't want this file usage lingering around, do we?

```
/**
 * Implements hook_ENTITY_TYPE_delete() for the Importer
   config entity type.
 */
function products_importer_delete(\Drupal\Core\Entity\
   EntityInterface $entity) {
   if ($entity->getPluginId() !== 'csv') {
      return;
   }

   $fid = _products_importer_get_fid_from_entity($entity);
   $file = Drupal::entityTypeManager()->getStorage
      ('file')->load($fid);
```

```
\Drupal::service('file.usage')->delete($file, 'products',
    'config:importer', $entity->id());
}
```

Most of what we are doing in this specific version of hook_entity_delete() is the same as before. However, we are using the delete() method of the file.usage service but passing the same arguments. These $type and $id parameters are actually optional, so we can "un-use" multiple files at once. Moreover, we have an optional fifth parameter (the count) whereby we can specifically choose to remove more than one usage from this file. By default, this is 1, and that makes sense for us.

Finally, we also want to account for the cases in which the user edits the importer entity and changes the CSV file. We want to make sure the old one is no longer marked as used for this Importer. And we can do this with hook_entity_update():

```
/**
 * Implements hook_ENTITY_TYPE_update() for the Importer
   config entity type.
 */
function products_importer_update(\Drupal\Core\Entity\
  EntityInterface $entity) {
  if ($entity->getPluginId() !== 'csv') {
    return;
  }

  /** @var \Drupal\products\Entity\ImporterInterface
    $original */
  $original = $entity->original;
  $original_fid = _products_importer_get_fid_from_entity
    ($original);
  $new_fid = _products_importer_get_fid_from_entity
    ($entity);
  if ($original_fid !== $new_fid) {
    $original_file = Drupal::entityTypeManager()->
      getStorage('file')->load($original_fid);
    \Drupal::service('file.usage')->delete($original_file,
      'products', 'config:importer', $entity->id());
    $file = Drupal::entityTypeManager()->getStorage('file')
      ->load($new_fid);
    \Drupal::service('file.usage')->add($file, 'products',
```

```
            'config:importer', $entity->id());
    }
}
```

We are using the specific variant of this hook that only gets fired for Importer entities. Just like we've been doing so far. And as I mentioned, we can access the original entity (before the changes have been made to it) like so:

```
$original = $entity->original;
```

And if the File ID that was on the original entity is not the same as the one we are currently saving with it (meaning the file was changed), we can delete the usage of that old File ID. Of course, we also track the usage of the newly uploaded file instead.

Processing the CSV file

Now that our plugin configuration works—and uploaded files are properly managed and marked as used—it's time to implement the getData() method by which we process the CSV file of the Importer entity. The result needs to be an array of product information, as expected by the import() method we saw earlier. So, we can have something like this:

```
/**
 * Loads the product data from the CSV file.
 *
 * @return array
 */
protected function getData() {
  $fids = $this->configuration['file'];
  if (!$fids) {
    return [];
  }

  $fid = reset($fids);
  /** @var \Drupal\file\FileInterface $file */
  $file = $this->entityTypeManager->getStorage('file')->
    load($fid);
  $wrapper = $this->streamWrapperManager->getViaUri($file->
    getFileUri());
  if (!$wrapper) {
    return [];
```

```
        }

        $url = $wrapper->realpath();
        $spl = new \SplFileObject($url, 'r');
        $data = [];
        while (!$spl->eof()) {
            $data[] = $spl->fgetcsv();
        }

        $products = [];
        $header = [];
        foreach ($data as $key => $row) {
            if ($key == 0) {
                $header = $row;
                continue;
            }

            if ($row[0] == "") {
                continue;
            }

            $product = new \stdClass();
            foreach ($header as $header_key => $label) {
                $product->{$label} = $row[$header_key];
            }
            $products[] = $product;
        }

        return $products;
    }
```

First, quite expectedly, we check for the existence of the File ID in the configuration and load the corresponding File entity based on that. To do this, we use the entity manager we injected into the plugin base class. But then comes something new.

Once we have the File entity, we can ask it for its URI, which will return something like this: `public://products.csv`. This is what is stored in the database. But in order to turn that into something useful, we need to use the *stream wrapper* that defines this filesystem. And to get that, we use the `StreamWrapperManager` service (`stream_wrapper_manager`), which has a handy method of returning the *stream wrapper* instance responsible for a given URI—`getViaUri()`. And once we have our `StreamWrapperInterface`, we can use its `realpath()` method to get the local path of the resource. We will come back to *stream wrappers* a bit later in this chapter, and it will make more sense. But for the moment, it's enough to understand that we are translating a URI in the `scheme://target` format into a useful path that we can use to create a new PHP-native `SplFileObject` instance, which, in turn, we can use to process the CSV file easily.

When creating the `SplFileObject`, we used the external URL of the file. This worked just fine, and we were able to also demonstrate how we can get our hands on the external URL if we ever need to. But, as we will see in the next chapter, it will also work directly with the stream URI, and we will switch to this approach instead.

With three lines of code, we are basically done getting all the rows from the CSV into the `$data` array. However, we also want to make this data look a bit more like what the JSON resource looked like—a map where the keys are the field names and the values are the respective product data. And we also want this map to contain PHP standard objects instead of arrays. Therefore, we loop through the data, establish the CSV header values, and use those as the keys in each row of a new `$products` array of objects. Our end result will look exactly like the product information coming from the decoded JSON response.

And with this, we are done. Well, not quite. We still need to inject the `StreamWrapperManager` service (`stream_wrapper_manager`) into our plugin. But you should know how to do that by now, so I will let you do it on your own.

Nothing we don't yet know how to do. However, there is one thing I'd like to point out here. In *Chapter 7, Your Own Custom Entity and Plugin Types*, I mentioned how, at the time, I believed the Guzzle HTTP client is a service that would be useful to all Importer plugins. Well, I was clearly wrong, as the CSV-based one we just created now doesn't need it, so there is no reason why it should be injected into it. What we need to do here is remove this dependency from the base plugin class and only use it in the JSON importer. However, I leave this up to you as homework.

Our CSV Importer plugin is now complete. If we did everything correctly, we can now create a new Importer entity that uses it, upload a correct CSV file, and import some Product entities via our `Drush` command. How neat.

Our own stream wrapper

At the beginning of this chapter, we briefly talked about stream wrappers and what they are used for. We saw that Drupal comes with four stream wrappers that map to the various types of file storage it needs. Now it's time to see how we can create our own. And the main reason why we would want to implement one is to expose resources at a specific location to PHP's native filesystem functions.

In this example, we will create a very simple stream wrapper that can basically only read the data from the resource. Just to keep things simple. And the data resource will be the product images hosted remotely (the ones we are importing via the JSON Importer). So there will be some rework there to use the new stream wrapper instead of the absolute URLs. Moreover, we will also learn how to use the site-wide settings service by which we can have environment-specific configurations set in the `settings.php` file and then read by our code.

The native way of registering a stream wrapper in PHP is by using the `stream_wrapper_register()` function. However, in Drupal, we have an abstraction layer on top of that in the form of services. So, a stream wrapper is a simple tagged service, albeit with many potential methods. Let's see its definition, which we add to the `products.services.yml` file:

```
products.images_stream_wrapper:
  class: Drupal\products\StreamWrapper\
    ProductsStreamWrapper
  tags:
    - { name: stream_wrapper, scheme: products }
```

Nothing too complicated. The service is tagged with `stream_wrapper`, and we use the `scheme` key to indicate the scheme of the wrapper. So the URIs will be in this format:

`products://target`

One important thing to note about stream wrapper services is that we cannot pass dependencies to them. The reason is that they are not instantiated in the normal way (by the container) but arbitrarily by PHP whenever some of its methods need to be called. So if we need to use some services, we'll have to use the static way of loading them.

The stream wrapper service class needs to implement `StreamWrapperInterface`, which comes with a lot of methods. There are many possible filesystem interactions that PHP can do, and these methods need to account for them all. However, we will only be focusing on a few specific ones that have to do with reading data. After all, our resources are remote and we don't even have a clue how to make changes to them over there. So for the rest of the methods, we will be returning FALSE to indicate that the operation cannot be performed.

Let's see this big class then:

```php
namespace Drupal\products\StreamWrapper;

use Drupal\Component\Utility\UrlHelper;
use Drupal\Core\StreamWrapper\StreamWrapperInterface;
use Drupal\Core\StringTranslation\StringTranslationTrait;

/**
 * Stream wrapper for the remote product image paths used
   by the JSON Importer.
 */
class ProductsStreamWrapper implements
  StreamWrapperInterface {

  use StringTranslationTrait;

  /**
   * The Stream URI
   *
   * @var string
   */
  protected $uri;

  /**
   * @var \Drupal\Core\Site\Settings
   */
  protected $settings;

  /**
   * Resource handle
   *
   * @var resource
   */
  protected $handle;

  /**
```

```
 * ProductsStreamWrapper constructor.
 */
public function __construct() {
  // Dependency injection does not work with stream
    wrappers.
  $this->settings = \Drupal::service('settings');
}


/**
 * {@inheritdoc}
 */
public function getName() {
  return $this->t('Product images stream wrapper');
}


/**
 * {@inheritdoc}
 */
public function getDescription() {
  return $this->t('Stream wrapper for the remote location
    where product images can be found by the JSON
      Importer.');
}


/**
 * {@inheritdoc}
 */
public static function getType() {
  return StreamWrapperInterface::HIDDEN;
}


/**
 * {@inheritdoc}
 */
public function setUri($uri) {
  $this->uri = $uri;
```

```
}

/**
 * {@inheritdoc}
 */
public function getUri() {
  return $this->uri;
}

/**
 * Helper method that returns the local writable target
 *   of the resource within the stream.
 *
 * @param null $uri
 *
 * @return string
 */
public function getTarget($uri = NULL) {
  if (!isset($uri)) {
    $uri = $this->uri;
  }

  [$scheme, $target] = explode('://', $uri, 2);
  return trim($target, '\/');
}

/**
 * {@inheritdoc}
 */
public function getExternalUrl() {
  $path = str_replace('\\', '/', $this->getTarget());
  return $this->settings->get('product_images_path') .
    '/' . UrlHelper::encodePath($path);
}

/**
```

```
  * {@inheritdoc}
 */
public function realpath() {
  return $this->getTarget();
}


/**
  * {@inheritdoc}
 */
public function stream_open($path, $mode, $options,
  &$opened_path) {
  $allowed_modes = array('r', 'rb');
  if (!in_array($mode, $allowed_modes)) {
    return FALSE;
  }
  $this->uri = $path;
  $url = $this->getExternalUrl();
  $this->handle = ($options && STREAM_REPORT_ERRORS) ?
    fopen($url, $mode) : @fopen($url, $mode);
  return (bool) $this->handle;
}


/**
  * {@inheritdoc}
 */
public function dir_closedir() {
  return FALSE;
}


/**
  * {@inheritdoc}
 */
public function dir_opendir($path, $options) {
  return FALSE;
}
```

```php
/**
 * {@inheritdoc}
 */
public function dir_readdir() {
  return FALSE;
}


/**
 * {@inheritdoc}
 */
public function dir_rewinddir() {
  return FALSE;
}


/**
 * {@inheritdoc}
 */
public function mkdir($path, $mode, $options) {
  return FALSE;
}


/**
 * {@inheritdoc}
 */
public function rename($path_from, $path_to) {
  return FALSE;
}


/**
 * {@inheritdoc}
 */
public function rmdir($path, $options) {
  return FALSE;
}


/**
```

```php
 * {@inheritdoc}
 */
public function stream_cast($cast_as) {
  return FALSE;
}


/**
 * {@inheritdoc}
 */
public function stream_close() {
  return fclose($this->handle);
}


/**
 * {@inheritdoc}
 */
public function stream_eof() {
  return feof($this->handle);
}


/**
 * {@inheritdoc}
 */
public function stream_flush() {
  return FALSE;
}


/**
 * {@inheritdoc}
 */
public function stream_lock($operation) {
  return FALSE;
}


/**
 * {@inheritdoc}
```

```php
   */
  public function stream_metadata($path, $option, $value) {
    return FALSE;
  }


  /**
   * {@inheritdoc}
   */
  public function stream_read($count) {
    return fread($this->handle, $count);
  }


  /**
   * {@inheritdoc}
   */
  public function stream_seek($offset, $whence = SEEK_SET)
    {
    return FALSE;
  }


  /**
   * {@inheritdoc}
   */
  public function stream_set_option($option, $arg1, $arg2)
    {
    return FALSE;
  }


  /**
   * {@inheritdoc}
   */
  public function stream_stat() {
    return FALSE;
  }


  /**
```

```
 * {@inheritdoc}
 */
public function stream_tell() {
  return FALSE;
}


/**
 * {@inheritdoc}
 */
public function stream_truncate($new_size) {
  return FALSE;
}


/**
 * {@inheritdoc}
 */
public function stream_write($data) {
  return FALSE;
}


/**
 * {@inheritdoc}
 */
public function unlink($path) {
  return FALSE;
}


/**
 * {@inheritdoc}
 */
public function url_stat($path, $flags) {
  return FALSE;
}


/**
 * {@inheritdoc}
```

```
  */
  public function dirname($uri = NULL) {
    return FALSE;
  }
}
```

The first thing to look at is the constructor in which we statically load the `Settings` service and store it as a class property. And speaking of which, we also define a `$uri` property to hold the actual URI this wrapper *wraps* and a `$handle` property to hold a generic PHP resource handle.

The `getName()` and `getDescription()` methods are pretty straightforward and are used for identifying the stream wrapper, while the `getType()` method returns the type of stream. We'll go with the hidden type because we don't want it visible in the UI. It's strictly for programmatic use so that we can read our product images. Do check out the available types and their meanings by looking at the `StreamWrapperInterface` constants.

Then, we have a getter and setter for the `$uri` property by which the Drupal `StreamWrapperManager` can create an instance of our wrapper based on a given URI. The `getTarget()` method is actually not in the interface but is a helper to extract a clean target from the URI (the target being the second part of the URI that comes after `scheme://`). And we use this method in `getExternalUrl()`, which is quite an important method responsible for returning an absolute URL to the resource in question. But here we also use our `Settings` service to get the `product_images_path` key. If you remember at the beginning of the chapter, we saw that the path to the public filesystem is defined in the `settings.php` file like so:

```
$settings['file_public_path'] = 'sites/default/files';
```

That `$settings` variable is the data array that is wrapped by the `Settings` service. So we want to do the same when defining our own remote path to the product images:

```
$settings['product_images_path'] = 'http://path/to/the
  /remote/product/images';
```

This way we are not committing to Git the actual remote URL and we can also change it later if we want. And this is the URL we are reading inside the `getExternalUrl()` method.

The other pillar of our read-only stream wrapper is the ability to open a file handle to the resource and allow us to read the data from it. And the `stream_open()` method does this as it gets called when we run either `file_get_contents()` or `fopen()` on our URI. Using the `$mode` parameter, we ensure that the operation is read-only and return `FALSE` otherwise—we do not support *write* or other flags.

Any mode can have `b` appended to it to indicate that the file should be opened in binary mode. So, where `r` indicates read-only, `rb` indicates read-only in binary mode.

The third argument is a bitmask of options defined by PHP. The one we're dealing with here is `STREAM_REPORT_ERRORS`, which indicates whether or not PHP errors should be suppressed (for instance, if a file is not found). The second is `STREAM_USE_PATH`, which indicates whether PHP's include path should be checked if a file is not found. This is not relevant to us, so we ignore it. If a file is found on the include path, then the fourth argument, (`$opened_url`), should be set with the file's real path.

What we do then is translate the URI into the absolute URL of the external resource so that we can open a file handle on it. And in doing so, we make use of the `STREAM_REPORT_ERRORS` option to either prepend the `@` to the `fopen()` function or not (doing so suppresses errors). Finally, we store the reference to the resource handle and return a Boolean based on it to indicate whether the operation succeeded.

Finally, we also implement the `stream_read()`, `stream_eof()`, and `stream_close()` methods so that we can actually also stream the resources if we want to. As for the rest of the methods, as already mentioned, we return `FALSE`.

All we have to do now is clear the cache and make use of our stream. As long as we have a valid URL declared in the `settings.php` file, our stream should work fine. And here are the kinds of things we could do with a URI like this:

```
$uri = 'products://tv.jpg';
```

To get the entire file content into a string, we can do this:

```
$contents = file_get_contents($uri);
```

Or we can use the example from the beginning of the chapter and stream the file bit by bit:

```
$handle = fopen($uri, 'r');
$contents = '';
while (!feof($handle)) {
  $contents .= fread($handle, 8192);
}
fclose($handle);
```

All these file operations, such as opening, reading, checking the end of a file, and closing, are possible due to our `stream_*()` method implementations from the wrapper.

And finally, maybe now it's also a bit clearer what we did when writing the CSV Importer and using the `StreamWrapperManager` to identify the stream wrapper responsible for a given URI, and based on that, the real path of the URI.

To end the section on stream wrappers, let's do some clean-up work by refactoring our `JsonImporter::handleProductImage()` method a bit. Our logic there involved hardcoding the URL to the remote API, which is really not a good idea. Instead, now that we have our stream wrapper, we can go ahead and use it. We can replace this:

```
// This needs to be hardcoded for the moment.
$image_path = '';
$image = file_get_contents($image_path . '/' . $name);
```

With this:

```
if (!file_exists('products://' . $name)) {
  return;
}
$image = file_get_contents('products://' . $name);
```

It's that simple. And now we can control the remote URL from outside the Git repository and, if it changes, we don't even have to alter our code. Granted, solely for this purpose, implementing a stream wrapper seems a bit excessive. After all, you can simply inject the `Settings` service and use the URL in the Importer plugin itself allowing for the same kind of flexibility. But we used the opportunity to learn about stream wrappers and how to create our own. And we even managed to find a small use case in the process.

Working with unmanaged files

Working with *unmanaged* files is actually pretty similar to doing so with *managed* files, except that they are not tracked in the database using the File entity type. There is a set of helper functions similar to what we've seen for *managed* files that can be accessed through the `FileSystem` service I mentioned earlier. Let's see some examples.

To save a new file, we do almost like we did before with *managed* files:

```
$image = file_get_contents('products://tv.jpg');
// Load the service statically for quick demonstration.
$file_system = \Drupal::service('file_system');
$path = $file_system->saveData($image, 'public://tv.jpg',
  FileSystemInterface::EXISTS_REPLACE);
```

We load the file data from wherever and use the `saveData()` method on the service the same way as we did with `FileRepositoryInterface::writeData()`. The difference is that the file is going to be saved but no database record is created. So the only way to use it is to rely on the path it is saved at and either try to access it from the browser or use it for whatever purpose we need. This method returns the URI of where the file is now saved or `FALSE` if there was a problem with the operation. So if all went well with the previous example, $path would now be `public://tv.jpg`.

And just like with the *managed* files, we also have a few other helpful methods in that service, such as `move()`, `copy()`, and `delete()`. I recommend you inspect that service to get more details on how these methods work.

Private filesystem

The private filesystem is used whenever we want to control access to the files being downloaded. Using the default public storage, users can get to the files simply by pointing to them in the browser, thereby bypassing Drupal completely. However, `.htaccess` rules prevent users from directly accessing any files in the private storage, making it necessary to create a route that delivers the requested file. It goes without saying that the latter is a hell of a lot less performant, as Drupal needs to be loaded for each file. Therefore, it's important to only use it when files should be restricted based on certain criteria.

Drupal already comes with a route and Controller ready to download private files, but we can create one as well if we really need to. For example, the Image module does so in order to control the creation and download of image styles—`ImageStyleDownloadController`.

The route definition for the default Drupal path looks like this:

```
system.files:
  path: '/system/files/{scheme}'
  defaults:
    _controller: 'Drupal\system\FileDownloadController::
      download'
    scheme: private
  requirements:
    _access: 'TRUE'
```

This is a bit of an odd route definition. We have a `{scheme}` parameter, which will be the actual file path requested for download. The URI scheme itself defaults to `private`, as illustrated by the signature of `FileDownloadController::download()`. Moreover, access is allowed at all times as Drupal delegates this check to other modules—as we will see in a minute.

If we look inside `FileDownloadController::download()`, we can see that it isn't actually much that it is doing itself. However, we also note that in the first line, it looks for the query parameter called `file` in order to get the URI of the requested file:

```
$target = $request->query->get('file');
```

But based on the route definition, we don't even have this parameter. This is where *Path Processors* come into play, more specifically, implementations of `InboundPathProcessorInterface`. These are tagged services that get invoked by the routing system when building up the routes by the requested path. And essentially, they allow the alteration of a given path as it comes in.

The core *System* module implements its own path processor for the purpose of handling the download of private files:

```yaml
path_processor.files:
  class: Drupal\system\PathProcessor\PathProcessorFiles
  tags:
    - { name: path_processor_inbound, priority: 200 }
```

It's a simple tagged service definition whose class needs to implement the correct interface that has one method. In the case of `PathProcessorFiles`, it looks like this:

```php
/**
 * {@inheritdoc}
 */
public function processInbound($path, Request $request) {
  if (strpos($path, '/system/files/') === 0 && !$request->
    query->has('file')) {
    $file_path = preg_replace('|^\/system\/files\/|', '',
      $path);
    $request->query->set('file', $file_path);
    return '/system/files';
  }
  return $path;
}
```

The goal of this method is to return a path that can be the same as the one requested or changed for whatever reason. And what Drupal does here is check whether the path is the one defined earlier (that starts with /system/files/) and extracts the requested file path that comes as the first argument after that. It takes that and adds it to the current request parameter keyed by file. Finally, it returns a cleaner path called simply /system/files. So this is why the FileDownloadController::download() method looks there for the file path.

Turning back to the Controller, we see that it essentially checks for the file and, if it is not found, throws a 404 (NotFoundHttpException). Otherwise, it invokes hook_file_download(), which allows all modules to control access to the file. And these can do so in two ways: either by returning -1, which denies access or by returning an array of headers to control the download for that specific file. By default, files in the private filesystem cannot be downloaded unless a specific module allows this to happen.

So what does this mean? If we have a file in the private filesystem, we need to implement hook_file_download() and control access to it. Let's see an example of how this might work by assuming we have a folder called /pdfs, whose files we want to make accessible to users that have the administer site configuration permission:

```
/**
 * Implements hook_file_download().
 */
function module_name_file_download($uri) {
  $file_system = \Drupal::service('file_system');
  $dir = $file_system->dirname($uri);
  if ($dir !== 'private://pdfs') {
    return NULL;
  }

  if (!\Drupal::currentUser()->hasPermission('administer
    site configuration')) {
    return -1;
  }

  return [
    'Content-type' => 'application/pdf',
  ];
}
```

This hook receives as an argument the URI of the file being requested. And based on that, we try to get the name of the folder it's in. To do this, we use the file_system service again.

If the file is not in the private filesystem inside the /pdfs folder, we simply return NULL to signify that we don't control access to this file. Other modules may do so (and if none do, access is denied). If it is our file, we check for the permission we want and return -1 if the user doesn't have it. This will deny access. Finally, if access is allowed, we return an array of headers we want to use in the file delivery. In our case, we simply use the PDF-specific headers that facilitate the display of the PDF file in the browser. If we wanted to trigger a file download, we could do something like this instead:

```
$name = $file_system->basename($uri);
return [
  'Content-Disposition' => "attachment;filename='$name'"
];
```

We use the filesystem service to determine the file name being requested and adjust our headers accordingly to treat it like an attachment that has to be downloaded.

And that is all there is to it. If we want more control (or a different path to download the files), we can implement our own route and follow the same approach. Without, of course, the need to invoke a hook, but simply handling the download inside the controller method. For example, this is what FileDownloadController::download() does to handle the actual response:

```
return new BinaryFileResponse($uri, 200, $headers, $scheme
  !== 'private');
```

This type of response is used when we want to deliver files to the browser, and it comes straight from Symfony.

Images

In this section, we are going a bit deeper into the world of images in Drupal while keeping the focus on module developers.

Image toolkits

The Drupal Image toolkits provide an abstraction layer over the most common operations used for manipulating images. By default, Drupal uses the GD image management library that is included with PHP. However, it also offers the ability to switch to a different library if needed by using the ImageToolkit plugins:

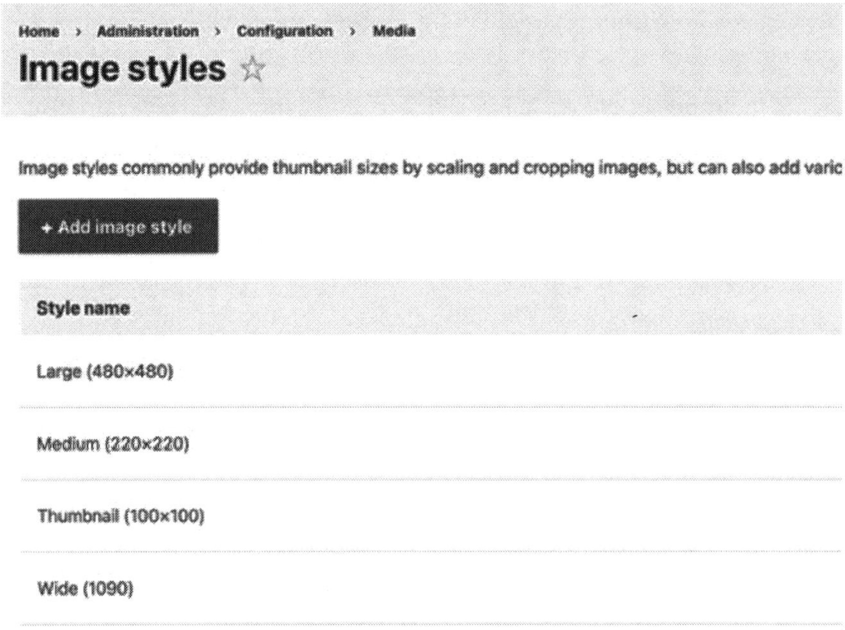

Figure 16.3: Image toolkit configuration UI

For instance, a contributed module could implement the `ImageMagick` library for developers who need support for additional image types, such as TIFF, which GD does not support. However, only one library can be used at a time as it needs to be configured site-wide.

Programmatically manipulating images using a toolkit involves instantiating an `ImageInterface` object that wraps an image file. This interface (implemented by the `Image` class) contains all the needed methods for applying the common manipulations to images, as well as saving the resulting image to the filesystem. And to get our hands on such an object, we use the `ImageFactory` service:

```
$factory = \Drupal::service('image.factory');
```

The role of this factory is to create instances of `Image` using a given toolkit. And it works like this:

```
$image = $factory->get($uri);
```

The second parameter to this method is the `ImageToolkit` plugin ID we want the `Image` object to work with. By default, it uses the default toolkit configured for the entire application.

And now we can use the manipulation methods on the `ImageInterface` to change the file:

```
$image->scale(50, 50);
$image->save('public://thumbnail.jpg');
```

In this example, we scale the image to 50 x 50 and save it to a new path. Omitting the destination in the `save()` method would mean overwriting the original file with the changed version. If you need to perform such manipulations manually, I encourage you to explore the `ImageInterface` for all the available options.

Image styles

Even though, as we've seen, we can handle image manipulations programmatically ourselves, typically this is done as part of *Image Styles*, which can be created and configured via the UI. These involve the application of several possible *Image Effects* in order to create image variations used in different places:

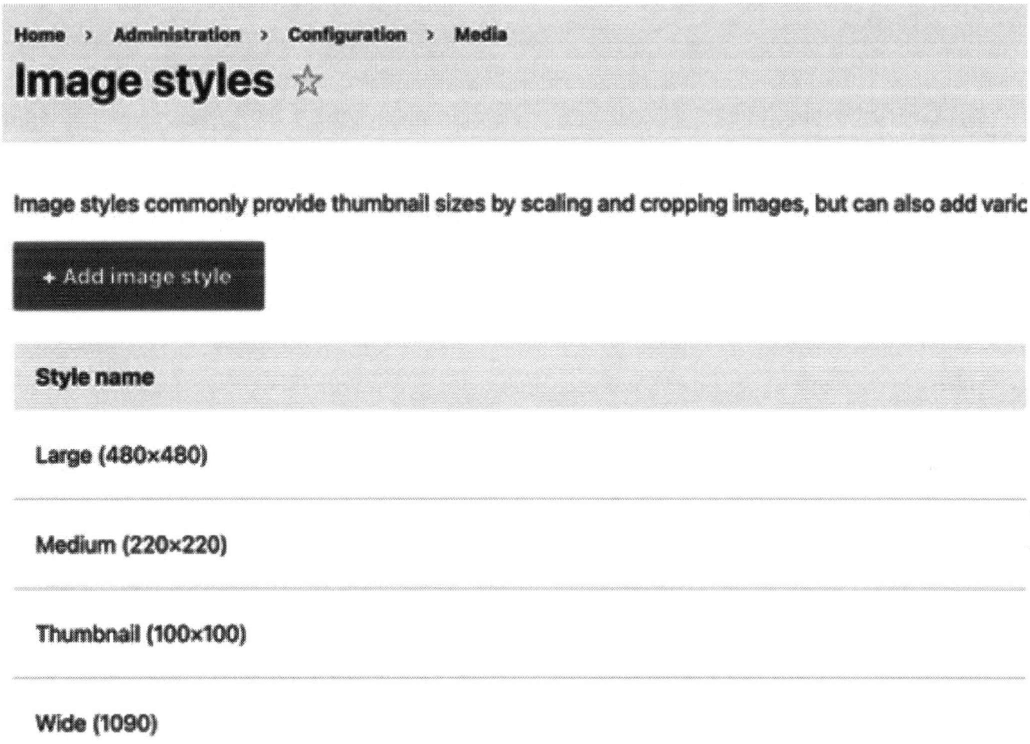

Home > Administration > Configuration > Media

Image styles ☆

Image styles commonly provide thumbnail sizes by scaling and cropping images, but can also add varic

+ Add image style

Style name

Large (480×480)

Medium (220×220)

Thumbnail (100×100)

Wide (1090)

Figure 16.4: Default image styles in Drupal

The image styles themselves are configuration entities that store configuration specific to the `ImageEffect` plugins they work with. Once they are created in the UI, we can make use of them in various ways. The most typical way is to use the image style in the `display` configuration of an entity field or even in Views when rendering an image field.

If you remember, at the beginning of the chapter we created the image field on the product entity but we did not configure a display. So for the moment, the imported images do not show up on the main product page. But we can add some display configuration to our base field definition so that images are shown with a specific image style:

```
->setDisplayOptions('view', array(
  'type' => 'image',
  'weight' => 10,
  'settings' => [
    'image_style' => 'large'
  ]
))
```

In this example, we are using the default `image` field formatter plugin, which can be configured to use an image style. So, under the `settings` key, we reference the `large` image style configuration entity that comes with Drupal core. Omitting this would simply just render the original image. Make sure you check back to *Chapter 7, Your Own Custom Entity and Plugin Types*, and *Chapter 9, Custom Fields*, if you are a bit fuzzy on the base field definitions.

Rendering images

In *Chapter 4, Theming*, we talked about theme hooks and how we use them in render arrays to build output. And we also saw a few examples of theme hooks that come with Drupal core and that can be used for common things (such as links or tables). But images are also something we'll often end up rendering, and there are two ways we can do so (both using theme hooks defined by Drupal core).

First, we can use the `image` theme hook to simply render an image. And it's pretty simple to use it:

```
return [
  '#theme' => 'image',
  '#uri' => 'public://image.jpg',
];
```

And this will render the image as is. We can also pass some more options, such as the *alt*, *title*, *width*, or *height*, all of which are applied to the image tag as attributes, as well as an array of any other kinds of attributes we may want. Check out `template_preprocess_image()` for more information on how this works.

Alternatively, the Image module defines the `image_style` theme hook, which we can use to render the image using a given image style:

```
return [
  '#theme' => 'image_style',
  '#uri' => 'public://image.jpg',
  '#style_name' => 'large',
];
```

This theme hook works pretty much the same way, except that it has an extra parameter for the ID of the `ImageStyle` entity we want to use. And the rest of the parameters we find on the `image` theme hook can also be found here. In fact, `image_style` delegates to the `image` theme hook under the hood.

Finally, we may also find ourselves in a situation in which we need to get our hands on the URL of an image using a given image style. We need to work with the `ImageStyle` configuration entity for this:

```
$style = \Drupal::entityTypeManager()->getStorage
    ('image_style')->load('thumbnail');
$url = $style->buildUrl('public://image.jpg');
```

Once we load the image style we want, we simply call its `buildUrl()` method, to which we pass the URI of the file for which we want the URL. The first time this URL is accessed, the image variation gets created and stored to disk. Future requests will load it directly from there for improved performance.

Summary

We are closing this chapter after covering a lot of different topics that have to do with working with files in Drupal.

We started with a couple of introductory sections in which we outlined some general concepts, such as the various filesystems (storages) that Drupal uses, as well as how stream wrappers come into play for working with them. We also introduced the different ways to work with files: *managed* versus *unmanaged*.

Next, we dove into working with *managed files* and created an image field on our Product entity type so that we could import images into it. The other example of working with *managed* files had us create a new Product importer based on a CSV file of data, and we also saw how to upload, read, and process such a file, as well as manually track its usage. As a parenthesis, we introduced a very powerful feature of Drupal that allows us to hook into the entity CRUD operations and perform actions whenever these are fired. This is a majorly important technique module developers typically use in Drupal.

We then switched gears and implemented our own stream wrapper to serve our imaginary remote API that stored the product images. Moreover, we talked about working with *unmanaged* files and some of the functions we can use for this—things similar to *managed* files except the method names are different and there are no File entities or usage tracking them.

We then continued with the private filesystem and talked about what this serves and how we can work with it to control access to our own files. This, as opposed to allowing users to bypass Drupal and download files from the public filesystem.

Finally, we finished the chapter with a look at the APIs surrounding images and how we can use toolkits to process images, both manually and as part of image styles. And even more useful, we saw how we can render images in all sorts of ways and get our hands on the image style URLs.

In the next chapter, we will look at automated testing and how we can ensure that our code works and that we don't introduce regressions along the way.

17
Automated Testing

Automated testing is a process in which we rely on special software to continuously run pre-defined tests that verify the integrity of our application. To this end, automated tests are collections of steps that cover the functionality of an application and compare triggered outcomes to expected ones.

Manual testing is a great way to ensure that a piece of written functionality works as expected. The main problem encountered by most adopters of this strategy, especially those who use it exclusively, is regression. Once a piece of functionality is tested, the only way that you can guarantee that regressions (or bugs) were not introduced by another piece of functionality is by retesting it. And as the application grows, this becomes impossible to handle. This is where automated tests come in.

Automated testing uses special software that has an API that allows us to automate the steps involved in testing functionality. This means that we can rely on machines to run these tests as many times as we want, and the only thing stopping us from having a fully working application is the lack of proper test coverage with well-defined tests.

There's a lot of different software available for performing such tests, and it's usually geared toward specific types of automated testing. For example, Behat is a powerful PHP-based open-source behavior testing framework that allows the scripting of tests that mirror quite closely what a manual tester would do—interact with the application through the browser and test its behavior. There are other testing frameworks that go much lower in the level of their testing target. For example, the PHP industry-standard tool PHPUnit is widely used for performing unit tests. This type of testing focuses on the actual code at the lowest possible level; it tests whether class methods work properly by verifying their output after providing them with different input. A strong argument in favor of this kind of testing is that it encourages better code architecture, which can be (partly) measured by the ease with which unit testing can be written for it.

We also have functional or integration tests, which fall somewhere in between these two examples. These go higher than the code level and enlist application subsystems in order to test more comprehensive sets of functionality, without necessarily considering browser behavior and user interaction.

It is not difficult to agree that a well-tested application features a combination of different testing methodologies. For example, testing the individual architectural units of an application does not guarantee that the entire subsystem works, just as testing only the subsystem does not guarantee that its individual components will work properly under all circumstances. Also, the same is true for certain subsystems that depend on user interaction—these require test coverage as well.

In this chapter, we will see how automated testing works in Drupal. More specifically, we will go through and explain all the testing methodologies available for us as module developers and provide examples for them with two tests each. By the end of this chapter, you'll be ready to write your own tests and be familiar enough with the code to further explore the testing capabilities available.

The main topics we will cover in this chapter are as follows:

- Testing methodologies in Drupal
- Registering tests
- Getting familiar with Unit, Kernel, Functional, and FunctionalJavaScript tests

Testing methodologies in Drupal

Drupal's PHP tests are all run by PHPUnit, which covers more testing methodologies than just those mentioned earlier. So, let's see what these are.

Drupal comes with the following types of PHP-level testing:

- **Unit**: Low-level class testing with minimal dependencies (usually mocked)
- **Kernel**: Functional testing with the kernel bootstrapped, access to the database, and only a few loaded modules
- **Functional**: Functional testing with a bootstrapped Drupal instance, a few installed modules, and using a Mink-based browser emulator (Goutte driver)
- **Functional JavaScript**: Functional testing using the Selenium driver for Mink, allowing the testing of JavaScript-powered functionality

As mentioned, all these test suites are built on top of PHPUnit and are, consequently, run by it. Based on the namespace the test classes reside in, as well as the directory placement, Drupal can discover these tests and know what type they are.

In this chapter, we will see examples of all of them as we go about testing some of the functionality we've been writing in this book.

PHPUnit

Drupal uses PHPUnit as the testing framework for all types of tests. In this section, we will see how we can work with it to run tests.

> **Important note:**
>
> In your development environment (or wherever you want to run the tests), make sure you have the composer dependencies installed with the `--dev` flag. This will include PHPUnit. Remember not to do this in your production environment as you can compromise the security of your application.

To run PHPUnit tests, we use the command line, and it's very easy to do so. To run an entire test suite (of a certain type), we must navigate to the Drupal core folder (this works in a normal Drupal site installation where the vendor folder is located there):

```
cd core
```

And run the following command:

```
../vendor/bin/phpunit --testsuite=unit
```

This command goes back a folder through the vendor directory and uses the installed phpunit executable.

If you are following along with the GitHub repository that accompanies this book, the vendor folder is placed elsewhere, and there is a PHPUnit configuration file at the root of the project. So, to achieve the same as what we've done here, you would run from the root folder:

```
./vendor/bin/phpunit --testsuite=unit
```

Going forward, we will assume a regular Drupal installation where the PHPUnit configuration file is in the core folder.

As an option, in the previous example, we specified that we only want to run unit tests. Omitting that would run all types of tests. However, for most of the others, there will be some configuration needed, as we will see in the respective sections. If we want to run a specific test, we can pass it as an argument to the phpunit command (the path to the file):

```
../vendor/bin/phpunit tests/Drupal/Tests/Core/Routing/
    UrlGeneratorTest.php
```

In this example, we run a Drupal core test that tests the `UrlGenerator` class. Alternatively, we can run multiple tests that belong to the same *group* (we will see how tests are added to a group soon):

```
../vendor/bin/phpunit --group=Routing
```

This runs all the tests from the `Routing` group, which contains the `UrlGeneratorTest` we saw earlier. We can run tests from multiple groups if we separate them with commas.

Also, to check what the available groups are, we can run the following command:

```
../vendor/bin/phpunit --list-groups
```

This will list all the groups that have been registered with PHPUnit.

Finally, we can also run a specific method found inside a test by using the `-filter` argument:

```
../vendor/bin/phpunit --filter=testAliasGeneration
    UsingInterfaceConstants
```

This is one of the test methods from the same `UrlGeneratorTest` we saw before and is the only one that would run.

Registering tests

There are certain commonalities between the various test suite types regarding what we need to do in order for Drupal (and PHPUnit) to be able to discover and run them.

First, we have the directory where the test classes should go. The pattern is this: `tests/src/[suite_type]`, where `[suite_type]` is the name of the test suite type this test should be. It can be one of the following:

- **Unit**
- **Kernel**
- **Functional**
- **FunctionalJavascript**

So, for example, unit tests would go inside the `tests/src/Unit` folder of our module.

Second, the test classes need to respect a namespace structure as well:

```
namespace Drupal\Tests\[module_name]\[suite_type]
```

This is also pretty straightforward to understand.

Third, there is a certain metadata item that we need to have in the test class PHPDoc. Every class must have a summary line describing what the test class is for. Only classes that use the `@coversDefaultClass` attribute can omit the summary line. Moreover, all test classes must have the `@group` PHPDoc annotation indicating the group they are part of. This is how PHPUnit can run tests that belong to certain groups only.

So, now that we know how to register and run tests, let's look at unit tests and see how we can write our own.

Unit tests

As briefly mentioned at the beginning of the chapter, unit tests are used for testing single *units* that make up the code architecture. In practice, this means testing individual classes, especially the methods they contain and what they should be doing. Since the testing happens at such a low level, they are by far the fastest tests that can be run.

The logic behind unit tests is quite simple: after providing input, the test asserts that the method output is correct. Typically, the more *input -> output* scenarios it covers, the more stable the tested code is. For example, tests should also cover unexpected scenarios, as well as exercise all the code contained in the tested methods (such as forks created by *if/else* statements).

The programming pattern of dependency injection—objects should receive as dependencies other objects they might need—becomes critical when it comes to unit testing. The reason is that if class methods work with the global scope or instantiate other objects, we can no longer test them cleanly. Instead, if they require dependencies, we can *mock* them and pass them within the context of the executed tests. We will see some examples of this shortly. But before we do that, let's create a simple class that can be easily tested using a unit test.

A typical example is a simple calculator class. It will take two numbers as arguments to its constructor and have four methods for performing basic arithmetic on those numbers. We'll put this into our *Hello World* module:

```
namespace Drupal\hello_world;

/**
 * Class used to demonstrate a simple Unit test.
 */
class Calculator {

  protected $a;
  protected $b;
```

```
public function __construct($a, $b) {
  $this->a = $a;
  $this->b = $b;
}

public function add() {
  return $this->a + $this->b;
}

public function subtract() {
  return $this->a - $this->b;
}

public function multiply() {
  return $this->a * $this->b;
}

public function divide() {
  return $this->a / $this->b;
}
}
```

Nothing very complicated here. You could argue that a calculator class should not get any dependencies but instead pass the numbers to the actual arithmetic methods. However, this will work just fine for our example and is a bit less repetitive.

Now, let's create the first unit test to make sure that this class behaves as we expect it to. In the previous section, we saw which directory these need to go in. So, in our case, it will be /tests/src/Unit. And the test class looks like this:

```
namespace Drupal\Tests\hello_world\Unit;

use Drupal\hello_world\Calculator;
use Drupal\Tests\UnitTestCase;

/**
 * Tests the Calculator class methods.
 *
```

```php
 * @group hello_world
 */
class CalculatorTest extends UnitTestCase {

  /**
   * Tests the Calculator::add() method.
   */
  public function testAdd() {
    $calculator = new Calculator(10, 5);
    $this->assertEquals(15, $calculator->add());
  }

  /**
   * Tests the Calculator::subtract() method.
   */
  public function testSubtract() {
    $calculator = new Calculator(10, 5);
    $this->assertEquals(5, $calculator->subtract());
  }

  /**
   * Tests the Calculator::multiply() method.
   */
  public function testMultiply() {
    $calculator = new Calculator(10, 5);
    $this->assertEquals(50, $calculator->multiply());
  }

  /**
   * Tests the Calculator::divide() method.
   */
  public function testDivide() {
    $calculator = new Calculator(10, 5);
    $this->assertEquals(2, $calculator->divide());
  }

}
```

First, you notice that the namespace corresponds to the pattern we saw in the previous section. Second, the PHPDoc contains the required information: a summary and the `@group` tag. Third, the class name ends with the word `Test`. Finally, the class extends `UnitTestCase`, which is the base class we need to extend for all unit tests.

> **Important note:**
> All types of test class names in Drupal need to end with the word *Test* and extend the relevant base class that provides specific code for that type of test.

Then, we have the actual methods that test various aspects of the `Calculator` class and which always must start with the word `test`. This is what tells PHPUnit that they need to be run. These methods are the actual standalone tests themselves, meaning that the `CalculatorTest` class has four tests. Moreover, each of these tests runs independently of the others.

Since the `Calculator` arithmetic is very simple, it's not difficult to understand what we are doing to test it. For each method, we are instantiating a new instance with some numbers, and then we *assert* that the result from the arithmetic operation is equal to what we expect. The base class provides a multitude of different assertion methods that we can use in our tests. Since there are so many of them, we are not going to cover them all here. We will see more as we write more tests, but I strongly recommend that you check the base classes of the various types of test suites for methods that start with the word `assert`. A great way to do this is also to use an IDE that autocompletes as you type the method name. It can be very handy.

With this, we can already run the test and see whether it passes. Normally, it should because we can do math in our heads and we know it's correct:

```
../vendor/bin/phpunit
../modules/custom/hello_world/tests/src/Unit/
   CalculatorTest.php
```

The result should be green:

```
OK (4 tests, 4 assertions)
```

However, earlier I mentioned that a good test also accounts for unexpected situations and negative responses. We have not done so very well in our example. If we look at `testAdd()`, we can see that the assertion is correct with those two numbers. But what if we later go to the `Calculator::add()` method and change it to this by accident:

```
return 15;
```

The test will still pass, but will it actually be a true positive? Not really, because if we pass different numbers, the calculation won't match anymore. So, we should test these methods with more than just one set of numbers to prove that the math behind the `Calculator` class is valid.

So, instead, we can do something like this:

```
$calculator = new Calculator(10, 5);
$this->assertEquals(15, $calculator->add());
$calculator = new Calculator(10, 6);
$this->assertEquals(16, $calculator->add());
```

This way, we are sure that the addition operation works correctly. One trade-off in this is that we have a bit of repetitive code, especially if we have to do this for all the other operations as well.

Generally, when writing tests, repetition is much more acceptable than when writing the actual code. Many times, there is nothing you can do about it as the code will seem very repetitive. However, in our case, we can actually do something by using the `setUp()` method, which is called by PHPUnit before each test method runs. Its purpose is to perform various preparation tasks that are common for all the tests in the class. However, don't take this to mean that it runs only once and then is used by all. In fact, it runs before each individual test method.

So, what we can do is something like this:

```
/**
 * @var \Drupal\hello_world\Calculator
 */
protected $calculatorOne;

/**
 * @var \Drupal\hello_world\Calculator
 */
protected $calculatorTwo;

/**
 * {@inheritdoc}
 */
protected function setUp(): void {
  parent::setUp();
  $this->calculatorOne = new Calculator(10, 5);
  $this->calculatorTwo = new Calculator(10, 2);
}
```

We create two class properties, and inside the setUp() method, we assign to them our calculator objects. A very important thing to keep in mind is to always call the parent of this method because it does very important things for the environment setup, especially as we move to Kernel and Functional tests.

Now, the testAdd() method can look like this:

```
public function testAdd() {
  $this->assertEquals(15, $this->calculatorOne->add());
  $this->assertEquals(12, $this->calculatorTwo->add());
}
```

Much cleaner and less repetitive. Based on this, you can extrapolate and apply the same changes to the other methods yourself.

Mocked dependencies

Seldom are tested classes so simple as our calculator class. Most of the time, they will have dependencies that in turn also have dependencies. So unit testing becomes a bit more complicated. In fact, the ease with which unit tests are written has become a litmus test for the quality of the code being tested—the less complicated the unit test, the better the code.

As our second example of writing unit tests, let's go into the "real world" and test one of the classes we wrote in this book, namely, the UserTypesAccess class. If you remember from *Chapter 10, Access Control*, we created this service to be used on routes as an access checker. Although we can write functional tests that verify that it works well as part of the access system, we can also write a unit test to check the actual code in the access() method. So, let's get started.

The first thing we need to do is to create the class (respecting the directory placement as well as the class namespace):

```
namespace Drupal\Tests\user_types\Unit;

use Drupal\Tests\UnitTestCase;

/**
 * Tests the UserTypesAccess class methods.
 *
 * @group user_types
 */
class UserTypesAccessTest extends UnitTestCase {}
```

So far, things look like our previous example—we have the PHPDoc information, and we are extending the `UnitTestCase` class. So let's write a test for the `access()` method of the `UserTypesAccess` class. However, if you remember, this method takes two arguments (a user account and a route object), and also uses the entity type manager, which is injected in the class. So, that is where the bulk of the complexity lies. What we need to test is the return value of the method depending on these arguments—basically, whether it will allow or deny access if the user account has certain values found on the route.

In unit testing, dependencies are usually mocked. This means PHPUnit will create empty lookalike objects that behave as we prescribe them to, and we can use these as the dependencies. The way to create a simple mock object is this:

```
$user = $this->createMock('Drupal\user\Entity\User');
```

The `$user` object will now be a mock of the Drupal `User` entity class. It, of course, won't do anything, but it can be used as a dependency. To actually make it useful, we need to prescribe some behavior for it based on what the tested code does with it. For example, if it calls its `id()` method, we need to prescribe this behavior. We can do this with *expectations*:

```
$user->expects($this->any())
  ->method('id')
  ->will($this->returnValue(1));
```

This tells the mock object that for every call to the `id()` method on it, it should return the value 1. The `expects()` method takes in a matcher, which can be even more restrictive. For example, instead of `$this->any()`, we can use `$this->once()`, which means that the mock object can have its `id()` method called only once. Check out the base class for the other available options, as well as what you can pass to the `will()` method—although `$this->returnValue()` is going to be the most common one. Finally, if the `id()` method takes an argument, we can also have the `with()` method to which we pass the value of the expected argument in the matcher.

A more complex way of creating a mock is by using the mock builder:

```
$user = $this->getMockBuilder('Drupal\user\Entity\User')
  ->getMock();
```

This will get the same mock object but will allow some more options in its construction. I recommend checking out the PHPUnit documentation for more information as this is as deep as we are going to go in this book on mocking objects.

Now that we know a bit about mocking, we can proceed with writing our test. To do this, we need to think about the end goal and work our way back to all the method calls we need to mock. Just as a reminder, this is the code that we need to test:

```php
public function access(AccountInterface $account, Route
  $route) {
  $user_types = $route->getOption('_user_types');
  if (!$user_types) {
    return AccessResult::forbidden();
  }
  if ($account->isAnonymous()) {
    return AccessResult::forbidden();
  }
  $user = $this->entityTypeManager->getStorage('user')->
    load($account->id());
  $type = $user->get('field_user_type')->value;
  return in_array($type, $user_types) ?
    AccessResult::allowed() : AccessResult::forbidden();
}
```

So, at first glance, we see that we need to mock `EntityTypeManager`. The method arguments we will instantiate manually with some dummy data inside. However, mocking `EntityTypeManager` is going to be quite complicated. A call to its `getStorage()` method needs to return a `UserStorage` object. This needs to also be mocked because a call to its `load()` method needs to return a `User` entity object. Finally, we also need to mock that because a call to its `get()` method is also expected to return a value object.

As I mentioned, we will proceed by going backward from our end goal. So, we can start with instantiating the types of `AccountInterface` objects we want to pass, as well as the route objects:

```php
/**
 * Tests the UserTypesAccess::access() method.
 */
public function testAccess() {
  // User accounts
  $anonymous = new UserSession(['uid' => 0]);
  $registered = new UserSession(['uid' => 2]);

  // Route definitions.
```

```
    $manager_route = new Route('/test_manager', [], [],
        ['_user_types' => ['manager']]);
    $board_route = new Route('/test_board', [], [],
        ['_user_types' => ['board']]);
    $none_route = new Route('/test_board');
}
```

And the new *use* statements at the top:

```
use Drupal\Core\Session\UserSession;
use Symfony\Component\Routing\Route;
```

Basically, we want to test what happens for both types of users: anonymous and registered. When instantiating the `UserSession` objects (which implement `AccountInterface`), we pass in some data to be used with it. In our case, we need the user `uid` because it will be requested by the tested code when checking whether the user is anonymous or not.

Then, we create three routes: one where managers should have access, one where board members should have access, and one where no one should have access (as indicated by the `_user_types` option on the route). Do refer back to *Chapter 10, Access Control*, if you don't remember what this functionality is about.

Once this is done, we instantiate our `UserTypesAccess` class, with a view to calling its `access()` method with various combinations of our account and route objects:

```
$access = new UserTypesAccess($entity_type_manager);
```

And the new *use* statement at the top:

```
use Drupal\user_types\Access\UserTypesAccess;
```

However, we don't yet have an entity type manager, so we need to mock it. Here is all the code we need to mock the entity type manager to work for our tested code (this goes before the code we wrote so far in this test):

```
// User entity mock.
$type = new \stdClass();
$type->value = 'manager';
$user = $this->getMockBuilder('Drupal\user\Entity\User')
    ->disableOriginalConstructor()
    ->getMock();
$user->expects($this->any())
```

```
  ->method('get')
  ->will($this->returnValue($type));


// User storage mock
$user_storage = $this->getMockBuilder
  ('Drupal\user\UserStorage')
  ->disableOriginalConstructor()
  ->getMock();
$user_storage->expects($this->any())
  ->method('load')
  ->will($this->returnValue($user));


// Entity type manager mock.
$entity_type_manager = $this->getMockBuilder
  ('Drupal\Core\Entity\EntityTypeManager')
  ->disableOriginalConstructor()
  ->getMock();
$entity_type_manager->expects($this->any())
  ->method('getStorage')
  ->will($this->returnValue($user_storage));
```

First of all, you will notice that the entity type manager is only mocked at the very end. We first need to start the call chain, which ends with a User entity object field value. So, the first block mocks the User entity object, which expects any number of calls to its `get()` method to which it will always return a `stdClass()` object with the property `value` that is equal to the `manager` string. This way, we are mocking the entity field system accessor.

Important note

While using the mock builder to create our mocks, we can use the `disableOriginalConstructor()` method to prevent PHPUnit from calling the constructor of the original class. This is important to prevent the need for all sorts of other dependencies that don't actually impact the tested code.

Now that we have the User entity mock, we can use it as the return value of the `UserStorage` mock's `load()` method. This, in turn, is the return value of the entity type manager mock's `getStorage()` method. So, all the code we wrote means that we have mocked the following chain:

```
$this->entityTypeManager->getStorage('user')->load
  ($account->id());
```

It doesn't really matter what we pass to the `load()` method, as we will always have that one user entity that has the `manager` user type.

Now that everything is mocked, we can use the `$access` object we created earlier and make assertions based on calls to its `access()` method:

```
// Access denied due to lack of route option.
$this->assertInstanceOf(\Drupal\Core\Access
  \AccessResultForbidden::class, $access->access
    ($registered, $none_route));

// Access denied due to user being anonymous on any of the
  routes
$this->assertInstanceOf(\Drupal\Core\Access\
  AccessResultForbidden::class, $access->access($anonymous,
    $manager_route));
$this->assertInstanceOf(\Drupal\Core\Access\
  AccessResultForbidden::class, $access->access
    ($anonymous, $board_route));

// Access denied due to user not having proper field value
$this->assertInstanceOf(\Drupal\Core\Access\
  AccessResultForbidden::class, $access->access
    ($registered, $board_route));

// Access allowed due to user having the proper field
  value.
$this->assertInstanceOf(\Drupal\Core\Access\
  AccessResultAllowed::class, $access->access(
    $registered, $manager_route));
```

The return value is always an object that implements an interface—either `AccessResultAllowed` or `AccessResultForbidden`—so that is what we need to assert. We are checking four different use cases:

- Access denied if there is no route option
- Access denied for anonymous users on any of the routes
- Access denied for registered users with the wrong user type
- Access allowed for registered users with the proper user type

So, with this, we can run the test and should hopefully get a green result:

```
../vendor/bin/phpunit
../modules/custom/user_types/tests/src/Unit/
  UserTypesAccessTest.php
```

This is the basics of writing unit tests. There are many more types of assertions, and you'll end up mocking quite a lot of dependencies in Drupal. But don't be put off by the slow pace encountered at first as things will become faster as you get more experience.

Kernel tests

Kernel tests are the immediate higher-level testing methodology we can have in Drupal and are actually integration tests that focus on testing various components. They are faster than regular Functional tests as they don't do a full Drupal install, but use an in-memory pseudo installation that is much faster to bootstrap. For this reason, they also don't handle any browser interactions and don't install any modules automatically.

Apart from the code itself, Kernel tests also work with the database and allow us to load the modules that we need for running the test. However, unlike the Functional tests we will see next, Kernel tests also require us to manually trigger the installation of any database schemas we need. But we will see how we can do this in the two examples we cover in this section.

Before we can work with Kernel tests, though, we need to make sure we have a connection to the database, and that PHPUnit is aware of this. Inside the core folder of our Drupal installation, we find a phpunit.xml.dist file, which we need to duplicate and rename to phpunit.xml. This is the PHPUnit configuration file. Normally, this file should already be ignored by Git, so no need to worry about committing it to the repository.

In this file, we find an environment variable called SIMPLETEST_DB where we can specify the connection to the database using the format shown in the following commented code:

```
mysql://username:password@localhost/databasename
  #table_prefix
```

Once that is in, PHPUnit will be able to connect to the database in order to install Drupal for Kernel tests as well as Functional and FunctionalJavaScript tests.

If you are following along with the GitHub repository accompanying this book, this configuration file is found in the root folder and is already prepared for running all the types of tests we cover in this book.

> **Important Note:**
>
> As a rule of thumb, you should opt for Kernel tests over Functional tests whenever browser interactions are not necessary, and Kernel tests are enough to do the job. The reason is that a suite full of tests can end up taking a long time to run so you should make it as performant as possible.

TeamCleaner test

Now that we have that covered, it's time to write our first Kernel test. And a nice simple example can be to test the `TeamCleaner` queue worker plugin we created in *Chapter 14, Batches, Queues, and Cron*. If you are wondering why this cannot be tested using the ultra-fast unit testing methodology, the answer is that its single method doesn't return anything. Instead, it alters database values that we need to access in order to check it happened correctly.

The test class goes naturally in the `tests/src/Kernel` folder of our module and can start off like this:

```
namespace Drupal\Tests\sports\Kernel;

use Drupal\KernelTests\KernelTestBase;

/**
 * Test the TeamCleaner QueueWorker plugin.
 *
 * @group sports
 */
class TeamCleanerTest extends KernelTestBase {}
```

The namespace is consistent with the ones we've seen so far, and we have the correct PHPDoc annotations to register the test. Moreover, this time, we are extending from `KernelTestBase`.

The first thing we need to do is specify which modules we want loaded when running this test. For our case, this is the `sports` module, so we can add a class property that contains this name:

```
/**
 * {@inheritdoc}
 */
protected static $modules = ['sports'];
```

Specifying a list of modules here does not actually install them but simply loads and adds them to the service container. So yes, we have access to the module and code as well as the container. But that also means that schemas defined by these modules are not actually created, so we need to do that manually. The same is true for the configuration the module is shipped with. But we can handle these things in the `setUp()` method or in the actual test method itself. We'll opt for the latter because, in this case, we only have one test method in the class. And the whole thing can look like this:

```
/**
 * Tests the TeamCleaner::processItem() method.
 */
public function testProcessItem() {
  $this->installSchema('sports', 'teams');
  $database = $this->container->get('database');
  $fields = ['name' => 'Team name'];
  $id = $database->insert('teams')
    ->fields($fields)
    ->execute();

  $records = $database->query("SELECT id FROM {teams} WHERE
    id = :id", [':id' => $id])->fetchAll();
  $this->assertNotEmpty($records);

  $worker = new TeamCleaner([], NULL, NULL, $database);
  $data = new \stdClass();
  $data->id = $id;
  $worker->processItem($data);
  $records = $database->query("SELECT id FROM {teams} WHERE
    id = :id", [':id' => $id])->fetchAll();
  $this->assertEmpty($records);
}
```

And the *use* statement:

```
use Drupal\sports\Plugin\QueueWorker\TeamCleaner;
```

Since the `TeamCleaner` plugin removes teams, it's enough to only install the `teams` table. We can do that using the parent `installSchema()` method, to which we pass the module name and table we want installed. We don't actually deal with players, so we should avoid doing unnecessary work, such as the creation of the `players` table.

Then, very similar to how we do it in real code, we get the database service from the container and add a record to the teams table. This will be the test record that we delete, so we remember its $id. But before we test this, we want to make absolutely sure that our record got saved. So we query for it and assert that the result is not empty. The assertNotEmpty() method is another helpful assertion that we can use when dealing with arrays.

Now that we are certain the record is in the database, we can "process" it using our plugin. So, we instantiate a TeamCleaner object, passing all its required dependencies—most importantly, the database service. Then, we create a simple object that mimics what the processItem() method expects and call the latter while passing the former to it. At this point, if our plugin did its job correctly, the team record should have been deleted from the database. So, we can query for it and this time assert the opposite of what we did before: that the query comes back empty.

And with this, our test is finished. As always, we should run it and make sure it passes:

```
../vendor/bin/phpunit ../modules/custom/sports/tests/src/
    Kernel/TeamCleanerTest.php
```

And that is a very simple example of using Kernel tests for testing a component, particularly one that integrates with the database. We could have used a Functional test as well, but that would have been overkill—it would run slower and make no use of the benefits that it offers over Kernel testing, such as browser integration.

> **Note**
>
> We went with an almost Unit-like approach here by manually instantiating the TeamCleaner plugin class and passing dummy data to it. The cool thing about Kernel tests is that we could have even used the worker plugin manager and instantiated the plugin with that instead.

CsvImporter test

After this simple example, let's write another test that illustrates a more complex scenario. And we will write one that tests the CsvImporter plugin we created in the previous chapter.

There is quite a lot of functionality that goes into this plugin and working with it—we have the actual importing, the plugin and configuration entity creation, the user interface for doing so, and so on. It's a very good example of functionality that can benefit from multi-methodology test coverage. In this respect, we start with testing its underlying purpose, that of the product import, for which we don't need browser interactions. This means that we can use a Kernel test.

Like we wrote the previous test, we can start with the class like so (this time in the `products` module):

```
namespace Drupal\Tests\products\Kernel;

use Drupal\KernelTests\KernelTestBase;

/**
 * Tests the CSV Product Importer
 *
 * @group products
 */
class CsvImporterTest extends KernelTestBase {}
```

Nothing new so far.

Next, we need to specify the modules we need loaded. And here we have a bigger list:

```
/**
 * {@inheritdoc}
 */
protected static $modules = ['system', 'csv_importer_test',
    'products', 'image', 'file', 'user'];
```

Only the `products` module may seem obvious to you at this point, but all the rest are also needed. The `system`, `image`, `file`, and `user` modules are all somehow needed for dealing with the file upload and storage process that is needed for the `CsvImporter` plugin.

> **Important Note:**
> It's not always so easy to figure out which modules are needed, so it will involve a bit of a trial-and-error process, at least in the beginning. A typical scenario is to run the test and notice failures due to missing functionality. Tracking this functionality to a module and specifying this module in the list is how you usually end up with a complete module list, especially when the test is complex and needs a wide range of subsystems with dependencies.

But you may be wondering what's with the `csv_importer_test` module there. Often, you may need to create modules used only for the tests—usually because they contain some configuration you want to use in your testing. In our case, we did so to demonstrate where these modules would go and to add a `products.csv` test file that we can use in our tests.

Tests modules go inside the `tests/modules` folder of the module that contains the tests that use them. So, in our case, we have `csv_importer_test` with its `info.yml` file:

```
name: CSV Importer Test
description: Used for testing the CSV Importer
core_version_requirement: ^10
type: module
package: Testing
```

And the mentioned CSV file we will use is right next to it:

```
id,name,number
1,Car,45345
2,Motorbike,54534
```

Now that we have covered that, we can write the test method:

```
/**
 * Tests the import of the CSV based plugin.
 */
public function testImport() {
  $this->installEntitySchema('product');
  $this->installEntitySchema('file');
  $this->installSchema('file', 'file_usage');
  $entity_type_manager = $this->container->get
    ('entity_type.manager');
  // Assert we have no products in the system.
  $products = $entity_type_manager->getStorage('product')
    ->loadMultiple();
  $this->assertEmpty($products);

  $csv_path = $this->container->get
    ('extension.path.resolver')->getPath('module',
      'csv_importer_test') . '/products.csv';
  $csv_contents = file_get_contents($csv_path);
  $file = $this->container->get('file.repository')->
    writeData($csv_contents, 'public://simpletest-
      products.csv', FileSystemInterface::EXISTS_REPLACE);
  $config = $entity_type_manager->getStorage('importer')->
```

```
  create([
  'id' => 'csv',
  'label' => 'CSV',
  'plugin' => 'csv',
  'plugin_configuration' => [
    'file' => [$file->id()]
  ],
  'source' => 'Testing',
  'bundle' => 'goods',
  'update_existing' => true
]);
$config->save();

$plugin = $this->container->get('products
  .importer_manager')->createInstanceFromConfig('csv');
$plugin->import();
$products = $entity_type_manager->getStorage('product')
  ->loadMultiple();
$this->assertCount(2, $products);

$products = $entity_type_manager->getStorage('product')->
  loadByProperties(['number' => 45345]);
$this->assertNotEmpty($products);
$this->assertCount(1, $products);
}
```

And the *use* statement at the top:

```
use Drupal\Core\File\FileSystemInterface;
```

The initial setup here is a bit more complicated, partly because of Kernel tests not installing module schemas. Using the parent `installEntitySchema()` method, we can install all the necessary tables for the Product and File content entities. However, since we are working with managed files, we also need to install the `file_usage` table manually. It is not technically an entity table. Again, there is no shame in arriving at these steps using trial and error.

Now that we have the basics set up, we can do a sanity check and ensure that we don't have any product entities in the database. There is no reason why we should have any, but it doesn't hurt to ensure it. This guarantees a valid test since our goal will be to later assert the existence of products.

Then we create a managed File entity by using the `products.csv` file from the `csv_importer_test` module. The `ExtensionPathResolver::getPath()` method is a very common way of retrieving the relative path to a module or a theme, regardless of where it is actually located. And we save the contents of this file into the `public://` filesystem of the testing environment. Keep in mind, though, that after the test runs successfully, this file gets removed as Drupal cleans up after itself.

Next, we need to create an Importer configuration entity that uses the CSV-based plugin to run the import. And instead of doing it through the UI, we do it programmatically. Using the storage handler, we create the entity as we learned in *Chapter 6, Data Modeling and Storage*. Once we have that, we use the Importer plugin manager to create an instance based on this configuration entity (to which we gave the ID `csv`). And finally, we run the import of the products.

Now, for the assertions, we do a double-check. Since our test CSV contains two rows, we load all the product entities again and assert that we have a total of two. No more, no less. And here we see another useful assertion method for working with arrays: `assertCount()`. But then we get a bit more specific and try to load a product that has a field value (the `number`) equal to an expected number from the test CSV file. And assert that it is, in fact, found as well.

We could even do some more assertions. For example, we can check that all the Product field values have been set correctly. I'll let you explore ways in which you can do this—either by querying based on these values or asserting equality between field values and their expected ones. But it's important to not go overboard as it will impact speed and, in some cases, add insufficient value to the test coverage to compensate for it. The trick is to find the right balance.

Finally, with our test in place, we can run it:

```
../vendor/bin/phpunit
../modules/custom/products/tests/src/Kernel/
  CsvImporterTest.php
```

And this test should pass as well.

In the previous section, we looked at Kernel tests and said that they are basically integration tests that focus on components rather than interactions with the browser. In the next section, we'll go one level up and talk about fully-fledged functional tests, otherwise called browser tests (due to the name of the base class we need to extend).

Functional tests

Functional tests in Drupal use a simulated browser (using the popular Mink emulator) that allows users to click links, navigate to pages, work with forms, and make assertions regarding HTML elements on the page. What they don't allow is testing JavaScript-based interactions (see the next section for those).

Functional tests extend the `Drupal\Tests\BrowserTestBase` class, which is integrated with PHPUnit like the ones we've seen before. The base class contains loads of methods both for asserting things and for shortcuts to perform Drupal (and web)-related tasks: creating users, entities, navigating to pages, filling in and submitting forms, logging in, and so on. And just like before, each test (class method) runs in isolation, so things such as content and users cannot be shared across multiple tests but would have to be recreated (perhaps using the `setUp()` method as we've already seen).

Browser tests perform a full Drupal installation with a minimal number of modules (using the *Testing* installation profile). This means that we can specify to install other modules as well, and the schema for these also gets installed. Moreover, it's also important to understand that the resulting installation has got nothing in common with our current development site. Any configuration we need, we have to create. There are no users, no content, and no files. So, it is a brand new, parallel installation that runs for the duration of one single test and gets cleaned up as it finishes.

Configuration for Functional tests

Before writing our Functional tests, we need to turn back to our `phpunit.xml` file and change some environment variables. Apart from the `SIMPLETEST_DB` variable we adjusted earlier, we also have the `SIMPLETEST_BASE_URL` and `BROWSERTEST_OUTPUT_DIRECTORY`. The first is used to know where the application can be accessed in the browser. The latter is the directory where output data can be saved by PHPUnit and needs to be an absolute local path (for example, a folder in the local `files` folder):

```
/var/www/sites/default/files/browser-output
```

Moreover, make sure the user running the test has permissions to write into the `sites/simpletest` folder as that is where the virtual filesystem is created for each test. The easiest way to do it is to change the folder ownership to the web server user that runs the process. In the case of Apache, this is usually `www-data`.

Hello World page test

The first Functional test we will write is for the *Hello World* page we created and the functionality behind it. We will test whether the page shows the correct *Hello World* message, also depending on the value found in the configuration. So, let's create the class for it, naturally in the `hello_world` module, inside the `tests/src/Functional` folder:

```
namespace Drupal\Tests\hello_world\Functional;

use Drupal\Tests\BrowserTestBase;

/**
```

```
 * Basic testing of the main Hello World page.
 *
 * @group hello_world
 */
class HelloWorldPageTest extends BrowserTestBase {}
```

You can really see the consistency with the other types of tests. But in this case, as mentioned, we extend from `BrowserTestBase`.

Also, like before, we can configure several modules we want installed:

```
/**
 * {@inheritdoc}
 */
protected static $modules = ['hello_world', 'user',
  'node'];
```

We will need the User and Node modules for the second test we run, which will go in the same class as this one.

Additionally, we also need to tell the test what Drupal theme it should use:

```
/**
 * {@inheritdoc}
 */
protected $defaultTheme = stark;
```

We go with Stark, which doesn't contain core markup.

But let's proceed with the first, easier test:

```
/**
 * Tests the main Hello World page.
 */
public function testPage() {
  $expected = $this->assertDefaultSalutation();
  $config = $this->config('hello_world.custom_salutation');
  $config->set('salutation', 'Testing salutation');
  $config->save();

  $this->drupalGet('/hello');
```

```
$this->assertSession()->pageTextNotContains($expected);
$expected = 'Testing salutation';
$this->assertSession()->pageTextContains($expected);
}
```

If you remember, our /hello page shows a greeting depending on the time of day, unless an administrator has overridden that message through a configuration form. So, we start this test by asserting that with a fresh install that has no override, we see the time-based greeting. And for that, we create a separate assertion message since it's a bit wordy and we will reuse it:

```
protected function assertDefaultSalutation() {
  $this->drupalGet('/hello');
  $this->assertSession()->pageTextContains('Our first
    route');
  $time = new \DateTime();
  $expected = '';
  if ((int) $time->format('G') >= 00 && (int) $time->format
    ('G') < 12) {
    $expected = 'Good morning';
  }

  if ((int) $time->format('G') >= 12 && (int) $time->format
    ('G') < 18) {
    $expected = 'Good afternoon';
  }

  if ((int) $time->format('G') >= 18) {
    $expected = 'Good evening';
  }
  $expected .= ' world';
  $this->assertSession()->pageTextContains($expected);
  return $expected;
}
```

The very first thing we do here is use the drupalGet() method to navigate to a path on the site. Do check out the method signature for all the options you can pass to it. And the first assertion we make is that the page contains the text *Our first route* (which is the page title). The parent assertSession() method returns an instance of WebAssert, which contains all sorts of methods for asserting the presence of elements on the current page in the Mink session. One such method is the generic `pageTextContains()` with which we simply check that the given text can be found anywhere on the page.

Although in quite a lot of cases asserting the presence of a text string is enough, you may want to ensure that it is actually the right one (to avoid false positives). For example, in our case, we could check that it is really the page title that is rendered inside an `<h1>` tag. We can do it like so:

```
$this->assertSession()->elementTextContains('css', 'h1',
    'Our first route');
```

The `elementTextContains()` method can be used to find an element on the page based on a locator (CSS selector or XPath) and assert that it contains the specified text. In our example, we use the CSS selector locator, and we try to find the `<h1>` element.

If all of that is okay, we proceed with asserting that the actual salutation message is present on the page. Unfortunately, we have to duplicate quite some code because it is dependent on the time of day.

Going back to our actual test method, we can proceed knowing that the message is showing correctly on the page. And the next thing we want to test is the following: if there is a `hello_world.custom_salutation` configuration object with a `salutation` value that is what should be shown. So, we programmatically create it. Next, we again navigate to the same path (we essentially reload the page) and check that the old message is not shown anymore and that the new one is instead.

So, if we run this test:

```
../vendor/bin/phpunit
../modules/custom/hello_world/tests/src/Functional/
    HelloWorldPageTest.php
```

...darn. We get an error:

```
Behat\Mink\Exception\ResponseTextException: The text "Good
    evening world" appears in the text of this page, but it
        should not.
```

It's as if we didn't even override the salutation message. But we did.

The problem is caching. Keep in mind, we are navigating these pages as anonymous users, and caching is enabled on the site like in normal scenarios. In *Chapter 11, Caching*, I made a note about this particular problem—the `max-age` property only bubbles up to the page level for the dynamic page cache (logged-in users) and not for anonymous users.

> **Important Note:**
>
> This is a great example of automated testing shedding light on mistakes we introduce while developing and that we don't notice. We most likely wrote our functionality while having caching disabled and/or always visiting the page as a logged-in user. It's an easy mistake to make. Luckily, automated testing comes to the rescue.

The solution to this problem can be found using an all-out cache kill switch. This means that we need to alter our logic a bit to tell Drupal to never cache the pages where our salutation component is shown. This is the price we pay for the highly dynamic nature of our functionality, and it's always a good exercise to evaluate whether it is worth it. There are, of course, much more complicated (and creative) solutions for this, but we will opt for the simple kill switch.

The kill switch is easy to use. It's a service called `page_cache_kill_switch` that we need to inject into our `HelloWorldSalutation` service. By now you should know how to do that so I won't repeat it here.

Next, at the beginning of the `getSalutation()` and `getSalutationComponent()` methods, we simply have to add this line:

```
$this->killSwitch->trigger();
```

And now if we run this test, we should get a green result.

Hello World form test

The second Functional test we will write should test the salutation override form itself. In the previous one, we interacted with the configuration API directly to make changes to the configuration value. Now we will see whether the form to do so actually works. But since we can reuse quite a lot from the previous test, and they are very closely related, we can add it to the same class:

```
/**
 * Tests that the configuration form for overriding the
   message works.
 */
public function testSalutationOverrideForm() {
  $expected = $this->assertDefaultSalutation();
  $this->drupalGet('/admin/config/salutation-
    configuration');
  $this->assertSession()->statusCodeEquals(403);
  $account = $this->drupalCreateUser(['administer site
    configuration']);
```

```
$this->drupalLogin($account);
$this->drupalGet('/admin/config/salutation-
  configuration');
$this->assertSession()->statusCodeEquals(200);
$this->assertSession()->pageTextContains('Salutation
  configuration');
$this->assertSession()->elementExists('css', '#edit-
  salutation');

$edit = [
  'salutation' => 'My custom salutation',
];
$this->submitForm($edit, 'op');
$this->assertSession()->pageTextContains('The
  configuration options have been saved');
$this->drupalGet('/hello');
$this->assertSession()->pageTextNotContains($expected);
$this->assertSession()->pageTextContains('My custom
  salutation');
}
```

We start this test in the same way, asserting that the hour-dependent message is shown. This also proves that each test runs in its own independent environment and changes to the configuration in one test have no impact on the other. They all start with a blank slate.

Then we navigate to the configuration form page and assert that we do not have access. For this, we use the `statusCodeEquals()` assertion method to check the response code. This is good because we need to be logged in with a user that has a certain permission.

> **Note**
>
> The access restrictions on the configuration form allow any user that has a certain permission. For this reason, our test should focus on that permission rather than something else that may indirectly include this permission. For example, it should not assume that a user with the administrator role has that permission.

So we create a new user account using the handy `drupalCreateUser()` method, whose first parameter is an array of permissions the user should have. We can then use the resulting User entity with the `drupalLogin()` method to log in. Under the hood, this navigates to the user login page, submits the form, and then asserts that everything went well. Now we can go back to the configuration form page and should have access— something that we also assert. In addition, we assert that we have the page title and that we have the salutation text field HTML element on the page. We do so using the `elementExists()` method, using the CSS selector. Again, check out `WebAssert` for all sorts of assertion methods that help you identify things on the page.

Now it's time to submit the form and override the salutation message. And we do this with `submitForm()`, whose most important parameter is an array of values to fill in the form elements, keyed by the `name` parameter of the individual form HTML element. In our case, we only have one. Do check out the documentation of this method for more information on all the things you can do with it. Once the form is submitted, the page will reload, and we can assert the presence of the confirmation message. And finally, we can go back to the `/hello` path and assert that the old message is no longer showing but the new overridden one does so instead.

Running the test class again should now include this new test as well, and everything should be green. In the next section, we'll bring JavaScript into the picture so that we can also test the more dynamic browser integrations. But already you can notice that Kernel tests are much faster to run if you don't need to interact with a browser.

Functional JavaScript tests

The last type of PHP tests we can write in Drupal is the JavaScript-powered Functional test. `FunctionalJavascript` tests are useful when we want to test more dynamic client-side functionality such as JavaScript behaviors or Ajax interactions.

They are an extension of the regular Functional tests, but which use WebDriver. The latter is an API that allows things like Selenium to control browsers such as Chrome or Firefox. Drupal uses Chrome for this so make sure you have Selenium installed and working with the Chrome driver. We won't cover this here because it depends on your local environment and the current latest versions. But if you are following along with the GitHub repository accompanying this book, you should be all setup.

Assuming you have Selenium running, we can write some tests. But only after we add another environment variable to the PHPUnit configuration file (ensure the Selenium endpoint is correct for you):

```
<env name="MINK_DRIVER_ARGS_WEBDRIVER" value='["chrome",
  null, "http://localhost:4444/wd/hub"]'/>
```

Time test

If you remember from *Chapter 12, JavaScript and Ajax API*, we added to our Hello World salutation component a little time widget that displays the current hour in real time if the salutation is not overridden. This component is powered by JavaScript, and more importantly, appended to the page using JavaScript.

Moreover, in the previous section, we wrote a Functional test for the Hello World page in which we asserted the presence of the salutation message. However, the actual time widget would never show up there because the Mink driver used in these types of tests does not support JavaScript. So if we want to test that, we need to write a `FunctionalJavascript` test.

As expected, these tests follow the same patterns for the directory placement and namespaces. So our first test class can start like this:

```
namespace Drupal\Tests\hello_world\FunctionalJavascript;

use Drupal\FunctionalJavascriptTests\WebDriverTestBase;

/**
 * Testing the simple Javascript timer on the Hello World
   page.
 *
 * @group hello_world
 */
class TimeTest extends WebDriverTestBase {}
```

By now most of the above code should be clear. However, the base class we extend this time is the `WebDriverTestBase` class, which itself is a child of `BrowserTestBase`. Interestingly, it doesn't add much to the mix apart from configuring the test to use Selenium Web Driver and adding a few JavaScript-specific helper methods. This is to demonstrate that most of the difference between Functional and FunctionalJavascript tests is determined by the actual Mink driver.

One extremely handy addition, though, is the ability to take screenshots. Often when testing frontend interactions, things don't go as we thought and we don't understand why. The parent `createScreenshot()` method allows us to save a full-page screenshot at any given moment that we can investigate for debugging purposes. All we have to do is pass in the name of the file we want to be saved. So do check that out.

Moving on with our test, let's add the modules we want to be enabled:

```
/**
 * {@inheritdoc}
 */
protected static $modules = ['hello_world'];
```

As expected, the Hello World module is enough.

And the theme to use in the test installation:

```
/**
 * {@inheritdoc}
 */
protected $defaultTheme = 'stark';
```

Now the very simple test method can look like this:

```
/**
 * Tests the time component.
 */
public function testSalutationTime() {
  $this->drupalGet('/hello');
  $this->assertSession()->pageTextContains('The time is');

  $config = $this->config('hello_world.custom_salutation');
  $config->set('salutation', 'Testing salutation');
  $config->save();

  $this->drupalGet('/hello');
  $this->assertSession()->pageTextNotContains('The time
    is');
}
```

We are using the exact same assertion techniques as before, but because JavaScript is enabled, the time widget text should show up now. And like before, we also test that if the salutation method is overridden, the time widget does not show up.

CsvImporter test

When learning about Kernel tests, we wrote a test for the `CsvImporter` that focused on the importing functionality given an existing Importer configuration entity (which we created programmatically). However, another important angle of this functionality is the process of creating this configuration entity as we are relying on Ajax to dynamically inject form elements related to the selected Importer plugin. So let's write a test for that as well.

Just as before, the test class can start with something like this:

```
namespace Drupal\Tests\products\FunctionalJavascript;

use Drupal\FunctionalJavascriptTests\WebDriverTestBase;

/**
 * Testing the creation/edit of Importer configuration
 *   entities using the CSV importer
 *
 * @group products
 */
class ImporterFormTest extends WebDriverTestBase {}
```

Let's set the default theme:

```
/**
 * {@inheritdoc}
 */
protected $defaultTheme = 'stark';
```

And like always, let's enable some modules:

```
/**
 * {@inheritdoc}
 */
protected static $modules = ['image', 'file', 'node',
  'products', 'csv_importer_test'];
```

If we try to run a test with these modules, it will fail because the Products module will be enabled before the Image one. And, if you remember, we created an Image field on the Product entity, but we forgot to make the image module a dependency on it. So let's add this quickly to the `products.info.yml` file:

```yaml
dependencies:
  - drupal:image
```

> **Important Note:**
>
> The Node module is enabled because it defines the `access content` permission, which is used by the core `machine_name` form element. And this element is used on the Importer entity form so we'll need it in order for the tests to actually work.

Even though we only write one test method, there is quite a bit of preparation for it that we might want to reuse elsewhere. Plus, it also looks cleaner to be separated from the actual test method. So we can add a `setUp()` method instead:

```php
/**
 * {@inheritdoc}
 */
protected function setUp(): void {
  parent::setUp();
  chmod('public://', 0777);
  $csv_path = \Drupal::service('extension.path.resolver')->
    getPath('module', 'csv_importer_test') .
      '/products.csv';
  $csv_contents = file_get_contents($csv_path);
  $this->file = \Drupal::service('file.repository')->
    writeData($csv_contents, 'public://simpletest-
      products.csv', FileSystemInterface::EXISTS_REPLACE);
  $this->admin = $this->drupalCreateUser(['administer site
    configuration']);
  ProductType::create(['id' => 'goods', 'label' =>
    'Goods'])->save();
}
```

And the new *use* statements:

```
use Drupal\products\Entity\ProductType;
use Drupal\Core\File\FileSystemInterface;
```

As expected, the first thing we do is the same thing as we did in the previous test—load the test CSV file from the `csv_importer_test` module and "upload" it to Drupal, creating a new managed File entity. But before that, we set permissions to allow the files to be uploaded to the test site's public folder. Depending on your testing setup, this may not be needed.

Then, we create an administrator user account that has the permission needed for creating Importer configuration entities, as well as a bundle for the Product entity so that we can create products. We didn't need to worry about the bundle in the previous test because we created the Importer configuration programmatically. But now, through the UI, a bundle needs to exist in order to select it.

The resulting File entity and admin user account we store on class properties, so we should also define those:

```
/**
 * @var \Drupal\file\FileInterface
 */
protected $file;

/**
 * @var \Drupal\Core\Session\AccountInterface
 */
protected $admin;
```

And with this, we are ready to write our empty test method and start filling it up step by step:

```
/**
 * Tests the importer form.
 */
public function testImporterForm() {}
```

We can start with the basics:

```
$this->drupalGet('/admin/structure/importer/add');
$assert = $this->assertSession();
$assert->pageTextContains('Access denied');
```

We navigate to the form for creating importer configuration entities and assert that the user does not have access. This is because, by default, we are browsing as anonymous users. Next, we need to log in and try this again:

```
$this->drupalLogin($this->admin);
$this->drupalGet('/admin/structure/importer/add');
$assert->pageTextContains('Add importer');
$assert->elementExists('css', '#edit-label');
$assert->elementExists('css', '#edit-plugin');
$assert->elementExists('css', '#edit-update-existing');
$assert->elementExists('css', '#edit-source');
$assert->elementExists('css', '#edit-bundle');
$assert->elementNotExists('css', 'input[name="files
   [plugin_configuration_csv_file]"]');
```

We use the same `drupalLogin()` method and navigate back to the form. This time we assert that we have the title as well as various HTML elements—the form elements used for creating the entity. Moreover, we also assert that we do not have the element for uploading the CSV file because that should only show up if we select that we want to use the CSV Importer plugin.

It follows we do just that:

```
$page = $this->getSession()->getPage();
$page->selectFieldOption('plugin', 'csv');
$this->assertSession()->assertWaitOnAjaxRequest();
$assert->elementExists('css', 'input[name="files
   [plugin_configuration_csv_file]"]');
```

Using the `getSession()` method, we get the current Mink session, from which we can get the object representing the actual page we are looking at. This is a `DocumentElement` object that can be traversed, inspected, and manipulated in all sorts of ways. I recommend you check out the `TraversableElement` class for all the available methods.

One such method is `selectFieldOption()`, by which we can specify the locator of an HTML select element (ID, name, or label) and a value, and it will trigger the selection. As you know, this is supposed to make an Ajax request bringing in our new form elements. And using `assertWaitOnAjaxRequest()` on the `JSWebAssert` object, we can wait until that is complete. Finally, we can assert that the file upload field is present on the page.

Next, we proceed with filling in the form:

```
$page->fillField('label', 'Test CSV Importer');
$this->assertJsCondition('jQuery(".machine-name-
   value").html() == "test_csv_importer"');
$page->checkField('update_existing');
$page->fillField('source', 'testing');
$page->fillField('bundle', 'goods');
$wrapper = \Drupal::service('stream_wrapper_manager')->
   getViaUri($this->file->getFileUri());
$page->attachFileToField('files[plugin_configuration
   _csv_file]', $wrapper->realpath());
$this->assertSession()->assertWaitOnAjaxRequest();
$page->pressButton('Save');
$assert->pageTextContains('Created the Test CSV Importer
   Importer.');
```

The generic fillField() method is useful for things such as text fields, while the checkField() method is expectedly useful for checkboxes. The locator for both is again either the ID, the name, or the label of the element.

We also use the assertJsCondition method to have the execution wait until a JavaScript change has happened on the page. And we do this to ensure that the entity machine name field has been currently filled in.

Next, with the help of the stream wrapper of the file that we uploaded, and more specifically, its realpath() method, we attach the file to the field using the attachFileToField() method. This triggers an Ajax request, which again we wait to complete. Lastly, we use the pressButton() method to click on the submit button and then assert that we have a confirmation message printed out (the form has been saved and the page refreshed).

Now to check that the operation went through properly:

```
$config = Importer::load('test_csv_importer');
$this->assertInstanceOf(\Drupal\products\Entity\
   ImporterInterface::class, $config);

$fids = $config->getPluginConfiguration()['file'];
$fid = reset($fids);
$file = File::load($fid);
$this->assertInstanceOf(\Drupal\file\FileInterface::class,
   $file);
```

And the new *use* statements:

```
use Drupal\file\Entity\File;
use Drupal\products\Entity\Importer;
```

We load the configuration entity using the ID we gave it and then assert that the resulting object is an instance of the correct interface. This checks whether we saved the entity. Next, we load the File entity based on the ID found in the Importer configuration entity and assert that it itself also implements the correct interface. This proves that the file got saved and the configuration is correct.

Instead of checking the rest of the field values programmatically, in the same way, we opt for navigating to the edit form of the Importer entity and asserting that the values are pre-filled correctly:

```
$this->drupalGet('admin/structure/importer/
   test_csv_importer/edit');
$assert->pageTextContains('Edit Test CSV Importer');
$assert->fieldValueEquals('label', 'Test CSV Importer');
$assert->fieldValueEquals('plugin', 'csv');
$assert->checkboxChecked('update_existing');
$assert->fieldValueEquals('source', 'testing');
$page->hasLink('products.csv');
$assert->fieldValueEquals('bundle', 'Goods (goods)');
```

The `fieldValueEquals()` and `checkboxChecked()` methods are handy for checking field values. Moreover, we also use the `hasLink()` method to check whether there is a link with that name on the page. This is to prove the uploaded file is shown correctly:

Figure 17.1: Plugin configuration for CSV Importer

And finally, since the bundle field is a reference field and not a simple text field, we need to construct the value the testing framework actually sees there, which is in this pattern: `Label (ID)`.

And with this, our test is complete, and we can run it in its entirety:

```
../vendor/bin/phpunit
../modules/custom/products/tests/src/Kernel/
    CsvImporterTest.php
```

Summary

In this chapter, we talked a bit about automated testing in Drupal. We started with an introduction about why it's useful and, in fact, important to write automated tests, and then briefly covered a few of the more popular types of software development testing methodologies.

Drupal has the capability for quite a lot of methodologies, as we've seen. We have unit tests—the lowest level form of testing that focuses on single architectural units and which are by far the fastest-running tests of them all. Then we have Kernel tests, which are integration tests focusing on lower-level components and their interactions. Next, we have Functional tests, which are higher-level tests that focus on interactions with the browser. And finally, we have the FunctionalJavascript tests, which extend the latter and bring Selenium and Chrome into the picture to allow the testing of functionalities that depend on JavaScript.

We've also seen that all these different types of tests are integrated with PHPUnit so we can run them all using this tool. This means that all the different types of tests follow the same "rules" for registering them with Drupal, namely, the directory placement, the namespacing, and the PHPDoc information.

The world of automated testing is huge, and there can be no single chapter in a book that can cover all the different ways something can be tested. For this reason, especially for beginners, the journey toward good test coverage is full of trial and error and even has the occasional frustration. But out of this, we get stable code that works always, and that is protected from regressions.

In the next and final chapter, we will take a look at a few things we can do to protect our Drupal applications from malicious attacks.

18
Drupal Security

Writing secure code is an important aspect of any web application. Preventing ever-so-creative hacking techniques can be really daunting, and this is partly the reason why we, as developers, sometimes choose a well-established framework with solid and up-to-date security measures baked right in.

Drupal is a CMS that takes security very seriously. The community has a dedicated security team that is always on the lookout for vulnerabilities and advises core contributors and module developers on ways to fix potential vectors of attack. It is also responsible for the fast mitigation of any such issue and disseminating the correct information to the affected parties.

When it comes to out-of-the-box installation, Drupal has come a long way in addressing many security concerns present in previous versions. For this reason, in this chapter, we will talk about some of the most prominent security features that Drupal comes with out of the box and that are directly related to our work as module developers. Moreover, we will take a look at some tips for ensuring that the modules we write respect the security standards Drupal prides itself on.

The topics we will cover in this short and final chapter are related to protecting our applications from:

- Cross-Site Scripting (XSS)
- SQL Injection
- Cross-Site Request Forgery (CSRF)

Cross-Site Scripting (XSS)

With the adoption of Twig as the templating system, prevention against XSS attacks has been significantly improved. There are two main consequences of this adoption. The first one addresses the need for separating presentation from business logic. In other words, themers and developers can no longer directly access Drupal's APIs, nor can they run SQL queries from templates. To expose any such functionality, Twig extensions and filters can be used, but they require the logic to be encapsulated inside a module.

The second consequence is in the form of Twig auto-escaping. This means that any string not specifically marked as safe will be escaped by Twig using the native PHP `htmlspecialchars()` function.

Sanitization methods in Drupal

Twig auto-escapes any string that is output using the normal notation, as follows:

```
{{ variable_name }}
```

However, there are cases in which the variable has already been marked safe, and Twig no longer escapes it. This is usually in the case of `MarkupInterface` objects, such as `FilteredMarkup` or `FormattableMarkup`. In these cases, Twig assumes that the strings they wrap have already been sanitized and that they can be output as they are. Of course, it is then up to us, as module developers, to ensure that we don't use any such objects with strings that contain unsanitized user input.

Let's look at a popular example of such an object we use all the time, and then we will talk about the different ways we can sanitize our user input.

If you remember, throughout this book we used the `t()` function (and the `StringTranslationTrait` method), which returns a `TranslatableMarkup` object used for translating strings. Printing such an object inside Twig will prevent auto-escaping because Twig already considers it safe. Moreover, if you remember, this applies to the main string only, as any placeholders we use do get escaped:

```
$object = t('This does not get escaped but this does:
  @safe', ['@safe' => 'This can be unsafe as it will be
    escaped'])
```

Even if there were no security implications, we should not be passing user input or variables to `TranslatableMarkup`, as that hinders the actual purpose of these objects—to translate the string. However, for other `MarkupInterface` objects, there are a few ways we can treat user input or strings of a dubious origin in order to prepare them for Twig:

- `Drupal\Component\Utility\Html::escape()`: This is the strictest sanitization function used to print plain text. It uses PHP's `htmlspecialchars()` to convert special characters to HTML entities.

- `Drupal\Component\Utility\Xss::filter()`: This filters HTML to prevent XSS attacks. It allows a few basic HTML elements.

- `Drupal\Component\Utility\Xss::filterAdmin()`: This is a very permissive XSS filter that allows through most HTML elements apart from things like `<script>` or `<style>`. It should be used only for known and safe sources of input.

- `Drupal\Component\Utility\UrlHelper::filterBadProtocol()`: This strips dangerous protocols from URLs. It should be used before printing the HTML attribute value when the URLs are obtained from user input or unsafe sources.

So, depending on the case, using one of the previous sanitization methods will prevent XSS attacks when dealing with markup that Twig doesn't escape.

Double escaping

Since Twig already does much of the work for us, it's also important not to go overboard with escaping. Veteran Drupal 7 developers may have a tendency to escape things like there is no tomorrow, but this can have unintended consequences. For example, imagine the following scenario:

```
return [
  '#theme' => 'my_custom_theme',
  '#title' => 'The cow\'s got milk.',
];
```

Since Twig is auto-escaping, the following string will be printed:

```
The cow's got milk.
```

So there is no visible change as the string was safe. However, imagine that we were overzealous with our sanitization and did this:

```
return [
  '#theme' => 'my_custom_theme',
  '#title' => Html::escape('The cow\'s got milk.'),
];
```

Then, we would get the following title:

```
The cow&#039;s got milk.
```

That is because the first time it is escaped, Drupal turns the apostrophe into an HTML entity ('). However, the browser renders it correctly, so we don't actually see it. The second escaping turns the individual characters from that HTML entity into *their* respective HTML entities. In this case, the & character gets turned into &. So, the entire string is no longer properly readable by the browser.

I now draw your attention for a moment to *Chapter 4, Theming*. In that chapter, we saw that the #markup and #plain_text properties already serve to sanitize the user input passed through them. The first uses the Xss::filterAdmin() method, whereas the latter uses the Html::escape() method. So, keep in mind that if you use those as part of your render arrays, you may not need further sanitization.

SQL Injection

SQL Injection remains a very popular vector attack on vulnerable applications that incorrectly make use of database drivers. Luckily, by using the Drupal database abstraction layer, we go a long way toward ensuring protection against such vulnerabilities. All we have to do is use it correctly.

When it comes to Entity queries, there isn't much we can do wrong. However, when using the Database API directly, as we did in *Chapter 8, The Database API*, we have to pay attention.

Most of the time, vulnerabilities have to do with improper placeholder management. For example, we should never do things like this:

```
$database->query('SELECT [column] FROM {table} t WHERE
    t.name = ' . $variable);
```

This is regardless of what $variable is—direct user input or otherwise. Because by using that direct concatenation, malicious users may inject their own instructions and complete the statement in a different way than intended. Instead, we should use code like we did in *Chapter 8, The Database API*:

```
$database->query("SELECT [column] FROM {table} t WHERE
    t.[name] = :name", [':name' => $variable]);
```

In other words, use placeholders that will then be sanitized by the API to ensure that no characters are allowed to form malicious statements.

Drupal comes with an additional security improvement when it comes to SQL injection vulnerabilities—single statement executions. Up until recently, the PHP PDO driver (which Drupal extended since Drupal 7) did not have a flag in place to inform MySQL to execute only a single statement at a time. Theoretically, vulnerabilities caused by appending multiple statements were possible (with one painful example of an attack that marked the Drupal community forever—SA-CORE-2014-005). However, this has been changed, and Drupal now sends this flag via PDO to the database engine to prevent multiple statements from being executed at once. So, we get this extra bit of protection.

Cross-Site Request Forgery (CSRF)

CSRF attacks are another popular way that applications can be overtaken, by forcing a user with elevated privileges to execute unwanted actions on their own site. Usually, this happens when certain URLs on the application trigger a process simply by being accessed through the browser (and by being authenticated): for example, deleting a resource.

The most important thing to consider in this respect is to never have such actions happening simply by accessing a URL. To help with this, we have the powerful Form API, which already had token-based CSRF protection embedded from previous versions of Drupal. So basically, you can create forms whose submit handlers perform potentially damaging actions (as we learned in *Chapter 2, Creating Your First Module*) or even add a second layer using a confirmation form (as we saw in *Chapter 6, Data Modeling and Storage*, and *Chapter 7, Your Own Custom Entity and Plugin Types*, when talking about entities). The latter is actually recommended for when the action is irreversible or has greater implications.

Although the Form API should account for most use cases, we may also encounter the need to declare a callback URL that directly handles the process. And, to protect ourselves from CSRF attacks, we can use the CSRF token system, as we saw in *Chapter 10, Access Control*, when we talked about the various types of access control. I recommend that you check out that chapter for more information on this topic.

Summary

Drupal has come a long way with locking down its APIs to attack vulnerabilities. Of course, this does not mean it's perfect, nor that a bad developer cannot create security holes. For this reason, it's extremely important to pay attention to the security implications of all the code you write, follow the standards (including the OWASP checklist), and be aware of what contributed modules you use (to at least be covered by the Drupal security team). Moreover, it's also very important to keep up to date with security announcements from the Drupal security team as new vulnerabilities may be discovered and updates required to remedy them. These are more time-sensitive in some cases than others, but it's always good to stay up to date as quickly as possible (by following the communication from the Drupal security team). Luckily, though, historically speaking, Drupal has not had many security crises—at least not compared to other open-source frameworks out there. So, from a security standpoint, it has a good reputation. However, do not take this to mean that you, as a module developer, are unburdened by the heavy responsibility of keeping your application safe.

In this chapter, we discussed three traditional vulnerabilities web applications usually face, how Drupal stands against these, and what we as module developers can, and should, do to protect ourselves from them: XSS, SQL Injection, and CSRF. Of course, there are many more things that we can do from an application and server maintenance point of view. However, these fall outside the scope of what this book focuses on. I strongly encourage you, though, to read all the available documentation on security in Drupal and keep yourself informed.

Wow. Can you believe you just finished the last chapter of this book and you can finally go play ping pong? Box of 4 kittens. Yes, do take that needed break as it was not an easy journey, although I hope a productive one. Once you are done, and back in front of the keyboard, I strongly encourage you to revisit the sections that seemed more complicated to you. Do this while checking and navigating the Drupal core code to understand and see for yourself the concepts in action. No resource will ever be better than the code itself, and the main goal of this book was to point you in the right direction. There are so many more cool things to learn and this process never stops. If you are interested, you will learn every day. I do.

Index

Packtpub.com

Subscribe to our online digital library for full access to over 7,000 books and videos, as well as industry leading tools to help you plan your personal development and advance your career. For more information, please visit our website.

Why subscribe?

- Spend less time learning and more time coding with practical eBooks and Videos from over 4,000 industry professionals

- Improve your learning with Skill Plans built especially for you

- Get a free eBook or video every month

- Fully searchable for easy access to vital information

- Copy and paste, print, and bookmark content

Did you know that Packt offers eBook versions of every book published, with PDF and ePub files available? You can upgrade to the eBook version at packtpub.com and as a print book customer, you are entitled to a discount on the eBook copy. Get in touch with us at customercare@packtpub.com for more details.

At www.packtpub.com, you can also read a collection of free technical articles, sign up for a range of free newsletters, and receive exclusive discounts and offers on Packt books and eBooks.

Other Books You May Enjoy

If you enjoyed this book, you may be interested in these other books by Packt:

Drupal 10 Development Cookbook - Third Edition

Matt Glaman, Kevin Quillen

ISBN: 9781803234960

- Create and manage a Drupal site's codebase
- Design tailored content creator experiences
- Leverage Drupal by creating customized pages and plugins
- Turn Drupal into an API platform for exposing content to consumers
- Import data into Drupal using the data migration APIs
- Advance your Drupal site with modern frontend tools using Laravel Mix

Digital Marketing with Drupal

José Fernandes

ISBN: 9781801071895

- Explore the most successful digital marketing techniques
- Create your digital marketing plan with the help of Drupal's digital marketing checklist
- Set up, manage, and administer all the marketing components of a Drupal website
- Discover how to increase the traffic to your Drupal website
- Develop and implement an e-commerce marketing strategy for your Drupal Commerce store
- Manage your daily marketing activities using Drupal
- Get started with customizing your consumers' digital experience
- Find out what's next for Drupal and digital marketing

Packt is searching for authors like you

If you're interested in becoming an author for Packt, please visit authors.packtpub.com and apply today. We have worked with thousands of developers and tech professionals, just like you, to help them share their insight with the global tech community. You can make a general application, apply for a specific hot topic that we are recruiting an author for, or submit your own idea.

Share Your Thoughts

Now you've finished *Drupal 10 Module Development*, we'd love to hear your thoughts! Scan the QR code below to go straight to the Amazon review page for this book and share your feedback or leave a review on the site that you purchased it from.

https://packt.link/r/1837631808

Your review is important to us and the tech community and will help us make sure we're delivering excellent quality content.

Download a free PDF copy of this book

Thanks for purchasing this book!

Do you like to read on the go but are unable to carry your print books everywhere?

Is your eBook purchase not compatible with the device of your choice?

Don't worry, now with every Packt book you get a DRM-free PDF version of that book at no cost.

Read anywhere, any place, on any device. Search, copy, and paste code from your favorite technical books directly into your application.

The perks don't stop there, you can get exclusive access to discounts, newsletters, and great free content in your inbox daily

Follow these simple steps to get the benefits:

1. Scan the QR code or visit the link below

https://packt.link/free-ebook/9781837631803

2. Submit your proof of purchase
3. That's it! We'll send your free PDF and other benefits to your email directly

Made in the USA
Monee, IL
20 August 2024

64186712R00319